✿ THE ✿
CIVIL WAR
✿ IN ✿
50
OBJECTS

THE

—◦◊◦—

CIVIL WAR

IN

—◦◊◦—

50

OBJECTS

HAROLD HOLZER

AND THE

NEW-YORK HISTORICAL SOCIETY

—◦◊◦—

With an Introduction by Eric Foner

VIKING

VIKING
Published by the Penguin Group
Penguin Group (USA) Inc., 375 Hudson Street, New York, New York 10014, USA

USA | Canada | UK | Ireland | Australia | New Zealand | India | South Africa | China

Penguin Books Ltd, Registered Offices: 80 Strand, London WC2R 0RL, England
For more information about the Penguin Group visit penguin.com

Illustration credits
Plate no. 50–1: Courtesy of David Rubenstein
Other illustrations from the collection of the New-York Historical Society

LIBRARY OF CONGRESS CATALOGING-IN-PUBLICATION DATA
Holzer, Harold.
The Civil War in 50 objects / Harold Holzer and the New-York Historical Society ; with an introduction by
    Eric Foner.
pages   cm
Includes bibliographical references and index.
ISBN 978-0-670-01463-7 (hardcover)—ISBN 978-1-101-61311-5 (ebook) (print)
1. United States—History—Civil War, 1861–1865—Antiquities. 2. United States—History—Civil War,
    1861–1865—Museums. 3. United States—History—Civil War, 1861–1865—Anecdotes. 4. United
    States—History—Civil War, 1861–1865—Collectibles. 5. New-York Historical Society. I. Foner, Eric. II.
    New-York Historical Society. III. Title.
E646.H65 2013
973.7075—dc23
2013001532

Printed in the United States of America
10   9   8   7   6   5   4   3   2   1

Book design by Carla Bolte

PEARSON

❧ TO ❧

RICHARD GILDER

Chairman Emeritus of the New-York Historical Society

and

ROGER HERTOG

Chairman of the New-York Historical Society

———❀❀❀———

For the inspiration to find usable lessons from the past

[W]e cannot escape history.
We . . . will be remembered in spite of ourselves.

—Abraham Lincoln

Annual Message to Congress, December 1, 1862

CONTENTS

✥ FOREWORD ✥

O N A WINTRY EVENING IN 1804, THE NEW-YORK HISTORICAL SOCIETY was founded by eleven visionary men as a permanent means of preserving the historical record of America's past. All of the founders had lived through a time when the streets of New York City were riotous with rebellion and economic uncertainty, when much of the city was burned in the wake of British occupation during the Revolutionary War. They had also lived through the birth of the new nation and George Washington's inauguration as first president of the United States, in New York, the nation's first capital. With a keen sense of the importance of their own historical moment and a strong consciousness of the challenges ahead, they laid the groundwork for a vast collection of documents, books, art, and artifacts that would be a guide and inspiration for generations to come. Early on these men declared that the Society's vision was not to be "limited to a single State, or district, but extend to the whole Continent." Thus the New-York Historical Society became the first institution in America to collect the history of the nation.

Fifty-nine years later, as civil strife burst upon the streets of New York City again, with draft riots and bloodshed over threats to the union of the American states, the New-York Historical Society had become one of the greatest American history libraries in the country and the only important museum in New York. It was foreseeable that a great proportion of the wealth of objects collected in relation to the Civil War would soon find its way onto the Society's bookshelves and into its galleries and halls. Presaging a Civil War collection that would eventually tell the history of the period uniquely, gifts began arriving almost immediately after the end of the war: the Civil War library of General John Watts de Peyster; the collection of Daniel Parish Jr., comprising more than twenty-one thousand slavery pamphlets, over sixty-five hundred manuscripts, and twelve hundred photographs dealing with the Civil War; two Civil War swords; the Meserve collection of actual Civil War photographs, including Lincoln, mounted in twenty-eight folio volumes (one of four sets made); the personal papers of General Franz Sigel, the popular Civil War hero of the German citizens of New York, numbering over a thousand pieces; and Thomas Nast's preliminary oil sketch for *Departure of the Seventh Regiment for the War*. The Society's collections around the Civil War continued to grow over the next century, reaching an unparalleled breadth and depth when, as part of its bicentennial celebrations in 2004, the Gilder Lehrman Collection, a unique archive of primary sources in American history, was placed on deposit at the Society and made available to researchers. Among the Gilder Lehrman Collection's great Civil War treasures are general orders; orderly books; recruitment broadsides; maps, photographs, and newspapers; and the journals, official dispatches, and personal letters of military commanders, politicians, soldiers, and civilians. The archive includes letters and diaries written by statesmen, soldiers, and civilians that provide extraordinary perspectives on virtually every aspect of the Civil War, including battles, life on the home front, Lee's surrender, Lincoln's assassination, and prisoner-of-war experiences. Thousands of soldiers' letters and diaries, most of them unpublished, capture the experience of the common soldier and his family in great detail.

For many years now, the history of the Civil War has come to life for scholars, students, and the historically minded general public through objects in the New-York Historical Society. But today, as the sesquicentennial of the war is commemorated, the collection occupies an even greater place of privilege. It is our good fortune to be able to share fifty of our million or so Civil War objects with readers of this book. Even the most avid Civil War buffs among you will discover much that will appear new! We are fortunate to have as author and guide the great Lincoln scholar Harold Holzer. Eric Foner, the renowned historian of the Civil War and Reconstruction, has written an introduction of great substance that, as always with the best historians, is provocative of thought. I am grateful to my colleague the New-York Historical Society's historian and vice president, Valerie Paley, for her work as part of the team. My colleagues Jean Ashton and Linda Ferber and their library and museum staffs were instrumental in suggesting objects from which the fifty presented in this book were drawn. It was Wendy Wolf's idea to do this book, and I thank her and her Viking colleagues for recognizing our collection and staff as uniquely suitable for the task. I am also pleased to acknowledge the generosity of David Rubenstein for his special loan of the Thirteenth Amendment.

It was most fortunate for the New-York Historical Society to have Roger Hertog answer the call to take over the chairmanship of the board of trustees in 2007, when the visionary Richard Gilder stepped down. His leadership has promoted and supported a resurgence of interest in the American story and the rebirth of our venerable institution as central to culture in New York.

LOUISE MIRRER
PRESIDENT AND CEO
NEW-YORK HISTORICAL SOCIETY

⚜ PREFACE ⚜

I BEGAN WRITING ABOUT ABRAHAM LINCOLN AND THE AMERICAN CIVIL War nearly forty years ago and have been conducting research ever since at institutions all over the world. But it did not take me long to realize that one of the most comprehensive collections existed in my own hometown. As I learned, few institutions in this country so richly represent the full range of the Civil War experience on both the battlefront and the home front, from its causes to its results, as does the New-York Historical Society and the treasures it has preserved. Still, until I began working on this project, I had no idea just how deep and comprehensive that collection actually is. I suspected it could help to punctuate or perhaps illustrate the Civil War story, but I quickly discovered how beautifully and completely it can actually tell that story—and with palpable emotion, drama, significance, and power.

No wonder. As I learned in examining acquisition files for this project, the Society has been dedicated to amassing a definitive record of slavery, secession, rebellion, and reunion from the time these movements first roiled the city and the nation, and the depth of today's holdings bears witness to its unflagging dedication to that aspiration ever since. Adding strength to strength, countless other items not officially part of the permanent collection now repose within its walls as well, on long-term individual loan or in the form of large, accessioned archives sheltered here for years—most notably the renowned Gilder Lehrman Collection. By any measure, the combination of all these resources is more than comprehensive; it is nothing short of incomparable. It was high time that a representative sampling testified to that preeminence, and this book is the result—a start really—offering what amounts to a highlight history of the Civil War era as told through a sampling of the New-York Historical Society's abundance of treasures large and small.

In truth, the Society houses so many important and eclectic Civil War items—many of which I confess I never even knew existed until asked to write this book, despite years of research here—that the task of selecting the most compelling "top fifty" for this book proved nearly impossible. My hope is that the items, more or less chronologically arranged on the following pages, not only tell the story of the war itself but also convey the encyclopedic nature of the institution's holdings. Readers should know that there is much more where all this came from.

The Society's original focus on the unfolding history of the war fortuitously coincided with the democratization of American museums. It also accompanied a growing national mania for reunions, memoirs, and monuments dedicated to preserving the wartime experience as a cautionary lesson to a reunited but still wounded America. Having commenced its determination to acquire this material while the war still raged, the Historical Society never lost sight of its original interest. It has since amassed, through donation and purchase alike, a remarkable variety of documents, artifacts, relics, and images from the period. Nearly all reflect high levels of creativity, an abiding sense of patriotism (on both sides), genuine historical relevance, and the degree of passion that inspired both their creation, often under duress, and their subsequent paths from private hands into a public resource.

Today the museum's galleries, archives, and library abound with material evoking both the military and the civilian experience of this horrific period—original pieces that New Yorkers once wore, carried, wrote, painted, sculpted, commissioned, or collected, in an effort, as the historian Michael Kammen has described the phenomenon, to "remind Americans of the human sacrifices and honors won in the struggle for worthy causes."

Under the expert guidance of the New-York Historical Society's leadership, the fifty treasures chosen from among many offer a novel way to tell the national, state, city, and intensely personal stories of the war, from the vantage points of both the famous and the anonymous,

military and civilian, black and white, men and women—all surely
representing what their original owners or creators believed was their
own commitment to "worthy causes." Naturally, the focus falls inevitably on New York City; however, the archive not only tells the story of
how a great war affected the nation's greatest metropolis but also includes valuable generic material produced elsewhere and collected by
New Yorkers who served in the war on both sides of the conflict or who
moved here afterward to remake their lives. Eventually, they decided
that the Society—New York's oldest museum—was the ideal institution
to house their mementos.

Not all the treasures presented on these pages constitute material
that historians ordinarily call "important." To be sure, the book includes
the collection's most extraordinary Civil War items—and there are
many: the original model for the war's greatest technological marvel, the
ironclad USS *Monitor;* a copy of General Grant's handwritten terms for
Confederate surrender; Abraham Lincoln's modest scribbled estimate of
his chances for reelection; the revolutionary Thirteenth Amendment to
the U.S. Constitution; and a chilling handwritten account of Lincoln's
assassination by one of the guests occupying his box at Ford's Theatre—
along with significant works of art and one-of-a-kind letters and diaries.
But we took pains to include as well the more personal and unusual relics in the collection, equally rare and unique if less widely known or influential: a handwritten prison newspaper created by lonely and isolated
Confederate captives; a small American flag flown from a Manhattan
residence during the send-off for the city's first Union regiment; a primitive cipher key used to decode secret messages sent to Confederate
forces; a small piece of cardboard adorned with purloined uniform buttons; a Civil War drum once pounded to rally soldiers into battle; a flamboyant full-dress Zouave uniform; an officer's footlocker still packed
with original personal belongings; and a wobbly but decipherable example of penmanship by a determined veteran amputee learning to write
again with a new prosthetic arm—to name but a few.

With its understandable focus on New York, the Historical Society,
perhaps more than any other collection in the country, testifies to how
very close the nation's largest municipality came to anarchic bedlam of

its own during the Civil War—an important but often-neglected story. For here is evidence of its mayor's brazen effort to take New York out of the Union to preserve lucrative trade with the Confederacy; a fully preserved draft wheel used in Manhattan to draw the names of the first conscripts on the day the draft riots exploded; and a charred Bible dramatically rescued from the Colored Orphan Asylum on Fifth Avenue after rioters heartlessly set fire to the building. And from the opposite side of the story, here too are relics testifying to the mammoth civilian effort to fund the care and feeding of federal troops, to the liberating initial impact of the Emancipation Proclamation, and to the maiden effort to enlist African American regiments to fight for union and freedom. With its many other treasures and curiosities, the collection yields a tangible history of heroic survival, in some cases clung to proudly for generations until ultimately acquired for safekeeping by an institution dedicated to their preservation, study, and exhibition.

It may seem odd at first glance that so many people of the late nineteenth century, the survivors of a population so sharply reduced by injury and disease between 1861 and 1865, chose to remember at all a ghastly experience they might have been wiser to forget. In fact, many writers of the day, from the North as well as the South, did urge Americans to put the war behind them and reunite as if nothing had ever divided them. As the historian David Blight has shown, such advice did little to inhibit public enthusiasm for veterans' groups and monuments but did succeed for a time in marginalizing African Americans from national memory, not to mention erasing their claims to the fairly won benefits of Union victory. Those who doubt that some New Yorkers, however conflicted, stubbornly preserved such recollections anyway need only search the records of the Historical Society to find proof of a decisive African American Civil War experience and a strong will to enshrine the evidence.

Above all, readers will surely note that the arc of black freedom constitutes the most important thread running through this book—just as it defined the war itself, much as subsequent generations did to obscure that reality. "All knew," as Lincoln insisted in his second inaugural address, that slavery was, "somehow, the cause of the war." And all knew by

1863 that emancipation would be its effect. It is thus no accident that the very first relic appearing in this book is a heartbreaking little iron manacle once used to shackle a slave child and that the final treasure on these pages is a signed copy of the document that symbolically broke *all* such shackles forever—the constitutional amendment outlawing slavery throughout the United States. In between can be found remarkable items that dramatize and illuminate in altogether new ways America's convulsive struggle to redefine itself and, in the end, to make good, after more than four score years, on the original promise of the Declaration of Independence that all men are created equal.

HAROLD HOLZER

❧ INTRODUCTION ❧

Nearly a century and a half after its conclusion, the Civil War remains the central event in American history. The reasons for the war's continued relevance lie not only in its great accomplishments—the preservation of the Union and the destruction of slavery—but in the fact that it raised so many questions that remain fundamental to Americans' understanding of themselves as a nation. What should be the balance of power between local authority and the national government? Who is entitled to American citizenship? What are the concrete meanings of freedom and equality? These questions remain subjects of controversy today. In that sense, the Civil War is not yet over.

The Civil War permanently affected the future course of the development of the United States. It changed the nature of warfare, gave rise to today's American nation-state, and destroyed the greatest slave society the modern world has known. In the physical destruction it brought to the South, the economic changes it produced throughout the nation, the new technologies it diffused, and the new ideas it spawned, the war altered the lives of several generations of Americans. The war produced a loss of life unprecedented in the national experience. Recent estimates suggest that over 700,000 combatants perished in the conflict, nearly outnumbering those who died in all other American wars combined. For those who lived through it, the Civil War would always remain the defining moment in their lives.

The Civil War is sometimes called the first modern war, although what constitutes "modernity" in warfare is a matter of interpretation. Certainly, it was the first war in which mass armies confronted each other on the field of battle wielding weapons of slaughter created by the Industrial Revolution. It was the first war, except the Crimean, in which the railroad transported troops and supplies, the first in which railroad junctions such as Chattanooga, Atlanta, and Petersburg became major military objectives. It was the first to demonstrate the superiority of ironclads over wooden ships, thus revolutionizing naval warfare, the first in which balloons observed the enemy's lines and the telegraph made possible instantaneous communications between generals. The war saw the introduction of armored trains, hand grenades, and even primitive submarines.

Most important of all, the war took place soon after a revolution in arms manufacture had replaced the traditional musket, accurate only at short range, with the more modern rifle and bullet, easier to load and deadly at six hundred yards or more because of its grooved barrel. This development changed the nature of combat, giving those on the defensive—usually Southern armies—an immense advantage over attacking forces. By the end of the war, in the eastern theater, combat approximated what would later become typical of World War I, with armies fighting from behind elaborate trenches and fortifications for months on end. The war of rifle and trench produced the appalling casualty statistics of Civil War battles. At Gettysburg, there were fifty thousand dead, wounded, and missing. Total casualties numbered well over a million, in an American population of around thirty-two million.

Medical care during the Civil War was primitive; far more men perished of disease and inadequate treatment of wounds than on the battlefield. The Civil War was also the first in which large numbers of Americans were held in military prisons. Fifty thousand men died in these prisons, victims of overcrowding and inadequate diet and medical attention.

The war's brutal realities were brought home with unprecedented immediacy to the public at large. Especially in the North, newspapers reported the results of battles on the following day and published long lists of the casualties. Via mass-produced images of camp and battle scenes, the infant art of photography carried the experience of war into millions of American homes. Although the camera at this time could only capture static scenes—for action, the press relied on artists' sketches, which they published as engravings—it was the photograph that, as the *New York Times* put it, became "the Clio of the war." Beginning in 1862, when photographers entered the battlefield to take pictures of the dead at Antietam, the horror of modern war became tangible. "Let him who wishes to know what war is," wrote Oliver Wendell Holmes, "look at this series of illustrations."

Historians have long debated whether the Union's victory was inevitable. Certainly, the Union overshadowed the Confederacy in manpower and economic resources. The population of the North and the loyal border states numbered over twenty million, while only nine million persons lived in the Confederacy, nearly four million of them slaves. In manufacturing, railroad mileage, and financial resources, the North far outstripped the South. But the Union, which had to conquer an area as large as western Europe, also had a far greater task. Moreover, the early Northern generals, trapped in an older conception of warfare as a genteel pursuit carried on by small, professional armies, proved unable to bring the North's advantages in manpower and technology to bear on the battlefield. Not until 1864, when Ulysses S. Grant engaged in a long-term war of attrition against Lee's forces and William T. Sherman brought the wrath of his army to the heart of Georgia, did the North find generals attuned to the realities of modern war.

Like the American patriots during the War of Independence, the Confederates could lose battle after battle and still win the war, if their opponents tired of the conflict. Thus, civilian morale—the will to fight—was a key military resource, and political leadership was crucial to victory. Lincoln proved far more successful than his Confederate counterpart, Jefferson Davis, in mobilizing public sentiment.

"It is war," declared the nineteenth-century German historian Heinrich von Treitschke, "which turns a people into a nation." The Civil War created the modern national state in America. It also profoundly altered the federal government's relationship to the American economy. To mobilize the North's economic resources, the Lincoln administration instituted the first national banking system and national currency; levied the first national taxes on income; imposed the first highly protective tariffs; and laid the foundation for the first transcontinental railroad. The transfer of political power at Washington from Southern planters to allies of Northern industrialists and merchants created the political conditions in which the United States emerged by century's end as the greatest economic power on earth.

If the Civil War forms part of the nineteenth-century process of nation building, Lincoln's Union was rather different from the nations being constructed in Europe. It was conceived as neither the reclamation of ancestral lands nor the institutional embodiment of a common ancestry, language, or culture. Rather, Lincoln insisted, the nation was the incarnation of a universal set of ideas centered on political democracy and human liberty. Indeed, he said, the ideals of the Declaration of Independence enabled immigrants—who could not "trace their connection by blood" to the nation's birth—to nevertheless be fully accepted as American. The war had a universal significance precisely because the United States, by self-definition, embodied the idea that government should rest on popular consent and that all men should be free. These principles, of course, had been enunciated by the founding fathers but fatally compromised by the existence of slavery. Only with the destruction of slavery could the United States seriously claim to represent to the world the principle of human liberty.

Everyone of that generation, Lincoln said in his second inaugural address, understood that slavery was "somehow" the war's cause. Slavery lay at the root of the crisis that produced the war, and Union victory eradicated slavery from American life, bringing the entire nation, in Lincoln's words, a "new birth of freedom." Yet the war left it to future generations to confront the numerous legacies of slavery and to embark on the still unfinished quest for racial justice.

As early as the debates over the Declaration of Independence and the Constitution, slavery had been a divisive issue in American politics. By the 1850s, slavery had expanded relentlessly westward, while in the North a dynamic economy based on free labor had been consolidated. In that decade, the issue of slavery's further expansion and long-term future shattered the political system. The election of Lincoln, a man publicly committed to stopping slavery's spread and to seeking its "ultimate extinction," propelled most of the slave states to leave the Union and form the Confederate States of America. The South's refusal to accept the legitimacy of a Lincoln presidency and his refusal to accept secession led directly to war.

Begun to preserve the old Union, the war eventually became a crusade for emancipation, producing one of the greatest social revolutions of the nineteenth century. The old image of Lincoln single-handedly abolishing slavery with the stroke of his pen has long been abandoned, for too many other Americans—politicians, reformers, soldiers, and slaves themselves—contributed to the coming of emancipation. Nonetheless, the Emancipation Proclamation, issued on January 1, 1863, profoundly altered the nature of the war and the future course of American history.

It was the proclamation, more than any other single wartime event, that transformed a war of armies into a conflict of societies. Although it freed few slaves on the day it was issued, since it applied almost exclusively to areas under Confederate control, it made protecting the freedom of the emancipated slaves a task of the Union army, ensuring that Union victory would produce a social revolution within the South and a redefinition of the place of blacks in American life. Emancipation liquidated the largest concentration of property in the United States. In 1860, the economic value of slaves as property exceeded the combined value of all the nation's railroads, banks, and factories. There could now be no going back to the prewar Union. A new system of labor, politics, and race relations would have to replace the shattered institution of slavery.

The war linked Union and liberty in a potent new combination. Emancipation demonstrated that the newly empowered national state could expand the realm of freedom. Among reformers, the war inspired a shift from antebellum anti-institutionalism, which saw the purification of the individual as the route to social change, to a state-centered vision in which political power could be harnessed to social betterment. Emancipation would long remain a model of social change, a touchstone for movements demanding other forms of liberation.

The war not only ended slavery but produced a radical change in the answer to the question, who is an American? Before 1860, the definition of those entitled to enjoy the "blessings of liberty" protected by the Constitution was defined by race. In the *Dred Scott* decision of 1857, the Supreme Court decreed that no black person could be a citizen of the United States. The enlistment of 200,000 black men in the Union armed forces during the second half of the war altered blacks' relationship to the nation. Within the army, black soldiers were anything but equal to white. They were confined to segregated units and initially paid less than whites. Nonetheless, by proving themselves in battle and playing a central role in winning the war, blacks staked a claim to equal citizenship in the postwar Republic. The inevitable consequence of black military service, one senator observed in 1864, was that "the black man is henceforth to assume a new status among us." Before the Civil War, the abolitionist movement, a small minority of the Northern population, had advanced the idea of a national citizenship whose members enjoyed the equal protection of the laws, regardless of race. In the war's aftermath, this principle was written into the laws and the Constitution.

Like all wars, the conflict encouraged an identification of patriotism with unconditional loyalty to the existing administration. North and South, dissent was widely viewed as akin to treason. Nonetheless, as the war progressed, it exacerbated existing social tensions within both societies and created new ones. Many Northerners attuned to traditional notions of local autonomy feared the growing power of the national government and resented the fact that manufacturers and financiers were reaping the profits of wartime prosperity while workers saw their wages undermined by inflation. The prospect of a sweeping change in blacks' status called forth a racist reaction. By 1863, as casualties mounted, Northern Democrats subjected the Lincoln administration to withering criticism. In that year, the introduction of conscription (with men able to avoid military service if they were wealthy enough to pay a penalty or provide a substitute) provoked the New York City draft riots. This assault upon all the symbols of the new order being created by the war—draft offices, the homes of wealthy Republicans, industrial establishments, and the city's black population—became the most violent civil upheaval in the nation's history other than the South's rebellion itself. The Confederacy, too, was racked by internal conflict.

After an initial burst of patriotic enthusiasm, many non-slaveholders became convinced that they were bearing an unfair share of the war's burdens.

After the war ended, the loyalties it had created helped the Republican Party retain national dominance into the twentieth century. The Grand Army of the Republic, the organization of war veterans, became a fixture of Republican politics and a presence in every Northern community. In the South, the Confederate experience came to be remembered as the Lost Cause, a noble struggle for local rights and individual liberty (with the defense of slavery conveniently forgotten).

Slowly, the Southern understanding of the war gained national dominance. It became a cliché that the South lost on the battlefield but won the battle over historical memory. By the turn of the century, as soldiers from North and South fought side by side in the Spanish-American War, the Civil War was recalled as a conflict of brother against brother in which both sides fought for noble causes—union for the North, local self-determination for the South. The displacement of slavery from a central role in the war's causes and conduct accorded with the new racial realities of the age of Jim Crow and the national retreat from the ideal of racial equality. Not until the 1960s, under the impact of the civil rights revolution, did most historians restore emancipation to center stage in their accounts of the Civil War, and it has remained there ever since.

However we remember the Civil War, there is no doubt that it transformed the nation. As the abolitionist Wendell Phillips put it soon after the war ended, Americans were "never again to see the republic in which we were born."

ERIC FONER

THE

CIVIL WAR

IN

50

OBJECTS

PLATE 1-1

1

Chains That Bind

Slave Shackles Intended for a Child, ca. 1800

IN 1841, A FUTURE PRESIDENT OF THE UNITED STATES BOARDED A CANAL boat just outside Louisville, Kentucky, and then watched in horror as a group of shackled slaves came into view on deck. As he soon learned, the poor souls were being transported to the Deep South—there to be sold into almost unimaginably cruel bondage in sweltering rice and cotton fields.

Abraham Lincoln never got the scene out of his mind. He was on his way home to Illinois at the time after spending nearly six weeks vacationing at his best friend's plantation. Being served there by enslaved people night and day never seemed to bother him or nag in the least at his conscience. But the sight of the shackled slaves heading south burned itself indelibly into his memory.

"They were chained six and six together," he painfully recalled. "A small iron clevis was around the left wrist of each, and this fastened to the main chain by a shorter one at a convenient distance from the others; so that the negroes were strung together precisely like so many fish upon a trot-line. In this condition they were being separated forever from the scenes of their childhood, their friends, their fathers and mothers, and brothers and sisters, and many of them, from their wives and children, and going into perpetual slavery where the lash of the master is proverbially more ruthless and unrelenting than any other where." Lincoln seemed particularly bewildered that the restrained slaves seemed happy, sang songs, played cards, and "cracked jokes," immune to their fate or, more likely, bravely determined to make the best of it. He was so haunted by the scene that he admitted it still made him "miserable" thirteen years later.

But even Lincoln probably never saw shackles quite as haunting as the tiny pair in plate 1–1. This gruesome relic of slavery was designed to restrain a mere child. Experts have determined that this particular set of manacles—also called bilboes (perhaps because they were first made in Bilbao, Spain, for use by the Spanish armada)—dates to about 1800, showing that little had been done to improve them over the preceding decades, for they closely resemble similarly crude shackles recovered from the wreck of the slave ship *Henrietta Marie,* which sank off the coast of Florida a hundred years earlier, in 1700.

Some slave masters and ship captains might cushion such restraints with a layer of rope, but if they did, it was primarily to prevent abrasions and infections that might reduce a slave's market value. Most slave traders of the period used restraint as a precaution, precisely as the owners of another eighteenth-century slave ship, the *Dispatch,* made clear in their instructions to their captain: "Keep 'em shackled and hand Bolted fearing their rising or leaping Overboard, to prevent which let always a Constant and Carfull watch be appointed to which must give the strictest Charge for the preservation of their own lives, so well as yours and on which the voyage depends." In other words, shackles were necessary on these voyages so captives would not jump into the sea to escape their fate or revolt against their kidnappers. After all, the Africans were valuable cargo: they simply had to be secured.

Bilboes like those in plate 1–2 often linked two people together. So the modern viewer must conclude that two different children, perhaps members of the same uprooted family, might once have been restrained by these crude shackles. The more compassionate ship captains would chain their cargo only when the ships remained in tantalizing sight of their African homeland—or when they first approached an unknown port in the Americas. That was when the captives were most likely to stir in anger or fear and attempt an escape. The slave trade historian George F. Dow discovered a document in which a captain writing in the late

Slave shackles, ca. 1866

seventeenth century admitted: "When our slaves are aboard we shackle the men two and two, while we lie in port, and in sight of their own country, for 'tis then they attempt to make their escape, and mutiny." Still, only on the rarest occasions were restraints forced on women or children; the cruelty or fear that inspired these particular contraptions is almost incomprehensible. As the writer Corey Malcom has persuasively written, the people of any age restrained by devices like these "were barely considered human, and would never again be free."

Just as surviving bilboes evoke a visceral impression of bondage, surviving evidence of *un*shackling animates a more joyful part of slave history: the breaking of chains that came with liberation, in forms both symbolic and vividly real. Since 1921, the New-York Historical Society has also owned a set of shackles once literally cut from the ankles of a pretty seventeen-year-old Georgia slave named Mary Horn by Lieutenant Colonel William W. Badger of the 176th Regiment, New York Volunteers, who served as provost marshal of Sumter County, Georgia, during

PLATE 1–2

the early days of Reconstruction. Mary's owner, an unrepentant former judge and legislator from the town of Americus, had reportedly fastened the shackles on her ankles to keep her away from her lover, George, who lived on a nearby plantation. Only when the 176th marched into the neighborhood did George demand that his fiancée's humiliating restraints be removed.

The amazing part of this story is that these events appear to have taken place in 1866—the year *after* the Civil War ended, well after slaves like Mary and George had been legally freed under the terms of the Thirteenth Amendment to the Constitution. The reality was that former masters continued to hold immense power over their former "people," inciting much violence bred by what a contemporary described as "fierce misunderstandings" and "brutal ignorance." With Badger installed in the neighborhood, George summoned the courage to report the judge's treatment of his beloved, protesting that the ex-master had forbidden the two to see each other, much less get married. Mary had tried running away, but George's former owner had returned her to the judge, who then forged the shackles to restrain her. For weeks she had been forced to work in the cornfields with the painful restraints tearing at her legs.

Colonel Badger listened to George's story and quickly issued a summons. The girl was duly brought to him, still wearing the chains, her ankles "wrapped with rags to prevent their galling the flesh." George himself held Mary over an anvil while Colonel Badger pierced the rivets with a cold chisel and freed her—retaining the odious souvenir for himself. The colonel then performed some kind of ceremony joining George and Mary in matrimony and advised the newlywed husband to protect his wife with his life. The old judge was tried by a military court and punished, but he subsequently returned to his plantation. A year later, George reportedly killed Mary's former master during a melee with the stubborn judge's former slaves. In a way, justice had finally been done.

2

———∽∽∽———

The Human Face of Slavery

Daguerreotype of Caesar: A Slave, ca. 1850

ALL WE KNOW FOR CERTAIN ABOUT "CAESAR," THE ELDERLY EX-SLAVE who gazes so poignantly across time from the justly famous pre–Civil War daguerreotype in plate 2–1, would fill no more than a long caption. Yet what the breathtaking portrait conveys about the system that kept Caesar in bondage for much of his life—yet apparently failed to deprive him of his spirit and his dignity—speaks volumes.

We have precious little reliable documentation about the subject himself—only traditional stories asserting that Caesar was the very last slave manumitted in New York State and that he endured so long in bondage that he outlived three or four generations of masters on the Nicoll family estate in Bethlehem, New York, west of Albany. According to the inscription on his marble tombstone, Caesar was born in 1737 and died in 1852—which would mean he lived to be an astounding 115 years old.

Caesar was born the property of Rensselaer Nicoll, the descendant of an extremely wealthy New York family, and grew up as the playmate of his master's son Francis, who took him as his own possession when he married and moved to a nearby estate. When an aging Nicoll lapsed into senility, Caesar was tasked with the daily job of rocking him to sleep in an oversized cradle. After the old man's death, Nicoll's widow passed Caesar on to her son, who assigned him responsibility for the family stables. Caesar may even have driven the Nicoll family on their annual

winter sleigh rides to New York City. One only hopes that he got to see something of the countryside during these rare sojourns. As it turned out, Caesar survived this owner, too, but when New York in 1808 enacted a law freeing all slaves under sixty-five, the old servant was already seventy and thus ineligible. Although his own children and grandchildren secured their liberty, Caesar was passed down from generation to generation like a family keepsake.

Certainly, some of that legendary survival instinct shows vividly in this portrait: Caesar's strong expression suggests uncompromised vigor and dignity. He cannot conceal the triumph of endurance. His fixed stare,

PLATE 2–1

his handsome attire, and the firm way he grips his staff all suggest that he believes—as the viewer is surely meant to appreciate—that he has earned every single year of his unimaginable life in bondage. Caesar reflects not only vitality under oppression but indomitability.

But why were such visual documents created in the first place, since they could only testify to the ubiquity and inhumanity of slavery and inevitably incite opposition to the institution? Odd as it may seem, some of the same masters who kept their human property in dehumanizing shackles—sometimes literally, as we have seen—occasionally, perplexingly, ushered them to local photographers to record their images. In many cases, we might even assume, the subjects of such mementos were house slaves beloved, in some perverse sense, by the white families they served. Caesar, needless to say, was a natural subject for such a memento. Because of his advanced age he was a curiosity—and also perhaps a highly useful living testament to the benevolence with which slaveholders insisted they treated their chattel. How else, after all, could a slave survive to 115 unless he was well cared for? Apparently, he had already inspired a portrait in another medium. In 1849, an artist named G. W. Woodward had executed a profile sketch of the living marvel as he sat dozing in a chair. Then, around 1850, his current master's son persuaded Caesar to sit for this daguerreotype.

On other occasions, for altogether different reasons, so-called slave pictures were commissioned by abolitionists in the North to demonstrate the humanity of indefatigable African Americans who had fled or survived bondage. In some famous cases (such as a widely reproduced photograph of a slave whose scarred back was vividly lacerated by years under the whip), they were clearly meant as atrocity pictures designed to inspire popular revulsion against the institution.

Caesar was alive when New York State rather reluctantly enacted its first "manumission" law in 1799 (Pennsylvania, Connecticut, and Rhode Island had banned slavery earlier). New York's Act for the Gradual Abolition of Slavery promised eventual freedom to slaves born after July 4, 1799, but not all at once. Males remained enslaved until the age of twenty-eight, females until the age of twenty-five—which meant Caesar and others of his older generation did not qualify for freedom: they were reclassified as "indentured servants" but remained technically in bondage. Thus only in 1827 did slavery as such disappear altogether in the Empire State. Even then, part-time residents of the state were still permitted to bring slaves to New York. Seven years later, in 1834, white rioters attacked a free black community in Manhattan, driving most of its residents out and destroying their homes. Not until 1841 were all forms of slavery banned entirely, and it is conceivable that Caesar did not actually gain his legal freedom until then.

If the ca. 1850 date attributed to Caesar's daguerreian portrait is accurate, then the image is also embedded with a powerful historical irony. That year, Congress, led by Senators Henry Clay and Stephen A. Douglas, cobbled together a package of bills meant to take the steam out of the percolating national debate over slavery expansion. For four years thereafter, the legislation did successfully keep the slavery genie in the bottle. But included among the planks of the famous Compromise of 1850 was a toxic provision requiring citizens in all the states to return fugitive slaves to their masters. The result was particularly painful to progressive New Yorkers. Enactment of the new legislation meant the nullification of the state's long-standing Personal Liberty laws, which had offered some hope of justice and safety to runaways. New York's free African American community reacted to the 1850 compromise with outrage, forming committees to resist enforcement of the Fugitive Slave Act, holding mass protest rallies, and publishing disparaging editorials. One of those who came close to proposing violence to protect black fugitives was technically a fugitive slave himself: Frederick Douglass, now a well-known orator and editor and an increasingly influential voice for abolition. "If the American revolutionists had excuses for shedding but one drop of blood," he contended, "then have the American slaves excuses for making blood flow 'even unto the horse bridles.'"

That August, just before President Millard Fillmore approved the compromise, Douglass appeared in Cazenovia, in upstate New York, to address the two thousand delegates to the Fugitive Slave Convention, called especially in protest. In a declaration urging American slaves to flee from slavery notwithstanding the new law, Douglass held out hope to an abandoned population. "You are ever in our minds, our hearts," he assured them. "We cannot forget you, our brethren, for we know your sufferings . . . because we know from experience, what it is to be an American slave. So galling was our bondage, that, to escape from it, we suffered the loss of all things, and braved every peril, and endured every hardship. . . . [Do] not despair of your deliverance."

Artists and photographers observed these seismic shifts too, and slowly began integrating the African American, if not into society itself, then at least into the visual culture of mid-nineteenth-century America. Subtly at first, these images testified to the inhumanity of the slave system and the ability of African Americans, given the opportunity, to rise above what the scholar Albert Boime called the "brute" status to which so many whites had relegated them. Every time such an image suggested a subject's humanity, Boime contends, it reemphasized the "grotesque" incongruity of slavery in a nation conceived and dedicated to the proposition that all men are created equal.

Does Caesar represent the courage of surviving fugitives—or of slaves who had simply served for so many decades that their oppressors died off, leaving them free at last by virtue of longevity alone? It is impossible to know his full story for certain. But for all its mystery his powerful image still serves in a sense to illustrate the portentous advice to slaves with which Frederick Douglass ended his August 21, 1850, open letter reflecting on that year's compromise legislation: "Be prayerful—be brave—be hopeful. 'Lift up your heads, for your redemption draweth nigh.'"

Final redemption for all the enslaved people who continued in hopeless bondage was what the Civil War turned out to be about.

3

Old Kentucky Home

Negro Life at the South,
Painting by Eastman Johnson, 1859

THE SENTIMENTAL NOTION OF HOME MEANT VERY DIFFERENT THINGS to Americans in different sections of the country, both before and during the Civil War. But to nearly all, home stood for family love and nurture, and represented the crucible of religious faith and secular patriotism—what the historian Drew Gilpin Faust later called "the altar of sacrifice."

Ultimately, for many Southerners, home also came to symbolize a romanticized ideal worth fighting the central government to preserve intact, notwithstanding all its flaws—especially when it came to race. Little noticed in this conflicting set of understandings was what "home" indeed was for enslaved people at the time. Invariably, it was primitive, ramshackle, crowded, and unsanitary; cold in winter and broiling in summer; and lacking all but the most rudimentary furnishings and implements. In some cases, slave owners kept their "people" in worse settings than they kept their animals.

The artist Eastman Johnson (1824–1906) offered one of the best-known views ever painted of so-called slave life, an interpretation that usually strikes modern eyes as retrograde and clichéd to the point of embarrassment (even though, significantly, it was soon followed by a metamorphosis in the artist's own attitude toward slavery and freedom).

Here, in a phrase, is the visual embodiment of the dangerous myth of the "happy slave"—an argument that fueled pro-slavery intransigence for generations: the fiction that their cheerful nature demonstrated that slaves were better off as chattel. Under closer observation, however, Johnson's canvas offered a far more subtle and complex commentary on slave life of the day.

First of all, in a literal sense, the painting's title, while technically accurate, was somewhat misleading just the same. A viewer of that time—and today—would understandably infer that the scene purports to show slave life as it existed in the Deep South. Actually, Johnson ventured no farther than his father's neighborhood in Washington, D.C., to paint this genre scene. The family had relocated there from Maine in 1853, when the elder Johnson secured a government job with the U.S. Navy. Eastman, the talented youngest of eight children, meanwhile pursued art studies in Boston, Düsseldorf, Paris, and The Hague before opening a studio in New York City in 1859. That year, apparently on a visit to his father, Eastman simply asked family servants to assemble in front of their quarters in the backyard and pose there as models. Other sources give a local slave dwelling or the rear of a run-down nearby tavern as the setting. Either way, it is probably safe to assume that the crumbling roof, broken windows, and cluttered lawn were all products of the artist's imagination.

The central figure in the composition, a benign elderly man, merrily plays his banjo as a mother urges her small child to join in and dance—a motif popular with many artists of the day, including Thomas Eakins. Oblivious to the squalor, a young couple cuddles romantically in the foreground while an old woman observes the scene by leaning out of an upstairs window. Meanwhile, a beautifully attired white woman enters the scene from the main house—we are surely meant to believe—to observe the amusements. As one critic of the day insensitively maintained, her arrival cast "a refinement over the scene, and as she is not startled, we need not be, at witnessing the innocent enjoyment of negro Southern life."

Other viewers, of course, could be left with the impression that even in the grip of slavery black people remained incurably jolly—and that perhaps slave life was not so bad after all. Here, in the words of the

PLATE 3–1

publication the *Albion,* was a "truthful . . . glance at the *dolce far niente* of our colored brethren." It is important to note, however, that not all viewers of the day concurred with this rosy perspective. In fact, from the outset, whether the picture was meant to "support or condemn slavery," in the scholar John Davis's words, was a matter of lively debate.

Writing in 1867, the pioneering art critic Henry T. Tuckerman was quick to observe that the artist had acquired a "peculiar fame" for "his delineation of the negro," adding: "One may find in his best pictures of this class a better insight into the normal character of that unfortunate race than ethnological discussion often yields. The affection, the humor, the patience and serenity which redeem from brutality and ferocity the civilized though subjugated African, are made to appear in the creations of this artist with singular authenticity." From the beginning some critics regarded the painter—and this painting—as antislavery. One such contemporary labeled the work "a sort of 'Uncle Tom's Cabin' of pictures," and another acknowledged that it was "as telling as a chapter from 'Slavery as It Is,' or a stirring speech from the Antislavery platform."

One thing remains certain: the canvas was enormously popular in its time—even among white liberals, and this in an era of sectional conflict inflamed to the boiling point by the inhumane 1857 *Dred Scott* decision and the 1858 Lincoln-Douglas debates. When the picture was exhibited at New York's National Academy of Design in the year of John Brown's raid on Harpers Ferry (1859), it drew rave reviews and immediately earned Johnson membership in the prestigious association.

It also quickly acquired a nickname, "Old Kentucky Home"—after the wildly popular seven-year-old minstrel song by Stephen Foster that emphasized happy old "darkies" living lives of bliss ("The young folks roll on the little cabin floor, / All merry, all happy, and bright!"), though the song also conceded that they actually endured miserable lives of toil ("The head must bow and the back will have to bend, / Wherever the darky may go. / A few more days and the trouble all will end, / In the field where the sugar-canes grow"). This song, too, has been misunderstood, for Frederick Douglass later credited the Foster tune with evoking sympathy for enslaved people. Johnson's complex painting, open to the same variety of interpretations, may have prompted a similar response.

Many critics of the day immediately saw the picture as more than the sum of its parts. As one period writer shrewdly observed: "How fitly do the dilapidated and decaying negro quarters typify the approaching destruction of the 'system' that they serve to illustrate. . . . Yet this dilapidation, unheeded and unchecked, tells us that the end is near."

Negro Life at the South was auctioned off in 1867. The following year, the painting already known as "the artist's masterpiece" fetched the staggering sum of six thousand dollars—a small fortune in its time—when it was acquired next by the sugar-refining magnate and major collector Robert L. Stuart. By then, Eastman Johnson had significantly expanded his own artistic horizons, sufficiently so to move beyond representations like *Negro Life* that might be misconstrued as supportive of slavery. His epiphany came in March 1862, when he personally witnessed a fugitive slave family fleeing on horseback into Union lines near Centreville, Virginia. The scene apparently called to his mind the flight of the Holy Family into Egypt. The artist who, according to some interpretations, had helped perpetuate the retrograde image of enslaved blacks as happy in their bondage now produced an exhilarating image called *A Ride for Liberty—the Fugitive Slaves,* showing a father, mother, and child dashing off toward freedom, emancipating themselves.

In the space of just three years, Eastman Johnson himself was also liberated.

GREAT SALE
OF
HORSES, CATTLE,
NEGROES & OTHER
FARM STOCK
THIS DAY AT
PUBLIC AUCTION

THE SLAVE AUCTION

4

For Sale to the Highest Bidder

The Slave Auction, Sculpture by John Rogers, 1859

PAINTERS LIKE EASTMAN JOHNSON MIGHT GENERATE CONFLICTING responses to their ambiguous work. However, there was no mistaking the intentions of John Rogers's mass-produced plaster sculptural group *The Slave Auction,* which reached the public in 1859, the same tumultuous year as *Negro Life at the South.* The rigidly posed and rather homely piece has lost much of the power it held over audiences in the months leading up to the Civil War. But in its day, it was clearly meant to provoke—at a time when Northern abolitionists and Southern fire-eaters were furiously busy provoking each other.

Rogers (1829–1904) was an ambitious and entrepreneurial artist who developed a genius for imagining and mass-producing scenes and subjects—even controversial ones—in forms customers found suitable for display in their homes. In this regard, his works became the three-dimensional analogues of the wildly popular lithographs of Currier & Ives, which also alternated between sentimental and politically charged subjects. With *The Slave Auction*—one of the first of the plaster casts that came to be known as Rogers Groups—the sculptor dramatically launched himself as an artist to be reckoned with. "I think it will be [by] far the most powerful group I have ever made," he predicted in October 1859, when he moved to New York to cast the work. That month, of course, John Brown conducted his raid on Harpers Ferry—and Rogers's work took on new urgency and, for some, new drawbacks. "I have got

PLATE 4–1 (opposite)

a magnificent negro on the stand," Rogers wrote, describing the portraiture in the final design. "He fairly makes a chill run over me when I look at him. . . . The auctioneer I have rather idealized and made such a wicked face that Old Nick himself might be proud of it—two little quirks of hair give the impression of *horns*. The woman will be as more nearly white and she and the children will come in gracefully. I am entirely satisfied to stake my reputation on it and imagine the present excitement on the subject will give it great popularity."

Though the final plaster indeed won immediate praise from antislavery critics, the work failed to find many customers, however hard Rogers labored to market it. He invited friends to examine and comment on his preliminary model "in order to make any alterations that might strike them before it is too late"—a method the art historian Michael Leja has called a "primitive form of the focus group." Rogers admitted in frustration, "The Slave Auction tells such a strong story that none of the stores will receive it to sell for fear of offending their Southern customers." As an alternative, Rogers hit upon the ingenious idea of pushcart marketing—selling copies on the street—retaining a man he described as "a good looking negro to carry them around on a sort of tray, with an appropriate notice printed on the front." Fortuitously, the African American salesman encountered the New York abolitionist Lewis Tappan, who immediately bought one of the first copies and even recommended other likely customers. But Rogers quickly came to realize that the group's "strong story" still proscribed its appeal in the divided city of New York.

In abolition-minded Boston, moreover, Rogers hurt his chances to earn significant royalties in a more sympathetic community when he resisted the idea of raising the sculpture's selling price. "I think it is going to take," he predicted, "and I expect to make a good profit at $1.50. I want them to go off and be popular even at a present sacrifice so as to have them scattered round and be known." A Boston shop set the price high anyway, but when the proprietor tried to hike it again, Rogers put his foot down. "You know that they are not intended for rich people's parlors, but for the more common houses in the country," the sculptor insisted. "The abolitionists here have advised me to put them at $3.00 and many think that is too high. As I want them popular, they must be put low or else nobody but the rich will buy them and they would not want them in their parlors. . . . Large sales and small profits is the motto I must stick to."

In the end, this particular group generated neither. "I sell less of it than almost any other group," he finally reported. Critical acclaim did come his way. An abolitionist Chicago paper lauded the piece as "a work of genius," predicting of Rogers: "He and his work will be heard of hereafter." The *National Anti-Slavery Standard* raved: "If the primary object of Art were ornament merely, this group might be objected to on account of the painfulness of its subject; but if moral instruction be one of its legitimate offices, the work is certainly worthy of the highest commendation." But popularity for this particular group never materialized. It may have sold no more than thirty casts altogether. Perhaps the scene depicted in *The Slave Auction* seemed too barbaric to qualify as decoration, even if the *Independent* heartily recommended it as "worth a thousand of the commonplace, classical, and comparatively costly pieces of household ornament and art, that everywhere meet the eye." Most white homeowners, even those committed to the fight against slavery, were not yet ready to adorn their sitting rooms with images of suffering people of color. And there was no mistaking the fact that this sculpture was intended to horrify, not just enhance a parlor.

Idealized or not, it was certainly based on reality—and perhaps motivated by a specific, widely reported event that took place that same year. In March 1859, a mammoth slave auction shamelessly occurred at a racecourse near Savannah, Georgia, attracting throngs of eager buyers. Some four hundred slaves went on the block there, and the mass sale was so well advertised it inspired the *New York Tribune*'s antislavery editor, Horace Greeley, to dispatch a correspondent to report on the dehumanizing proceedings. The reporter sent back a gruesome description of both the presale exhibition and the actual bidding for human flesh—all written in a matter-of-fact style that brilliantly conveyed the horror of the scene without overreaching for sympathy. The story appeared on March 9, 1859, and it is conceivable John Rogers read enough of it to inspire his artistic response:

The negroes were examined with as little consideration as if they had been brutes indeed; the buyers pulling their mouths open to see their teeth, pinching their limbs to find how muscular they were, walking them up and down to detect any sign of lameness, making them stoop and bend in different ways that they might be certain there was no concealed rupture or wound; and in addition to all this treatment, asking them scores of questions relative to their qualifications and accomplishments. All these humiliations were submitted to without a murmur and in some instances with good-natured cheerfulness. . . .

The expression on the faces of all who stepped on the block was always the same, and told of more anguish than it is in the power of words to express. Blighted homes, crushed hopes and broken hearts was the sad story to be read in all the anxious faces. Some of them regarded the sale with perfect indifference, never making a motion save to turn from one side to the other at the word of the dapper Mr. Bryan [the auctioneer], that all the crowd might have a fair view of their proportions, and then, when the sale was accomplished, stepping down from the block without caring to cast even a look at the buyer, who now held all their happiness in his hands. Others, again, strained their eyes with eager glances from one buyer to another as the bidding went on, trying with earnest attention to follow the rapid voice of the auctioneer. . . . And so the Great Sale went on for two long days, during which time there were sold 429 men, women and children. There were 436 announced to be sold, but a few were detained on the plantations by sickness.

However disturbing, the report failed to include the most dehumanizing of all slave auction practices—the intimate, sometimes groping physical examination, usually conducted behind a screen but sometimes in full view of a cackling audience. One Northerner visiting Richmond in 1852 looked on in shock as a slave for sale was ushered behind one such screen, "his trowsers [*sic*] stripped down to his feet and his shirt pushed up on to his waist as though his *private parts*, behind and spine, thighs & legs were the parts most desirable to be perfect. I saw the fellows laugh as they looked at his privates."

There is no mistaking the specificity of the lettering inscribed on the auctioneer's block Rogers sculpted: "GREAT SALE OF HORSES, CATTLE, NEGROES & OTHER FARM STOCK THIS DAY AT PUBLIC AUCTION." The reporter covering the Savannah auction for the *Tribune* had contended that words were inadequate to the scene. But John Rogers was fully up to the challenge. When *The Slave Auction* failed to take the public by storm, a disappointed Rogers went off for a while to study art in Rome. But he soon returned and never again wavered from his commitment to mass-produced sculpture for the popular market—visualizations of the recognizable incidents of everyday life, no matter how painful.

By 1860, the *New York Tribune* would contend, admittedly with a touch of hyperbole: "John Rogers is as familiar a name to Americans as that of the modern martyr, John Brown, and perhaps more so."

Rogers would take up the Civil War as a theme in several subsequent statuettes, most famously the 1864 group in the Society's collection, *The Wounded Scout, a Friend in the Swamp,* which according to the sculptor showed "an escaped slave leading off & protecting a wounded soldier." The abolitionist poet Lydia Maria Child hailed it as "a significant lesson of human brotherhood for all the coming ages." Rogers sent a copy of the plaster to President Lincoln, who in one of the few letters he ever wrote to an artist, acknowledged the gift on June 13, 1864:

Mr. John Rogers
New-York.
I can not pretend to be a judge in such matters; but the Statuette group "Wounded Scout"—"Friend in the Swamp" which you did me the honor to present, is very pretty and suggestive, and, I should think, excellent as a piece of art. Thank you for it.
                    Yours truly, A. Lincoln

Rogers always insisted that his plaster groups were "not intended for rich people's parlors but more for common houses & the country." But now one of them occupied a place in the most famous residence in the nation: the White House.

5

Weapon of Last Resort

"John Brown" Pike, ca. 1857–1859

A T FIRST GLANCE, IT LOOKS LIKE A WEAPON DATING TO THE MIDDLE Ages, not to the modern antebellum battle against American slavery. But this long, sharp wood-and-steel pike was specifically designed and manufactured to arm what some called a heroic assault for freedom—and what others branded a mad act of lawless terrorism.

With its protagonists so armed, "John Brown's effort was peculiar." So said Abraham Lincoln when he delivered his Cooper Union address in New York City on February 27, 1860—an oration many contemporaries (including Lincoln himself) believed responsible for catapulting him to the presidency. In an otherwise elaborate, even belabored, two-hour defense of the federal government's power to intervene against the spread of slavery, Lincoln spent at most two *minutes* on the most explosive news story of the time: the John Brown raid. The famous Cooper Union speech is seldom associated with the even more famous and controversial Harpers Ferry incident, but the fact is that John Brown's raid—and Brown's swift execution—occurred only a few months before Lincoln traveled to speak in New York. To say the affair was still very much on the minds of most Americans in February 1860 would be an understatement.

PLATE 5–1

But Lincoln barely mentioned it. Mainstream Republicans like the Illinois Republican—battling for the party's center without violating antislavery principles that had inspired formation of the new party in the first place—had ample reason to minimize, or even dismiss, the John Brown controversy. Determined to halt the spread of slavery into the new western territories, they were careful to disassociate themselves from radical abolitionists who wanted to end slavery everywhere, and immediately, even at the cost of blood. That kind of advocacy, however humane it may seem to modern Americans, alarmed moderate Northerners and struck terror in the hearts of white Southerners, who believed that if abolitionists succeeded in liberating their slaves, blacks would overwhelm, murder, or, worst of all, intermarry with them. Their incurable racial paranoia was in one sense understandable: in South Carolina, for example, the black population—slave and free—actually outnumbered the white. Unsuccessful as John Brown's raid proved, except as a symbolic act, it confirmed the worst fears of slaveholders, who reacted to the insurgency by further tightening their already brutal grip on human beings they regarded as their "property."

By the end of the decade preceding the Civil War, the Connecticut-born John Brown (1800–1859) was no stranger to the tactic of armed resistance to slavery. Once a struggling cattle farmer and leather tanner, he had been converted to the abolitionist cause in 1837, when he learned that a mob had murdered the antislavery editor Elijah Parish Lovejoy in Alton, Illinois. That year, Brown took a public vow: "Here, before God, I consecrate my life to the destruction of slavery."

For most of the next two decades, Brown worked in Massachusetts organizing antislavery rallies and constructing an Underground Railroad system to speed the safe escape of runaways. As the nation otherwise tilted more decidedly toward the slave power, Brown became increasingly radicalized. When he learned that the Compromise of 1850 would include a federal law mandating the capture and return of fugitive slaves, he formed what he called the League of Gileadites to shield escapees who

reached his vicinity, and he pledged to use force when necessary to protect them. Eventually, Brown received a generous grant from the wealthy abolitionist leader Gerrit Smith to resettle near Lake Placid in upstate New York, where he continued his passionate advocacy for freedom. In 1855, Brown attended an antislavery convention in Albany, most of whose delegates cautioned against resorting to violent means to advance the cause of abolition. Brown vehemently disagreed. At the time, western settlers were locked in furious combat over the slavery issue in so-called Bleeding Kansas, a territory roiling in an acrimonious dispute over the future status of slavery there. In response to an outbreak of violence by pro-slavery "Border Ruffians," who attempted to menace settlers into supporting a constitution that consecrated slavery, Brown hit upon the idea of leading an expedition of his own to Kansas to do battle with pro-slavery forces. Enraged upon learning that the Border Ruffians had attacked the antislavery town of Lawrence, Kansas, in May 1856 and burned the local newspaper office and hotel, he vowed revenge. On May 24, he orchestrated a bloody massacre of pro-slavery settlers along the banks of Pottawatomie Creek. Brown's followers dragged five men from their homes and hacked them to death with broadswords.

From that point, the violence in Kansas only escalated. In early June, Missourians under General John W. Reid marched a well-armed force into the territory to defend slavery interests, burning out antislavery settlers, sacking the town of Lawrence, and killing one of Brown's sons at Osawatomie. Though vastly outnumbered, Brown's force somehow regrouped in the nearby woods, set up a stout line of defense, and engaged in battle with the Missourians, killing or wounding forty soldiers and losing only one more man on their side. Brown eventually agreed to a truce and prisoner exchange and was allowed to leave Kansas unmolested to regroup and plan his next move. By then, "Osawatomie Brown" had become a messianic hero to abolitionists in the North and a symbol of Northern agitation and terror to outraged Southerners. The nation "had reached a point," Brown maintained, "where nothing but war can settle the question."

For the next two and a half years, Brown labored to raise money to finance another dramatic thrust against slavery: this time, an actual armed invasion of Virginia. By now, he was fully converted to armed insurrection and, according to some, unbalanced by zealotry, family losses, and megalomania. That did not inhibit wealthy New Englanders from contributing to his latest plot. William Lloyd Garrison, editor of the *Liberator*, became one of the most prominent funders. John A. Andrew, who went on to serve as governor of Massachusetts during the Civil War, donated twenty-five dollars. Frederick Douglass provided both advice and moral support, although he later advised Brown not to launch an armed attack into slave territory.

In March 1858, Brown commissioned a Collinsville, Connecticut, metal maker named Charles Blair to forge 950 pikes—spear-like weapons shaped like bowie knives at their tips. When he took his small band of followers into Virginia, he expected hundreds, if not thousands, of slaves to flock to him. When they did, he planned to supply them with these pikes, which required little or no training to use. Each pike was individually stamped with a number; the Society's example is marked "101." With these he intended to arm Southern slaves unaccustomed to firearms in a bid to foment a region-wide revolt. As Brown confidently told Douglass, "When I strike, the bees will begin to swarm." His initial target would be western Virginia. Brown planned his raid carefully, going so far as to chart the outlines of a provisional government he hoped to establish once he conquered Southern territory and liberated and empowered enslaved blacks. He continued working to raise money to finance his planned armed revolt. Meanwhile—almost as if to stay in practice—he joined raiding parties on a mission in the slave state of Missouri and in one bold move freed eleven enslaved people and helped spirit them off to freedom in Canada.

In the fall of 1859, an unusually large group of out-of-town visitors quietly took rooms at a modest inn in Hagerstown, Maryland. The bearded old gentleman with the cold eyes who checked in with his boys registered the party as "I. Smith and Sons." If the boarders aroused suspicion there, it went unreported. By July, the mysterious "Smith" had moved his entire group to a nearby rented farm. Here "Mr. Smith"—none other than John Brown, of course—gathered a force of sixteen white and five black men and hatched his final plan to cross into Virginia and capture the federal arsenal at Harpers Ferry. The armory along the river there housed some 100,000 weapons, and Brown believed a stealth attack would not only arouse a slave revolt but provide sufficient weapons to equip the revolutionaries for a long march farther into the South. Once they expanded their movement, Brown had convinced himself, slaves would get word of the insurrection, abandon their plantations en masse, and join his crusade, effectively destroying the institution of forced labor in Virginia and, eventually, the entire South. If he could hold the arsenal for just two days, he believed, the slave population would flock to his cause. Once the pikes with which he planned to arm slaves arrived from Connecticut in late September, he was ready. This is one of the original weapons.

On Sunday, October 16, 1859, Brown led eighteen of his men in a daring sunrise raid against the Harpers Ferry arsenal. There they easily overcame the sole watchman who guarded the facility, Brown proclaiming to the frightened guard: "I came here from Kansas and this is a slave state. I have possession of the United States armory and if the citizens interfere with me, I must burn the town and I will have blood." In quick order Brown's force secured a nearby bridge and captured a number of hostages, including a major prize: Lewis Washington, a great-grandnephew of the first president, whom they menaced and robbed at his home, liberating his slaves—who numbered only three. News of the occupation spread quickly when Brown's men attacked, briefly halted, but then inexplicably freed an eastbound train, which sounded the alarm once it steamed out of town. At 7:05 a.m., its conductor frantically wired the railroad: "Express train bound east, under my charge, was stopped this morning at Harper's Ferry by armed abolitionists. They have possession of the bridge and the arms and armory of the United States. Myself and Baggage Master have been fired at, and Hayward, the colored porter, is wounded very severely, being shot through the body." Ironically, the first casualty of John Brown's Raid thus turned out to be a free black man.

Within hours, telegraph operators confirmed early reports and spread the alarm all the way to Washington that Osawatomie Brown had invaded Virginia. Meanwhile, white residents of the community took up arms of their own, organized into an impromptu militia, and aimed gunfire at the arsenal from the surrounding hills, effectively keeping Brown pinned down. Brown then ordered his men to collect inside the facility's secure-looking brick engine house. Here the raiders barricaded themselves inside, trapped, for a last stand. Within thirty-six hours, a company of U.S. Marines arrived on the scene, commanded by a remarkably handsome, mustached colonel named Robert E. Lee. The future Civil War general ordered one of his lieutenants—J. E. B. Stuart, another officer destined for later fame—to approach the engine house bearing a white flag to offer Brown safety if he surrendered immediately. "No," came the reply, "I prefer to die here." Lee's forces promptly opened fire, then rammed open the heavy doors with a large wooden ladder and easily overpowered the insurgents after a brief but bloody struggle inside. Another Lee lieutenant, Israel Greene, leaped at Brown from one of the fire engines and struck at him with his saber, making a deep cut on the back of his neck. "Instantly, as Brown fell," Greene later recalled, "I gave him a saber thrust in his left breast." The thin blade struck something hard and bent in two, saving Brown's life—at least temporarily. When the smoke cleared, ten of the raiders lay dead or dying, including two more of Brown's sons. Lee quickly established control of the strategically and symbolically crucial federal facility and held Brown for questioning inside the engine house before hauling him off to jail in nearby Charles Town.

Amid the debris of the brief but bloody encounter at Harpers Ferry—reports of whose suppression were now spreading throughout the nation—soldiers found Brown's cache of modern rifles and confiscated them. They discovered as well clusters of primitive-looking pikes. Ironically, none of the handful of African Americans who had joined John Brown's raid had known how to use the curious weapons.

Some of the marines on the scene picked up individual spears and hauled them off as souvenirs. John Brown's personal arsenal of freedom was dispersed, and in John Greenleaf Whittier's words, "Nevermore may yon Blue Ridges the Northern rifle hear, / Nor see the light of blazing homes flash on the negro's spear." But John Brown's cause was gathering attention and momentum. The Mississippi senator Jefferson Davis may have branded it "a startling revelation of . . . hatred and fanaticism." But insisting to critics and skeptics that Brown was not insane, Frederick Douglass pointed out: "Moral considerations have long since been exhausted upon slaveholders. It is in vain to reason with them. One might as well hunt bears with ethics and political economy for weapons, as to seek to 'pluck the spoiled out of the hand of the oppressor' by the mere force of moral law. Slavery is a system of brute force. It shields itself behind *might*, rather than right. It must be met with its own weapons. . . .

"Like Samson," Douglass insisted, Brown had "laid his hands upon the pillars of this great national temple of cruelty and blood, and when he falls, that temple will speedily crumble to its final doom, burying its denizens in its ruins." But like the proverbial hunter chasing bears with ethics, John Brown had tried to launch a modern revolution with spears.

6

John Brown's Body

John Brown's Blessing,
Painting by Thomas Satterwhite Noble, 1867

J OHN BROWN'S TRIAL WAS SWIFT (HIS REQUEST FOR A DELAY WAS denied), the verdict unsurprising, and the death sentence fully anticipated. After a weeklong proceeding, the Charles Town, Virginia, court convicted Brown of "conspiring with slaves to commit treason and murder" and ordered him to be hanged.

Brown proved a model of deportment during the trial, seemingly content with his approaching martyrdom and pleased that so many journalists were on hand to observe and report the proceedings. He seemed to one military observer a "crafty old fiend," pretending to be too weak to listen one moment, but occasionally sitting upright to make an emphatic point or two to the judge. Meanwhile, as expected, editorial comment ran along strict geographic lines, with New England newspapers describing Brown as something of a saint and a typical opposition journal branding him and his band as "a handful of crazed fanatics."

Before the judge pronounced the death sentence, the ailing old warrior summoned the strength to make an impassioned closing statement, expressed with quiet dignity, but with enough passion to send chills through the South nearly as powerful as the October raid itself. Ralph Waldo Emerson later expressed the opinion that the words were surpassed in beauty only by the Gettysburg Address. But Brown's final

PLATE 6-1

condemnation against the slave power did little to win sympathy, much less clemency:

> In the first place, I deny everything but what I have all along admitted: of a design on my part to free slaves. I intended certainly to have made a clean thing of that matter, as I did last winter, when I went into Missouri and there took slaves without the snapping of a gun on either side, moving them through the country, and finally leaving them in Canada. I designed to have done the same thing again on a larger sale. That was all I intended. I never did intend murder, or treason, or the destruction of property, or to excite or incite slaves to rebellion, or to make insurrection. . . . Had I interfered in the manner which I admit, and which I admit has been fairly proved . . . in behalf of the rich, the powerful, the intelligent, the so-called great, or in behalf of any of their friends, either father, mother, brother, sister, wife or children, or any of that class, and suffered and sacrificed what I have in this interference, it would have been all right. Every man in this Court would have deemed it an act worthy of reward rather than punishment.

On December 2, 1859, Brown read one more time from the Bible and wrote a final statement: "I, John Brown, am now quite certain that the crimes of this guilty land will never be purged away but with blood." At eleven in the morning, the jailer John Avis, accompanied by Sheriff James W. Campbell, warrant in hand, led John Brown from his cell and down the jailhouse steps, ready to usher him into a horse-drawn cart scheduled to take him a short distance to the gallows. Brown wore a black cashmere suit, a collarless cotton shirt, and red slippers. According to some accounts, his hands were tied.

What supposedly happened next, however, became the stuff of myth that transcends history. By some reports forced to walk from the jail with the noose already hanging loosely from his collar, Brown reportedly surveyed the scene before him: a crowd of two thousand hostile whites and a few sympathetic African Americans, all held in check by soldiers wearing the almost comical-looking Colonial-style uniforms of the local Jefferson Guard. And then Brown caught sight of a black woman and her baby pressing to the front of the throng. According to legend, the woman dramatically held her small child in her outstretched arms and asked Brown to pronounce his blessing. If the doomed man really spoke at this point, we have no record of his words, but one newspaper insisted that Brown bent his head low, leaned across the porch railing, muttered a prayer, and kissed the child's brow. In truth, the overwhelming show of force had efficiently kept the crowd far from the scene, and his jailers certainly would not have allowed their prisoner to offer such a dangerous and potentially inciteful gesture. Moreover, it is hard to imagine that local slaves were given a day off from their labors to pay their respects to a man their owners believed an abolitionist madman who meant to see them liberated.

Inaccurate or not, the reports alone were enough in some quarters to transform Brown's image overnight from maniac to martyr, inspiring poets and artists for the next generation. The deification became as extreme as the vitriol. Ralph Waldo Emerson, for example, predicted that "the new saint" would "make the gallows as glorious as the cross." John Greenleaf Whittier spoke for many abolitionists when he published "Brown of Osawatomie" in the New York *Independent* just three weeks after the execution:

> *John Brown of Osawatomie spake on his dying day:*
> *"I will not have to shrive my soul a priest in Slavery's pay;*
> *But let some poor slave-mother whom I have striven to free,*
> *With her children, from the gallows-stair put up a prayer for me!"*

> *John Brown of Osawatomie, they led him out to die;*
> *And lo! a poor slave-mother with her little child pressed nigh:*
> *Then the bold, blue eye grew tender, and the old harsh face grew mild,*
> *And he stooped between the jeering ranks and kissed the negro's child!*

> *The shadows of his stormy life that moment fell apart,*
> *And they who blamed the bloody hand forgave the loving heart;*
> *That kiss from all its guilty means redeemed the good intent,*
> *And round the grisly fighter's hair the martyr's aureole bent!*

Needless to say, the drama and the verse soon inspired artists, too. None had been on hand to witness, much less record, Brown's final moments, but with imagination, talent, and a keen understanding of the appeal of legend over fact, they expanded the myth further. But Brown's emergence as a divinity could prove powerful and convincing even when handled more subtly.

One artist who did so was the Kentucky-born painter Thomas Satterwhite Noble (1835–1907), a late bloomer where the cause of antislavery was concerned. Reared on a Lexington plantation, Noble grew up being ministered to night and day by slaves, then studied art in Europe. Shortly before the Civil War, Noble's father freed his laborers, and the family set an example for the community by hiring all of them back for wages. That bold gesture was not enough, however, to persuade Thomas to fight for the Union. Instead, like many Kentuckians, he cast his lot with the South and rose to the rank of captain in the Confederate army, serving for a time as a staff aide to the governor of Louisiana. After the war he settled in St. Louis, then moved to New York to establish himself as an artist, and there he unexpectedly emerged as something of an abolitionist painter. Perhaps Noble was telling the truth when he argued in 1861 that his only quarrel with Lincoln's government had revolved around the somewhat specious issue of states' rights, not slavery. Other secessionists offered the same explanation, although few contemporaries doubted that the "right" that Southern states wanted primarily to protect was of course the right to own slaves.

In any event, the war, or Confederate defeat, or perhaps emancipation, somehow transformed Noble, because he soon produced a series of sympathetic canvases titled *Past, Present, and Future Conditions of the Negro*—now sadly lost—followed by a bravura 1865 painting depicting (and implicitly condemning) the last sale of slaves on the steps of the St. Louis courthouse. This was the same building, many contemporaries surely knew, where the *Dred Scott* case had been first heard before making its way in 1856 to the U.S. Supreme Court (where the ruling that black men had no rights that "a white man was bound to respect" inflamed abolitionists like John Brown). In 1867, Noble turned his attention to the most controversial abolitionist of them all: Brown himself.

Immune to the dubious legend of the final kiss, Noble focused instead on the purported blessing, basing his extravagantly bearded portrait of Brown on period photographs but giving him the air of a biblical prophet. He showed the Jefferson Guards in their anachronistic uniforms and merely guessed at the likenesses of Brown's captors, a detail that proved so uncannily accurate it moved the Cincinnati journalist Murat Halstead, who had witnessed the scene, to inquire whether Noble had been on hand too. (He had not—though somewhere in the crowd that day stood a civilian who had obtained a special pass to the hanging, so eager was he to see Brown dangle from the rope. Perhaps a few of the other onlookers at the execution noticed that rather famous Maryland actor among them: John Wilkes Booth.)

Thomas Noble's finished painting, showing the condemned man placing his hand on the slave child's head, was widely exhibited before arriving at the New-York Historical Society in 1939 and lavishly praised from the start, with one nineteenth-century critic extolling its "marvellous power." More to the point, it helped usher in the decisive image of John Brown as a latter-day Moses. It certainly marked the artist's full conversion on the slavery issue. There is evidence that the painter's courage was enough to get him in trouble back in Kentucky. In 1867, a newspaper reported that Noble had jeopardized his "position at home by representing so unwelcome a matter to the South."

The historian Albert Boime has persuasively argued that Thomas Noble's melodramatic picture helped establish John Brown as the quintessential white patriarch who selflessly gave up his life for the liberty of others. Not everyone at the time shared this belief, of course, not even all opponents of slavery, but there is little doubt that after his hanging, Brown emerged into abolitionist nobility—propelled to this mythic status by an artist named Noble, no less.

By the time the first Union troops began heading south to the defense of Washington, D.C., in April 1861, they were singing a new song that crystallized this metamorphosis. More than a year before these soldiers began chanting Julia Ward Howe's newer lyrics to the same tune attributed to one William Steffe, the soldier Thomas Brigham Bishop's version, "The John Brown Song," seemed to perfectly capture the spirit of the Union fighting for its own existence—and something more:

John Brown's body lies a-mouldering in the grave;
John Brown's body lies a-mouldering in the grave;
John Brown's body lies a-mouldering in the grave;
His soul is marching on!
Glory, glory, hallelujah! Glory, glory, hallelujah!
Glory, glory, hallelujah!

His soul is marching on!

PLATE 7–1

7

The Animal Himself

Right Hand of Abraham Lincoln,
Cast by Augustus Saint-Gaudens, 1886,
from 1860 Original by Leonard Wells Volk

HERE IS THE GARGANTUAN HAND OF A FRONTIER RAIL-SPLITTER, champion wrestler, and acclaimed prairie debater who always strove to refrain from gesturing while he spoke in public because his paws were so large it made him appear as if he were swatting bees. Here, too, is the oversized hand that would one day sign the Emancipation Proclamation and grasp the text of both the Gettysburg Address and the second inaugural.

There is no shortage of irony in the fact that this cast, which ranks among the most influential sculptures ever made of the quintessential Republican Abraham Lincoln, was executed by a relative—albeit by marriage—of Lincoln's lifelong archrival in politics, the Democrat Stephen A. Douglas. Though but a side story to an amazing saga of artistic ingenuity and the triumph of marketing over originality, it serves to remind us that much of nineteenth-century art, especially mass-produced popular art, was inspired by profit, not philosophy.

Leonard Wells Volk (1828–1895) was a moderately talented journeyman sculptor who had studied in Rome, then relocated to Chicago, where he produced a workmanlike statue of the patron who had helped arrange his trip abroad: his wife's cousin the controversial U.S. senator

Life Mask of Abraham Lincoln,
bronze cast by Augustus Saint-Gaudens, 1886,
from 1860 original by Leonard Wells Volk

PLATE 7–2

known to the public as the "Little Giant." Evidently where Volk was concerned, art should be nonpartisan. When he learned in March 1860 that Douglas's nemesis Abraham Lincoln would soon be in Chicago to represent a client in what promised to be a lengthy railroad case, he persuaded him to visit his Dearborn Street studio to pose for a likeness. Volk clearly felt he would be well-advised to produce a portrait of the politician who had so vigorously engaged his cousin in their widely covered debates for the U.S. Senate two years earlier (the sculptor had witnessed one of their earlier encounters). Lincoln had gone on to lose that 1858 contest, but the defeat had not halted his steady rise to national prominence. Now one of the leading Republican antislavery advocates in the West, he was being widely discussed as a candidate for the presidency.

Volk was the first artist, aside from photographers, for whom Lincoln consented to pose. It is possible he had begun to realize that to be taken seriously as a statesman, he had to make himself more readily available to painters and sculptors. Lincoln was amenable to Volk's plan but had no idea what was expected of him. "I have never sat before to sculptor or painter. . . . What shall I do?"

Volk promised to make the sculpting process as efficient as possible by first creating a plaster cast of Lincoln's face, which he would then use as a model for the proposed statue, limiting the need for protracted sittings. All that the subject needed to do was allow his face to be smothered in plaster and wait an hour for it to harden. The sculptor would be left with a perfect intaglio cast of Lincoln's features—something like a photographic negative—into which he could pour fresh wet clay to make a positive "print." Intrigued, Lincoln offered to have his hair cut before his appointment, but Volk cautioned him not to trim it too short: he wanted the cast to look like the Lincoln his neighbors and supporters knew. Meanwhile, Volk measured Lincoln against his studio wall and pronounced him exactly one foot taller than his diminutive cousin-in-law Douglas.

As it turned out, Lincoln hardly enjoyed the actual process of sitting for the life mask. After the wet plaster had hardened on his face for about sixty minutes, with nothing but straws inserted into his nostrils to help him breathe, Volk had trouble easing it off. Lincoln, the sculptor remembered, then "bent his head low and took hold of the mold, and gradually worked it off without breaking or injury," adding compassionately, "It hurt a little, as a few hairs of the tender temples pulled out with the plaster and made his eyes water." At least the painful experience did not dissuade Lincoln from returning to Volk's studio and sitting a few more times for a bust, as promised. On one of these occasions, Volk asked Lincoln to remove his coat, vest, and shirt, and pull down his undershirt as well, so he could model his subject's brawny shoulders. Lincoln cooperated but was evidently embarrassed by the ordeal, for when the sitting was over, he fled so quickly he failed to realize he had hastily gotten dressed in the studio without pulling up the top half of his union suit. When he reached the street, a passerby pointed out that he was trailing its two dangling sleeves behind him. Lincoln sheepishly returned to the artist's headquarters, where Volk helped to reassemble his outfit, after which "out he went with a hearty laugh at the absurdity of the thing."

When Volk completed the statuette, Lincoln was suitably impressed, telling another sculptor: "In two or three days after Mr. Volk commenced my bust, there was the animal himself!" The following month, the Republican Party indeed chose Lincoln as its nominee for the presidency, and Volk's project took on new urgency. Though yet to realize the commercial potential of his unique Lincoln life mask, the sculptor became more determined than ever to create his planned life-sized statue. To accomplish it, he decided he must also obtain casts of Lincoln's "two great hands."

Literally overnight, Volk rushed downstate to the nominee's Springfield hometown and proposed to apply plaster to him yet again—this time to his extremities. Once again, Lincoln agreed to undergo the ordeal and named the following morning for the sitting.

Early on May 19, 1860, Volk reappeared at Lincoln's home at the appointed hour, only to find his subject's right hand badly "swollen as compared with the left, on account of excessive hand-shaking the evening before." His left appeared lean and sinewy as usual, the right disproportionately bulbous. But Volk had no time to wait for the swelling to subside and decided to proceed as planned. To minimize the distortion, he suggested that the candidate clutch something in his puffy right hand so the difference between the two would be less apparent.

"I wished him to hold something in his right hand, and he looked for a piece of pasteboard, but could find none," Volk recalled in a reminiscence published in the *Century Magazine* in 1881. "I told him a round stick would do as well as anything. Thereupon he went to the woodshed, and I heard the saw go, and he soon returned to the dining-room (where I did the work), whittling off the end of a piece of broom-handle. I remarked to him that he need not whittle off the edges."

"Oh, well," Lincoln replied, "I thought I would like to have it nice."

When Volk finished casting the right hand, he began applying plaster to the left, and Lincoln felt the need to explain a barely detectable imperfection. "You have heard that they call me a rail-splitter," he told the sculptor, "and you saw them carrying rails in the procession Saturday evening; well, it is true that I did split rails, and one day, while I was sharpening a wedge on a log, the axe glanced and nearly took my thumb off, and there is the scar, you see."

Back in Chicago, Volk took an unusual amount of time to find a venue for the planned work. Not until 1876—eleven years after Lincoln's death—was it finally unveiled in the Springfield state capital. The final work presented Lincoln as a liberator, clutching not a sawed-off, whittled-down broomstick but the Emancipation Proclamation. Although he had enjoyed more life sittings with Lincoln than almost any other artist of the day, Volk's bearded figure looked too squat and bulky, the face oddly generic. Ultimately, though he had commissioned not only life casts to help him fashion a lifelike figure but also a remarkable photograph of a full-figured Lincoln, Volk was unable to make his own statue look very lifelike or realistic at all.

In the 1880s, however, Volk belatedly realized the commercial potential of his earlier portraits of the clean-shaven Lincoln, which he had been wise enough to patent at the time of their creation. He authorized a number of large and small plaster and bronze copies of his 1860 bust, some draped, some in the classical "Hermes" or "nude" style. And he began mass-producing copies of the life mask as well and, ultimately, of the hands. Plaster, bronze, and modern-blend copies have abounded in the marketplace ever since.

It comes as no surprise that the sculptor George Grey Barnard appreciatively called Volk's early work "the best thing done in Lincoln's life time." The mask and the casts show the future president on the threshold of war and greatness. The contents of Volk's studio burned in the 1871 Chicago fire, but the life mask and hands survived: the sculptor carried them wherever he traveled, even overseas. And in ubiquitous replicas they have endured in popularity as have no other artistic representations of the man.

Moreover, subsequent generations of sculptors—from Daniel Chester French to Augustus Saint-Gaudens—acknowledged a major debt to Volk. Both French and Saint-Gaudens used his originals as guides to fashion works of their own. Few modern viewers realize that the marble hands grasping the throne-like chair of the Lincoln Memorial and the hand clutching his lapel in the great monument at Lincoln Park in Chicago owe their inspiration—and their lifelike detail—to Volk's pioneer castings. The bronze hand in the New-York Historical Society collection in fact was Saint-Gaudens's own—the very bronze from which he sculpted his acclaimed Lincoln statue. Volk may have intended his casts as a model for his own work, but they live primarily in the work of many others.

Richard Watson Gilder, the nineteenth-century poet and editor who organized a committee to purchase the life mask and hands from Volk when the sculptor was near the end of his life, later wrote verses that beautifully expressed his belief, shared by many contemporaries, that no other portraits had ever come as close as Volk's did to capturing the "majestic ghost" of Lincoln:

> *This bronze doth keep the very form and mold*
> *Of our great martyr's face. Yes, this is he:*
> *That brow all wisdom, all benignity;*
> *That human, humorous mouth; those cheeks that hold*
> *Like some harsh landscape all the summer's gold;*
> *That spirit fit for sorrow, as the sea*

For storms to beat on; the lone agony
Those silent, patient lips too well foretold.
Yes, this is he who ruled a world of men
As might some prophet of the elder day—
Brooding above the tempest and the fray
With deep-eyed thought and more than mortal ken.
A power was his beyond the touch of art
Or armed strength—his pure and mighty heart.

8

⟞⟋⟍⟝

Secession, New York Style

To the People of Louisiana,
their Executive and Representatives Greeting,
Broadside, January 29, 1861

D URING THE SO-CALLED GREAT SECESSION WINTER BETWEEN ELECTION
Day 1860 and Inauguration Day 1861, the Southern states were not
the only territories whose leaders seemed determined to reevaluate their
relationship in and loyalty to the American Union. As these extraordinary documents attest, so did a place many people—now, and even
then—considered the quintessential city of the North: New York.

Few realized at the time how deeply interconnected the city's economy had become with the institution of slavery and the export of cotton.
City leaders looked on nervously as seven Southern states—and commercial partners—seceded from the Union even before Abraham Lincoln departed his Springfield hometown for his inauguration as
president. Before Lincoln ever reached Washington, or uttered a word of
official policy, the seceded states had formed a provisional government,
ratified a new pro-slavery Constitution, and sworn in a president of their
own—Jefferson Davis of Mississippi.

Lincoln's eleven-day inaugural journey to Washington beginning February 11, 1861, nonetheless proved a sensation with the public, attracting
hundreds of thousands of onlookers to see and hear the virtually unknown leader in town squares and train depots across the North—more

To the People of Louisiana, their Executive and Representatives Greeting:

WE THE PEOPLE OF THE CITY OF NEW YORK, in Mass-Meeting assembled, taking into consideration the distracted state of the country, and the imminence of Civil War; and believing that the specific rights and demands of the South are imperfectly understood, not only in this great metropolis but in all the North—have appointed *and by these Presents do appoint, citizens*—

JAMES T. BRADY,

CORNELIUS K. GARRISON,

and APPLETON OAKSMITH,

our *Commissioners*; to proceed to the States of SOUTH CAROLINA, GEORGIA, FLORIDA, ALABAMA, MISSISSIPPI and LOUISIANA, to confer with the PEOPLE of such States, their GOVERNORS, CONVENTIONS and REPRESENTATIVES, as to what measures are best calculated to preserve PEACE and SECURE THE RIGHTS OF THE SOUTH; and at the same time to obtain from such States and such People a precise and distinct statement of DEMANDS; and an avowal of what measures they are prepared to adopt to avert the calamity of CIVIL WAR.

Said Commissioners are further empowered to represent the People of this city in any convention or conventions held or to be held in any of the Southern States or in the District of Columbia.

AND WE THE PEOPLE OF THE CITY OF NEW YORK hereby call upon all persons or People, Governments or States, and the executive, administrative, military and judicial deparments thereof to give our said COMMISSIONERS safe-conduct, and to extend to them, and each of them, all necessary protection, support and aid.

In witness whereof, we have hereunto caused our Chairman, duly elected by our Representatives from the different Wards of this City in Mass-meeting assembled at the Cooper Institute, to affix his signature, in the City of New York, this twenty-eighth day of January, in the year of our Lord one thousand eight hundred and sixty-one.

OFFICE OF THE MAYORALTY OF THE CITY OF NEW YORK:—

I, FERNANDO WOOD, Mayor of the City of New York, hereby certify that on the twenty-ninth day of January, in the year of our Lord one thousand eight hundred and sixty-one, personally appeared before me James De Peyster Ogden, known to me to be the citizen described in the above credentials, and who, as Chairman of a Mass Meeting of the People of this City, has affixed his signature thereto, and acknowledged the execution thereof.

I further certify that I am personally acquainted with the said Commissioners above named, that they are citizens of New York and gentlemen entitled to high consideration.

In witness whereof I have hereunto set my hand and my official seal in the city of New York, on the day and year first above named.

PLATE 8–1

people than had ever cast eyes on any American president. But contemporaries also understood that it was not the only such spectacle unfolding in the country: it was playing out against the threatening backdrop of a rival inaugural trip in the South, and along his "meandering" journey Lincoln was often greeted with partisan hostility in Northern newspapers loyal to the defeated Democratic Party.

No doubt the weary president-elect looked forward with especially keen anticipation to his arrival in New York City on February 19, 1861. Here, almost exactly one year earlier, he had made his triumphant East Coast oratorical debut at Cooper Union, then a newly opened college in Manhattan. That speech, he later commented appreciatively, together with a flattering photograph made earlier the same day by Mathew Brady at his handsome new Broadway gallery, helped elect him. Perhaps Lincoln had forgotten that despite the enthusiastic reception he had generated among local Republicans and antislavery newspapermen in February 1860, the city ended up voting against him for president that November by a margin of more than two to one. In fact, the smoldering sectional crisis notwithstanding, New York remained hostile to Republicans in general and the president-elect in particular. If Lincoln needed a reminder of the challenges he still faced in (and from) the nation's leading commercial city, he got a jolting wake-up call soon after his arrival.

The procession of carriages that took him and his family to the Astor House, a sumptuous hotel opposite City Hall, was as impressive as any the metropolis had witnessed, comparable even to the parade the Prince of Wales had enjoyed when he came through town not long before. But spectators along Lincoln's route offered little of the same fervor. *Frank Leslie's Illustrated Newspaper* was not the only one of the city's many periodicals to report "much respect" but "little enthusiasm" for the president-elect. Riding in an open coach drawn by six black horses (the same carriage, many noticed, that had been used by the future Edward VII), Lincoln could observe flags "flung to the breeze" and a few banners here and there conveying messages of welcome and good luck. But the crowds south of Twenty-third Street thinned out noticeably, and when Lincoln arrived at the Astor House, a large throng may have been on hand to witness his arrival but offered more in the way of stares than cheers. Among the locals trapped in the traffic jam that day, perched on the top deck of a horse-drawn omnibus and thus ideally positioned to observe the scene, was Walt Whitman, who remembered: "There were no speeches, no compliments, no welcome." The poet found the absence of excitement chilling—and vaguely threatening:

> All was comparative and ominous silence. The new comer look'd with curiosity upon that immense sea of faces, and the sea of faces return'd the look with similar curiosity. In both there was a dash of something almost comical. Yet there was much anxiety in certain quarters. Cautious persons had fear'd that there would be some outbreak, some mark'd indignity or insult to the President elect on his passage through the city, for he possess'd no personal popularity in New York, and not much political. No such outbreak or insult, however, occurr'd. Only the silence of the crowd was very significant to those who were accustom'd to the usual demonstrations of New York in wild, tumultuous hurrahs.

Added Whitman: "I ha[d] no doubt (so frenzied were the ferments of the time) many an assassin's knife and pistol lurk'd in hip or breast-pocket there—ready, soon as break and riot came."

From there, at least politically, things for Lincoln went from bad to worse. After a rest and a welcoming levee at his hotel, he ventured across Broadway the next morning for an awkward public reception hosted at City Hall by the mayor of New York, Fernando Wood—out of the frying pan, as it turned out, and directly into the fire.

The mayor, an ardently pro-South Democrat, had already decided, as Lincoln well knew, that the best way for New York to maintain preeminence during the sectional crisis and prevent any potential threat to its lucrative trade with the slaveholding South was to secede from the Union, too, and form some sort of independent republic. On January 7, 1861, some seven weeks before Lincoln's visit, Wood had formally asked the city's Common Council why the municipality should not "disrupt the bands which bind her to a venal and corrupt master—to a people and a party that have plundered her revenues, attempted to ruin her commerce, taken away the power of self-government, and destroyed the Confederacy of which she was the proud Empire City?"

"As a free city," Wood suggested, New York "would have the whole and united support of the Southern States, as well as all the other States to whose interests and rights under the Constitution she has always been true." The breathtaking proposal offered an unimaginable alternative to loyalty: "Amid the gloom which the present and prospective condition of things must cast over the country, New York, as a *Free City*, may shed the only light and hope of a future reconstruction of our once blessed Confederacy." After all, Wood argued, if "the Government is dissolved . . . it behooves every distinct community, as well as every individual, to take care of themselves." Wood was careful to avoid recommending "the violence implied in these views." But he provocatively reminded the Common Council of an old rallying cry: "freedom, 'peaceably, if we can; forcibly, if we must.'" Reading the proclamation, the New York lawyer George Templeton Strong called the mayor "a cunning scoundrel," noting that Wood "sees which way the cat is jumping and puts himself right on the record . . . giving the best possible offence to his allies of the Southern Democracy."

A careful reading of the twenty-page *Communication from His Honor the Mayor, Fernando Wood,* an original pamphlet copy of which resides in the New-York Historical Society collection, points out a major backstory behind the initiative. Wood was not only fearful of losing trade rights with the South; he also saw secession as an opportunity to separate the city from the rest of New York State, whose legislature had imposed objectionable taxes and exerted unwelcome control over municipal construction projects. In short, the mayor wanted to be as free from Albany as from Washington. Naturally enough, his promise of tax relief and open trade intrigued the worried merchant class and in the bargain appealed to workers, many foreign-born, who had no desire to fight against slavery and see free African Americans competing with them for unskilled jobs. Hundreds of businesses in the city, as the writers Anne Farrow, Joel Lang, and Jenifer Frank accurately pointed out, "were connected to, or dependent upon, cotton . . . merchants, shippers, auctioneers, bankers, brokers, insurers, and thousands of others." What-

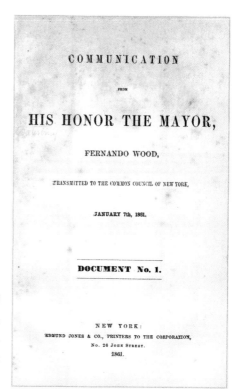

*Communication from
His Honor the Mayor,
Fernando Wood,
January 7th, 1861*

ever the complex nature of the local politics animating Wood's message, it was interpreted at the time principally as an audacious salvo against the incoming Lincoln administration—and one that came close to outright treason.

Three weeks later, Wood outdid himself with an even more extraordinary document—an original copy of which is also at the New-York Historical Society: an official communication, stamped with the city seal, addressed to the governors, senators, and representatives of all the seceded states. The message announced the appointment of three New York "commissioners" instructed to proceed to South Carolina, Georgia, Florida, Alabama, Mississippi, and Louisiana to discuss ways to "preserve PEACE and SECURE THE RIGHTS OF THE SOUTH." In other words, Wood planned to assume the status of a chief of state designating ambassadors to negotiate concessions to states in rebellion against the

PLATE 8–2

federal government. While the emissaries were in the Southern capitals, of course, they could remind officials of New York's willingness to maintain commercial ties. Not long thereafter, Wood went further still, earning condemnation in some quarters for unashamedly approving the shipment of arms through the city bound for the South.

Wood's "communication" naturally struck a responsive chord among those of his constituents who were skeptical of Lincoln. New York was bitterly divided, increasingly populated by immigrants with little natural allegiance to American institutions and openly contemptuous of people of color. A tireless organization man from the beginning of his political career with a knack for working the city's feuding clubhouses to his own benefit, Wood had won election to the House of Representatives as a Democrat before the age of thirty. From 1855 to 1858, he served his first term as mayor, a tenure characterized by bitter disputes with the state legislature over management of the corrupt and fractured police force. After narrowly losing a bid for reelection in 1857, Wood earned a second term in 1859 and was midway through his new, equally fractious administration when President-elect Lincoln passed through town. The writer John Bigelow, who was well acquainted with the mayor, called Wood "the handsomest man I ever saw, and the most corrupt man that ever sat in the Mayor's chair."

Now, on February 20, 1861, he formally, almost defiantly welcomed the president-elect from behind the symbolic safety of George Washington's old desk, which adorned City Hall's splendid second-floor Governor's Suite. As Lincoln stood impassively before him, Wood ostentatiously lectured him with a statement urging him to use his "exalted powers" to make certain the country returned to "its former harmonious, consolidated, and prosperous condition." Wood made no secret in his remarks of his concern that New York's "commercial greatness" was being "endangered" by the crisis that, the mayor strongly implied, Lincoln had done too little to avert.

In his careful response, Lincoln calmly deflected the assault—and in the process let much of the air out of New York's secession trial balloon. Repeating a message he had offered in several predominantly Democratic towns along his tour, he thanked Wood and the city for welcoming him even though they "do not by a majority agree with me in political sentiments."

Then he got to the main point. "There is nothing," he declared, "that can ever bring me willingly to consent to the destruction of this Union, under which not only the commercial city of New York, but the whole country, has acquired its greatness." Responding indirectly to the city's overt secession initiatives, he coolly added: "I understand a ship to be made for the carrying and preservation of the cargo, and so long as the ship can be saved, with the cargo, it should never be disbanded." The language was oblique, to be sure, but the message was inescapable. Privately, Lincoln was even clearer and more self-confident—adapting a different but unmistakably firm metaphor: "I reckon that it will be some time before the front door sets up housekeeping on its own terms." If Wood really expected that Lincoln would offer him the concessions and conciliation he had thus far refused to offer the South, he was disappointed. The mayor, a local newspaper reported, "got nothing."

Lincoln would never appear in public in New York again. But the city's brief and potentially devastating flirtation with secession ended. Lincoln's New York troubles would continue, but the idea that the nation's principal port could declare its independence died aborning. Two months later, once Fort Sumter came under attack, Fernando Wood pledged allegiance to the Union, and his recent and highly questionable initiatives faded from memory. The surviving evidence of New York's bizarre effort to establish its independence as a free city serves as a reminder of a crucial and fearful interregnum during which a political misstep or rhetorical overreaction might have threatened what was left of the Union and changed the course of history. Asked by the London *Times,* "What would New York be without slavery?" a Southern editor is said to have replied: "The ships would rot at her docks; grass would grow in Wall Street and Broadway, and the glory of New York, like that of Babylon and Rome, would be numbered with the things of the past."

That dire prediction was about to be put to the test.

PLATE 9-1

9

—✺✺✺—

Where the Civil War Began

South-Western Angle of Fort Sumter,
Charleston Harbor, S.C., April 15, 1861,
Photographic Print by Alma A. Pelot

W HEN HIS INAUGURAL CEREMONIES ENDED AND HIS PRESIDENCY officially began, Abraham Lincoln found waiting for him on the desk in his White House office a series of desperate messages from the commander of a beleaguered federal garrison in Charleston Harbor: Fort Sumter. Robert Anderson, a native Kentuckian who wished above all else that North and South could separate without violence, had bad news to report. His 127 men were fast running out of provisions. They could not last much longer without fresh supplies. Hostile forces surrounded the five-sided fort, which presented impregnably thick walls east to the sea but stood at the center of newly erected batteries to the north, south, and west. Built to withstand foreign attack in the large harbor's main channel, the fort was more vulnerable to assault from domestic foes.

The Lincoln administration thus faced a critical series of fundamental decisions virtually from its first moments in power. Above all was the question of to whom all the Charleston forts rightfully belonged. South Carolina insisted that since Sumter sat on a man-made island within its sovereign territory, it could rightfully claim ownership. But even Lincoln's predecessor, the Democrat James Buchanan, had insisted that since it had been built with federal funds, it belonged to the entire nation. Buchanan had even ordered a ship to supply it in January 1861, but the *Star of the West* quickly turned back when it came under fire from batteries on the shoreline. Now the choice fell to Lincoln: abandon the installation and withdraw the men, averting or postponing a showdown; or draw a line in the sand at Sumter and insist on the right to maintain a federal presence there. The very future of the Union might depend on his decision.

In communications to General-in-Chief Winfield Scott even before he took office, Lincoln had made his views abundantly clear. Scott should be "as well prepared as he can," Lincoln advised him, "to either *hold,* or *retake,* the forts, as the case may require, at and after the inauguration." Though he had toned down the equally bellicose language he originally drafted for his inaugural address, Lincoln left little doubt where he stood when he rose to deliver his most important speech to date on March 4, 1861: "All the power at my disposal will be used to hold, occupy, and possess the property and places belonging to the Government."

The unresolved subject dominated the new president's initial Cabinet meetings, but if Lincoln thought his newly appointed ministers would rally around his inclination to maintain Fort Sumter, he was mistaken. Secretary of State William H. Seward initially believed that Anderson should withdraw his men and that the government should make its stand at the nearby, more easily defended Fort Pickens off the coast of Florida. General Scott, too, endorsed the idea of abandoning Sumter. Earlier, the politician whom Lincoln had defeated for the presidency, the still-respected Democratic senator from Illinois, Stephen A. Douglas, had introduced a congressional resolution calling for withdrawal of all the garrisons in the seceded states north of Florida. Only the West Point graduate Postmaster General Montgomery Blair argued for holding the Charleston fort. None of the other secretaries seemed inclined to risk the government's reputation by fighting for Sumter—a battle, everyone agreed, the vastly outnumbered garrison was unlikely to win. By April 8, Anderson, whose total loyalty to the Union Lincoln still doubted, confided anxiously to Adjutant General Lorenzo Thomas: "We have not oil enough to keep a light in the lantern for one night. . . . We shall strive to do our duty, though I frankly say that my heart is not in this war, which I see is to be thus commenced. That God will still avert it, and cause us to resort to pacific means to maintain our rights, is my ardent prayer."

Jefferson Davis, now president of the Confederate States of America, had a similar choice to make. He knew that Fort Sumter posed no real military threat to Charleston, since most of its guns pointed toward the ocean, while its other weapons were incapable of doing much damage onshore. In a letter to South Carolina's new governor, Francis W. Pickens, he argued: "The little garrison in its present position presses on nothing but a point of pride." But pride was more than enough to move the two sides inexorably toward conflict. South Carolinians, Pickens included, believed the fact that Anderson had moved his garrison from the vulnerable Fort Moultrie to Sumter amounted to an act of outright aggression. Insisting that "there was obviously no other course to be pursued," the governor authorized batteries to be installed around the shoreline and aimed at the federal fort.

For a time, Lincoln bowed to his advisers' caution and opted for delay. Meanwhile, continuing to cling to the fantasy that secessionists constituted only a well-organized minority throughout the South, he sent emissaries to South Carolina to take the measure of the state's alienation from the Union. But the president's trusted friend Ward Hill Lamon reported back that Union sentiment there no longer existed. The only exception was a cantankerous old judge named James Petigru, who had insisted that South Carolina was too small to be a nation and too large to be an insane asylum. His neighbors dismissed him as a crank and ignored him.

After Lamon's return to Washington, Lincoln decided to reprovision Fort Sumter with food and other essentials, but not guns or ammunition, and ordered a naval squadron to proceed to Charleston. But in a stroke of political genius he announced his intentions in advance to Governor Pickens, throwing what the historian Craig L. Symonds has called "the burden of decision making" to Jefferson Davis. If Davis decided to allow the fort to take on new provisions, he would be perceived as backing down. If the Confederate president opted to interrupt the expedition with an act of overt hostility, he would be seen as the aggressor. The historian James McPherson has aptly described Lincoln's game-changing strategy as "heads I win, tails you lose." Pressed to the wall, Davis chose to attack, and on the Confederacy fell the burden of starting the Civil War.

At 3:20 a.m. on April 12, Anderson received and rejected a final demand that he surrender and abandon Fort Sumter. A little more than an hour later, as civilians ringed the shore and crowded the rooftops of the mansions on the Battery to watch the spectacle, Confederate batteries commanded by the flamboyant brigadier general Pierre Gustave Toutant Beauregard opened fire, commencing a bombardment that lasted some thirty-four hours. By the time the Union supply ships appeared over the horizon, delayed by a gale wind, the shelling had become so fierce they were forced to remain outside the harbor. Inside the city, meanwhile, the diarist Mary Boykin Chesnut heard the first guns and excitedly scribbled this entry: "The heavy booming of a cannon—I sprang out of bed, and on my knees, prostrate, I prayed as I have never prayed before." The secessionist firebrand Edmund Ruffin, given the "highly appreciated compliment" of unleashing the first shot, seemed irritated when the Union garrison did not offer a "hostile defense," worrying that if the fort fell without fighting back, it "would have cheapened our conquest."

Anderson's defenders had ample reason to offer only token resistance; some of their guns were unmounted or facing the wrong direction, and they had precious little ammunition left on hand. In addition, Anderson wanted to ensure that the full onus for initiating hostilities fell on the secessionists, and he waited until full light before returning fire. For several hours the garrison in the fort simply hunkered down. The soldiers huddled outdoors on the parade grounds, ordered there for fear that a shell might ignite what was left in the powder magazines. Not until 7:00 a.m., two and a half hours after the bombardment began, did Fort Sumter begin to return fire. Fires broke out during the barrage, and the men began to experience trouble breathing. During a lull in the bombardment shortly after noon on April 13, a Confederate emissary rowed back out to the fort under a flag of truce, finding Sumter now shrouded in smoke like a smoldering volcano and capable of offering only sporadic return fire toward the shore. Again the Confederates asked for surrender, and this time Anderson capitulated. The next day, after a formal flag-lowering ceremony during which a weapon exploded amid a hundred-gun salute, resulting in the only human casualty of the entire siege, the Union defenders left to board the supply ships now waiting to transport them north.

Once a bulwark against possible enemy invasion, Fort Sumter evolved literally overnight into an icon of Confederate independence and resistance. Even as the city began mobilizing for the further defense of South Carolina, pleasure boats thronged the harbor to get a closer look at the prize, while photographers rushed to the island to make visual records of the place where the rebellion had started—certain that the results would become treasured, and profitable, keepsakes. Among the most vivid, and probably the very first, was the work of a man named Alma A. Pelot, a camera operator employed by one of Charleston's most prominent photographers, Jesse H. Bolles. Authorized to set up his cameras inside the fort by General Beauregard himself, Pelot took this amazing view of Confederates huddling inside the grounds of the battered installation on the very first day of its occupation. Scrawled beneath this historic image is the handwritten inscription "South-western angle of Fort Sumter, showing portion of officers Quarters on the gorge, and soldiers barracks on the west side of Parade [ground], with part of flag staff. Charleston Harbor, S.C. April 15 1861. Approved G. T. Beauregard Brig. Genl."

The following day, the *Charleston Mercury* proudly announced that a "young native Artist" had "taken full and perfect representations of the internal appearance of Fort Sumter, on the morning after the surrender." The newspaper, which had earlier rallied the state toward secession, made it clear from the outset that the images were treated as more than ephemeral illustrations, noting: "These pictures for the time will afford appropriate ornament for our Drawing Rooms, Scrap Books and Albums, and a most acceptable present to distant and anxious friends. Well our citizens could see them, and especially our patriotic ladies, who may now have a hand in taking Fort Sumter." Within days the

Bolles studio had increased its advertising buy after announcing the project with the following notice on April 17:

FORT SUMTER.

PHOTOGRAPHIC REPRESENTATIONS
OF THE

Internal Appearance of Fort Sumter,

TAKEN ON THE MORNING
AFTER THE SURRENDER,
EXHIBITING FIVE DIFFERENT VIEWS.
WILL BE READY FOR DELIVERY
THIS AFTERNOON, 17TH INST.,
AT BOLLES TEMPLE OF ART,
CORNER OF KING AND LIBERTY STREETS

For the next four years, America would be consumed by a war of armies, a war of words, and a war of images—with pictures like this often providing the home front not just with newsworthy depictions of distant battlegrounds but with talismans capable of stimulating assurance, indignation, and fortitude. These photographs did more than merely illustrate; they inspired, helping to build national pride on each side of the war and serving to steel both Northern and Southern families for unforeseeable confrontations yet to come.

10

⸻∽⁂∽⸻

"Flagmania"

Flag, 1861

HERE IS A SIMPLE-ENOUGH-LOOKING RELIC WITH SUCH RICH AND complex meaning it requires an entire volume to unravel its full story. The absence of seven Southern state delegations in Congress after the initial wave of secession made possible the admission of the new state of Kansas to the Union on January 29, 1861, America's thirty-three-star flag instantly becoming outdated. Had flag makers attempted to calibrate the net effect of all this addition and subtraction on the Union itself—and on the number of white stars traditionally arrayed on the background field of blue—the flags of 1861 might have been almost unrecognizable that tragic year.

As it happened, unionists and Northern flag makers alike resolutely refused to downsize the star-spangled banner. Kansas statehood—without slavery, the subject of years of bloody battle there—had been achieved at great political and human cost. Now, with war looming, too much emotion and symbolism had been invested in its admission, and in the national flag itself, to permit further tinkering. As early as his February journey from Springfield to Washington for his inauguration, President-elect Abraham Lincoln himself saw evidence of this almost defiant patriotism as he was repeatedly greeted along his cross-country itinerary by Union men proudly waving new thirty-four-star American flags. In a sense, the ubiquity of these all-or-nothing 1861 flags echoed

PLATE 10-1

Lincoln's own frequently repeated (if to many unconvincing) argument that secession was an impossibility.

In the emotional highlight of his inaugural journey, Lincoln reached the founding city of Philadelphia on February 21, 1861. Here was much more evidence of patriotism than he had experienced in hostile New York. On Washington's Birthday the following morning, Lincoln ascended a makeshift wooden platform accompanied by his youngest son, Tad, and in the highlight of an emotional ceremony hoisted a giant version of the new thirty-four-star flag outside Independence Hall, the birthplace of the United States. It was 6:00 a.m. on a bitterly cold day, but hundreds of onlookers filled the historic plaza to watch the event.

"I propose to say that when that flag was originally raised here it had but thirteen stars. I wish to call your attention to the fact, that, under the blessing of God, each additional star added to that flag has given additional prosperity and happiness to this country." Lincoln told the crowd to rousing cheers that only "passion" and "ill temper" could prevent "the new star" from remaining "there to our permanent prosperity." Someday, he further predicted, the country would count "five hundred millions" of "happy and prosperous people"—and, he implied, an infinite number of representative white stars on the national banner.

Few people standing there in the plaza that frigid morning knew that just hours before, Lincoln had learned that an assassination plot awaited him when he reached the pro-slavery city of Baltimore. Convinced that the threat was credible, Lincoln had reluctantly agreed to alter his original plans and travel through that city incognito after a brief stop at Harrisburg. For now, the only hint of danger he confided came in the dramatic highlight of his Independence Hall address. With the murder plot undoubtedly on his mind, he contemplated the moment that had brought him to this emotional flag-raising ceremony and unexpectedly proclaimed: "I would rather be assassinated on this spot, than to surrender it." And then, with the oversized flag waving above the plaza, Lincoln was on his way.

Lincoln evaded the threat in Baltimore, but two months later America's new flag came under attack from the Confederate batteries in Charleston. The four thousand shells fired onto the fort during the day-

and-a-half-long attack claimed no casualties except for a horse. The only notable exception was the American flag, shot down at one point, then rehoisted on a "jury mast extemporized on the parapet," and ultimately lowered respectfully by its overpowered Union defenders. Major Robert Anderson, commanding the garrison, demanded and won the right to salute the flag as it was slowly taken down in formal surrender ceremonies the next morning. He later took particular pride in the fact that he left "with colors flying and drums beating . . . and saluting my flag with fifty guns." Anderson was allowed to depart Charleston with the flag in his custody. He had every hope of being buried with it one day.

But almost immediately, Anderson—and the flag of Sumter—enjoyed a triumph. Although the major admitted he did not know whether he would be greeted in New York with a parade or a court-martial, his arrival in the city elicited "a popular outburst of loyalty to the Union . . . a thrilling and almost supernatural thing to those who participated in it"—and this in a municipality that had voted overwhelmingly against Abraham Lincoln and the Republican Party that now ruled what was left of the United States. During Lincoln's recent visit to New York, even the pro-Republican *Times* would concede that the only things the New York "ladies" waved at Lincoln were "their handkerchiefs." Anderson's visit prompted a quite different response. "The heather is on fire," cheered an excited observer in Massachusetts. "The whole population, men, women, and children, seem to be in the streets with Union favors and flags."

Nowhere was this phenomenon more vividly apparent than in New York, where the price of flags quickly skyrocketed in the wake of unprecedented popular demand. The colors were soon visible everywhere. "It was a period when the flag—*the Flag*—flew out from every housetop," one contemporary marveled. On April 19, Major Anderson himself appeared in public atop the pediment of a jewelry company building on lower Broadway to greet volunteers from the 7th Regiment as they marched off to the defense of Washington. The elite company, which included a number of artists and writers, was off for a ninety-day enlistment that, nearly everyone on the streets that day no doubt believed, would be marked by both the beginning and the end of this rebellion.

*Study for "Departure of the Seventh Regiment for the War,
April 19, 1861," by* Thomas Nast, ca. 1865–1869

The city's busiest boulevard was arched that day with a virtual canopy of red, white, and blue. Flags flew from windows as far as the eye could see, while onlookers along the thronged parade route waved flags of their own. Most prominent of all in this sea of patriotic color was the actual, tattered, sacred flag of Fort Sumter, unfurled over the street where Anderson now stood to inspire the recruits as the 7th Regiment paraded downtown.

One of the flags in use that memorable day—the banner in plate 10–1—hung outside a Fifth Avenue window, probably just north of the spot where that street intersects with Broadway. Before the soldiers of the 7th Regiment marched past, Mrs. John E. Forbes, the grandmother of one Irving McKesson, made certain her new thirty-four-star flag flew proudly to salute the departing volunteers. Ninety-four years later, McKesson's wife presented the relic to the New-York Historical Society— an extraordinary reminder of an unprecedented patriotic phenomenon.

PLATE 10–2

But what the *New York World* soon dubbed "flagmania" was only be-ginning. Just one day after the 7th set off for Washington, a crowd esti-mated as high as 100,000 thronged Union Square for what an observer described as "the most immense and astonishing demonstration ever seen in this or . . . any country." Speaker after speaker mounted a plat-form that stood before the square's famous bronze equestrian statue of George Washington to offer pro-Union speeches. The backdrop was es-pecially sensational, as the usually pristine sculptural icon was itself draped by Fort Sumter's oversized American flag. From one end of town to another on that memorable day, the response to Sumter was "in the flag of our country—waving from every steeple and Schoolhouse, from City Hall and Court House, from every shop window and market stall, and on the head-gear of every horse in the busy street."

The city's picture publishers provided alternatives to decorate family homes in honored places above the parlor hearth. They quickly churned out dozens of "flagmania" engravings and lithographs, many showing young soldiers toting "the flag of our Union," swords brandished, often accompanied by an inspiring verse meant to pour more on the fire of the Sumter outrage.

PLATE 11-1

11

——⟨⟨⟨⟨⟩⟩⟩⟩——

The Palmetto and the Snake

Confederate Palmetto Flag, 1861

ONE OF THE MORE UNLIKELY RELICS IN THE NEW-YORK HISTORICAL Society's Civil War collection is this handkerchief-sized cotton flag. Less than a foot square in overall dimensions and somewhat tattered, it retains evidence of the vivid blue with which its unknown creator painted it in 1861, around the same time South Carolina declared its independence from the Union and joined the Confederacy.

According to the donor who presented the banner to the Society at war's end, this state flag flew proudly in Charleston during the Confederate bombardment of Fort Sumter—waving in that day's strong winds as a testament to Southern defiance during the opening hours of the Civil War.

The design for South Carolina's new state flag, featuring a white palmetto tree set against an azure field, with a white crescent moon tucked into its upper hoist corner, had been formally adopted only three months earlier. But its inspiration could be traced all the way back to 1765, when foes of the British Stamp Act angrily toted blue flags in their protest parades, most of them featuring an emblem pattern composed of three crescent moons—increasingly interpreted as a defiant symbol of liberty. Just such a flag flew from Charleston's Sullivan's Island when it came under attack by the British fleet in June 1776. It was said that the city's defender, the patriot colonel William Moultrie, credited an impenetrable wall of palmetto tree logs at the site of the fort subsequently named for him with saving the island from destruction by enemy shells. In tribute, South Carolina added an upright palmetto tree to the state flag in 1861, as if to serve notice to Union forces that it would again, and always, be prepared to resist what it regarded as invasion.

The flag's other dominant symbol, the coiled snake, dated to the Colonial period. Benjamin Franklin had issued his famous woodcut, "Join, or Die," in 1754, showing a snake sliced into pieces, each representing a different disconnected colony. The image was meant to call to mind an ancient legend that held that if a snake was cut into sections, it would return to life if joined back together before the sun went down. By adapting and visualizing this myth, Franklin meant to inspire the squabbling colonies to make themselves stronger through national unity. The coiled-snake motif eventually appeared on American currency, on military uniforms, and of course on flags—the generic snake eventually replaced by an indigenous American rattlesnake, the pieces restored and inseparable, and a new slogan in place to ward off aggressors: "Don't tread on me."

By the outbreak of the Civil War, the combination of all these potent emblems in South Carolina iconography served to vivify the assertion of the seceded states that they were fighting a noble battle for their independence and liberty little different from the struggles of the founders against Great Britain during the Revolutionary War era. As the historian Reid Mitchell has pointed out, "The flag itself was the emblem of the community that sent companies and regiments into the field. . . . Their flags linked them to their homes." Since flags were usually made by women, they required protection much as the soldiers' wives and mothers needed protection. "The flag was the physical tie between the homelife they had left and fought for and the war into which they were plunged." Yet the fact that South Carolina felt compelled to maintain its own flag at a moment of emerging Southern nationalism testified as well to the challenges facing a new Confederate nation founded on states' rights: some of its own component parts still considered themselves independent republics. Not for a while longer did the Stars and Bars come into general use in all areas of the Confederacy. The problem with the Stars and Bars motif was that it so closely resembled the Stars and

Confederate Navy Jack, or "Southern Cross," 1861–1865

Stripes, especially on the battlefield. For that reason the Confederate general P. G. T. Beauregard designed a separate "battle flag" based on the St. Andrew's cross.

Nevertheless, artists on both sides returned frequently to the palmetto-and-snake motifs throughout the Civil War—both to further sanctify the idea of Southern independence and, from the other side, to brand it as outright treason.

It would be unfair to conclude that Confederate nationalism waned over the course of the Civil War simply because patriotic emblems grew scarcer or, conversely, that emblems grew scarcer because nationalism waned. The truth has little to do with demand or patriotism. In fact, so much of Southern industry began focusing on war production, so many artists and artisans took up arms, that neither the time nor the manpower remained on hand to supply a full panoply of civilian goods. Imports, meanwhile, declined precipitously as a result of the Union

PLATE 11–2

blockade. Through all the deprivation, flags retained their special romance, and it was not unusual for an engraver assigned to "official" work in the Confederate Treasury or Post Office departments to place a flag prominently on currency or stamps. And when Lost Cause artists reinvigorated Confederate memory after 1865, flags and flag bearers resumed their dominant place retrospectively. Artists like William L. Sheppard and Allen C. Redwood made flag bearers objects of special attention and reverence, illustrating the legend that those bearing the colors almost always fell picturesquely and passed their banners to an eager comrade before either soldier or flag hit the ground. The reality was more complicated, but one story that has the ring of truth involved an enlisting officer who told a potential recruit that he would be especially proud to carry the regimental flag because it bore the words "Victory or Death."

The enlistee replied, "I object to the motto."

"Why so?" inquired the officer. "How shall it be changed?"

The recruit answered: "Make it victory or pretty damned badly wounded, and I'm your huckleberry."

If enthusiasm varied, so did the use of enthusiasm-generating symbols. Toward the end of the war, the snake symbol that had begun appearing frequently in American cartoons created in the North was no longer the coiled rattler symbolizing American defiance but the equally venomous new symbol of Northern Democratic opposition to the war: the copperhead. New York, Boston, and Philadelphia artists might depict Jefferson Davis strung up from a symbolic palmetto or hanging from the proverbial sour apple tree of derisive song. In one end-of-war print titled "Young America," the nation was symbolized by the cherubic infant Hercules, seen choking the life out of the two serpents dispatched by a jealous Hera, according to Greek myth, but redeployed now to remind Northerners that national survival had been threatened by the reptilian offenses of sedition and rebellion. The palmetto and snake, once used to represent liberty and endurance, came in the end to reference treason.

That makes it doubly ironic that in June 1865, E. C. Estes, the business manager and secretary of the executive committee for the National

Freedman's Relief Association, sent this flag to George H. Moore, librarian of the New-York Historical Society, accompanied by the following affidavit: "Herewith is a small Palmetto Flag which was in use by the Rebels during the attack on Fort Sumter. Mr. Chs. C. Leigh obtained it in that vicinity some years ago. He is certain of its genuineness, and when about to leave home a month ago, at my suggestion deemed it best to send it to you."

At the time, the association was busy collecting clothing and cash not for unrepentant white advocates of the Lost Cause but for ex-slaves uprooted and impoverished by the war. Perhaps Estes and Leigh meant this only as a prize of war. It did not seem to occur to the generous donor that the flag had once represented the last defense *against* the freedom of the once-enslaved people his organization was now endeavoring to sustain.

A GREAT RUSH

Cost what it may,

The Nation must be Saved!

TO JOIN THE

36TH REGIMENT

NEW YORK VOLUNTEERS,

Commanded by COLONEL W. H. BROWN.

This fine Regiment, one of the best in the Army of the Potomac, has been an active participant in the engagements on the Peninsula, and particularly distinguished itself during the "SEVEN DAYS' FIGHTING," having captured the Colors of the 14th North Carolina Regiment at the Battle of Malvern Hill. The term of enlistment of this Regiment will be out in

NINE MONTHS.

DON'T WAIT TO BE DRAFTED!

THE USUAL BOUNTY GIVEN.

Recruiting Office, No. 17 CENTRE STREET,
BETWEEN CHAMBERS AND READE STREETS.

Lieut. G. H. MOORE, Recruiting Officer.

BAKER & GODWIN, Printers. Printing-House Square. Opposite City Hall. New York.

PLATE 12–1

12

⟞᯽⟝

To Arms!

A Great Rush to Join the 36th Regiment,
New York Volunteers, Woodcut, ca. 1862

O N APRIL 15, 1861, PRESIDENT LINCOLN OFFICIALLY ACKNOWLEDGED the existence of a rebellion against the U.S. government. Based on a 1795 law giving him the power to arm the states' militias in an emergency, he issued a proclamation calling for seventy-five thousand volunteers to "re-possess the forts, places, and property which have been seized from the Union" by "combinations too powerful to be suppressed by the ordinary course of judicial proceedings, or by the powers vested in the Marshals by law." Four days later he ordered a blockade of Southern ports. The aggressive response masked a desperate situation. The South housed the majority of federal arsenals, now falling like dominoes into Confederate hands. And in 1861 the American standing army boasted a paltry sixteen thousand men, most of them assigned to duty at remote western forts guarding settlers against Indians.

Northern states responded to the proclamation with alacrity, but within weeks four more Southern states forced now to choose between secession and suppression of their sister states not only formally refused to raise regiments for Lincoln but abandoned the Union entirely: Tennessee, Arkansas, North Carolina, and Virginia joined the Confederacy. Border slave states like Kentucky and Maryland resisted the call for volunteers and teetered on the brink of secession as well. In July, Lincoln asked a special session of Congress for "the legal means for making this contest, a short, and a decisive one." After this, no one doubted that a real civil war had begun, even though confident Northerners continued to believe it would be brief.

Because the Militia Act that authorized Lincoln to call for volunteers specifically limited their service to ninety days, many idealistic Northerners rushed into service expecting to endure no more than a three-month duty characterized by more glory than danger. Only later did the administration turn to three-year recruitment and eventually resort to military conscription to fill increasingly demanding state quotas for more men.

The first volunteers had a difficult—and dangerous—time reaching the national capital. On April 19, the day Lincoln ordered the blockade, a mob of pro-secessionist Marylanders attacked troops from the 6th Massachusetts Volunteers as they attempted to change railroad lines in Baltimore—along the same perilous route Lincoln himself had originally planned to take when he passed through that city en route to Washington for his inauguration six weeks earlier. Lincoln had altered his plans, but the soldiers could not. Waiting for them as horses pulled their railroad cars across town, angry onlookers jeered, waved Confederate flags, and threw stones before gunfire rang out. As many as four civilians and nine soldiers died in the riot. Fears mounted that Washington itself was now vulnerable to attack.

When the governor of Maryland, Thomas Hicks, reacted to the outbreak of violence by requesting that federal troops stop using his state as a passageway to the defense of Washington (further insulting the president by proposing that the British ambassador serve as mediator between North and South), Lincoln summoned Hicks and the mayor of Baltimore, George W. Brown, for an emergency meeting. It proved more a confrontation than a conference. The president used the occasion to issue a blunt statement that left little doubt that he expected volunteers not only to continue coming forward but to come forward through Maryland:

You, gentlemen, come here to me and ask for peace on any terms, and yet have no word of condemnation for those who are making war on us. You express great horror of bloodshed, and yet would not lay a straw in the way of those who are organizing in Virginia and elsewhere to capture this city. The rebels attack Fort Sumter, and your citizens attack troops sent to the defense of the Government, and the lives and property in Washington, and yet you would have me break my oath and surrender the Government without a blow. There is no Washington in that—no Jackson in that—no manhood nor honor in that. I have no desire to invade the South; but I must have troops to defend this Capital. Geographically it lies surrounded by the soil of Maryland; and mathematically the necessity exists that they should come over her territory. Our men are not moles, and can't dig under the earth; they are not birds, and can't fly through the air. There is no way but to march across, and that they must do. But in doing this there is no need of collision. Keep your rowdies in Baltimore, and there will be no bloodshed. Go home and tell your people that if they will not attack us, we will not attack them; but if they do attack us, we will return it, and that severely.

The president hoped he had secured the right of passage through Maryland, but when troops still had not appeared in Washington by the night of April 23, Lincoln's aides found him standing "alone and silent" before the huge windows on the second floor of the White House, gazing "long and wistfully . . . down the Potomac in the direction of the expected ships; and, unconscious of other presence in the room, at length broke out with irrepressible anguish in the repeated exclamation, 'Why don't they come! Why don't they come!'" Two days later he authorized Lieutenant General Winfield Scott to arrest the members of the Maryland legislature, if necessary, to prevent their assembling at Annapolis with the avowed purpose of instituting secession proceedings. When the first battered volunteers of the 6th Massachusetts finally limped into Washington, Lincoln greeted them personally, saying: "I begin to believe that there is no North. The Seventh Regiment is a myth. Rhode

Island is another. You are the only real thing." But then New York's 7th at last made its way into town, covering the final twenty miles from Annapolis on foot, prepared to fight secessionists all along the way if necessary. Finally, Washington was secured.

New York responded to the first call for volunteers—its initial quota was seventeen regiments—with a rush of patriotic fervor and an unprecedented commitment to service. "Cost what it may," thundered one recruiting poster, "the Nation must be Saved!" On Sunday, April 21, George Templeton Strong attended Sabbath services at New York City's Trinity Church and was electrified by the divine coincidence of the epistle of the day from the book of Joel: "Prepare War; wake up the mighty men: let all the men of war draw near. . . . Beat your plowshares into swords. . . . Multitudes, multitudes in the Valley of Decision . . . because they have shed innocent blood in their land." By the following evening, prominent New Yorkers, Strong among them, had organized a volunteers' association to manage recruitment efforts. New York's 7th Regiment marched down Broadway and off to the defense of Washington "through a tempest of cheers two miles long," while a parade of the 69th Irish Brigade attracted a large crowd of what the incurable blue-blooded snob Strong called "Biddies . . . sobbing and sighing." According to Strong, too old to fight but sufficiently imbued with war fever to agree to train recruits in rifle marksmanship: "Both regiments looked as well as one has a right to expect of levies raised on such short notice. The uniformed companies looked and marched well."

In May, the stakes increased when Lincoln asked for another forty-two thousand volunteers, this time for a term of three years, and added a call for eighteen thousand sailors for the navy. Individuals eager to claim command of a new company or regiment conducted most of this recruiting. Absent any government recruiting offices—at least initially—these ambitious would-be captains and colonels competed with one another to organize units for the war. The New-York Historical Society boasts a number of posters that were once displayed in shopwindows, on fences, and on trees to attract volunteers. "Pension! Bounty! Extra Pay!" promised one. Another, promoting the Harris Light Cavalry, touted its "beautiful camp at Scarsdale, near New Rochelle, New York" as if it were a vacation retreat, adding that "6 Sergeants and 8 corporals to each company will be selected from the best privates in the ranks."

Yet another such poster heralded "75 More Recruits Wanted for the Anthon Battalion of Light Artillery Now Quartered at Camp Green, Mount St. Vincent, Central Park, N.Y.," adding the alluring promise of "$50 cash bounty immediately upon enlistment and $100 at the end of the war!"

The New York print publisher Baker & Godwin, which had issued a Lincoln campaign lithograph just a few months earlier, now produced a large notice asking for volunteers for the Twelfth New York Artillery, which breathlessly announced: "The conscription will soon commence! Avoid it and secure the Bounties and help to man the forts! Awake! The Enemy Are Upon Us." The offer included a $402 bounty from the federal government and $75 more from the state, and the poster provided the useful detail that recruiters were ready to accept volunteers at offices on both Broadway and South Street. Baker & Godwin contributed other stellar examples of the genre, including a magnificent hand-colored, two-by-three-foot "Recruits Wanted" broadside offering Brooklyn recruits a $75 bounty and a month's pay in advance to serve three years under Colonel Anthony Conk's "Senatorial Regiment." The appeal to patriotism was visual as well as mercenary. The woodcut featured a barefoot and appealingly buxom goddess of liberty sitting atop a cannon beside a large American eagle, holding the national shield and a ribbonlike banner declaring: "Respond to Your Country's Call!" In the background sat a paddle-wheel ship and a lighthouse to suggest unthreatened commerce and by contrast the now-iconic walls of Fort Sumter, its tattered flag flying. Surmounting all was a liberty cap illuminated by a sunburst indicating that the war had become as much about freedom as reunion and revenge.

The resulting early rush of patriotism nationwide was compromised by confusion, disorganization, and corruption, but somehow the Union came close to meeting its manpower quotas. The North was ready to make the war a short one as advertised, though the South had other ideas. New York exceeded its original quota many times over, organizing sixty-six regiments by the end of 1861.

One of the gaudiest among all the Society's recruitment posters is the richly illustrated "A Great Rush / Cost what it may," a poster issued in 1862 to attract recruits for the 36th Regiment, New York Volunteers, a unit commanded by a colonel named W. H. Brown. Though this handsome example of the Union's insatiable appetite for manpower dates to the year after recruiting officially commenced, it beautifully represents the ongoing push for volunteers.

By the time this poster appeared, Lincoln had asked for yet another 500,000 men, and there was no going back. By the end of the war, by one estimate, more than 2.7 million had served in the federal armed forces and over a million in the Confederate.

13

━━━◦/◦/◦━━━

Uniform Courage

Zouave Uniform, ca. 1861–1863

INTACT SURVIVING CIVIL WAR UNIFORMS IN FINE CONDITION ARE RARE and precious enough, but the gorgeous, impeccably preserved Zouave costume that has resided in the New-York Historical Society collection since 1948 may be unique. The exotic woolen outfit—boasting additional elements made of linen, cotton, metal, bone, and even wood— was worn by Private David P. Davis of the 5th New York Volunteer Infantry, a unit known as Duryee's Zouaves or the "Red-Legged Devils," through some of the bloodiest engagements of the eastern theater. Davis was one of thousands of early Union recruits who went into action at the most terrifyingly modern battles in world history incongruously dressed like Algerian soldiers from previous generations. Anachronisms or not, by the end of the war some seventy-five Zouave regiments had fought on the Union side and about twenty-five regiments on the Confederate. All of them enlisted and fought in flamboyant attire like this as long as their costumes held out. They proved hard to maintain and virtually impossible to replace.

In their baggy red pantaloons, short cape-like jackets, white puttees, gold-trimmed wraparound sashes, and fez-style tasseled hats of distinctly Middle Eastern inspiration (they even wore turbans for dress occasions!), Zouaves turned out to be easy marks—their uniforms' vivid hues made them targets. But for a while, fey and affected as their apparel may look to modern eyes, Zouaves were widely considered the roughest

PLATE 13–1

and toughest men in Union service. Eventually, most Zouave regiments shed the distinctive costumes, if only because it grew increasingly difficult to find materials to repair them. But a few units did stubbornly cling to the uniform (the 114th Pennsylvania, also known as Collis's Zouaves d'Afrique, served in full dress from 1862 until the end of the war because, it was explained, they were "men of pride and culture"). The gradual disappearance of these colorful Zouave fighters, as the historian Mark E. Neely Jr. and I have written, constituted what amounted to "a reversal of the caterpillar's progress toward butterfly."

The French had first brought the Zouave "look" home from their wars in North Africa in the 1830s (the name derived from a colorfully attired Berber tribe from Algeria's Jurjura Mountains known as the Zouaoua) and adapted it for their own elite units in the Crimea. Observing them there, the future Civil War general George B. McClellan praised the French Zouaves as "the most reckless, self-reliant, and complete infantry that Europe can produce," adding admiringly: "With his graceful dress, soldierly bearing, and vigilant attitude, the Zouave at an outpost is the beau-ideal of a soldier." There was no denying that though to modern eyes they made soldiers look not unlike harem dancers, the uniforms came to convey unrivaled fearlessness. "Nobody knows anything about these men who has not seen them in battle," wrote Thomas Wentworth Higginson, a white abolitionist who later became an officer in an all-black Union regiment. *There is a fierce energy about them beyond anything of which I have ever read,* unless it be the French Zouaves. It requires the strictest discipline to hold them in hand." Not everyone concurred. The artist Winslow Homer created several famous canvases of Zouaves smoking pipes or pitching quoits in camp, but even an art critic of the day who lauded the works as "remarkably fine" could not help speculating about the inutility of Zouave uniforms in combat, deriding the "flaming scarlet and blue . . . with which some departmental lunacy has clothed a large portion of our heroes."

In fact, one of the war's first Union heroes had helped introduce and popularize the Zouave style in America, and his early death cemented the Zouaves' reputation for manhood and courage. Ephraim Elmer Ellsworth, who hailed from upstate New York, won prewar fame as the drillmaster of an elite and gaudily uniformed outfit called the U.S. Zou-ave Cadets, by some accounts the first Americans to dress in this dis-tinctive style. Ellsworth may have had a hand in designing the uniforms himself, but it was one of his cadets who described their attire with all the deadpan earnestness of a twenty-first-century fashion writer: "A bright red chasseur cap with gold braid; light blue shirt with moire an-tique facings; dark blue jacket with orange and red trimmings; brass bell buttons, placed as close together as possible; a red sash and loose red trousers; russet leather leggings, buttoned over the trousers, reaching from ankle halfway to knee; and white waistbelt." When the Ellsworth unit made an appearance at the New York Academy of Music for a "grand dress" demonstration of its gymnastic drill routines, the *New York Times* rapturously declared, "The name Zouave is just now a house-hold word."

Ellsworth's elite unit went on to win a national drill team champion-ship and then toured the West performing its acrobatic routines to the accompaniment of a brass band. Later Ellsworth headed to Illinois, where he fell under the thrall of Abraham Lincoln, studying for a time in Lincoln's Springfield law office before joining a handpicked cadre of military officers and civilians who accompanied the president-elect as bodyguards on his inaugural journey to Washington. The spruce, di-minutive Ellsworth, who became a huge favorite with the entire Lincoln family, initially hoped for appointment to a desk job in the War Depart-ment, but when it stalled, he impatiently returned to New York and or-ganized a company of local firemen into an eleven-hundred-man Zouave regiment, deploying them to the defense of Washington in the spring of 1861. Lincoln personally swore them in on May 5.

That month, itching for action, Ellsworth grew increasingly offended by the sight of a mammoth Confederate flag constantly flying from atop the Marshall House, an undistinguished hotel in Alexandria, Virginia, just across the Potomac River from the White House—technically Con-federate territory since Virginia had seceded in April. On May 24, Ells-worth defiantly marched a company of soldiers into the city and climbed up to the hotel rooftop himself, where he tore down the flag and headed downstairs clutching it as a trophy of war. But the hotel's indignant proprietor, James W. Jackson, met Ellsworth as he descended the staircase and fired at him at close range with a double-barreled shotgun, killing him instantly. The little colonel, the first Union officer to die in the war, was only twenty-four years old. Reflecting widespread outrage at the news, George Templeton Strong predicted that his "murder will stir the fire in every northern state." In Strong's opinion, Ellsworth "could hardly have done such service as his assassin has rendered the country."

Recognizing similar propaganda value in the tragedy, and no doubt deeply mourning his death as well, Lincoln consecrated Ellsworth's sacrifice and helped elevate him to the status of national martyr by hosting his funeral in the East Room of the White House. He also sent a magnificent condolence letter to the young man's bereaved parents, lamenting in part:

> In the untimely loss of your noble son, our affliction here, is scarcely less than your own. So much of promised usefulness to one's country, and of bright hopes for one's self and friends, have rarely been so suddenly dashed, as in his fall. In size, in years, and in youthful appearance, a boy only, his power to command men, was surpassingly great. This power, combined with a fine intellect, an indomitable energy, and a taste altogether military, constituted in him, as seemed to me, the best natural talent, in that department, I ever knew.

Amid the Ellsworth mania it was forgotten by most Northerners that the colonel's so-called avenger, the innkeeper Jackson, was himself shot dead on the spot by a Union corporal. Jackson, too, became a martyr, no less celebrated for his sacrifice in the Confederacy as was "the gallant Ellsworth," the quintessential Zouave hero, in the Union. But with significantly greater publishing power, and a public blessed with much more disposable income to spend on decorative pictures, the Northern hero emerged the more famous by far. More than four dozen prints of Ellsworth flooded the marketplace in 1861.

Following Ellsworth's virtual canonization, so many Zouave regiments organized in tribute, imitation, or both that one French-language newspaper proudly commented: *"Il pleut des Zouaves"* ("It is raining

Zouaves"). Like all regiments, they varied in ability, but their extravagant uniforms always made them stand out. New York uniquely combined ethnic pride and fashion appeal when it organized one such unit, the Phoenix Regiment of Corcoran Zouaves, which its commanders described as a "splendid Regiment of Irish volunteers" composed of "as fine a lot of fellows as ever followed the Green Flag to Battle." In the words of a verse accompanying its original recruitment poster: "Oh, come and wear a green cockade / And learn the soldier's glorious trade; / 'Tis of such stuff a hero's made— / Then come and join the Bold Brigade."

Unfortunately, far less is known about Private David P. Davis, whose son donated his intact uniform to the New-York Historical Society more than eighty years after the end of the war. But according to archival records, Davis enlisted at the age of twenty-six on May 9, 1861—only two weeks before Ellsworth died so spectacularly in Alexandria—mustering into service at Fort Schuyler in the Bronx before heading south to the front. Before the end of his two-year service, Davis saw action in the Peninsula Campaign, the Second Battle of Bull Run, Antietam, Fredericksburg, and Chancellorsville. He survived them all—flamboyantly dressed like this.

Ephraim Elmer Ellsworth (1837–1861),
photographic print, ca. 1861

PLATE 13–2

14

⟨ση⟩

Divided Loyalties

Letter from Howard Cushing Wright
to His Mother, 1861

NOT EVERY NEW YORKER VOLUNTEERED TO FIGHT FOR THE UNION, or even support the Union cause, even in the wake of such patriotism-generating events as the attack on the Stars and Stripes at Fort Sumter, the flag-suffused rally at Union Square, and the martyrdom of the local celebrity Colonel Ellsworth. For some, what was often called "the Southern way of life" proved irresistibly alluring.

One such New Yorker was Howard Cushing Wright, whose cool-headed letter to his mother declaring his unwavering allegiance to the Confederacy appears on these pages. Wright was born in the city around 1837; his father was a banknote engraver from Maine, and his mother was a well-known educator who hailed from Charleston. No doubt the Sumter episode alone inspired fascinating table conversation in the Wright household in April 1861. One wonders what Mrs. Wright said of the action at her onetime hometown—or what her son made of it. A war many historians have described as brother against brother may have seemed to the Wrights more like a mother-against-father dispute. In fact, most of their children sided with the Union. But the Wrights had apparently taken or sent their promising son on several trips to the South during his boyhood, and these sojourns clearly influenced him.

He was precocious from the start and an abundantly gifted writer. By

New Orleans, Monday, July

My dearest mother.

I received your letter through E.
Benedict & Co's office here yesterday and it was as
welcome as it was unexpected. I had not written
you for a long time because of not being sure
through communication but will trust this to
B. & Co's mail, so as to assure you, & through you
my dear sisters, of my good health and prosperity.
I received a letter from you & others from Zelly & Mr.
Patterson while at Pensacola. Coming from the
North, they were opened in the Army P.O., as was the
rule with letters from an enemy's country, although
the Lieut. in charge of the P.O., who was an old
friend, offered to forego the order in my case, which
I deemed unnecessary & improper to accede to. I am
glad to learn that you still have even moderate
health and are sustained by your indomitable
perseverance and pray earnestly that you may be
successful in your school enterprise. I am very
well pleased too, to see that Sister Nanny's name
has been published on the faculty list, as it will
give her a nominal standing that will be of use
to her in other exertions in the profession of music
for which I know she has an inclination of natural
taste and thereby will find it less laborious to
than instruction in the English branches. With good
fortune, too, it might become much more compen-
sating to her than any other branch of teaching
could be. I hope Phebe's pleasure trip will do her
good & that she will take more out-door exercise.
How well I see, in looking back, that she & Zelly
have both sacrificed themselves in an overstrained sense
of home duties toward their children.

PLATE 14-1

2

How deeply I deplore this terrible war,
at seems to place such a gulf between me
d those whom I love at home, I cannot well
lain in words; but I would not for the world
ve you think for a moment, my dear mother,
t the strength of my feelings in the cause
the South could in the slightest impair my
e for you all. No, it leads me to think oftener
d more tenderly of those at home. It is a
rible crisis when brother is arrayed against
ther, but should the one hesitate to oppose
grant wrong & criminal oppression because the
er sides with that wrong & oppression, even if
views it in a far different light?

Henry Patterson wrote me that by birth &
me my allegiance was due to the North. If a
d were born in a stable, would it be a colt?
cept among my own family I have no friends in
North — I owe it nothing. But how is it with
South? The period I passed in Bayoufara, in my
ildhood, made more impression upon me than
the rest of my boyish days. After returning North
lways felt a yearning I did not then understand
ard this section, & frequently looked forward to return-
g. My frivolous attempt to become a man of
siness in Corning &c's was the first great mistake
my life. People thought I was lazy & devoid of
nly ambition. It was because I was out of my
tural channel. The amount of labor in a
erent line that I have accomplished since then, has
nished other journalists. My next grand mistake
in the Home Circle. There my plans were good
I split on the rock of its business management.

the time war broke out, according to an account written many years later by his niece, young Howard had already established a small weekly literary journal in New York, developing a skill, a contemporary reported, for "composing serial sketches and romances." To help support himself, he sent additional contributions to a number of Louisiana newspapers and established a reputation there as well. Wright had already spent considerable time in the region and was devoted to Southern literature. When war broke out, he left for New Orleans.

On July 29, 1861, his spirits lifted by the unexpected Confederate victory at the First Battle of Bull Run (Manassas), Wright wrote home to his Southern-born mother to explain his decision to renounce the Union—probably to an audience of one who did not need much convincing, considering her origins. But as Wright's long letter shows, he certainly knew he was likely to lose the affection of other family members by pledging allegiance to the Confederacy. His letter reads more like a manifesto. Its calm formality suggests that he rather hoped his relatives could steer it into print.

After dispensing with family matters, Wright got right to the point, arguing passionately for states' rights, Southern independence, and the righteousness of slavery in what must rank as one of the most impassioned defenses of the Confederate cause ever composed. Though still largely unknown, it is eloquent enough to require a transcript rather than a summary:

> How deeply I deplore this terrible war, that seems to place such a gulf between me and those whom I love at home. I cannot well explain in words, but I would not for the world have you think for a moment, my dear mother, that the strength of my feelings in the cause of the South could in the slightest impair my love for you all. No, it leads me to think oftener and more tenderly of those at home. It is a terrible crisis when brother is arrayed against brother, but should the one hesitate to oppose flagrant wrong & criminal oppression because the other sides with that wrong & oppression, even if he views it in a far different light?
>
> Henry Patterson wrote me that by birth & home my allegiance was due to the North. If a kid were born in a stable, would it be a colt? Ex-

cept among my own family, I have no friends in the North—I owe it nothing. But how is it with the South? The period I passed in Bayou Sara, in my childhood, made more impression upon me than all the rest of my boyish days. After returning North I always felt a yearning I did not then understand toward this section, & frequently looked forward to returning. My frivolous attempts to become a man of business in Corning & Co's was the first grand mistake of my life. People thought I was lazy & devoid of manly ambition. It was because I was out of my natural channel. . . .

Northern papers boast of the unparalleled "rush to arms" of their people but what do the figures show? No deduction need be made from Northern population for slaves. Now if the North had "rushed to arms" as Louisianans have, [General Winfield] Scott would per force have 1,300,000 men at the seat of war and over 2,000,000 under arms and drilling, ready to respond to the first call of danger. And La. has not ceased sending troops to the field. Nearly every day companies are arriving from county parishes and others are getting up all over the city. Yes, my dear mother, I tell you with the solemn earnestness of truth, the people of the South are resolved, now that their stand of independence is taken, to maintain it to the bitter end. Thousands after thousands of their bravest men may be slaughtered in battle, they may be driven inch by inch from their homes on the border, but before they are conquered every courageous Southerner must be killed, every Southern dollar expended and there will be no longer a South—it will be but a worthless wreck. We are ready at any moment to put the torch to our entire cotton crop, destroy all our stored provisions, yes, to burn down our cities as the Russians did at Moscow, if necessary. But such sacrifices will not be required. Manassas has told us so. . . .

Now, then the South being determined to uphold the institution of slavery, in the belief that it was right, natural to their country, and God-ordained (vide the Sacred Scriptures), the best informed and most thoughtful have seen for years that the "irrepressible conflict" [the New Yorker William H. Seward's controversial prewar phrase for the inevitability of war] was a stern reality. The abolitionists did not boldly proclaim their real intentions in 1856 and 1860 because it would not have been politic, but they knew that by laboring with perseverance they could drive the South from one point to another until at length it would awake to its danger only to find itself helpless in the net which had been so slowly but surely drawn around it. . . . The Republican party gained control of the North and the Abolitionists gained control of the Republican party.

Southern statesmen saw the precipice to which their section was being so noiselessly drawn and they endeavored to awake the slumbering South. Many opened their eyes and myself among the number. I was not an earnest secessionist, on principle, from 1859, but a great many slept in their fancied security and indignantly protested against the cry of wolf because its fangs were not fastened in their throat.

But those who saw the danger resolved to save their country if possible. They knew that Lincoln would be elected and his administration could cripple the South in six months by removing our material to northern arsenals, by gaining unprincipled partizans among us through the disposal of office and federal patronage. Trusting to the ultimate vindication of his constituents, [John] Floyd [former president Buchanan's secretary of war] sent all the war material South that he could remove without arousing suspicion, that we might not be defenceless when we had to fight for our independence. Lincoln was elected & the news fell like a thunderbolt on those who had thought a majority at the North could never be deluded into hostility against them. Now spoke forth secession. "The irrepressible conflict is upon us—the South must choose at once between the abolition of slavery or independence—a year hence will be too late to take a stand—we will then be in chains!"

. . . Patriotism slept for awhile with some and the greed for gain and cowardly love of ease and safety kept others from coming forward. But the rapid succession of events that followed dashed the veil from before the eyes of the dim-seeing and awakened the latent patriotism of the luxuriant. Now we are eleven bonded States, Missouri is anxious to join us and poor outraged Maryland would, if she could. In Western Va & Eastern Tenn. there are plenty of abolitionists but our principle of government gives them the right to go where they please—to cast their lot with whichever government they desire. The South needs and wishes no unsympathizing hearts, no unwilling hands.

And now for the deduction—If slavery is right in the estimation of the South, she is right in upholding it. Consequently she is right in taking every necessary measure for defending it. Who but the individual menaced can be the judge of his danger? The South believed her institutions would be gradually destroyed by remaining in the Union & that the only way of preserving them was to set up an independent government, she had the right to do so precisely as the colonies had to declare their independence in 1776, when their cause of complaint was not the threatened destruction of their social system but simply a question of the pocket—taxes.

The North says that in seceding the South wanted to rob her. What baseless assertion! Has the South ever refused to arrange a friendly and equitable settlement of the national accounts? Why the North has never thought of letting her do it. The South, I believe, would gladly have consented at one time, even to get the worst of the bargain, than to be dragged into conflict with their brothers to maintain their rights. No, the Lincoln government thought it was able to rush out slavery, even if the South were destroyed with it, by arraying the host of the Northern States under that shallow but delusive cry of "the Union." This cry is but thoughtless sentiment—the stern and terrible facts of the times require men to go deeper down than buncombe. . . .

There seem to be three principle [*sic*] motives which bind together the North in this bloody, fratricidal war of extermination. First, the abolitionists think they see in it the eventual freedom of the slaves, whose alteration of social condition is to them dearer than the lives of millions of their own brothers. Second, the spirit of revenge arouses among the masses, and their desire to retrieve the mortification caused at first by the fall of Sumter & latterly by the rout of their great army at Manassas. Third, the love of ambition and gold, the war furnishing such a large number of military titles and "fat contracts." Thus, the Northern motive—springs of this war resolve themselves into four vices—fanaticism, revenge, vanity and avarice. These lead to crimes on a much larger scale that are inseparable from war—murder, arson, robbery and lying. Would it not have been better and more Christian to let the Southern Confederacy go out of the Union, right or wrong, with a fair settlement of the national accounts and an amicable treaty of commerce and friendship?

Who is there so stupid or even so prejudiced as to really and honestly believe that the South can now be forced back into the Union? What would a Union be worth, maintained by fire and sword? If a wife thinks she is wronged by her husband, and believing that he intends to ill-use her, leaves him, is there any honorable or chivalrous man who would advocate beating her and putting her in chains to prevent her running away? I am in no mood for boasting; because we have won such a signal victory at Manassas I do not look forward to a constant succession of triumphs; but this I do say, and leave its vindication to time & history—the South cannot be conquered. . . .

As my brothers-in-law, and perhaps my sisters, look upon me with deep sorrow for having espoused the cause of the South I have often longed to sit down and write them why I am heart and hand a secessionist, not that I expected to abate their Northern feelings a jot, (for a drop of rain can affect nothing falling in the midst of a desert of sand) but that they might understand and perhaps appreciate my feelings, should it become necessary for me to confront upon the battle field the man of that section in which I happened to be born. It is well that they should know that if I am not already in the ranks of Gen. Beauregard's army, it is not because I am unwilling to go or hesitate to wield a sword or bayonet against Northern men. [T]he South has plenty of men in the field to defend her soil and there are plenty more "eager for the fray." If these are not enough she will find plenty more, myself among the number. I pray God that in such an event I may not be confronted by one I love or esteem, but my duty to my country is my duty to God and to him I pray, as you pray, to bring this horrible war to an end.

The "horrible war" of course continued, and true to his word Wright enlisted as an officer in the 30th Louisiana Infantry and saw action at the Battle of Baton Rouge in 1862 and in the Confederate defense the following year of Port Hudson, a stronghold along the Mississippi River.

From there he was captured, imprisoned, paroled, and joined up to fight yet again.

Wright died in action on the battlefield on April 14, 1865—according to the date supplied by his niece to the Historical Society decades later. Although Lee had surrendered the Army of Northern Virginia five days earlier, effectively ending the war, skirmishes had continued to break out in North Carolina, Alabama, and several states in the West. Wright was reported to have "received a shot wound in the breast which caused instant death" during an artillery exchange at West Point, Georgia. Joseph Johnston surrendered the last standing Confederate army to William T. Sherman just twelve days later on the twenty-sixth.

Another casualty the very same day Howard Wright died was Abraham Lincoln, fatally shot at Ford's Theatre shortly after 10:00 p.m. Earlier on that same April 14, Major Robert Anderson, the commander who had lowered the U.S. flag in surrender at Fort Sumter four years earlier to the day, raised it anew in triumph at ceremonies there marking the end of the Civil War. By now, Sumter was a ruin, its walls battered by months of relentless shelling not by South Carolinians but by Union gunboats. Fireworks illuminated the harbor that night. Onlookers in Charleston no doubt recalled the beginning of the conflict, still not aware that Lincoln would soon become its final casualty and certainly unaware that a little-known New York writer named Howard Cushing Wright had fought against his section and his family, in his niece's words, showing himself "true to his convictions . . . a brave and loyal soldier who gave his life for the cause in which he believed." Wrote another eulogist: "The soil that he loved so well can not but lie tenderly on his faithful breast."

15

‒◦◦◦‒

Blarney from Bull Run?

*Return of the 69th (Irish) Regiment, N.Y.S.M. from
the Seat of War,* Painting by Louis Lang, 1862–1863

ASIDE FROM A FEW SURVIVING GIGANTIC CYCLORAMAS AND PETER
Rothermel's mural-sized paintings of the fighting at Gettysburg
commissioned by the state of Pennsylvania for its spacious capitol building, here is perhaps the largest-scale Civil War painting of them all. And
it is a true New York anomaly—a masterpiece of nineteenth-century
public relations designed, in a phrase so often used by modern market-
ers, to make lemons into lemonade.

Triumphal as the scene appears to the modern eye, the painting actually commemorates not the battle at which the men depicted in it had
fought but the safe return home to lower Manhattan of its survivors.
And these Irish Americans are veterans not of a resounding victory but
of a humbling defeat. Perhaps only in New York could ethnic pride swell
so grandly as to inspire a mammoth canvas more than seven by eleven
feet in size to honor a regiment that had achieved its greatest success
supervising a retreat. Recently restored to the full magnificence that
once dazzled both critics and viewers following years of deterioration in
storage, the panoramic picture now holds pride of place atop the museum staircase in the second-floor galleries opposite the New-York Historical Society library—repository of some of the surviving archives of
the very battle in which these soldiers fought.

94

To comprehend the onetime power of Louis Lang's *Return of the 69th (Irish) Regiment, N.Y.S.M. from the Seat of War* requires an understanding of who these men were—and how they got to and from the war in the first place. On April 23, 1861, just nine days after the surrender of Fort Sumter, the ten-year-old 69th Regiment of the New York State Militia responded to President Lincoln's call for volunteers and headed off to defend Washington under the command of the thirty-three-year-old colonel Michael Corcoran. Like most of his troops, Corcoran hailed from Ireland—in his case Carrowkeel in County Sligo. He had assumed command of New York's 69th in 1859.

A member of the influential Fenian Brotherhood in America as well as an active Democratic ward politician who held significant power as a school inspector and served on an influential committee overseeing judicial nominations, Corcoran had been highly successful in recruiting Irish Americans into the army. The Lincoln administration had made it clear that in order to promote loyalty among the North's diverse population—some of which, like the overwhelmingly Democratic Irish, opposed Lincoln politically—it wanted ethnic regiments formed and men we now call "hyphenated Americans" named to command them. By 1861, colonels and generals with foreign-sounding names like Schimmelfennig and Corcoran could be found leading Union soldiers into battle. Few proved very adept, but that is another story.

Corcoran's 69th, already widely known as the Irish Brigade, headed off by ship to Annapolis, then by rail to Washington, arriving at the capital on May 9, 1861, and making camp above the city at Arlington Heights. Assigned to join other units building up the defenses around Washington, the crack New York militia regiment needed only a week to construct its own 650-by-450-foot fortification, which the troops named in honor of their commander: Fort Corcoran. The grateful colonel asked the regimental chaplain, a Catholic priest named Thomas Mooney, to baptize its newly installed cannon with holy water. Father Mooney captured the mood of the hour by declaring, "Parents look forward to the first words of their children. I look forward to the first roar from the mouth of this babe." The archbishop recalled him.

On July 21, the Irish Regiment was ordered into the Battle of Bull Run

PLATE 15-1

in Northern Virginia as part of a brigade commanded by Colonel William T. Sherman. The 69th held its position manfully in the midst of a humiliating rout, losing forty-one men, then helped safeguard the Army of the Potomac's exposed rear flank during its hasty retreat back to Washington. But Michael Corcoran fell into enemy hands and became a prisoner of the Confederates. From captivity, he sent out the stirring message: "One half of my heart is Erin's, and the other half is America's. God bless America, and ever preserve her the asylum of all the oppressed of the earth, is the sincere prayer of my heart."

Though Corcoran continued to languish in confinement for more than a year, the twelve hundred volunteers of the Irish Brigade officially concluded their ninety-day enlistments once they returned to Washington from Manassas and then shipped back to New York under the command of Thomas Francis Meagher. They had served well in the midst of a demoralizing Union catastrophe, but even the most unflappable of these returning Bull Run veterans could not have expected the joyous reception the city offered them when they stepped off the steamer *John Potter* at Pier One at Battery Park in Manhattan on the morning of July 27. It was this jubilant scene that the artist Louis Lang painted in such monumental scale: a bravura depiction of a triumphant return that lacked nothing except the underpinning of a triumph. In a city where Irish pride trumped military accomplishment—and where sustaining morale remained a high priority—the boisterous reception seemed the most natural thing in the world. A critic of the day recognized that the picture emphasized not martial combat but "touching episodes that diversify the scene when the soldier becomes again the citizen."

Following their exuberant shoreline welcome, the ninety-day veterans of the 69th marched up Broadway to Union Square, then back down Fourth Avenue all the way to Grand Street to deposit their weapons at the Essex Market Armory. By August 3, the militia regiment had officially disbanded. It was left to Lang to immortalize a unique moment in early Civil War history: the glory of service for the sake of service.

He proved more than up to the challenge. Lang (1814–1893) was the son of a history painter and came to America from Germany as a young man after studying art in Stuttgart and Paris. By the early 1850s, he was

an established artist in New York and a member of the prestigious National Academy. No one is precisely sure who commissioned him to
paint the large picture of the return of the 69th, but the regiment itself is
the likeliest patron. It had an armory to decorate and a memory to preserve.

When completed in 1863, Lang's monumental canvas debuted on
public display at the Knoedler Gallery (formerly Goupil's) on Ninth
Street. It was an instant hit. A critic for the *New York Times* commented
favorably, noting that the incident it portrayed "gave scope to the artist;
allowing him to introduce the magnificent Bay of New-York as seen
from Bowling-green."

The influential periodical *Fine Arts* concurred: "The entrance of the
69th Regiment of N.Y. State Militia into this City . . . on its return from
its first brief and bloody campaign, was a popular ovation, especially
among the Irish residents of New York. The steady bearing and resolute
gallantry of the Sixty-ninth, in circumstances over which we have always passed lightly and which we would not willingly recall, fixed the
Sixty-ninth in the hearts of the people. The return, we say therefore, of
its shattered and hard-worn remains was regarded as a fete; and Mr.
Louis Lang, a very skilful and estimable artist here resident, has been
happy enough to select the most striking moment of their reception as
the subject of a large commemorative painting, now on exhibition at
Goupil's." For its part, the gallery wisely directed its exhibition publicity
at the Irish community. As its own advertising broadside proclaimed:
"Well may our adopted citizens be proud of a regiment that has nobly
sustained the glory and heroism of their native land, while defending the
flag of their adoption." As the art historian Barbara Dayer Gallati has as-
serted, the picture broke no new ground in heroic art—how could it,
with its focus instead on portraying identifiable local civilian celebrities?—but with its "brilliant accretion of detail" it provided "a complete
impression of an actual urban event" on a "scale . . . unmatched in
nineteenth-century American art."

Lang's highly romanticized scene—after all, it is very unlikely that
children and beautifully dressed girls lolled about in the street as men
and horses approached—was so well received that it seemed not to

matter that the man shown doffing his cap to the cheering crowd sandwiched between Castle Garden and the Washington Hotel was not the regimental hero. Michael Corcoran remained jailed in the South, and it had fallen to his replacement, Captain Thomas Francis Meagher, to get his enlistees home—and to receive the ovation of the welcoming crowd. "Col. Corcoran in Irons!" the *Albany Evening Journal* reported as late as September 5. "The traitors have special animosity against the gallant Colonel. He has, from the first, spurned every proposition to give his parole, or in any way to recognize the authority of the Rebel Government. . . . The announcement that their heroic Colonel is subjected to these indignities and humiliations will stir the warm blood of his friends." Lang cleverly included Corcoran in his scene in a detail in the lower right-hand corner of the canvas, where a newsboy can be seen hawking lithographs of the captured commander. As for the carefully delineated spectators shown cheering from nearby buildings and on the streets, Lang provided a useful "key" to their identities: many were portraits of the actual community leaders who had welcomed the regiment home. As the key reveals, the chaplain who had blessed Fort Corcoran a few months earlier was not among them. When New York's archbishop, John Hughes, learned that Father Mooney had "baptized" a cannon, he replaced him with Father Bernard O'Reilly, and it is O'Reilly who makes an appearance in the Lang canvas, tending to a Bull Run widow clutching her orphaned child.

Michael Corcoran finally gained his liberty in an August 1862 prisoner exchange. President Lincoln honored him and a few other newly liberated officers with a White House dinner on the eighteenth. The hero of the 69th eventually returned to New York and formed a new outfit, the Corcoran Legion, which subsequently saw action in a number of minor battles. Corcoran died young but not gloriously. Returning to the defense of Washington, he was riding alone three days before Christmas 1863 when he suffered a fatal accident, fracturing his skull when his horse fell on top of him.

As for the 69th, it reorganized with three-year recruits and returned to action later in 1861. Over the next few years, the Irish Brigade saw action on the Virginia Peninsula and at Second Bull Run and Antietam.

According to legend, the Confederate general Robert E. Lee was so impressed by its stubborn valor at another costly Union defeat at Fredericksburg that he dubbed the regiment "the Fighting 69th." True or not, the name stuck.

The painting, however, became an artistic curiosity of local interest to only those who recognized the represented figures. In addition, the depiction of the regiment's triumphal homecoming remained relevant just a short while, for not only did the soldiers return to the battlefront, but anti-Irish backlash following the 1863 draft riots further diminished the work's enduring attraction. In 1886, Lang donated the canvas to the Historical Society, where it remained on view until sometime after World War II. When curators rediscovered it in storage in 1977, it was in several pieces, which is how it remained until the beginning of the twenty-first century. The Williamstown Art Conservation Center reassembled the tattered fragments in time for the Society's grand reopening, after a three-year renovation, on November 11, 2011—fittingly, Veterans Day.

16

━━◦◦◦━━

"Reuniting" a Shattered Family

The Lincoln Family in 1861,
Painting by Francis Bicknell Carpenter, ca. 1865

ABRAHAM LINCOLN'S ELDEST SON, ROBERT, SPENT MUCH OF HIS father's presidency away at school in New England—he was enrolled at Harvard Law by the year Lincoln was assassinated—and his younger brother Willie died just eleven months into his father's term. In a way, it comes as little surprise that no surviving photographs show the Lincolns together before tragedy struck one, then another of them down.

Yet in another sense, the absence of such period pictures is astonishing. The briefly united family could easily have visited a photographer's studio together in that first wartime summer of 1861, when Robert arrived in Washington on school vacation and both younger boys were alive and well. The national mania for photographs was at its peak that year. The new *carte-de-visite* process made pictures far easier, and cheaper, to make and reproduce. The public collected images not only of their own families but of celebrities as well, filling their new leather albums with portraits of parents, children, and politicians alike. Yet no such sitting was ever arranged for or by the Lincolns. The family— principally Mary Lincoln, who generally hated the way she looked in photographs—never felt the need to commission a group picture, even though Mary enthusiastically collected family and celebrity *cartes* herself. For a time, the public appeared to have little interest of its own in seeing, much less owning, images of the president, his wife, and their three sons. The modern cult of the first family had not yet come into existence, and never would the Lincolns have another chance to immortalize themselves together. Robert, who came to regard the White House as a "gilded prison," spent most of his time away.

As for First Lady Mary Lincoln, who reacted to Willie's death by lapsing into protracted mourning, she later admitted she was fortunate if her busy husband could find time to visit her bedroom late at night merely to talk over the events of the day. The presidency was never conducive to family togetherness, and in the crucible of civil war it divided the Lincolns as much as it fractured families who sent fathers, brothers, husbands, and sons into battle—and often never saw them again.

Nonetheless, when the president himself died at the hands of an assassin in April 1865, Americans suddenly expressed a longing for retrospective visual assurances—however fanciful—that Lincoln had indeed enjoyed comfort in the bosom of his family while he lived. One particular New York–based artist was perfectly situated to capitalize on this demand. The man who deserved—but never truly received—full credit for brilliantly responding to this cultural yearning was the Homer, New York–born painter Francis Bicknell Carpenter (1830–1900). In 1864, armed with introductions from leading Republican politicians and further aided by a lifelong friendship with one of Lincoln's clerks, Carpenter talked his way into the White House and spent six months working there to create a heroic canvas of Lincoln reading the first draft of his Emancipation Proclamation to his Cabinet back in July 1862. The artist enjoyed life sittings with the president and his Cabinet officers and made many sketches of Lincoln's office. Ultimately, he painted the group gathered around a table there, in the spot they had first discussed Lincoln's most famous official act. Lincoln greatly admired the result. The huge canvas subsequently went on a national tour, earning critical raves and no small amount of fame for Francis Carpenter.

While laboring on his ambitious picture, which today hangs in the U.S. Capitol, Carpenter also got to observe Lincoln in loving exchanges with his surviving little boy, Tad. He believed that if "the worst of his adversaries" could only see the burdened president behind the scenes, it

PLATE 16-1

"would have melted their hearts." To Carpenter, "The President never seemed grander in my sight than when, stealing upon him in the evening, I would find him with a book open before him . . . with Little Tad beside him." In response, he so painted the two together for a tiny cameo picture he probably created expressly as a family keepsake. It remained unknown to the public for a century.

More important, Carpenter also accompanied Lincoln and Tad to Mathew Brady's photography studio in February 1864 principally to pose the president for a series of pictures meant to serve as models for his emancipation project. During the visit, he persuaded the president to sit for one photograph together with Tad, examining the photographer's oversized sample photograph album as if it were one of those books he often saw Lincoln reading to the boy. The resulting warm portrait of father and son might have served then and there to ameliorate the prevailing image of Lincoln (at least to his opponents) as a brutal warrior and harsh abrogator of constitutional liberties. But inexplicably it remained unpublished during the entire Civil War. Only after Lincoln's murder did Mathew Brady release the photograph to the public. It became an immediate bestseller, after which engravers and lithographers outdid themselves in a race to adapt the pose into imaginary composite group portraits of the entire, ill-fated family. None of these 1865 prints credited Carpenter for first posing the source model, and many of them took the liberty of converting the Brady prop album into a Bible in an effort to further sanctify the scene.

That left Carpenter to create the definitive, if no longer the first, pictorial statement about the private Lincoln. The usually enterprising artist was uncharacteristically lethargic in responding to the commercial appeal of such pictures. He did not take his idea for a Lincoln family portrait to the New York publisher John C. Derby until well after Lincoln's death. Nonetheless, Derby offered Carpenter the handsome sum of five hundred dollars to create a group portrait and hired the accomplished New York engraver John Chester Buttre to adapt it into a mezzotint. But Buttre had to wait.

Even as competitors rushed their cheap imitations to the market, Carpenter patiently wrote to Mary Lincoln to ask which photographic models he might consult to achieve the most accurate results. Mary recommended "the best likeness" of Robert taken "at [John] Goldin's" Washington studio the previous spring, apologizing that she had "none, unframed," to send him. She did share one relic from the Lincoln family album: a photograph of Willie and Tad together, taken in 1861. "Even in *that* likeness, of Willie," she lamented, "justice, is not done him, he was a very beautiful boy, with a most *spiritual* expression of face." Mary refused Carpenter's entreaties that she pose for a new photograph herself. It would be "utterly impossible," the grieving widow insisted, "in my present nervous state." Asked to propose an alternative, the ever-vain Mrs. Lincoln recommended "an excellent painted likeness of me, at Brady's in N.Y. taken in 1861. . . . I am sure you will like it." It is easy to see why Mary urged this particular model on the artist. The heavily retouched Brady image had miraculously carved inches from her ample posterior. Carpenter followed all of the widow's suggestions.

Using these models, Carpenter accomplished a handsome painting, but only "in *black* and *white*," he explained, "with the expressed purpose of facilitating the engraving. When that was completed, I fully intended to finish . . . the painting by adding color to the *flesh* . . . as well as to the *draperies*." He never did. Yet what the picture lacked in color, it more than made up for in skillful portraiture and the canny arrangement of figures and props: the composition showed the Lincolns seated around a modest, draped table bearing food as if set for an afternoon tea. Carpenter did not believe in "imaginary curtain or column, gorgeous furniture, or allegorical statue." Obviously pleased with the result, the print publisher, Derby, spent another $1,164 to get the chiaroscuro original engraved. It was finally issued in 1867. By then, unfortunately, many print buyers had already purchased group portraits of the Lincoln family, however inferior. The once-robust demand had faded. The Carpenter project had consumed so much time that the engraver, Buttre, was compelled to impose a mustache on the portrait of Robert Lincoln in recognition of the fact that the so-called Prince of Rails had in the intervening years grown from boy to man. Though titled *The Lincoln Family in 1861*, the composite in fact depicted its subjects as they appeared over a three-year period. Some copies of the engraving—including an example in the New-York

Historical Society—featured the very tinting and highlighted the very draperies that Carpenter had eschewed for his painting.

Francis Carpenter never got the credit he deserved for originating a powerful idea: sympathetically showing a quintessential public man— the president of the United States—in a private sphere alongside his wife and children. Until then, the genre had allowed for only a single famous example: the iconic domestic glimpse at George Washington and his family by Edward Savage. Carpenter did nothing less than launch an artistic revolution in how Americans perceive their elected leaders.

Carpenter's oil on canvas may look to modern observers like a colorless boilerplate—merely a family gathered woodenly around the proverbial dining room table. But the inspirational model for the composition—Lincoln reading a book to Tad—was in fact Carpenter's original invention, and only the painter's chronic insistence on perfection denied him the approbation he deserved for so brilliantly inventing a private life for the fallen Civil War president.

For a time, an appreciative Mary Lincoln lavished praise and attention on Francis Carpenter. When he arranged publication of an engraved portrait of the late president, she provided a rare and enthusiastic endorsement, calling it "the most perfect likeness of my beloved husband that I have ever seen." She felt betrayed, however, when Carpenter assembled his firsthand impressions of Lincoln—along with stories from contemporaries—into what turned out to be an enormously successful book called *Six Months at the White House*. Mary's chagrin escalated into fury when subsequent editions of the memoir were retitled *The Inner Life of Abraham Lincoln*. The woman who had once expressed "great pride" in "the success" of Carpenter's work now denounced him as a "silly adventurer . . . with whom my husband had scarcely the least acquaintance," scathingly adding: "This man . . . never had a dozen interviews with the late President and the latter complained more than once to me, that C[arpenter] presumed upon the privilege he had given C. to have the use of the State dining room, for a short time, whilst he was executing his painting. This was done in consequence of the rumor we had heard of his indigent circumstances."

In 1895, the sixty-five-year-old painter learned to his distress that his original Lincoln family painting had been sold to a New York collector for just fifty dollars by one George Probst, who had inherited Buttre's business when the veteran engraver died two years earlier. Probst insensitively boasted that he had rescued the long-discarded original "from a rubbish pile where it had lain for twenty-five to thirty years . . . forgotten by everybody." The proud new owner, Warren C. Crane, wasted no time in showing his acquisition to Carpenter. The artist admitted that he, too, had "forgotten all about the picture" but bristled that he had never actually sold it to Buttre, merely consigned it to be engraved. Despite his insistence that he had relinquished "only the *copyright* of this picture . . . and not the painting," and that the "incredible" fifty-dollar purchase price was "humiliating" to someone who had in his heyday commanded a thousand dollars and more for his portraits, Carpenter never regained ownership of his work.

Instead, Crane kept the black-and-white oil painting, preserved it, and ultimately donated this unique relic of the Civil War White House to the New-York Historical Society in 1909, the centennial year of Lincoln's birth. Certainly not the first, and probably not the most popular, domestic Lincoln image published after the president's death, it remains the most authentic behind-the-scenes study ever created of the Lincolns—a family shattered in life but evocatively reconceived by one New York artist's uncanny vision.

PLATE 17–1

17

―――⋘⊙∕⊙∕⊙⋙―――

Distant Drums

Snare Drum, ca. 1860–1865

A MONG THE MILITARY ARTIFACTS AT THE NEW-YORK HISTORICAL
Society is this magnificent double-headed tubular snare drum, its
wooden cylinder lavishly decorated with an expertly painted American
eagle whose outstretched wings are surrounded by a border of stars, a
red-white-and-blue shield of liberty at its feet. The animal-hide instrument is two-sided, indicating it was made to be used in battle, where,
like all such drums, it was employed to convey orders to troops. Even in
the confusing smoke and noise of combat, alert soldiers were trained to
rally around specific drumrolls that signaled either attack or retreat.

That this method of communication was effective was confirmed by
one Confederate general who appreciatively recalled a Union advance at
Antietam so brilliant it could have been inspired only by its regimental
band. He remembered that "this magnificent array moved to the charge,
every step keeping time to the tap of the deep-sounding drum." In this
sense, drums became something approaching the category of weapons
for their power to inspire precision. It is no surprise that the choicest
surviving examples boast patriotic inscriptions, and this particularly
fine relic is emblazoned with the motto "Union and Liberty." Its red
color indicates it was made for an artillery unit (blue drums signified
infantry).

According to the museum's files, the Society's drum was used during
the Civil War by one Philip Corell (1847–1935). Like many (but not all)

drummers, Corell enlisted as a mere fourteen-year-old. He initially joined the 99th New York Volunteer Infantry in 1861 and later served in Hancock's Veteran Corps, which contained regiments from New York, Pennsylvania, Maine, and Wisconsin. General Winfield Scott Hancock led his troops through the 1862 Peninsula and Maryland campaigns and fought with distinction at Fredericksburg, Chancellorsville, and Gettysburg. We do not know for sure whether Corell was on hand for all these engagements, but we can surmise that Hancock made ample use of musicians and drummers: any commander who acquired the nickname "The Magnificent" no doubt expected to be accompanied by marching bands.

At least Corell made it safely through all four years of the war and more, mustering out in 1866 and living almost seventy more years. Though plenty of camp musicians were adults, the romance attached to heroic "little drummer boys" resonated with the public. Corell was hardly the youngest drummer boy in the Union service. Traditionally, that distinction belongs to the Ohioan Johnny Clem, the famous "drummer boy of Shiloh," who joined up when he was only nine. Another source gives the youngest recorded drummer boy's age as seven. According to that unrivaled chronicler of Civil War statistics, E. B. Long, some thirty-eight hundred soldiers aged sixteen or younger actually served in the ranks of the federal army. The historian Bell I. Wiley calculated that 5 percent of Confederate soldiers were under eighteen. But that number surely did not include drummer boys, whose numbers were undoubtedly far larger, for each regiment needed one and the Union alone boasted more than thirty-five hundred regiments. According to one record, the U.S. Army placed orders for no fewer than thirty-two thousand drums between 1861 and 1865. A surviving roster for the regimental band of the 72nd Volunteer New York Infantry, a unit probably very much like Corell's 99th, boasted four separate musicians assigned, variously, to side and bass drums. Drummer boys almost always marched at the front—of both the band and the regiment itself.

Some regiments organized fife-and-drum bands that emphasized percussion over melody. A veteran of the 17th Maine remembered many a sunrise reveille promptly followed by the unforgettable sound of the

*Charles F. Mosby, Age 13. Confederate Drummer Boy,
Served Throughout the War,* photographic print, ca. 1865

PLATE 17–2

drumrolls. "The drums of one regiment commence their noisy rataplan, which is taken up by the 'Ear piercing fife and spirit stirring drum' of another, which is in turn echoed by another, till every drum corps of the brigade, with accompanying bugles and fifes, join in the din, and the morning air is resonant with the rattle of drums."

A powerful mystique thus grew up about drummer boys, nurtured along in large measure by poetry (Whitman extolled the "pride and joy" of "the stretch'd tympanum"), juvenile literature, and sentimental artists. The painter William Morris Hunt (1824–1879), for example, idealized one such young serviceman as a long-haired, open-shirted ragamuffin who appeared to have come right out of the barricades of the French Revolution. Hunt was not subtle: he symbolically positioned his drummer boy on a pedestal in acknowledgment of all such children's bravery. But despite its pretensions, the picture was surprisingly well received. Hunt followed this effort with a more realistic depiction titled *The Wounded Drummer Boy,* showing a child—perhaps the same drummer as he had depicted previously—now lying prostrate before his discarded instrument. Hunt's contemporary Eastman Johnson (1824–1906), who actually witnessed the Battle of Antietam, painted another unlikely scene he claimed to have observed firsthand there. He described his creation as "a drummer boy . . . disabled by a shot in the leg. As he lay upon the field," Johnson maintained, "he called to his comrades, 'Carry me and I'll drum her through.' They tied up his wound, a big soldier took him, upon his shoulders, and he drummed through the fight."

Such events probably never occurred, since drummer boys did not in fact "drum through the fight" during battles. They issued their rat-a-tat signals to announce attacks, after which they promptly headed to the rear to perform the other job to which they were assigned in combat: the grisly task of serving as stretcher bearers to remove the dead and the maimed. Another artist who left a singularly realistic portrait of this aspect of a drummer boy's life—at least in words—was Edwin Forbes, who observed in his memoir *Thirty Years After: An Artist's Story of the Great War,* published in 1890: "Painters of military pictures are fond of placing a broken drum in the fore-ground of their battle-scenes; but no representation could be more incorrect, for during a battle musicians and drummers are detailed to the rear for hospital service, and may often be found behind some fence enjoying a quiet cup of coffee."

Between engagements, drummer boys functioned in camp practically as servants, cleaning up campsites, barbering soldiers' hair, and drawing heavy pails of water from the nearest wells. During lulls in the action—and there were many more lulls than actions—they also served as part of the rhythm sections of their camps' military bands, pounding away during parades and drills, performing at impromptu evening concerts, and of course helping to rouse the soldiers before the crack of dawn. Thus they slept little themselves. The kindest soldiers collected funds to pay drummer boys something on the side and got small-sized uniforms made for them. The most brutal adults treated them abusively; what soldier, after all, enjoys being roused for reveille?

One painter who truly understood and acknowledged the stark life of the drummer boy in wartime was the New Englander Julian Scott, who in 1861 lied about his age to enlist at fifteen as a fifer in the 3rd Vermont Infantry. Scott went on to earn a Congressional Medal of Honor for valor under enemy fire, and when he began depicting scenes of the Civil War, he often showed drums and drummer boys on the sidelines of his pictures—where in fact they belonged. No one ever doubted their bravery, but the life of the drummer boy was far less glamorous than the one that most artistic observers mythicized. Scott's 1891 canvas, *Civil War Drummer Boys Playing Cards,* pointedly reminded viewers that the Civil War had exposed children to what one company musician described in a letter home as the "demoralizing influence the vices of army life have upon the minds of a great many." Where drummer boys were concerned, as Scott was pointing out, the war robbed a generation of its innocence.

We have no way of knowing where and under what circumstances Philip Corell played his drum during the Civil War—or how close he came to the kind of danger many artists vivified. But we do have his spectacularly preserved instrument, on which Corell's handwritten ink inscription is still visible, testifying to pride of ownership and faithfulness to duty: "Philip Corell / Co. F 5. Regt U.S. Vet. Vols. / 2nd BRIG. 1st DIV. 1st A, C. / Washington/D.C." As a handful of drummer boy photographs in the collection also show—all of them portraying young men proudly clutching oversized instruments like this one—their wartime experiences were likely the most exciting of their lives.

It surely surprised none of these veterans that Walt Whitman gave a particularly evocative title to his first collection of poems dedicated to the Civil War: *Drum-Taps*. And in one of the poems he described the power of the drum to stir a storm—this time of patriotism—right out of *King Lear:*

Beat! beat! drums!—blow! bugles! blow!
Through the windows—through doors—burst like a ruthless force,
Into the solemn church, and scatter the congregation,
Into the school where the scholar is studying;
Leave not the bridegroom quiet—no happiness must he have now
   with his bride,
Nor the peaceful farmer any peace, ploughing his field or gathering
   his grain,
So fierce you whirr and pound you drums—so shrill you bugles blow.

Beat! beat! drums!—blow! bugles! blow!
Over the traffic of cities—over the rumble of wheels in the streets;
Are beds prepared for sleepers at night in the houses? no sleepers
   must sleep in those beds,
No bargainers' bargains by day—no brokers or speculators—would
   they continue?
Would the talkers be talking? would the singer attempt to sing?
Would the lawyer rise in the court to state his case before the judge?
Then rattle quicker, heavier drums—you bugles wilder blow.

18

Thoughts of the Future— but Where?

Thoughts of the Future,
Painting by Edwin White, 1861

MONG THE MANY AMBIGUOUS DEPICTIONS OF AFRICAN AMERICANS that exist in the Society's—and nearly every—major collection of Civil War art and archives, Edwin White's powerful oil portrait remains one of the most intriguing. Massachusetts-born White (1817–1877), a self-taught genre painter with a fine reputation, had trained in Europe under Jacques-Louis David, exhibited at the National Academy, and earned distinction for a number of historical subjects (most prominently his 1859 *Washington Resigning His Commission,* for which he earned six thousand dollars) when he tackled the theme of freedom in this 1861 image. He did so not with a complex group composition in the manner of Eastman Johnson but with a haunting depiction of a solitary black working man—well dressed but, judging by his bare and deteriorating surroundings, impoverished even in freedom—reading the news of the day and perhaps pondering a better future outside the United States.

A poster marked "Hayti" can be seen tacked to a door in the background, suggesting specific aspirations to migrate to the black-led republic in the Caribbean. The man consults a newspaper, indicating that he is literate and fully capable of grasping his surroundings and aspiring

PLATE 18-1

to something better overseas. In other words, this is a colonization picture—meant to assure white people that black people wanted to leave America, even if such was never the case for any but a tiny minority. White's magisterial canvas has been on permanent loan from the New York Public Library since 1944.

For years, Frederick Douglass had tried to disabuse white Americans—even those like Henry Clay and, for a time, Abraham Lincoln, who believed in colonization as a philanthropic endeavor—of the notion that it was noble or even rational. In Douglass's contrary view, "the destiny of the colored American" was inexorably intertwined with "the destiny of America" and had to remain so.

Nonetheless, for years conflicted slave owners like Clay, who was known as the Great Compromiser, argued that the only way safely to end slavery in America was to facilitate the deportation of free blacks so that whites did not have to fear violent reprisals and would not have to live among free black citizens. With this supposedly eleemosynary purpose in mind, many moderates flocked to join the American Colonization Society, a group dedicated to this purpose. In a eulogy to Clay delivered in 1852, the former congressman Lincoln made no secret of his admiration for the man or his goal. He unapologetically endorsed words Clay had once employed to advance the idea of colonization: "There is a moral fitness in the idea of returning to Africa her children, whose ancestors have been torn from her by the ruthless hand of fraud and violence. Transplanted in a foreign land, they will carry back to their native soil the rich fruits of religion, civilization, law and liberty."

Not everyone agreed. "An attempt to remove" African Americans from the country, Frederick Douglass insisted, "would be as vain as to bail out the ocean. The whole naval power of the United States could not remove the natural increase of our part of this population. Every fact in our circumstances here marks us as a permanent element of the American people. . . . We shall never leave you." As Douglass put it: "We are Americans . . . and shall rise or fall with Americans."

White's rather opaque response to this unresolved debate was widely praised when it first went on view in New York in late 1861 at a sale organized to raise money for some sort of "Patriotic Fund." Commending the artist for eschewing "ridicule and obloquy" in his canvas, a critic for the antislavery weekly the *Independent* lauded as "magnanimous" White's sensitive "portrait of the janitor of the studio-building; a high, thought-ful brow, covered with a black skin, pondering a newspaper." As the critic interpreted the scene: "The black philosopher is reading the war news, and wondering what the future has in store for his race. The figure is full of feeling, and commands an involuntary respect for the dignified old serving man."

It appears impossible to pinpoint when the canvas acquired the name by which most people have identified it—*Thoughts of Liberia, Emancipation*—but it must have been later, since, for one thing, emanci-pation was not yet at the forefront of the national struggle to restore the Union when it was painted in 1861 and, for another, the background poster labeled "Hayti" clearly indicates that the painter intended the viewer to conclude that the subject of this portrait is pondering a future much closer to home than Africa. Certainly we are meant to infer from the poster tacked to the door in the background—itself a symbol of po-tentially dramatic exit and entrance—that the sitter is at least giving careful consideration to the thought of emigration nearby. Douglass, who called Haiti a "modern land of Canaan, where so many of our people are journeying from the rigorous bondage and oppression of our modern Egypt," abruptly canceled a trip of his own there when war broke out in the spring of 1861, saying: "This is no time for us to leave the country." Since Douglass declared himself—and other people of color—"ready to lend a hand in any way we can be of service," it is clear that from that day forward he was ruling out the Caribbean as an alternative even for those who had been "looking to that country for a home."

Over the years, this rugged portrait has inspired as many far-fetched interpretations as the dark-hued, nearly silhouetted masterpiece it most closely resembles—*Whistler's Mother.* One modern critic even attempted to tie White's picture directly to Lincoln himself, suggesting that in his lean, lank frame and haggard face, not to mention the stovepipe hat that can be seen in the foreground on the floor, the African American here bears more than accidental resemblance to the Emancipator. This interpreter went so far as to suggest that White intended "slyly" to probe the black "Lincoln" here "for what his response would be were he the one asked to establish a colony far from his home and the land of his birth." This may be overreaching, but in any case in the following year, 1862, Lincoln gave two unmistakable indications that his own "thoughts" had not strayed very far from those espoused by his lifetime hero, Clay.

In July 1862, Lincoln drafted an emancipation proclamation, and then, at the advice of his Cabinet, tabled it until its announcement could be sustained by a Union military victory. Throughout the summer, Lincoln impatiently waited for a success that did not come. In fact, the Army of the Potomac instead suffered another staggering setback at the Second Battle of Bull Run. To hasten the process of freedom, Lincoln meanwhile signed the Washington, D.C., compensated emancipation bill and two congressional confiscation acts and began intensive negotiations with Border State representatives to encourage these loyal slaveholding areas to agree to compensated emancipation on their own. But the Border State congressmen rejected the initiative, and with no other alternative Lincoln waited in frustration for the army to give him a victory so he could act alone on slavery in his capacity as commander in chief.

He had firmly made up his mind to do so, but over the next few weeks he gave every indication that he cared not a whit for the fate of the African American himself—a massive public relations feint that the beleaguered president believed crucial to guarantee that the majority of racist Northern whites accepted the proclamation when he finally published it.

In one such initiative, on August 14, Lincoln welcomed a delegation of free African Americans to the White House to discuss "emigration," marking the first time a president had hosted an official group composed of people of color. But the president hardly played the perfect host that day. Accompanied by an Associated Press reporter he had apparently instructed to record his remarks, Lincoln asked his visitors to be seated and then informed them that Congress had "appropriated . . . and placed at his disposition" money "for the purpose of aiding the colonization in some country of the people, or a portion of them, of African descent, thereby making it his duty, as it had for a long time been his inclination, to favor that cause."

"Your race are suffering," Lincoln bluntly told them, "the greatest wrong inflicted on any people. But even when you cease to be slaves, you are yet far removed from being placed on an equality with the white race." Without slavery, Lincoln continued in an astonishing exclamation, "the war could not have an existence." Then he got specific—and even more blunt:

> It is better for us both, therefore, to be separated. . . . The place I am thinking about having for a colony is in Central America. It is nearer to us than Liberia—not much more than one-fourth as far as Liberia, and within seven days' run by steamers. Unlike Liberia it is on a great line of travel—it is a highway. The country is a very excellent one for any people, and with great natural resources and advantages, and especially because of the similarity of climate with your native land—thus being suited to your physical condition.

As the stunned delegation sat in silence, Lincoln rambled on awkwardly, concluding by asking them to give a month's consideration of his proposals "for the good of mankind." The group withdrew and two days later sent a polite letter both commending the president for so "ably" making known his views and asking for more time to consult "with leading colored men in Phila New York and Boston upon the movement of emigration, to the point recommended in your address." The AP reporter dutifully wired an account of Lincoln's remarks, and the dispatch was widely published in the press; that is how Douglass learned of them.

Frederick Douglass, however, did not wait to consult with anyone. Only a few months after writing sympathetically that a "blind man can see where the President's heart is," the enraged abolitionist leader published a highly critical editorial in *Douglass' Monthly* condemning Lincoln for assuming "the language and arguments of an itinerant Colonization lecturer, showing all his inconsistencies, his pride of race and blood, his contempt for Negroes and his canting hypocrisy."

Douglass continued: "Illogical and unfair as Mr. Lincoln's statements are, they are nevertheless quite in keeping with his whole course from the beginning of his administration up to this day, and confirm the painful conviction that though elected as an anti-slavery man by Republican and Abolition voters, Mr. Lincoln is quite a genuine representative of American prejudice and Negro hatred and far more concerned for the preservation of slavery, and the favor of the Border Slave States, than for any sentiment of magnanimity or principle of justice and humanity."

There was some truth to Douglass's harsh judgment. Lincoln was indeed fearful that his imminent announcement of emancipation had the potential of frightening Kentucky and Missouri out of the Union, and he did believe that without their continued loyalty he must surrender the government and abandon the war to preserve the Union. But Douglass's reaction shows that Lincoln's speech to the delegation of free blacks had real sting and perhaps went too far. Though calculated to assure white voters that anything he did with regard to emancipation would be motivated by military necessity, not philanthropy, the comments obviously caused deep pain to many in the African American community.

Lincoln relieved some of that despair when he issued the preliminary proclamation on September 22, causing even the dubious Douglass to rejoice. But it would be a mistake to conclude that Lincoln's map to freedom thereafter followed a consistent path and included no more references to colonization. As late as December, in his annual message to Congress, he revealed that his administration was in the midst of negotiating a consular treaty with "Hayti." His message also included a proposed constitutional amendment authorizing Congress to appropriate funds "for colonizing free colored persons, with their own consent, at any place or places without the United States." That month, 453 African Americans sailed for Cow Island off Haiti to establish a new colony there under a dubious for-profit scheme Lincoln endorsed. The expedition proved a calamity, and Lincoln ordered a vessel to return 368 survivors to the mainland in 1864.

In the end, Lincoln actually spent only $38,000 of the $600,000 Congress appropriated for colonization, but there is no question that he actively pursued the idea of voluntary emigration of free blacks until at least mid-1863. Only when African Americans began fighting in the ranks for their own freedom did he conclude that they were fully entitled to coexist with whites in a biracial future society. The revolution in Lincoln's own mind portended a revolution in American society.

19

~~~∕o∕o∕~~~

There's Something in It

Half Model of the USS Monitor, 1862

IN MID-1861, THE CONFEDERATE NAVY LIFTED THE SUBMERGED HULL OF the wooden ship *Merrimack* from the shallow waters of the Portsmouth Naval Base, where it had been scuttled by evacuating Union forces. After that, Confederate authorities completely redesigned it, building a wooden casemate atop the hull and covering it with two layers of two-inch iron plates. The resulting vessel was too big, and the metal sheathing too heavy, for the hybrid failed to achieve much stability or speed: it steamed to a maximum of only six knots. But once launched, the renamed CSS *Virginia* managed to cause more devastation in one morning and afternoon than at any one-day battle in American naval history until the attack on Pearl Harbor on December 7, 1941—and survived its destructive debut unscathed to fight another day. Many worried observers of the time believed the *Virginia* might next have steamed up the Potomac and caused unanswerable destruction to Washington itself—ending the entire fight to save the Union, Secretary of War Edwin M. Stanton feared—had it not been for the technological marvel fortuitously en route to Virginia at that precise moment to engage it.

The Union's response was the truly revolutionary USS *Monitor,* made entirely in New York, whose original "plating" half model survives to this day in the Historical Society collection, the gift of the ship's highly efficient and well-paid builder, Thomas Fitch Rowland (1831–1907).

It was a model very much like this one that the Connecticut industrialist Cornelius Bushnell had lugged to Washington to show to Abraham Lincoln at the White House in early September 1861. Bushnell was convinced that a Swedish-born inventor working in Brooklyn, John Ericsson, had hit upon a brilliant advance in naval technology: what Ericsson described as "a floating battery absolutely impregnable to the heaviest shot or shell." Most daringly of all, the novel design featured a revolving gun turret, the first of its kind ever proposed and a direct forerunner of the rotating guns on modern warships.

Lincoln was certainly open to new shipbuilding ideas; he had once crafted his own wooden model of a vessel designed to lift itself buoyantly over river shoals—for which he became the only president before or after to receive a U.S. patent. But it is fair to say he had never seen anything quite like what Bushnell brought to him, a vessel designed to ride extremely low in the water while keeping afloat its heavy-gauge gun capable of firing in any direction it chose without altering the course of the ship. Lincoln examined the curious wood-and-metal scale model with intense interest and, suitably impressed, promised to accompany Bushnell to the Navy Department the very next morning to discuss the proposal further with the military professionals. There, Lincoln typically issued no direct orders to proceed with the scheme. But in his best frontier manner, he conveyed his undisguised interest by drawling: "All I can say is what the girl said when she put her foot into the stocking. It strikes me there's something in it."

Even with that prodding, the fusty naval board took its time mulling over the innovative proposal before ultimately awarding Ericsson a contract to create a test vessel. Work then commenced quickly at Rowland's shed-like Continental Iron Works in Greenpoint, Brooklyn, using metal from upstate Troy. Employees of the shipbuilding yard were required to take an oath of allegiance, and some initially balked, thinking it was a ruse to conscript them into the armed forces. In an interview with the *New York Times* in 1890, Rowland remembered that he had insisted on an unheard-of price to bring the plan to full realization, arguing that the construction schedule was so demanding that workers would be required to labor day and night, plus weekends, to speed production, increasing costs. Ericsson had no choice but to agree to Rowland's terms.

It was the inventor who proposed the name for the "floating battery at Greenpoint" in a letter to Assistant Secretary of the Navy Gustavus Vasa Fox. Desiring a title that would convey "the impregnable and aggressive nature of this structure," he noted that his "iron-clad intruder will . . . prove a severe monitor" to "the leaders of the Southern Rebellion." On these grounds, he wrote, "I propose to name the new battery *Monitor.*" The word ultimately evolved into a generic term for a whole series of similar vessels.

Because of the original bureaucratic delay, however, what became the original USS *Monitor* was not launched until the end of February 1862, when the *Times* reported (newspapers never quite understood that printing such news might alert the enemy) that "the iron-clad steamer *Monitor*" had been "put into commission . . . at the Brooklyn Navy-yard," adding: "Great exertions are being made to get the *Monitor* off at once, and she will doubtless sail in a day or two." Secretary of the Navy Gideon Welles wisely ordered it to be rushed to the vicinity of Hampton Roads, Virginia, where he presciently expected the refitted *Merrimack* to emerge at any moment from the Confederate naval yards at Norfolk and menace the wooden American fleet there. Just as feared, before the *Monitor* could be towed to Virginia—in fact, the ironclad almost capsized in choppy seas along the journey—the Confederate ironclad *Virginia* appeared on March 8 off Newport News and within hours rammed and sank the stately but antiquated USS *Cumberland,* shelled the

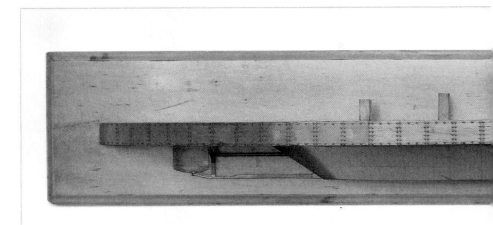

PLATE 19–1

majestic USS *Congress* into a smoldering ruin, and drove the USS *Minnesota* aground. Some 250 federal sailors died in the attacks, which all but spelled the approaching end of the wooden navy.

Shifting tides compelled the *Virginia* to withdraw for the day before it could finish off what was left of the federal armada, but when it appeared the next morning to continue the unchecked devastation, civilian onlookers watching breathlessly from the shoreline noticed a smaller, sleeker vessel steaming toward it from the opposite direction. From a distance, it appeared to be no bigger than an elongated lifeboat of some sort; it looked harmless enough to elicit the derisive nickname "Yankee cheese box on a raft." In truth, it was low-lying but formidable: 172 feet long by more than 41 feet wide. Moreover, it carried two eleven-inch Dahlgren smoothbore guns.

Over the next several hours, often with less than a hundred yards separating them, the USS *Monitor* held off the CSS *Virginia* in what became the most dramatic and unforgettable naval duel of the Civil War. The contest ended in a virtual draw. Shells from the *Virginia* could not penetrate the *Monitor* (one officer on the Confederate ironclad commented during the battle, "It is quite a waste of ammunition to fire at her. Our powder is precious . . . and I find I can do the *Monitor* as much damage by snapping my finger at her every five minutes"). But the *Monitor*'s guns proved equally incapable of penetrating the *Virginia*. Actually, the *Monitor*'s much-heralded turret malfunctioned during the

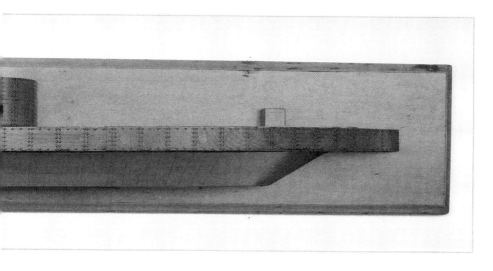

engagement, rotating uncontrollably, so that the crew was able to fire at the *Virginia* only when the guns swung around fully 360 degrees and the target came back briefly into view. No one died in the duel, and both sides claimed victory. But the arrival of the *Monitor* neutralized the offensive potential of the *Virginia* and allowed the Union navy to retain possession of Hampton Roads, which allowed McClellan's local campaign on the Peninsula to continue. (It subsequently ended in failure anyway.)

Despite all this, the so-called Battle of Hampton Roads proved the inspiration for the kind of art and poetry that seemed almost counterintuitive, since the battle between iron warships whose crews operated unseen from belowdecks rather than waving hats or climbing masts as at classic sea engagements of the past clearly heralded the end of romanticism in naval warfare. Inspecting the vessel for himself some time later, Nathaniel Hawthorne, for example, contended that the *Monitor* "could not be called a vessel at all; it was a machine." After seeing the ironclad, he wrote almost regretfully, "All the pomp and splendor of naval warfare are gone by. Henceforth there must come up a race of enginemen and smoke-blackened cannoneers."

"Hail to victory without the gaud," echoed Herman Melville in a similarly morose, almost sarcastic, vein. Here was "zeal that needs no fans / Of banners; plain mechanic power / Plied cogently in War now placed— / Where War belongs— / Among the trades and artisans." Lincoln, of course, saw nothing depressing in the *Monitor*'s achievement—quite the contrary. Irresistibly drawn to new technology, he visited Ericsson in early April, boarded the *Monitor* for a personal tour in early May while visiting nearby troops, and subsequently approved production of a fleet of similar ships. Naval warfare would never be the same again. As the *Monitor*'s chief engineer wrote to Ericsson after the battle: "Thousands have this day blessed you. . . . Every man feels that you have saved this place to the nation by furnishing us with the means to whip an ironclad frigate that was, until our arrival, having it all her own way with our most powerful vessels." Credit, even the exhausted crew agreed, went to the inventor and his invention.

In reality, the guns of both vessels fell silent after Hampton Roads. The *Virginia* never fired another shot in battle. The Navy Department meanwhile ordered the *Monitor* not to risk another engagement with its Confederate rival unless it posed a new threat to the federal fleet at Hampton Roads. The *Monitor*'s paymaster likened the orders to the manner in which "an over careful house wife regards her ancient china set—too valuable to use, too useful to keep as a relic, yet anxious that all should know what she owns & that she can use it when the occasion demands." The occasion never did. When Union forces later took Norfolk, Confederates determined their prize vessel could neither ascend the James River to Richmond nor survive in deep water, and they destroyed the *Virginia* before the enemy could capture it, in much the same way they often burned their own cotton rather than allow approaching Northern armies to seize crops. By New Year's Eve 1862, the *Monitor*, too, was no more. On the last day of its only year in active service, the legendary craft went to the bottom in a gale off Cape Hatteras.

Perhaps the quintessential artistic tribute to the pioneer ironclad *Monitor* is the Society's lithograph *The First Naval Conflict Between Iron Clad Vessels, In Hampton Roads, March 9th 1862*, the work of Endicott & Company of New York (plate 19–2). The central image in the composition, like most of the art inspired by the engagement, predictably depicted the one-on-one duel between the two ships at close range, the *Virginia* belching black smoke, the *Monitor* spewing white smoke (a pointed good-versus-evil contrast, though apparently their respective engines indeed generated just such contrasting flumes) at certain points of the battle. (The burning of coal produced black smoke on *both* ships; the firing of guns produced white smoke—again on both ships. It was up to the artist to decide what to emphasize.) Otherwise the Endicott print represented an important departure. It did not even include a portrait of Captain John Worden, the *Monitor*'s heroic commander, who was temporarily blinded and disabled during the battle. (In acknowledgment, Lincoln paid a courtesy call on the captain as well.) Moreover, it totally ignored the heroic crew who struggled in furnace-hot conditions to stabilize the turret and fire its guns. Instead, the picture focused on

The First Naval Conflict Between Iron Clad Vessels,
lithograph by C[harles]. Parsons, 1862

the inventor Ericsson, and in additional vignettes along the left and right borders detailed the ship's unique technological features. Next to Ericsson's portrait is a depiction of the *Monitor*'s "caloric engine." It was as if Herman Melville's predictions had come to life: honor was bestowed on the machine and its inventor rather than on the sailors.

The Union navy triumphed in the end but, just as Melville had noted, "without the gaud." When the *New York Times* marked John Ericsson's death in 1889 by dispatching a reporter to visit the builder Thomas Fitch Rowland at his Manhattan home, the correspondent could not help noticing there, still on proud display, a "model of the Monitor, handsomely finished, and with heads of Ericsson and others set in the frame."

But that was another model altogether. As the paper scrupulously noted: "The model by which the vessel was built hangs on the walls of the New-York Historical Society, to which it was presented by her builder." And there it has remained ever since.

PLATE 19–2

20

———— ❦ ————

Key to Confederate Victory?

Cipher Key, ca. 1861

ALEXANDER ROBERT CHISOLM (1834–1910) MAY HAVE DIED IN CIVILIAN luxury in New York after a long career as a stockbroker, merchant, and railroad investor. But in his rather more glamorous youth, he had served in the Civil War—on the Confederate side, no less—and most astonishingly of all as a personal aide and, in his own words, "confidential friend" to the flamboyant Louisiana-born Pierre Gustave Toutant Beauregard (1818–1893). Captain Chisolm was in fact serving at the general's side in Charleston, South Carolina, when Beauregard launched the April 1861 reduction of Fort Sumter. Chisolm's eventual role was quite specific: he had charge of sending and receiving coded messages, and plate 20–1 depicts the very deciphering key he used for that purpose—by Chisolm's own description, a "cipher code . . . in book form."

Chisolm was born on the large Coosaw Plantation in Beaufort, South Carolina, but when he was left fatherless at the age of two, his mother took him to stay with relatives in New York. After his mother, too, died in a carriage accident, Chisolm and his sister remained in the city, where they were raised by an aunt and uncle. When he came of age, he inherited the family plantation and its 250 enslaved people and returned south to grow rice and cotton on its 3,321 acres. After secession, the governor of South Carolina asked Chisolm to assign some of those slaves to the construction of batteries to be aimed at Fort Sumter from nearby Morris

Island. Chisolm requested an army commission in return and became a lieutenant colonel.

During the worsening Sumter crisis, Chisolm estimated that he took "five different communications" from the Charleston shoreline out to Major Robert Anderson, demanding his surrender. When he finally rowed out to report to the Union commander that Confederate batteries would shortly begin shelling the fort, he recalled that "Anderson was much affected stating that he would await our fire. He accompanied us to my boat cordially shaking our hands remarking 'If we never meet in this world again God grant that we meet in the next.'" Chisolm later observed that even after the bombardment "the exterior of the fort showed" nothing more than "slight indentations from our artillery fire," while "not a gun of its three tiers was dismounted." As he watched the departing federal garrison board ships to head north, Chisolm suddenly realized that it would have been "an impossibility to take" Sumter "by assault," adding: "That Anderson with his officers should have surrendered is still more to be wondered at, the only excuse for their action appears to be that they had become demoralized by the burning of the barracks, which did not explode the magazine or in any way effect the exterior of the fort." In one of the most interesting sections of his

PLATE 20–1

memoir, Chisolm expressed the belief that had Anderson "agreed to such a disgraceful giving up a Fort two years later, during the war, I believe they would all have been Court marshalled."

Chisolm saw subsequent action under Beauregard at the First Battle of Bull Run and reputedly led a successful cavalry charge at Cub Run Bridge. Confederate success in this first major engagement of the war was due to the timely arrival of rebel reinforcements from the Shenandoah valley. According to tradition—which may well be as much myth as history—Jefferson Davis was inspired to order those reinforcements to Manassas because of a secret message sent by the Confederate spy Rose O'Neal Greenhow. If so, that message may have been decoded on a contraption much like this one—or perhaps this very relic. Chisolm subsequently accompanied Beauregard west and served as an aide-de-camp, mostly as a scribe and confidential messenger, at Shiloh and other fronts before heading back to Charleston with the general for the long Confederate defense of the city against Union assault in 1862 and 1863, by which time, he noted, Sumter was a "great mass of ruins"—reduced, ironically, not by Confederate fire but by Union. Chisolm saw further action under Beauregard at such places as Battery Wagner, Drewry's Bluff, Savannah, and Petersburg.

After the war, he sought a pardon from President Andrew Johnson—reputedly the first Confederate officer to go to Washington for that purpose—and then sold his plantation and returned to New York, where he became a shipping merchant.

When Chisolm died at age seventy-five, the war had been over for nearly half a century. But he clearly still treasured his experience in Confederate military service. He had retained all his papers, which included scrapbooks, letters, notes, newspaper clippings, the manuscript of an unpublished, illustrated autobiography, and something more: the curious, fan-shaped cipher key that Chisolm had used in Beauregard's behalf to send, receive, and unscramble coded messages during the war. In 1912, Chisolm's son donated the entire lot to the New-York Historical Society, where he trusted it would be "more safely preserved than in my possession." Included in the trove was the battered cipher key.

Historians are not absolutely certain who adapted the ancient innovation of coded messages for modern war. In one form or another, armies had been using codes for centuries. We do know that a U.S. Army surgeon and cryptographer named Albert Myer, later chief signal officer, introduced a system of flag telegraphy known as "wigwag" that came into widespread use after 1861. The system used rapidly waving flags by day and substituted a system of shifting torches to send messages by night. Both iterations of course required recipients of the signals to have a dictionary, or key, at the ready to translate the coded signals into decipherable words and sentences. Myer later patented a cipher disk that aligned numbers and words in prearranged sequences so that signalmen could also rapidly and securely speak to each other in code by telegraph. Where cipher was concerned, the challenge was always to scramble messages in such a way that the enemy would have difficulty decoding them. But ciphering also required a system that the intended recipients of intelligence could unravel promptly enough to do some good during battle. It was an elusive goal, seldom completely met. But as a veteran of the corps named J. Willard Brown pointed out: "It does not do away with the utility of ciphers that they may be sometimes deciphered, for we must often use them, conscious that, with sufficient time and appliances, they can be interpreted; but knowing, also, that the time interpretation will require will render the message useless to the enemy." President Lincoln himself often requested that his messages to generals in the field be sent in code. At the top of such messages he characteristically scribbled—often misspelling the instruction—"Cypher."

Most military historians contend that Union cipher technology far outdistanced Confederate, perhaps because much of the latter remained faithful to the outdated sixteenth-century Blaise de Vigenère method. According to the best source on the complex subject, a study titled *Codes and Ciphers,* the Confederate general Albert Sidney Johnston employed a different system of shifting letters, known as "Caesar substitution," to communicate with General Beauregard during the Battle of Shiloh. Again, Chisolm's very cipher key may have been used to receive and decode that intelligence—which turned out to be insufficient to prevent a Union victory there in April 1862. True to the mystery and complexity that have always surrounded the story of coded messaging during the Civil War, the truth is hard to decipher.

The most Chisolm would explain about the system he used was scrawled in a note written on this relic in 1876: "Arrangement of cipher key used by Genl. G. T. Beauregard while in Command of Confederate Armies—the key words used being Our Navy our Pride." The veteran did usefully provide an example of how the system functioned, the sample being the coded cryptogram "XIERS.BMSN.J.DLBKXC.HZTHO." Unscrambled on Chisolm's key, the information translated into "Jones goes South to night." Presumably, there were always agents like Captain Chisolm at the other end of the telegraph lines to decode such alerts before the enemy did. All we know for certain is that few of these instruments of secret communication survive.

Chisolm, however, did survive. He married a general's daughter, thrived in business, and established a home in Manhattan and summer residences in Morristown, New Jersey, and Southampton, Long Island, where he helped found the Shinnecock Hills Golf Club. The only clues to his Civil War experience could be found in the occasional letters he wrote to the *New York Times* in 1893, 1894, and 1901, loyally defending Beauregard. Far kinder to his flawed old commander than history has been, Chisolm also contributed to the establishment of the Beauregard Monument Fund. Chisolm ended up a commander, too—of the New York camp of the Confederate Veterans.

21

⚯

Hidden Glory

An Episode of the War—
the Cavalry Charge of Lt. Henry B. Hidden,
Painting by Victor Nehlig, 1862

O N MARCH 9, 1862, A SMALL DETACHMENT COMPOSED OF FOURTEEN dragoons from Company H of the 1st New York Cavalry launched a valiant charge against a 150-man element of General Joseph Johnston's Confederate infantry in Northern Virginia. The Union men were under the command of a youthful, well-connected New York City–born lieutenant named Henry B. Hidden.

By one account, the rebels were at the time menacing the site of a bridge that Union soldiers were attempting to build at the Sangster railroad depot near Fairfax Station, Virginia. According to other descriptions, the Confederates were merely attempting an orderly withdrawal toward the Rappahannock River from Centreville and Manassas. Whatever the impulse for the charge, Hidden's surprise thrust initially scattered the much larger enemy force, and the mounted New Yorkers reportedly took thirteen Confederate prisoners. But at the peak of the brief and furious action, a bullet struck Hidden in the neck, killing him. He was only twenty-three years old. The vastly outnumbered members of the New York cavalry unit quickly fell into enemy hands.

Hidden and his cavalrymen might have been entirely forgotten, and the Battle of Sangster's Station, as it came to be known by veterans of the tiny engagement, might have languished even deeper in the shadows of Civil War history had it not been for the large, churning canvas that the painter Victor Nehlig (1830–1909) first exhibited at the National Academy of Design in 1863. *Gallant Charge of Lieut. Harry B. Hidden, at Sangster's Station, Virginia*, as it was called when it went on view at New York's Metropolitan Fair the following year, has understandably remained a favorite of museumgoers since Hidden's brother-in-law William H. Webb donated it to the Historical Society in 1875. Almost ever since, it has been known under a title that tends undeservedly to mute the high drama it portrays: *An Episode of the War—the Cavalry Charge of Lt. Henry B. Hidden.* Both the painting and the "episode" were of course much more.

That the canvas was created at all is remarkable enough. The obscurity of the event it celebrates was all but guaranteed when the action unfolded on the very same day the ironclads *Monitor* and *Virginia* fought their historic duel at Hampton Roads, and just one day after the

PLATE 21-1

crucial Battle of Pea Ridge in Arkansas, a Union victory that came at a cost of twenty-six hundred total casualties. Newspaper accounts understandably focused on the more important engagements that week on both land and sea. Hidden's pro-Union family, however, was determined to remember young Henry and the band of New York men who had refused to allow Confederate forces to march unmolested back to the Rappahannock River—and they clearly had the means to fund this pictorial tribute. The result created an immediate stir and generated a lasting memory. In an era of so-called war art, characterized principally by romanticized and reassuring depictions of stoic cavalier officers and lounging enlisted men safely gathered around tents and campfires, Nehlig's painting cast a new light on the harsh realities of war: it was not just ennobling; it was fast and furious and suggested genuine danger. Here was modern war in contemporary art.

Victor Nehlig hailed originally from Paris and had spent time in Cuba. At the beginning of the painter's career the art critic Henry T. Tuckerman urged him to focus his gifts on the depiction of historic events, especially the Civil War, calling this eventful period "a work for which his genius is admirably fitted." Nehlig heeded the advice. Early in the conflict he created a well-regarded depiction of Union volunteers "thronging" a park and then crafted a stirring portrait of a solitary "Picket-Guard" before turning to this bravura cavalry scene. Hailing Nehlig's masterwork as "a battle-piece" that "fully sustains his younger promise," the *New York Evening Post* in May 1863 judged the skirmish scene to be "one of the most spirited contributions to artistic history of Freedom's war."

America was still yearning for a level of history painting equivalent to the convulsive conflict it was experiencing. A few years after depicting this small incident, Nehlig would take on a much bigger theme: the 1862 Battle of Antietam.

What, then, inspired Nehlig to take on this less-than-epic subject? For one thing, Henry Hidden came from money; the Webbs were prominent shipbuilders, and painters naturally tended to portray martyrs whose families could pay for artistic tributes. Specifically who commissioned this painting has been lost to history, although it is reasonable to assume that Hidden's relatives, eager to consecrate his valor, were the patrons, since a member of the Webb family had it in his control ten years after war's end, when it was handed over to the Society.

Young Hidden had volunteered for service in the Union army on August 15, 1861, and quickly rose to the rank of first lieutenant. In Virginia, he served under the chronically recalcitrant general George B. McClellan, then commander of the Army of the Potomac, who insisted after Hidden's all but unacknowledged sacrifice that the otherwise unmolested Confederate withdrawal from Centreville had actually marked a triumph of his own leadership. In truth, McClellan's instinct for delay had allowed Johnston valuable time to retreat unscathed while the Union commander hesitated in the face of what he believed to be an army of over 100,000 men. When McClellan later reached and occupied the abandoned Confederate fortifications, it was evident that they had housed an army less than half that size and that many of the alleged weapons blocking his path were so-called Quaker guns—wooden decoys painted black to look like the real thing.

Hidden's contrasting, aggressive bravery was not forgotten—even if the action that lost him his life had no strategic value—thanks to his family. Absent Nehlig's painting it *would* have been forgotten, which, of course, is precisely why family members likely commissioned it. The episode remained a part of Civil War lore long after McClellan was discredited. In 1890, *Frank Leslie's Illustrated Newspaper* published an engraving of the Sangster's Station skirmish in its publication *The Soldier in Our Civil War*. The *New York Evening Post,* whose editor, William Cullen Bryant, was an acclaimed poet, published a poem called "First to Fall," inspired by and dedicated to the young lieutenant.

Hidden's overall contribution to Union victory was of course negligible, his fateful 1862 charge largely irrelevant, but his bravery, sacrifice, and lost promise earned a significant place in art, poetry, and narrative memory in the early days of the war. It helped that he was, like the martyred Ephraim Elmer Ellsworth before him, young, handsome, and genuinely worthy of a place in history, for scholars generally acknowledge Henry B. Hidden to be the first Union cavalry officer killed in action in the Civil War.

22

⟞ᴓᴓᴓ⟝

A Diarist in Action

Diary of William Rothert, 1861–1862

THE CIVIL WAR ERA INSPIRED A VAST AND ACCOMPLISHED LITERATURE from surprisingly talented diarists whose writing ability had remained largely unknown, and undemonstrated, during peacetime. Surely the most famous diarist on the Southern side was Mary Boykin Chesnut, wife of a former U.S. senator from South Carolina and later an aide to Jefferson Davis. Mrs. Chesnut eschewed "regrets or sad foreboding" in her accounts and instead dedicated her journal to "calm determination—and cool brains." Davis's wartime clerk John B. Jones also maintained a diary that offered historians unique insights into the day-to-day work of the Confederate government. The London *Times* war correspondent William Howard Russell, who was effectively banned from covering the front after Union officials frowned on his highly critical accounts of the Battle of Bull Run, had the last laugh with a wildly popular book, *My Diary North and South* (1863), a publishing success on both sides of the Atlantic.

One of the most remarkable of all personal Civil War journals, however, has never received the attention or appreciation it deserves: the small pocket diary of Private William Rothert of Company D of the 9th New York Volunteer Regiment (Hawkins's Zouaves). Rothert, who often added a sketch of one of his fellow Zouaves as an illustration, meticulously kept a daily account between August 1861 and July 1862, providing an important record of both routine life in camp and the jolting horror of battle action.

Rothert was a nineteen-year-old resident of New York when he enlisted in the flashy Zouave regiment. He did not make it past twenty. Rothert would die in action at the Battle of Antietam in September 1862. Two months earlier, inexplicably, as Robert E. Lee's army massed for the invasion of Maryland that would later cost the young private his life, William Rothert stopped keeping his diary. We do not know why.

On the eighty-three pages on which he wrote his surviving entries and drew his little pictures, Rothert recorded meticulous details about daily weather conditions and shed light on the often boring routine of army life. Although at first he saw little action himself, he did get to see a famous general or two, spied an occasional rebel, nearly drowned, made some mischief, endured mild punishment for his transgressions, went hungry, marked his twentieth birthday amid death and a freak accident in camp, and witnessed the arrival of escaped slaves seeking safety and freedom in the Union lines—fugitives he dismissed with racial epithets typical of the time. The summer heat was brutal, the fall winds bitter,

PLATE 22–1

the marches exhausting, the physical labor tiresome, and the rumors rife and often exaggerated, but Rothert's occasionally banal notations open a valuable window onto the life of a volunteer soldier on coastal duty during the first summer and fall of the Civil War—as the following excerpts show. And they culminate with a gripping account of Rothert's first battle action during General Ambrose E. Burnside's successful expedition to set up a Union stronghold along the coast of North Carolina. The history books show that Burnside succeeded in capturing Roanoke Island, where he seized thirty-two heavy guns and twenty-six hundred prisoners, then took New Berne, Beaufort, and Fort Macon. For these successes, Burnside earned promotion to major general. For his part, the Zouave private William Rothert gained no such acknowledgment—only the experience of a lifetime. As they say, he "saw the elephant."

1861

Camp Butler

Thurs Aug 1st [A]ll the liquor was thrown away by order of Gen But[ler]

Friday Aug 2nd Very fine and pleasant, warm eleven shots were fired at the pickets none of them taking effect.

Thursday Aug 8. Warm and pleasant expecting an attack 7,500 Rebels are at Little Bethel.

Monday Aug 12. Companies A and I have been so bad that the Colonel refused to give them anything to eat until they will do their duty. . . . Early at 3 o'clock this morning 4 niggers came from the other side of the river in a sail boat

Saturday Aug 24. Pleasant, a few rebels were seen scouting around last night. I was on the outer picket with a sergeant. Saw two rebel horsemen we both fired and they galloped off one of them was wounded tracks of blood seen on the leaves.

Camp Wool 3 miles from Fort Hatteras H[atteras] I[nlet]. N.C.

Thursday Sept 12 Building barracks

Saturday Sept 14 Had a little skirmish with about 200 cavalry none lost

Wednesday 18. Warm very heavy rain during the evening great trouble with mosquitoes

Thursday Sept 19. Warm the report is that 14000 men are to attack us

Saturday Sept. 21. Warm took 2 prisoners colored from mainland

Sunday Sept. 29 Pleasant Divine Service

Friday Oct. 4 Very warm the whole battalion started on a march this afternoon at 4 o'clock for the Light House where there were 1500 rebels landed marched until 11 o'clock when we bivouacked

Saturday Oct. 5 Got up at 3 o'clock and continued our march we arrived at the Light House but found no rebels they had retreated so we marched on our way back to camp where we reached at 9 o'clock in the evening a very tiresome sandy march

Monday Oct 7 Warm the rebels committing outrages on the inhabitants

Thursday Oct 17. Rainy buried a member of Co. G. a great many sick.

Sunday Oct 27 Chilly the party of the Indiana Regt were attacked last night

Tuesday Oct 29 Cold very heavy wind capsized in a boat had to swim a mile and a half to shore

Monday Nov 11 Steamer arrived giving the news that Charleston Beaufort and other places were taken Pleasant [The Union captured Beaufort, South Carolina, from its base at Port Royal on November 9.]

Tuesday Nov. 12 My birthday one of the member[s] of Co A died last night. One of the members of Co K Geo Bowers while attempting to draw a charge out of his musket accidentally went of[f] and shot him through the hand[.]

Thursday Nov 21 Cold we had a sham battle this afternoon a rebel steamer fired a few shells at the fort

Thursday Nov 28 Pleasant Thanksgiving day Gov [Edwin] Morgan issued a proclamation to have the Soldiers from the State of New York to rest and keep the day up with freedom

Sunday Dec 1 On Guard Warm an attack expected

Thurs Dec 5 Warm 2 Rebel steamers made their appearance this morning and after firing a few shots and taking up the Buoys left We were paid off today

Wednesday Dec 18. Warm I missed battalion drill and had to carry a
    Knap sack and musket for 2 hours which made me sweat
Thurs Dec 19. Warm we had a match battalion drill with the 48 Pennsyl-
    vania Regt today we beat them very badly we drilled at Camp Win-
    field about a mile and a half from our camp
Wednesday Dec 25 Christmas on Guard all quiet
Friday Dec 27 Warm on fatigue duty with the big launch to the Fort for
    provisions
Wed. Jan 1st 1862. New year I had a good square meal for the first time in
    a good while from on[e] of the Inhabitants which consisted of roast
    lamb some greens biscuit and Hoe Cakes & Coffee
Wednesday Jan 8 Warm a great many of the boys were drunk last night

Friday Jan. 24 Rain the company had to go after wood in all the rain and
    we got pretty well soaked there are 25 Gun Boats over the swash now[.]
    It is reported that 8 drowned Zouaves belonging to the 53 Regt were
    picked up on the bea[ch.]
Wednesday Jan 29th Warm 7 of us went out to see the fleet we stole a boat
    and sailed out and got back just at Retreat
Sunday Feb 2nd Warm & Pleasant. This afternoon we received orders to
    get ready in full heavy marching order in two hours to go on the expe-
    dition such a jumping & frolicking the boys went through was quite
    amusing & glad to hear they were going to leave Hatteras the Cooks
    and cooking 5 days ration & I spent most of the afternoon & evening in
    frying bacon.
Monday Feb 3. Warm Rainy We packed up this morning and marched to
    the Fort where we took the boat "Union" which took us over the swash
    to Ferry Boat "Eagle" where our quarters were in the horse road no cof-
    fee nor tea

The Gun Boat engagement Roanoke Island
Friday Feb. 7. It was rather foggy in the morning for some time but it soon
    cleared up & the fleet moved on The Gun Boats went up through the
    inlet & soon found the enemy who opened their batteries immediately
    When we followed up & had a splendid sight at the bombardment the

engagement commenced a[t] 12 o'clock & lasted until sun down when the troops were beginning to embark We go on board the [gun boat] Union & soon took us to shore where we landed & while some of the 25 Mass Regt were landing they were fired at by the rebels killing 1 man We were all drawn up in line and stacked arms and built fires which we sat by all night There was no sleep for us that night and rained all night

Saturday Feb 8. Cloudy & a slight rain falling we were aroused in the morning by some rebels firing at our pickets. Gen Burnsides then sent out 2 Regt to go out to attack a battery which was on the road they went and the battle soon began reinforcements were sent and soon the battle was at a terrible rage we were kept for a reserve At last it was our turn to attack the enemy & so we marched on to the battlefield while we were going there they were carrying in the wounded which was very sickening to behold When we came in reach of their bullets we had the order to deploy & kept firing for a while when we had the order to charge and our good old boys did so which we succeeded in gaining the battery & driving the enemy We had a very bad place to go through the battery was at the head of the road and on both sides of the road was a swamp which we had to go through up to our waists and our boys went through the charge splendidly and the battery was ours We then formed a line and went on again after the enemy and while we were after them some of the boys went through the dead bodies of the rebels and some found watches & even money we then came to a large field and we seen some rebels running across the field we immediately gave a chase and they took to some boats and we fired into them when one of them turned back & we took 7 prisoners among them was Gov Wise's son who was wounded We then camp & built fires in the field Then it rained all night and made it very unpleasant for us & we had nothing to eat. . . . [We] had 9 of our boys wounded and the Lt Col . . . who came up as a private in our Regt was killed instantly. . . . Our major says it was the biggest fight he ever saw and he was through 7 in Mexico[.]

In the dramatic days that followed the February 8 entry, Rothert and his compatriots rested a bit, went ashore to torch the town of Winton (the "fire made a great heat"), and took up a new position with the occupying force at Roanoke Island. In April, the regiment participated in a four-hour skirmish at South Mills in Camden County, North Carolina, where, Rothert wrote, the enemy "showered us with grape & cannister & musketry which was slaughtering us off like sheep & we had no support not even a man of another Regt was with us when we got the order to retreat to the woods." Then their task turned to "picking up our dead & wounded of which the field was lined with them" and falling back in a drenching rain, leaving the dying "to the mercy of the rebels."

Rothert made no mention of setting eyes on a female until he obtained a brief furlough to visit Edenton, the town nearest his new encampment at Fort Reno, where "the women were very afraid of us at first but they soon came & gave us flowers water &c." In the last entry of this irresistible account of soldier life, William Rothert and his regiment returned to Fort Norfolk "& encamped in tents." There the story—both astonishing and typical—abruptly ends.

23

———❦❦❦———

Tailor-Made Souvenirs of Battle

Military Buttons Mounted on Card, 1860–1864

SOLDIERS ON BOTH SIDES WERE MAD FOR SOUVENIRS OF THEIR SERVICE, and the collecting mania among invading and defending armies ran the gamut from the gathering of innocent tokens from detritus-littered battlefields, to the taking of trophies of war like pistols and swords, to the vulture-like theft of valuable personal property from helpless civilians, prisoners, and even corpses.

First Lieutenant Fred Mather of the 7th New York Heavy Artillery was one such souvenir hunter. His passion was for Confederate uniform buttons, a collection that he eventually mounted on a piece of rectangular cardboard. That was how it was displayed when it was donated to the Society by the New York Commandery of the postwar veterans of the Military Order of the Loyal Legion of the United States (MOLLUS). Judging by the handwritten descriptive notes on the display board, Mather did not particularly care whether he took the buttons from dead bodies on the battlefield or from living Confederate prisoners of war in federal custody. Included in the Mather trove are artillery and infantry buttons from casualties at Spotsylvania, and others, manufactured in locations from Birmingham, Alabama, to Waterbury, Connecticut, cut from the uniforms of enemy captives at Milford Station, Cold Harbor, Macon, and Charleston. Mather saw much action in 1864 and apparently wanted the folks back home to see evidence of it. The forced

Confederate Buttons.

gathered by Companion *Fred Mather,*

1st Lieut, 7th N. Y. Heavy Artillery

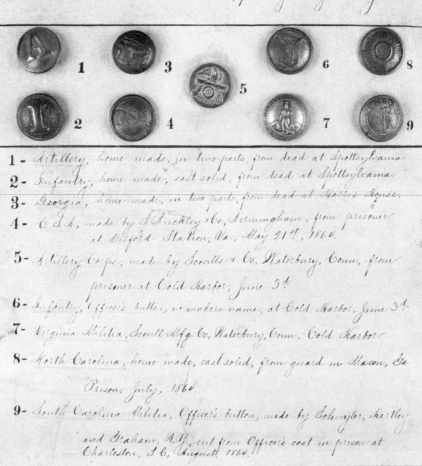

1- Artillery, home made, in two parts, from dead at Spottsylvania.

2- Infantry, home made, cast solid, from dead at Spottsylvania

3- Georgia, home made, in two parts, from dead at Harris House.

4- C. S. A., made by S. Buckley & Co, Birmingham, from prisoner
    at Milford Station, Va., May 21st, 1864.

5- Artillery Corps, made by Scovills & Co, Waterbury, Conn, from
    prisoner at Cold Harbor, June 3d.

6- Infantry, Officer's button, no maker's name, at Cold Harbor, June 3d.

7- Virginia Militia, Scovill Mfg Co, Waterbury, Conn, Cold Harbor

8- North Carolina, home made, cast solid, from guard in Macon, Ga.
    Prison, July, 1864.

9- South Carolina Militia, Officer's button, made by Schuyler, Hartley
    and Graham, N.Y., cut from Officer's coat in prison at
    Charleston, S.C, August, 1864.

PLATE 23-1

removal of the accoutrements of a uniform by an enemy guard was considered a gross humiliation to captives of the Civil War era.

Much less is known about a collection of eleven Confederate buttons mounted on a circular blue board, donated to the Society by the 7th Regiment National Guard in 1951 (plate 23–2). Like the Mather souvenirs, these dome-shaped brass buttons came from a variety of sources, as revealed in the various stamps they bear: "North Carolina"; a map of Alabama; "Virginia/Sic Semper Tyrannis" ("Thus Ever to Tyrants"); "Texas"; and "Animis Opibusque Parati" ("Prepared in Mind and Resources"), the motto of South Carolina. But one may safely conclude they were also gathered during the final twenty-four months of the war. The heartlessness that souvenir hunting often elicited manifested itself on the Confederate side, too. When a Southerner inspected the Bull Run battlefield in 1861, he found Yankee corpses disinterred, "and their skeletons & clothing . . . scattered all around." Relic hunters in search of Union buttons had dug up the graves to plunder the uniforms. Even Confederate prisoners at Andersonville did a healthy trade in buttons. The diarist Charles Wesley Homsher observed one hungry captive trading chews of tobacco for brass uniform buttons, and then, when he had gathered an even dozen, trading them to guards for a full plug of Cavendish tobacco plus two quarts of cornmeal. Guards in turn took what they called Union "Buttons with hens on" and painstakingly converted them into Confederate buttons to keep the lively, if pathetic, exchanges in full swing.

Inevitably, the lust for war booty went too far. John D. Billings, a Union veteran who served as a private under Daniel Sickles and Winfield Scott Hancock and went on to write the delightful *Hardtack and Coffee; or, The Unwritten Story of Army Life* in 1887, recalled that officers were at first especially hard on soldiers who did not respect Southern property rights during the first two years of fighting. "At the beginning of the war," Billings testified, "many generals were very fearful lest some of the acts of the common soldier should give offence to the Southern people. This encouraged the latter to report every chicken lost, every bee-hive borrowed, every rail burnt, to headquarters, and subordinates were required to institute the most thorough search for evidence that

Confederate buttons mounted on card, 1860–1865

should lead to the detection and punishment of the culprits, besides requiring them, to make full restitution of the value of the property taken. Our government and its leading officers, military and civil, seemed at that time to stand hat in hand, apologizing to the South for invading its sacred territory." After 1862, however, he concluded, "this kid-glove handling of the enemy had come to an end."

Indeed, William T. Sherman encouraged his army to "forage liberally on the country" during its famous March to the Sea, though it was specifically admonished about entering "the dwellings of the inhabitants." That did not prevent so-called bummers from occasionally pillaging valuables from these residences. As Billings remembered of these unfortunate civilians: "Sometimes the inhabitants were shrewd and watchful enough to scent danger and secrete the articles most precious to them till the danger was past; but not infrequently they were a little tardy in adopting such a measure, and were overhauled just before they had reached cover, and despoiled of the whole or a part of their treasure." Souvenir hunting rarely escalated to thievery, but when it did,

PLATE 23–2

some contemporaries took notice. One Iowa soldier recorded in his diary: "A member of the Company by the name of Locker was arrested for letting things stick to his fingers. Capt found a revolver upon him which he lost some time ago." The 149th New York Infantry acquired such a reputation for looting that one of its own brigade commanders admitted that the regiment "would yet steal the Southern Confederacy poor and take the shoes from off Gen. Lee's charger" if it could.

The collecting of war souvenirs was not limited to enlisted men. During the Union occupation of New Orleans, Union soldiers reportedly appropriated so much silverware from the town's civilian homes that their commanding officer, Benjamin F. Butler, acquired the derisive nickname "Spoons." The Union commander in chief, Abraham Lincoln, received his share of gifts as well, including an eagle-headed cane made from wood gathered from the vicinity of the 1863 Battle of Lookout Mountain and another crafted from the hull of the once-feared Confederate ironclad *Virginia.* In January 1865, a delegation visiting the White House from Philadelphia gave Lincoln "a truly beautiful and superb vase of skeleton leaves gathered from the battle-fields of Gettysburg." Lincoln responded with an appreciative little speech declaring that "so much has been said about Gettysburg, and so well said, that for me to attempt to say more may, perhaps, only serve to weaken the force of that which has already been said." Of course by then he had already said what *he* wanted to say about that most famous of wartime engagements—with the Gettysburg Address. The most famous present President Lincoln ever received came in a message from William T. Sherman on December 25, 1864: "I beg to present to you as a Christmas gift the city of Savannah with 150 heavy guns & plenty of ammunition & also about 25000 bales of cotton." Lincoln responded with "Many, many thanks."

Four months later, Lincoln was dead. Pieces of his clothing, locks of his hair, and remnants from the bloodstained pillow on which his injured head rested during his final hours all became talismanic souvenirs of their own.

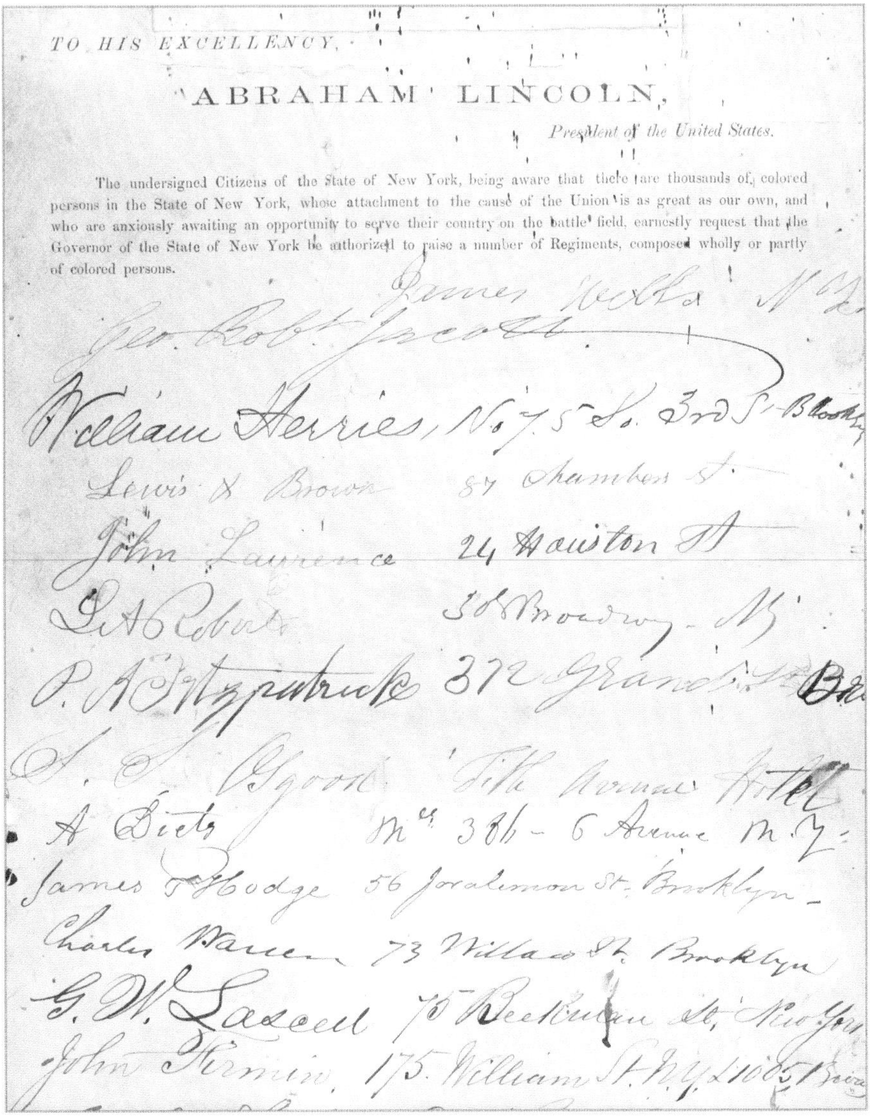

TO HIS EXCELLENCY,

ABRAHAM LINCOLN,

President of the United States.

The undersigned Citizens of the State of New York, being aware that there are thousands of colored persons in the State of New York, whose attachment to the cause of the Union is as great as our own, and who are anxiously awaiting an opportunity to serve their country on the battle field, earnestly request that the Governor of the State of New York be authorized to raise a number of Regiments, composed wholly or partly of colored persons.

Geo. Robt Jacott.   James Wells N.

William Herries,   No 75 So. 3rd St Brooklyn

Lewis & Brown   87 Chambers St.

John Lawrence   24 Houston St

Litt Roberts   38 Broadway N.Y

P. A Fitzpatrick   372 Grand St Ba

S. S. Osgood   Fifth Avenue Hotel

A Dietz   No. 386 - 6 Avenue N.Y.

James F Hodge   56 Joralemon St. Brooklyn

Charles Warren   73 Willow St. Brooklyn

G. W. Lascell   76 Beekman St. New York

John Firmin,   175 William St. N.Y & 1085 Broa

PLATE 24-1

24

⸺⟨∾∾⟩⸺

An Early Call to
Recruit Black Troops

*Petition to Abraham Lincoln
for Recruitment of Black Troops,* 1862

P RESIDENT ABRAHAM LINCOLN RECEIVED COUNTLESS PETITIONS ON
myriad subjects during the Civil War, but the New-York Historical Society can justifiably claim to own the lengthiest and most
impressive one ever created: a massive scroll some twenty-five feet long
containing the names of more than eight hundred New Yorkers urging
the recruitment of African Americans for military service in the summer of 1862.

In point of fact, a number of free black patriots had attempted to enlist in the Union army as soon as war broke out the previous spring, but
the Lincoln administration, ever fearful that any acknowledgment of racial tolerance might trigger secession movements in the Border States
along with political upheaval among Democrats in the North, refused to
accept them.

By the time the petition campaign's principal organizer, J. E. Gardner,
gathered his impressive roster of black recruitment advocates, Lincoln's
policies were changing. Slavery had been abolished in the nation's capital in April. The president's effort over the following weeks to rally
Border State congressmen around a plan to support gradual compensated

emancipation had stalled, but Lincoln continued to hope the loyal slave states would adopt it. Freedom for the region's 432,000 slaves—and the existence of another 129,000 free blacks in Delaware, Kentucky, Maryland, Missouri, and Washington, D.C.—unavoidably suggested a huge new pool of manpower for an army whose needs were expanding faster than white recruitments alone could satisfy. That same month, Congress officially authorized the president to admit black recruits, but Lincoln continued to resist the temptation to accept them into service. Unofficially, however, he offered no objections when Union forces began recruiting blacks to augment troop strength in areas like Kansas and the occupied sections of South Carolina and Louisiana. By the middle of the summer of 1862, following Union setbacks on the Virginia Peninsula, Lincoln had begun to consider emancipating slaves in the Confederacy as a military move. After all, the recalled federal commander George B. McClellan had constantly complained during the campaign that he lacked sufficient troop strength to defeat Robert E. Lee and the Confederates in their defense of Richmond.

Such were the prevailing issues when, on July 20, New Yorkers began signing their names to a preprinted petition addressed "TO HIS EXCELLENCY, ABRAHAM LINCOLN, President of the United States." The document continued:

> The undersigned Citizens of the State of New York, being aware that there are thousands of colored persons in the State of New York, whose attachment to the cause of the Union is as great as our own, and who are anxiously awaiting an opportunity to serve their country on the battle field, earnestly request that the Governor of the State of New York be authorized to raise a number of regiments, composed wholly or partly of colored persons.

One James Wells was the first to sign it, but the final list bore testimony not only to the widespread appeal of arming free blacks but also to the cultural and economic diversity of Manhattan, Brooklyn, Queens, and Westchester. It included a few Germans, a Jewish doctor, and Irish American patriots with monikers like O'Rourke, Flaherty, and O'Shea, as well as local royalty bearing elite names like Whitney, Vanderbilt, Pettigrew, Dodge, and Doubleday. When one William H. Hoogs signed the petition, he could not resist adding a pointed personal note: "For gds sake Abram to put the black to fighting." Expressing similar impatience, James M. Boyd added his own advice: "There is no good Reason why Negroes should be Exempt." F. C. Treadwell Sr. made sure to proudly list his age: seventy-one years. Perhaps the most intriguing name on the petition belonged to a crank who signed himself "John Brown of Harper's Ferry." Organizers struck it from the list.

At least one of the petitioners was a recognizable antislavery leader: Theodore Tilton edited the weekly newspaper the *Independent* and had sat on the platform on February 27, 1860, when Lincoln came to New York to deliver his Cooper Union address. He later appreciatively proposed that Lincoln's tombstone feature this epitaph: "He bound the nation, and unbound the slave."

Why this gargantuan petition was created in the form of a scroll has never been explained, nor have historians been able to unravel the most perplexing mystery it presents: Why was it never sent as intended to the president? Instead, the White House received a similarly worded variant bearing only seven signatures on a single sheet, among them those of Tilton; the Reverend Henry Ward Beecher, the minister of Brooklyn's Plymouth Church, where Lincoln had worshipped during his Cooper Union visit; and Fred. B. Perkins, a former *Independent* staffer and self-described "extreme Radical" who later wrote a book about the creation of Francis Bicknell Carpenter's painting of Lincoln's first reading of the Emancipation Proclamation to the Cabinet. Perkins offered a small clue to his enthusiasm for the petition when he later explained that at the time it was circulated, "officers commanding in one and another locality found it a physical impossibility to dispense with the services of the negroes." African Americans had become "fit material for enlistment . . . for a long time before the cautious President would determine that the hour was come for 'proclaiming liberty throughout all the land.'" Why the organizers of the recruitment drive sent a petition bearing seven names rather than a monster demand bearing eight hundred remains difficult to comprehend. Perhaps as an intentional slap, the version that ultimately made its way to the White House omitted the respectful title "His Excellency."

Meanwhile, Frederick Douglass maintained pressure of his own on Lincoln. Chiding him for evading "his obvious duty," he complained that "instead of calling the blacks to arms and to liberty he merely authorized the military commanders to use them as laborers, without even promising them their freedom at the end of their term of service to the government, and thus destroyed virtually the very object of the measure." Lincoln, Douglass concluded, suffered from a fatal "incapacity to do better."

Unbeknownst to all these critics, just two days after the date listed on the Society's mega-petition, Abraham Lincoln announced to his Cabinet—but, at their advice, tabled—a plan for an emancipation proclamation in the rebellious states.

For his part, Georgia's Howell Cobb predicted that the idea of black recruitment was destined to fail. "If slaves will make good soldiers," he warned, "our whole theory of slavery is wrong."

By war's end, the 200,000 or so African American men in arms proved Cobb's point.

25

⟨⟩⟨⟩

If My Name Ever
Goes into History,
It Will Be for This Act

By the President of the United States of America.
A Proclamation, Abraham Lincoln, 1863

O N NEW YEAR'S DAY MORNING, 1863, AS ABRAHAM LINCOLN WAS TO make the final Emancipation Proclamation official, he noticed a typographical error in the boilerplate language at the bottom of the beautifully handwritten "holograph" copy awaiting his signature. The template was supposed to read: "In witness whereof I have hereunto set my hand and caused the seal of the United States to be affixed." Though the flaw he spotted was minor and legally inconsequential, Lincoln decided he could not approve an imperfect document—not one as important as this—and instead ordered that, holiday notwithstanding, a government scribe redraft it. A hundred days earlier, Lincoln had issued a preliminary proclamation—an ultimatum giving the states in rebellion until this day to throw down their arms or risk forfeiting their slave property forever. Now that threat had come due. But Lincoln chose perfection over haste. While the scribe worked on a revision, the president energetically threw himself into a thronged White House reception and for the next several hours ushered in the year 1863 by greeting hundreds of visitors and shaking most of them by the hand.

BY THE PRESIDENT OF THE UNITED STATES OF AMERICA.

A Proclamation.

· · · · ·

Whereas, on the twenty-second day of September, in the year of our Lord one thousand eight hundred and sixty-two, a proclamation was issued by the President of the United States, containing, among other things, the following, to wit:

"That on the first day of January, in the year of our Lord one thousand eight hundred and sixty-three, all persons held as slaves within any State or designated part of a State, the people whereof shall then be in rebellion against the United States, shall be then, thenceforward, and forever, free; and the Executive government of the United States, including the military and naval authority thereof, will recognize and maintain the freedom of such persons, and will do no act or acts to repress such persons, or any of them, in any efforts they may make for their actual freedom.

"That the Executive will, on the first day of January aforesaid, by proclamation, designate the States and parts of States, if any, in which the people thereof, respectively, shall then be in rebellion against the United States; and the fact that any State, or the people thereof, shall on that day be in good faith represented in the Congress of the United States, by members chosen thereto at elections wherein a majority of the qualified voters of such State shall have participated, shall, in the absence of strong countervailing testimony, be deemed conclusive evidence that such State, and the people thereof, are not then in rebellion against the United States."

Now, therefore, I, ABRAHAM LINCOLN, PRESIDENT OF THE UNITED STATES, by virtue of the power in me vested as commander-in-chief of the army and navy of the United States, in time of actual armed rebellion against the authority and government of the United States, and as a fit and necessary war measure for suppressing said rebellion, do, on this first day of January, in the year of our Lord one thousand eight hundred and sixty-three, and in accordance with my purpose so to do, publicly proclaimed for the full period of one hundred days from the day first above mentioned, order and designate as the States and parts of States wherein the people thereof, respectively, are this day in rebellion against the United States, the following, to wit: ARKANSAS, TEXAS, LOUISIANA, (except the Parishes of St. Bernard, Plaquemines, Jefferson, St. John, St. Charles, St. James, Ascension, Assumption, Terre Bonne, Lafourche, St. Mary, St. Martin, and Orleans, including the City of New Orleans,) MISSISSIPPI, ALABAMA, FLORIDA, GEORGIA, SOUTH CAROLINA, NORTH CAROLINA, AND VIRGINIA, (except the forty-eight counties designated as West Virginia, and also the counties of Berkeley, Accomac, Northampton, Elizabeth City, York, Princess Ann, and Norfolk, including the cities of Norfolk and Portsmouth,) and which excepted parts are for the present left precisely as if this proclamation were not issued.

And by virtue of the power and for the purpose aforesaid, I do order and declare that all persons held as slaves within said designated States and parts of States are and henceforward shall be free; and that the Executive government of the United States, including the military and naval authorities thereof, will recognize and maintain the freedom of said persons.

And I hereby enjoin upon the people so declared to be free to abstain from all violence, unless in necessary self-defence; and I recommend to them that, in all cases when allowed, they labor faithfully for reasonable wages.

And I further declare and make known that such persons, of suitable condition, will be received into the armed service of the United States, to garrison forts, positions, stations, and other places, and to man vessels of all sorts in said service.

And upon this act, sincerely believed to be an act of justice warranted by the Constitution upon military necessity, I invoke the considerate judgment of mankind and the gracious favor of Almighty God.

In witness whereof I have hereunto set my hand and caused the seal of the United States to be affixed.

[L. S.] Done at the CITY OF WASHINGTON this first day of January, in the year of our Lord one thousand eight hundred and sixty-three, and of the Independence of the United States of America the eighty-seventh.

By the President:

Abraham Lincoln

Willia H Seward Secretary of State.

A true copy, with the autograph signatures of the President and the Secretary of State.

Jno. G. Nicolay
Priv. Sec. to the President.

Although African Americans and abolitionists had gathered at dawn in churches throughout the North awaiting the expected news that the president had issued the final emancipation order, no word of any kind came until early afternoon. Lincoln had spent much of the holiday at the reception. Now, as a handful of witnesses, including his private secretary, John G. Nicolay, and Secretary of State William H. Seward, looked on, Lincoln at last picked up a steel-tipped pen from the Cabinet table where he sat, dipped it in ink, held it to the proclamation, and then unexpectedly paused and set the pen down. After a few seconds passed, he took up the pen again and directed it toward the page once more, only to place it down a second time. Rumors had abounded in Washington for days that the president might, in the end, waver and decline to make the revolutionary order official after all. In New York, the diarist George Templeton Strong, for one, wondered whether "Lincoln's backbone" would "carry him through the work he is pledged to do. . . . If he come out fair and square," predicted Strong, "he will do the 'biggest thing' an Illinois jury-lawyer has ever had a chance of doing, and take high place among the men who have controlled the destinies of nations. If he postpone or dilute his action, his name will be a byword and a hissing till the annals of the nineteenth century are forgotten." Strong need not have worried. As Lincoln had only recently confided to a delegation of Kentuckians, he "would rather die than take back a word of the Proclamation of Freedom." Nevertheless, Seward and Nicolay surely wondered what Lincoln's unanticipated New Year's Day pantomime signified.

Finally, Lincoln turned to his perplexed secretary of state and explained: "I have been shaking hands since nine o'clock this morning, and my right arm is almost paralyzed. If my name ever goes into history it will be for this act, and my whole soul is in it. If my hand trembles when I sign the Proclamation, all who examine the document hereafter will say, 'He hesitated.'" For the next few moments, Lincoln sat silently and massaged his massive hands together. Finally, when he was satisfied that they had regained enough feeling, he "took up the pen again, and slowly, firmly wrote that 'Abraham Lincoln' with which the whole world is now familiar. He looked up, smiled, and said: 'That will do.'"

Indeed, it did. Although the Emancipation Proclamation is today

PLATE 25-1 (opposite)

perhaps the most misunderstood and underappreciated act of Lincoln's presidency, in its time it was regarded as truly revolutionary. Modern skeptics sometimes unfairly condemn Lincoln by pointing out that the proclamation freed slaves only in areas that were still under Confederate control, where Lincoln could not enforce it. The reason, of course, is that Lincoln drew his authority for the proclamation from his war powers as commander in chief and he could apply those powers only to areas in rebellion. Nevertheless, his act transformed the war overnight from a fight to restore the Union into one to destroy slavery altogether. It is no wonder that its author wanted his name to be as legible and firm as possible on the final document. Lincoln thought it was the "most important act of the nineteenth century."

As a piece of literature, however, the proclamation was immediately found sorely lacking. Frederick Douglass noticed it at once: "It was not a proclamation of 'liberty throughout the land, unto all the inhabitants thereof,' such as we had hoped it would be, but was one marked by discriminations and reservations." In the end, however, Douglass came to regard it as "a great and glorious step in the right direction." Still, as breathlessly as both North and South alike awaited the document, it remains astounding that more people did not clamor for copies once it was issued. Although countless publishers eventually did offer illustrative versions of the proclamation—the New-York Historical Society boasts several in its collection—the first examples appeared only in 1864 for the presidential campaign, and most rolled off the presses in 1865, after Lincoln's murder and martyrdom made his greatest act safe for celebration among previously recalcitrant white audiences. For the most part, the proclamation took the form of small booklets carried by Union soldiers to help them enforce its liberating terms when they seized rebel territory or of official war orders formally sent to generals in the field after January 1 (a copy of that order exists in the collection, too).

Today the scant surviving copies of the most famous of all these editions grace the best public and private Lincoln collections in the country. One such copy decorates the Oval Office. But when it first appeared, it was anything but popular.

The broadside featured here is one of a limited edition of just

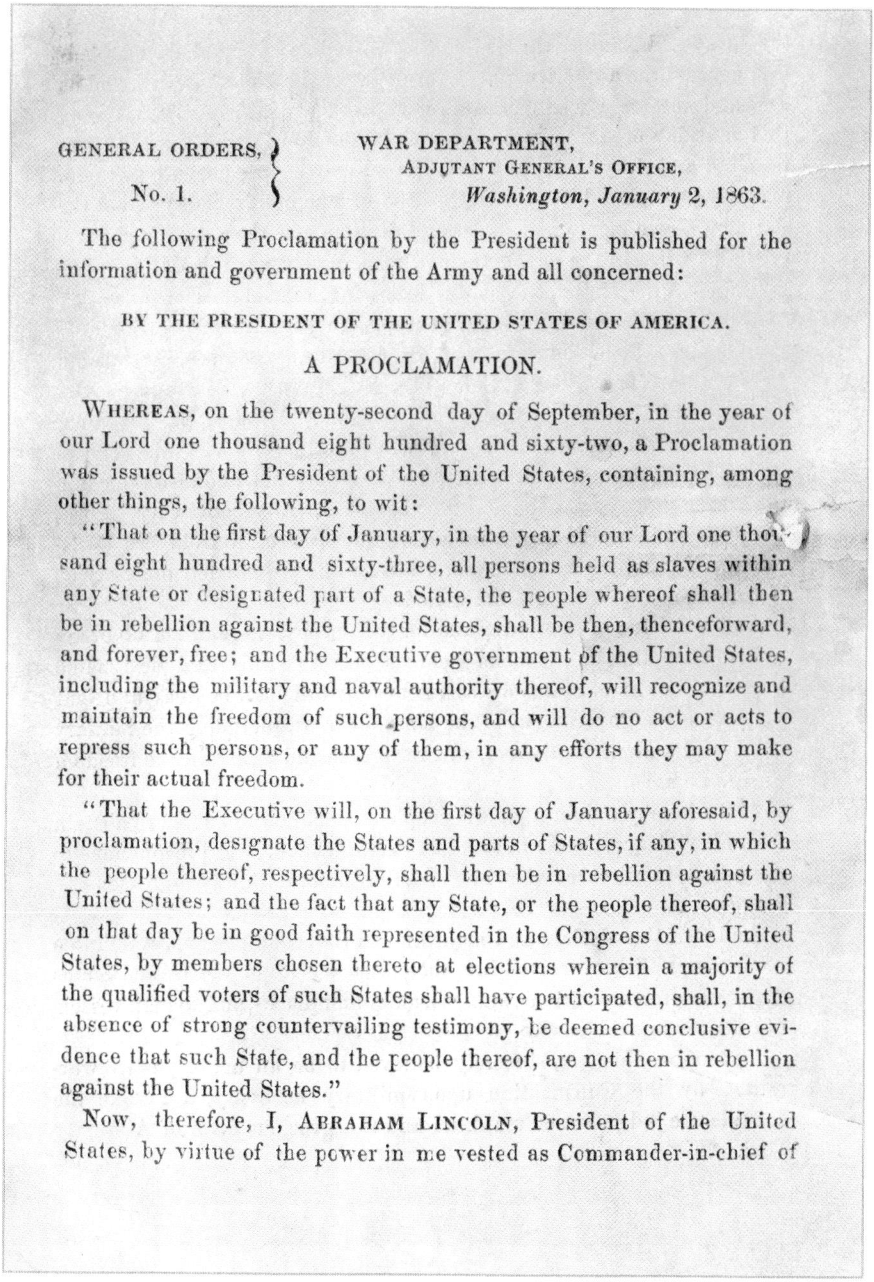

GENERAL ORDERS, }
No. 1. }

WAR DEPARTMENT,
ADJUTANT GENERAL'S OFFICE,
Washington, January 2, 1863.

The following Proclamation by the President is published for the information and government of the Army and all concerned:

BY THE PRESIDENT OF THE UNITED STATES OF AMERICA.

A PROCLAMATION.

WHEREAS, on the twenty-second day of September, in the year of our Lord one thousand eight hundred and sixty-two, a Proclamation was issued by the President of the United States, containing, among other things, the following, to wit:

"That on the first day of January, in the year of our Lord one thousand eight hundred and sixty-three, all persons held as slaves within any State or designated part of a State, the people whereof shall then be in rebellion against the United States, shall be then, thenceforward, and forever, free; and the Executive government of the United States, including the military and naval authority thereof, will recognize and maintain the freedom of such persons, and will do no act or acts to repress such persons, or any of them, in any efforts they may make for their actual freedom.

"That the Executive will, on the first day of January aforesaid, by proclamation, designate the States and parts of States, if any, in which the people thereof, respectively, shall then be in rebellion against the United States; and the fact that any State, or the people thereof, shall on that day be in good faith represented in the Congress of the United States, by members chosen thereto at elections wherein a majority of the qualified voters of such States shall have participated, shall, in the absence of strong countervailing testimony, be deemed conclusive evidence that such State, and the people thereof, are not then in rebellion against the United States."

Now, therefore, I, ABRAHAM LINCOLN, President of the United States, by virtue of the power in me vested as Commander-in-chief of

General Orders, No. 1, January 2, 1863, Abraham Lincoln

PLATE 25–2

forty-eight, originally printed in 1864 by two leaders of Philadelphia's pro-Lincoln Union League club, George Henry Boker and Charles Godfrey Leland. These two enterprising Republicans hatched the idea of publishing and selling twenty-one-by-seventeen-inch copies for the benefit of the U.S. Sanitary Commission. By then, Lincoln no longer had the original handwritten draft at his disposal, so Leland and Boker had to typeset a version from the published record.

The two spared no expense in producing faithful editions. Under the supervision of the State Department, they printed several rounds of drafts and proofs, and only when fully satisfied did they publish the final run of four dozen and send them off to Washington to be signed by Seward and the president.

Lincoln likely proved willing to participate in the project not only because of its promised benefit to wounded veterans but also, at least in part, out of gratitude to the Union League organization. It had awarded him an honorary membership in the Philadelphia chapter just eight months earlier, a tribute that the president accepted by pledging to the club's "patriotic" members—and potential supporters in his upcoming bid for reelection—"to do my duty in the trying times through which we are passing." Now he was doing that duty, repaying a political debt he no doubt expected would reap further dividends for his campaign in the coming months. But surely he was doing something more: aiding and abetting the transfiguration of a prosaic piece of writing into a canonical national treasure. And the chief beneficiary of such a metamorphosis would be Lincoln himself.

As promised, Boker and Leland went on to offer the signed broadsides at ten dollars apiece at the Philadelphia Great Central Sanitary Fair later that June—just days after Lincoln won his party's nod for a second term and the convention indeed proposed the Thirteenth Amendment to the Constitution abolishing slavery. The only piece of the plan that failed to fall into place was the anticipated public enthusiasm for the limited edition of Emancipation Proclamations. For while the Philadelphia fair attracted more than a hundred thousand visitors, several of the reproductions went unsold.

This remains difficult to comprehend, much less explain. Conceivably, it was a sign that not everyone, not even in the City of Brotherly Love, yet endorsed the liberty order enthusiastically enough to embrace it as an icon. If so, then skepticism reigned in Philadelphia, even though Lincoln made a rare trip from Washington to visit the fair personally, making three different speeches to enthusiastic audiences at both his hotel and Union League headquarters. To one audience he specifically declared that he hoped "my presence might do some good towards swelling the contributions of the great Fair in aid of the Sanitary Commission, who intend it for the soldiers in the field." Apparently, it did not—at least where the Leland-Boker edition was concerned.

The autographed proclamations were certainly not priced higher than the art, artifacts, machinery, and crafts on display and for sale. It cost two dollars merely to attend the fair, and multitudes did so, reportedly spending a total of one million dollars during its twenty-two-day run. Had the recent national convention politicized Lincoln and his order? Perhaps, but political campaigns in nineteenth-century America also tended to expand public demand for collectibles and display pieces associated with the candidates; they did not ordinarily suppress it.

One possible explanation for the lethargic response to the printings may be that the president was simply not popular at the time. After three years of bloody and costly war, the Northern public was growing deeply impatient with its leader, and Lincoln himself expected for a good while thereafter that he would be defeated in the fall election. And yet the Leland-Boker edition involved not thousands of souvenirs for purchase but only four dozen—each of them autographed by hand. Unless they were inadequately advertised or improperly identified at the fair, it remains almost incomprehensible that they did not sell out immediately. So it is reasonable to wonder whether their sluggish sales might then be attributable to the words themselves.

In the abstract the words had changed the war, changed the armed services, and changed the nation. But any prospective customer who carefully studied a copy at the Philadelphia fair might well have been reminded that, phrase for phrase, the proclamation was rather dull. Even the antislavery radical Karl Marx, writing from London, thought Lincoln's document called to mind "the trite summonses that one lawyer sends to an opposing lawyer, the legal chicaneries and pettifogging stipulations of an *actiones juris*"—a court case. Certainly capable of loftier prose, Lincoln had wanted a proclamation that would withstand legal challenges, not necessarily a call to sentiment and soul. He may have gotten what he wanted, but, for a time, enthusiasts like Leland and Boker paid the price—because prospective customers would not.

All we know for sure is that only five months later, the intrepid Philadelphia publishers suggested that the remainder of their unsold autographed editions "be disposed of" in some other way, again if possible "for the benefit of those who are now fighting for their country." That November—the very month of the presidential election—they sent five of the white elephant broadsides to offer at another Sanitary Commission–backed charity event: the National Sailors' Fair in Boston. There the remaining "autograph emancipation proclamations" presumably found an appreciative audience at last. At least we know of no more leftover copies or additional venues. They may even have been disposed of in what amounted to a bargain sale.

Ironically, the official holograph copy of the proclamation, which Lincoln had insisted be perfect so future generations would bear witness to his bold signature, has faded so badly over time that his handwriting is now barely legible. But the thickly inked autographs he provided for forty-eight copies of the document a year later look as if they were signed yesterday.

And though the words of the document remain uninspiring, and its immediate impact continues to be misinterpreted, the publishers Charles Leland and George Boker surely appreciated the truth of what the governor of their home state of Pennsylvania had said when Lincoln made the original act official: "The great proclamation of Liberty will lift the Ruler who uttered it, our Nation, and our age, above all vulgar destiny." As the journalist Frederic Perkins put it: "Notwithstanding all this guarded negation of statement and conditional assertion, yet such were the aspects of the war in the field, and of the public opinion of the North, that these two gigantic forces, embodying the moral sum total of the United States . . . inspired into the words of this short paper that whole and complete and immense meaning which has rendered it immortal."

26

—◦◦◦—

A Dentist Drills Lincoln

Writing the Emancipation Proclamation,
Etching by Adalbert Johann Volck, 1863

B Y THE MIDDLE OF THE SECOND YEAR OF THE CIVIL WAR, THE ELEVEN states of the Confederacy could boast only a handful of professional artists still actively pursuing their craft. The inescapable demands of military conscription meant the armed forces scooped up every able-bodied man for active duty, and the draft by no means excluded painters and engravers. Unfortunately for the South, this meant that potentially morale-building artworks introducing new Confederate military heroes and celebrating their significant battlefield triumphs never made it to the Southern home front. Any initial hope that English or French artists might step in and supply this need evaporated with the tightening of the Union blockade. When one blockade-runner did slip past the federal "anaconda" with a boatload of Scottish engravers on board, government officials promptly assigned these artists to the "official printmaking" that still held priority in the deprived region, meaning the design of Confederate currency and postage stamps.

The Confederacy actually lost one of its most talented propagandists— one who might well have made a significant difference in satisfying the yearnings of picture-starved Southern customers—before the fighting war even began. His disappearance had nothing to do with the blockade or the military draft. Rather, once the Lincoln administration headed off

secession in Maryland and imposed strict martial law in Baltimore, the local artist Adalbert Johann Volck (1828–1912) fell silent—or at least began working in secret. While he continued to churn out a breathtaking variety of anti-Union, pro-Confederate etchings at the highest level of artistic ingenuity and skill under the pseudonymous anagram "V. Blada," he did so for limited editions that circulated only among trusted friends who shared his political passions. Though the works achieved fame after the war, the ubiquity of later nineteenth- and twentieth-century reproductions long encouraged the mistaken belief that they originally appeared in significant quantities while the war raged. The truth is they did not; however capable, and inspired, Volck did not wield a mighty wartime pen. By the spring of 1861, this gifted would-be propagandist was all but driven underground. His rare *Confederate War Etchings* was first republished free from censorship in 1882. However limited its impact during the war, the ambitious portfolio stands as a remarkable testament to the resilience of Confederate patriotism in a Union-controlled border slave state. Notwithstanding censorship or racism, Volck either invented or illustrated some of the most intractable false-

PLATE 26–1

hoods attached to Union occupation and some of the most indelible mythology of the Lost Cause.

Born in Bavaria, Volck immigrated to America after the failed European revolutions of 1848 but, unlike most of his fellow Germans, headed not north but south to Maryland. While German-born leaders like Carl Schurz became major figures in the antislavery movement, Volck absorbed Southern values, graduating from the Baltimore College of Dental Surgery in 1852 and establishing a successful professional practice there. Always interested in drawing, he also joined the Allston Association, a local artists' club whose members proved passionately pro-secession and pro-Confederate. Union occupying forces came to consider the group a "nest of rebels." Astonishingly, there is no evidence that Volck ever received professional art training. He was entirely self-taught.

During the war, Volck seems to have become something of a Confederate agent as well, smuggling volunteers into the South and investing whatever money he earned from his dental practice in ultimately worthless Confederate bonds. His subsequent claims that he was also a blockade-runner, and briefly a prisoner in Fort Henry, were very likely efforts to bolster his Confederate credentials. In a century of searching, historians have unearthed no records to substantiate either boast. But Volck certainly became acquainted with Jefferson Davis's family either before or shortly after the war, and there is little doubt but that the Confederate president came at some point to know of his work. We just do not know when. After the war, Volck turned to oil painting, creating two portraits of the former general Robert E. Lee, one showing him meditating at Stonewall Jackson's grave, and the other sitting quietly in his study at Washington College—both as models for print reproductions meant to raise funds for a Lee statue. Volck also tried his hand at sculpture. But his considerable talents were definitely best suited to the delicate craft he practiced most skillfully: etching.

Infuriated by General Benjamin F. Butler's occupation of his home city, Volck made his artistic debut with a series of highly polished anti-Butler etchings in 1861. *Ye Exploits of ye Distinguished Attorney and General B.F.B. (Bombastes Furioso Buncombe)* savagely portrayed the New England–born general as a vain, corrupt, bloated, and baroquely costumed villain. One of these pictures suggested the general had declared himself "head of the church" in occupied Norfolk, where, Volck insisted, Butler had "sent their priests off to sweep the streets, cut down the crosses and substituted Union flags in their place." It was the first of many inflammatory calumnies—most false or ridiculously exaggerated—that Volck would reimagine in his work.

Volck next produced a broader collection he titled *Comedians and Tragedians of the North*. Like his subsequent work a marvel of acute portraiture, it exhibited a strong element of satirical humor but also revealed a streak of unapologetic racism. He depicted the Reverend Henry Ward Beecher as an African American and suggested that Lincoln and his fellow Republicans were Negro worshippers. Volck portrayed Secretary of War Simon Cameron as a thief (which he arguably was) and the pro-Union Maryland governor Thomas Hicks as a Judas. The artist reserved particular venom for Lincoln, whom he blamed for both Volck's own woes and those of the entire South. One of his earliest etchings devastatingly satirized Lincoln and Butler as Don Quixote and Sancho Panza. Another portrayed a frightened president hiding in fear on a freight car at the Baltimore railroad depot, recoiling from the mere sight of a hissing cat.

In 1863, Volck published the first edition of his masterwork, *Sketches from the Civil War in North America*. (The Society obtained its copy of the portfolio soon after its issue.) It was stamped with a false London imprint to disguise its Baltimore origins and thereby reduce the likelihood of seizure by Union army officials. What it lacked in circulation, however—the edition of two hundred was privately distributed—the *Sketches* more than made up for in raw power. In Volck's world, Northerners were plunderers, rapists, devils, and brutes; Southern men were invariably noble; white women brave, self-sacrificing, and virtuous victims of poverty and degradation; and slaves eternally grateful for their subjugation and determined to remain in bondage with their white masters. In one of his most extraordinary demonstrations of loyalty to his adopted "country," Volck produced an etching titled *Valiant Men "Dat Fite mit Sigel,"* depicting fellow German-born Union soldiers of General Franz Sigel's army killing helpless and innocent women and children.

No comparably graphic atrocity picture was ever produced by any other artist during the Civil War.

One of Volck's most unforgettably venomous efforts was inspired by the Emancipation Proclamation, which Northern artists, if they treated the subject at all, viewed as an almost sacred text inspired by the Constitution and the holy book and animated by Lincoln's own early life as a laborer. In an etching that has come to be known by the title *Writing the Emancipation Proclamation,* Volck took a rabidly contrary view, depicting Lincoln as a devilish-looking, slovenly figure sprawled across a cloven-hoofed desk—meant to symbolize satanic influences—and scribbling his document with ink drawn from an inkwell proffered by the winged Prince of Darkness himself. In Volck's extraordinary composition, Lincoln's foot rests rudely on a Bible as if to suppress its true guidance on slavery.

The walls of the room Volck imagined for this scene are decorated with a portrait of John Brown as a haloed saint, along with a celebratory depiction of the bloody—and successful—1791 slave uprising at Santo Domingo. On a table in the background in this improvised White House setting lies a liquor decanter and drinking glasses, suggesting that Lincoln must have composed his document under the influence of alcohol. (In fact, he was a teetotaler.) The window curtains are tied back with a vulture's head, while outside the birds of prey flock, presumably to feast on the devastated South. Perhaps the subtlest symbol in the entire scene is the almost indecipherable cloaked statue standing in the corner—a device that would have been recognizable to Volck's contemporaries, particularly his neighbors in Baltimore. It shows the national symbol, Columbia, partly covered over by a Scotch cap—a reference to the disguise that President-elect Lincoln allegedly wore to pass safely through Baltimore en route to his inauguration back in 1861. In an era in which most emancipation tributes were celebratory, Volck's over-the-top view of the muses that inspired Abraham Lincoln to compose his most important document—devil worship, drunkenness, sacrilege, tyranny, and cowardice—would have provided a powerful visual contradiction to otherwise unanswered sanctification pictures, had it been allowed to circulate the year it was created. But it was not.

Volck's love for the Confederacy proved as strong as his hatred for the Union, and he vividly depicted, or perhaps created, some of the most powerful legends in Lost Cause lore, including the hardships of cave life in besieged Vicksburg (see chapter 30); the God-fearing reverence of General Stonewall Jackson, whom he portrayed leading a prayer meeting in camp; the selfless sacrifice of impoverished Southern ladies sewing clothes for "boys in the army"; and the supposed loyalty of grateful black slaves hiding their white owners from rampaging Union troops.

In early 1862, Volck was inspired to visualize another tribute to Confederate generosity when he learned that General P. G. T. Beauregard had encouraged residents of the Mississippi valley "to send your plantation-bells to the nearest railroad depot, to be melted into cannon for the defense of your plantations." The plea caused an instant sensation throughout the South and no doubt gave rise to what turned out to be one of Volck's most evocative etchings, *Offering of Bells to Be Cast into Cannon*. The print took Beauregard's limited request one step further

Offering of Bells to Be Cast into Cannon,
etching by Adalbert Johann Volck, 1863

PLATE 26–2

and depicted an Episcopal priest, positioned like Christ revealing his stigmata, urging his parishioners to melt down their church bells for the holier purpose of providing metal for Confederate weaponry. As well-dressed white neighbors look on sadly, a cruelly caricatured slave willingly does the labor required to move the heavy bells into a forge. In etchings like these, Volck equated the Confederacy with Christianity, and the Union with sacrilege and satanism.

After the war, Volck told the Library of Congress that even though he had created nearly two dozen more original, unissued plates, he decided to suspend domestic publication once he became "a suspected man, and in daily fear of arrest." Then, after what he called "the deplorable murder of Lincoln," he further explained, "I thought it best to go into retirement and an officious friend persuaded me to let him take the last plates (20) to England and have them printed there."

Not everyone believed in his repentance. The Cincinnati war correspondent Murat Halstead, for one, never allowed himself to be convinced of Volck's allegedly "changed" sentiments. As he later complained of the artist's works: "We find these etchings full of the sharpest scorn and of rancorous hatred." To Halstead, they constituted "a record of the fierce animosities, the bitter resentments, the implacable prejudices, the passion, the frenzy and the ferocity of the war." They would undoubtedly have stung less if they had been crafted less brilliantly.

For his part, Adalbert Volck never entirely recanted the political beliefs he had so brilliantly evoked during the Civil War. But he did confess in 1905, four years before creating a carved silver shield for the Museum of the Confederacy in Richmond, dedicated to the "Brave Women of the South": "I feel the greatest regret ever to have aimed ridicule at that great and good Lincoln."

For some, his apology constituted too little and came much too late.

MEN OF COLOR, TO ARMS!

A Call by Frederick Douglass.

When first the Rebel cannon shattered the walls of Sumter, and drove away its starving garrison, I predicted that the war then and there inaugurated would not be fought out entirely by white men. Every month's experience during these two dreary years has confirmed that opinion. A war undertaken and brazenly carried on for the perpetual enslavement of colored men, calls logically and loudly upon colored men to help to suppress it. Only a moderate share of sagacity was needed to see that the arm of the slave was the best defence against the arm of the slaveholder. Hence with every reverse to the National arms, with every exulting shout of victory raised by the slaveholding Rebels, I have implored the imperilled nation to unchain against her foes her powerful black hand. Slowly and reluctantly that appeal is beginning to be heeded. Stop not now to complain that it was not heeded sooner. It may, or it may not have been best—that it should not. This is not the time to discuss that question. Leave it to the future. When the war is over, the country is saved, peace is established, and the black man's rights are secured, as they will be, history with an impartial hand, will dispose of that and sundry other questions. Action! action! not criticism, is the plain duty of this hour. Words are now useful only as they stimulate to blows. The office of speech now is only to point out when, where and how to strike to the best advantage. There is no time for delay. The tide is at flood that leads on to fortune. From east to west, from north to south the sky is written all over with "now or never." Liberty won by white men would lack half its lustre. Who would be free themselves must strike the blow. Better even to die free than to live slaves. This is the sentiment of every brave colored man among us. There are weak and cowardly men in all nations. We have them among us. They will tell you that this is the "whiteman's war;" that you will be "better off after than before the war;" that the getting of you into the army is to "sacrifice you on the first opportunity." Believe them not—cowards themselves, they do not wish to have their cowardice shamed by your brave example. Leave them to their timidity, or to whatever other motive may hold them back.

I have not thought lightly of the words I am now addressing to you. The counsel I give comes of close observation of the great struggle now in progress—and of the deep conviction that this is your hour and mine.

In good earnest, then, and after the best deliberation, I, now, for the first time during the war, feel at liberty to call and counsel you to arms. By every consideration which binds you to your enslaved fellow countrymen, and the peace and welfare of your country; by every aspiration which you cherish for the freedom and equality of yourselves and your children; by all the ties of blood and identity which make us one with the brave black men now fighting our battles in Louisiana, in South Carolina, I urge you to fly to arms, and smite with death the power that would bury the Government and your liberty in the same hopeless grave. I wish I could tell you that the State of New York calls you to this high honor. For the moment her constituted authorities are silent on the subject. They will speak by and by, and doubtless on the right side; but we are not compelled to wait for her. We can get at the throat of treason and Slavery through the State of Massachusetts.

She was first in the war of Independence; first to break the chains of her slaves; first to make the black man equal before the law; first to admit colored children to her common schools, and she was the first to answer with her blood the alarm cry of the nation—when its capital was menaced by rebels. You know her patriotic Governor, and you know Charles Sumner—I need add no more.

Massachusetts now welcomes you to arms as her soldiers. She has but a small colored population from which to recruit. She has full leave of the General Government to send one regiment to the war, and she has undertaken to do it. Go quickly and help fill up this first colored regiment from the North. I am authorized to assure you that you will receive the same wages, the same rations, the same equipments, the same protection, the same treatment and the same bounty secured to white soldiers. You will be led by able and skillful officers—men who will take especial pride in your efficiency and success. They will be quick to accord to you all the honor you shall merit by your valor—and see that your rights and feelings are respected by other soldiers. I have assured myself on these points—and can speak with authority. More than twenty years unswerving devotion to our common cause, may give me some humble claim to be trusted at this momentous crisis.

I will not argue. To do so implies hesitation and doubt, and you do not hesitate. You do not doubt. The day dawns—the morning star is bright upon the horizon! The iron gate of our prison stands half open. One gallant rush from the North will fling it wide open, while four millions of our brothers and sisters shall march out into Liberty! The chance is now given you to end in a day the bondage of centuries, and to rise in one bound from social degradation to the plane of common equality with all other varieties of men. Remember Denmark Vesey of Charleston. Remember Nathaniel Turner of South Hampton; remember Shields, Green, and Copeland, who followed noble John Brown, and fell as glorious martyrs for the cause of the slaves. Remember that in a contest with oppression, the Almighty has no attribute which can take sides with oppressors. The case is before you. This is our golden opportunity—let us accept it—and forever wipe out the dark reproaches unsparingly hurled against us by our enemies. Win for ourselves the gratitude of our country—and the best blessings of our prosperity through all time. The nucleus of this first regiment is now in camp at Readville, a short distance from Boston. I will undertake to forward to Boston all persons adjudged fit to be mustered into this regiment, who shall apply to me at any time within the next two weeks.

FREDERICK DOUGLASS.

Rochester, March 2, 1863.

PLATE 27-1

27

—o/o/o—

Frederick Douglass's Call to Arms

Men of Color, to Arms!
Broadside by Frederick Douglass, 1863

W HEN NEWS FIRST REACHED THE UNION ARMY IN THE FIELD THAT Abraham Lincoln had issued the Emancipation Proclamation on January 1, 1863, a regiment from the president's home state of Illinois promptly reacted by deserting, vowing to "lie in the woods until moss grew on their backs rather than help free slaves."

Ultimately, Lincoln's proclamation had a broader and much more positive effect on the federal fighting force—not only on its morale but also on its size and color. For it did more than offer freedom: for the first time it called specifically on African Americans "to garrison forts, positions, stations, and other places, and to man vessels of all sorts in said service." The result swelled the federal ranks and undoubtedly helped the Union win the war and end slavery.

On the heels of Lincoln's order, the House of Representatives passed a bill in March that specifically made free African Americans eligible to serve in the military for the first time. It gave the president new authority "to enroll, arm, equip, and receive into the land and naval service of the United States such number of volunteers as he may deem useful to suppress the present rebellion."

"Yes, there is a God," Thaddeus Stevens exulted after the bill sailed through, "an avenging God, who is now punishing the sins of this nation for the wicked wrongs which for centuries we have inflicted upon a blameless race." In the end, the Senate declined to take up the House bill on the grounds that Lincoln's proclamation had already accomplished the objective.

Soon thereafter, Secretary of War Edwin M. Stanton made the new state of things official, ordering the army "to arm, uniform, equip, and receive into the service of the United States" the first "volunteers of African descent." That same month the Union War Department officially opened its first Bureau of Colored Troops.

For the first few months of this revolutionary new era of black recruitment, however, manpower did not increase as quickly as the Lincoln administration had initially hoped. Massachusetts led the way as early as January with fund-raising and recruitment for a "separate corps," but the unavoidable fact remained that the state had few eligible African American residents. Governor John A. Andrew did what he could by raising the soon-to-become-legendary 54th Massachusetts, the first all-black regiment ever formed in a Northern state. Eager to do more, Governor Andrew recruited his friend and ally George L. Stearns, a onetime adviser to John Brown, and invited him to assume overall responsibility for African American recruitment. Stearns wisely invested in advertising and in the establishment of recruitment centers but soon concluded that he also needed African American leaders to spread the word among their own constituents. On February 23, Stearns made his way to Rochester, New York, to enlist the support of a man who proved vital to the recruiting effort: Frederick Douglass.

Douglass needed little convincing. As early as May 1861, he had published an editorial making clear his view that the swiftest and surest way to suppress the rebellion was to let *"the slaves and free colored people be called into service, and formed into a liberating army,* to march into the South and raise the banner of Emancipation among the slaves." Now the editor and orator quickly agreed to renew his call, and the result was a landmark editorial in *Douglass' Monthly* that was soon adapted into a separately printed, hugely influential, and justly renowned circular, a

Fred[erick] Douglass (1818–1895),
carte-de-visite (albumen print), n.d.

PLATE 27–2

copy of which the New-York Historical Society has owned since the year it was issued.

The Emancipation Proclamation was less than three months old when Douglass issued a proclamation of his own, titled *Men of Color, to Arms!* For the first time, as he told his readers (perhaps conveniently ignoring his earlier suggestions along the same line), he felt "at liberty to call and counsel you to arms. . . . I urge you to fly to arms, and smite with death the power that would bury the Government and your liberty in the same hopeless grave." With risk, he promised, would come liberty and equality. In a curiously self-serving introduction, Douglass confessed he was disappointed that the government had taken so long to heed his frequent advice that the country use "her powerful black hand" to suppress the rebellion. But then he said, "This is not the time to discuss that question. Leave it to the future." Instead, he issued what amounted to a bugle call to rally black volunteers:

> Action! action! not criticism, is the plain duty of this hour. Words are now useful only as they stimulate to blows. The office of speech now is only to point out when, where and how to strike to the best advantage. There is no time for delay. The tide is at flood that leads on to fortune. From east to west, from north to south the sky is written all over with "now or never." Liberty won by white men would lack half its lustre. Who would be free themselves must strike the blow. Better even to die free than to live slaves. This is the sentiment of every brave colored man among us. There are weak and cowardly men in all nations. We have them among us. They will tell you this is the "whiteman's war;" that you will be "[no] better off after than before the war;" that the getting of you into the army is to "sacrifice you on the first opportunity." Believe them not—cowards themselves, they do not wish to have their cowardice shamed by your brave example.

Three weeks after Douglass called on black men to volunteer, Lincoln wrote to Andrew Johnson, the pro-Union military governor of Tennessee, to urge him to support black recruitment, too. In quick order, Lincoln also authorized African American enlistment in Union-occupied areas of Florida, Louisiana, and the Mississippi valley. When commanders in the field resisted, he overruled them. Lincoln's military aide Henry Halleck, for example, ordered General Grant, who was initially reluctant, to free "all the slaves you can, and to employ those . . . to the best possible advantage against the enemy." The Union similarly ignored General Sherman's retrograde belief that the "Negro . . . is not the equal of the white man" and brushed off General Burnside's insistence that the "enrollment of these negroes is what the loyal people fear." As Lincoln told a group of church leaders visiting the White House in May, he "would gladly receive into the service not ten thousand but ten times ten thousand colored troops." By June 30, 1863, the first regiment of "U.S. Colored Troops" had mustered into service at Washington.

For a time, the Lincoln administration feared that the enlistment of black soldiers might depress the recruitment of white troops—that white soldiers would so intractably resent the arrival of black regiments they might refuse to fight alongside them, even though the "colored" units would improve their numerical advantage over the enemy and be entirely separate and commanded by white officers. To increase the likelihood that white soldiers supported the new arrivals, Lincoln rather shamefully agreed at first to pay black recruits a lower salary than white soldiers earned—a measure that Frederick Douglass, among others, bitterly resented. What was worse, black soldiers were compelled to pay for their uniforms, the cost deducted from their pay. (According to these strikingly inequitable rules, white privates earned thirteen dollars per month plus three dollars for clothing; black troops received only ten dollars a month and had three dollars of that deducted for uniforms.)

Nonetheless, some white soldiers still refused to accept their new comrades-in-arms. One soldier wrote home to complain that the conflict had "turned into a nigger war and all are anxious to return to their homes for it was to preserve the Union that they volunteered." Still, a significant number welcomed the additional manpower—there was safety in numbers, after all—and many even embraced the new crusade their arrival represented: not just reuniting the country but also destroying slavery. "I have no heart in this war if the slaves cannot go free," one such soldier declared. Another wrote home, "If the doom of slavery is not sealed by the war I shall curse the day I entered the Army or lifted a finger in the preservation of the Union."

In August, Frederick Douglass himself called at the White House to plead with Lincoln to provide black soldiers equal pay. The president welcomed him with a kind of stiff cordiality. Lincoln did concede that unequal pay was a "terrible remedy" but pledged that it was only temporary. "I assure you, Mr. Douglass," the president concluded, "that in the end they shall have the same pay as white soldiers." Lincoln did finally approve equal pay a year later.

The president never wavered from his commitment to enlist African Americans—or from his fury at pro-Union whites who objected. "I know as fully as one can know the opinion of others, that some of the commanders of our armies in the field who have given us our most important successes, believe the emancipation policy, and the use of colored troops, constitute the heaviest blow yet dealt to the rebellion," he wrote around the same time as Douglass's visit to the White House, "and that, at least one of those important successes, could not have been achieved when it was, but for the aid of black soldiers."

In words directed at his old neighbors back in Springfield, Lincoln proved especially blunt, suggesting that their continued resistance to black enlistment would damn them in history. When victory and peace finally came, he warned in a speech he asked an old neighbor to deliver for him, "there will be some black men who can remember that, with silent tongue, and clenched teeth, and steady eye, and well-poised bayonet, they have helped mankind on to this great consummation; while, I fear, there will be some white ones, unable to forget that, with malignant heart, and deceitful speech, they have strove to hinder it." By war's end, upwards of 180,000 African Americans had served in the Union army, with as many as 18,000 more in the Union navy.

28

———— ◊/◊/◊ ————

Suffered Severely
and Behaved Well

Emily J. Semmes to Paul Jones Semmes,
Letter, June 1, 1863

NEITHER DETERMINATION NOR BRAVADO EVER QUITE PREPARED
soldiers—elite officers and common soldiers alike—for the inde-
scribable horror of actual battle, the chilling experience they universally
called "seeing the elephant." For those who escaped one furious engagement unscathed only to face another, the sensations became more routine but no less frightening—or potentially deadly.

The Gilder Lehrman Collection—long on deposit at the New-York
Historical Society—boasts a unique series of personal letters written
just before and just after the Battle of Gettysburg by one combat-tested
Confederate officer who had previously fought at and survived the Peninsula Campaign and the Battle of Antietam and commanded the 2nd
Georgia Infantry in defense of Marye's Heights at Fredericksburg—all in
1862. The Gettysburg Campaign would prove to be his last.

Forty-eight-year-old Paul Jones Semmes had been born and raised on
a Georgia plantation and, after attending the University of Virginia,
returned to his home state and established a plantation of his own in the
town of Columbus, where he became a leading citizen. His was a military family. A celebrated cousin, Raphael Semmes, commanded the

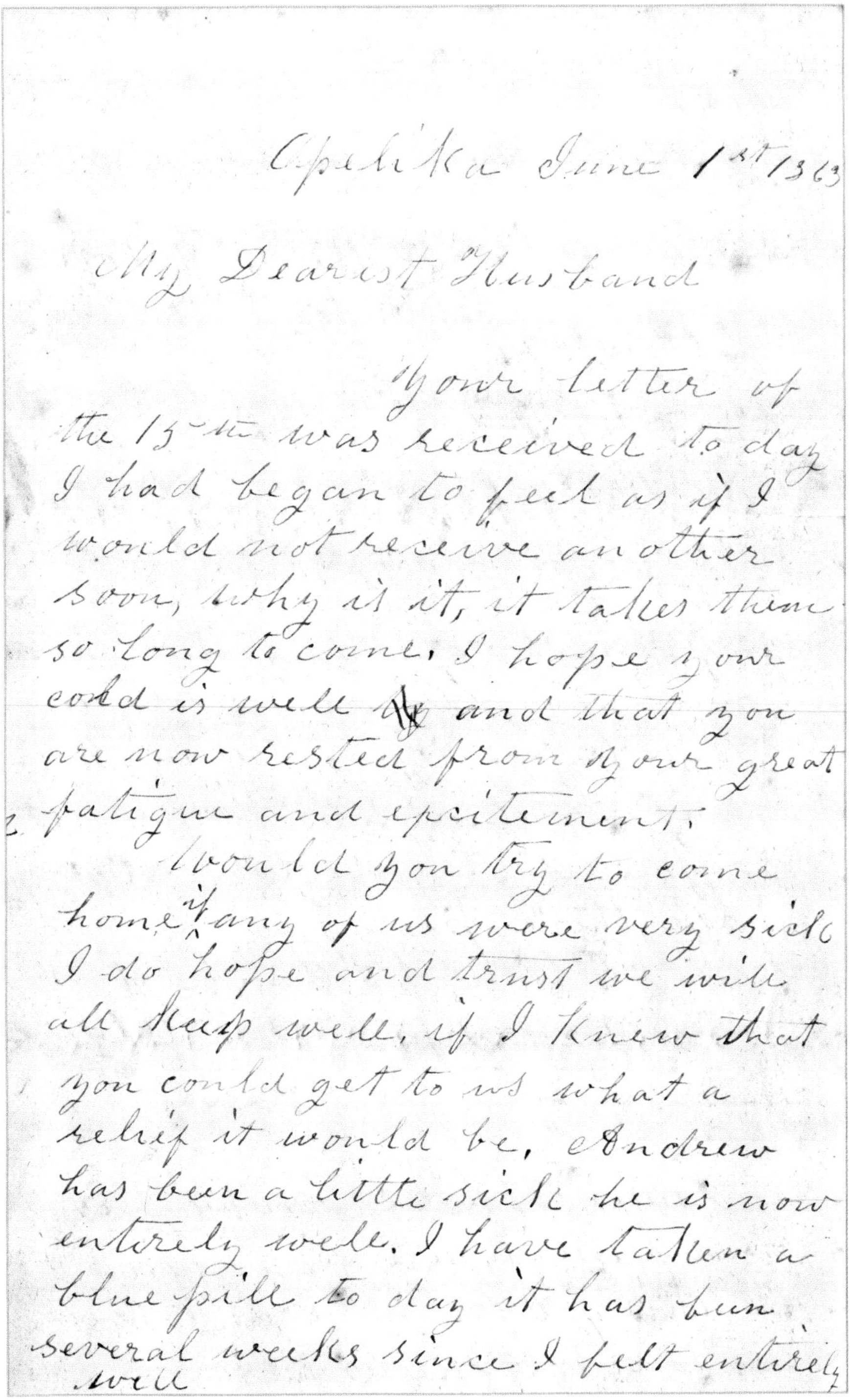

Apelika June 1st 1863

My Dearest Husband

Your letter of
the 15th was received to day
I had began to feel as if I
would not receive an other
soon, why is it, it takes them
so long to come, I hope your
cold is well and that you
are now rested from your great
fatigue and excitement.
Would you try to come
home if any of us were very sick
I do hope and trust we will
all keep well, if I knew that
you could get to us what a
relief it would be, Andrew
has been a little sick he is now
entirely well. I have taken a
blue pill to day it has been
several weeks since I felt entirely
well

PLATE 28-1

fabled Confederate commerce raider *Alabama*—something of an irony since Paul Jones, not Raphael, had been named for a naval hero. By the outbreak of the war, P.J., as he sometimes referred to himself, had already served for fourteen years as a captain in the Georgia state militia and had written a respected 1855 manual on infantry tactics. From 1860 to 1861 he worked as Georgia's quartermaster general, but after war broke out, the governor named him a colonel in charge of the state's newly organized 2nd Infantry Regiment. After serving in John Bankhead Magruder's division at the Battle of Seven Pines, Semmes was reassigned to Lafayette McLaws's division of James Longstreet's 1st Corps. As the Civil War historian Stephen W. Sears has pointed out, not one of McLaws's brigadiers—Semmes, Joseph Kershaw, William Barksdale, and William Wofford—"was a professional soldier, but each . . . made himself into a first-rate officer and combat leader."

In early May 1863, now a brigadier general, Semmes fought heroically once again in the astonishing Confederate victory at Chancellorsville. But in its aftermath, perhaps stunned by news of Stonewall Jackson's death a few days later, he took to contemplating his own mortality. "If my life can be spared," he poignantly wrote to his wife, Emily, from Culpeper, Virginia, on June 11, "we will have to return & live humbly & economically—If not spared, Oh! My Lord! What will become of my Dear, My Dear Family." A few days earlier, Emily had sent him a snippet of poetry along with "some flowers such as I wore on my bridal hat," perhaps as a birthday gift (Semmes was born on June 4). She assured her worried husband, "I spend nothing but what we are obliged to[;] we have now supplies to last until Christmas. Our garden is very good[;] we have had beans and squashes and Beets, we will very soon have an abundance of every thing and enough for you if you could get them." More important, she reported, even though their daughters had become so "proud" she prayed for them "that they may see their sin," their sons "go to Sunday school, and spend their Sunday better. . . . They study more at school and are improving." Providence, she prayed, would continue to watch over P.J. "Oh my darling," she wrote, "how grateful we ought to feel to the good Lord for your preservation through those terrible battles. It is in him I trust[;] he can do all things."

General Semmes, who "wept like a child" when he received his wife's letter and enclosure, accompanied his emotional reply with a frank admission that he feared his commanders no longer trusted him ("I believe that McLaws has attempted to poison Lee & Longstreet towards me," he confided). In the midst of these laments, he offered his wife some practical, if morbid, advice: his future was now so uncertain that Emily would be wise to renew his life insurance coverage.

But the war also had given Semmes a greater respect for religion; in fact, like many soldiers exposed to combat, and death, he had experienced a conversion. "I do humbly trust & pray to be carried safely through battle[.] I commit myself to God," he assured Emily. "I feel that though I have thus far escaped, the next Battlefield may be the last to me—the last of me. . . . The enemy confronts us with three times our force, & we are both to come in Conflict any day—indeed, a Battle I feel satisfied will not be postponed unless Hooker & his Army run away."

Semmes proved providential on several counts. Hooker did in fact disappear—but not by running away. Rather, in the wake of the general's humiliating defeat at Chancellorsville, Lincoln replaced him at the command of the Army of the Potomac with George G. Meade, and it was Robert E. Lee who made the next move, outnumbered though he was. Just weeks after his stunning victory in Virginia, Lee led his Army of Northern Virginia, Semmes included, into Pennsylvania, convinced that a second daring invasion of the North would extinguish Union morale and destroy its will to fight. What Semmes called the inevitable "next" battle would "be postponed" for only a few more weeks, and when fighting resumed, it would escalate to a level unknown before or since on this continent. The next encounter between Union and Confederate forces took place in the tiny town of Gettysburg.

On the hellish second day of fighting there, July 2, 1863, one Union officer observed shells exploding amid a terrified herd of cattle, "tearing" one cow "to pieces," with "others . . . torn and wounded. All were stampeded and were bellowing and rushing in their terror, first to one side and then to the other, to escape the shells that were bursting over them and among them." The officer admitted to terror of his own amid the unholy din, confessing: "Luckily the poor beasts were as much frightened as I was." At the peak of the enemy charge, the Union general Gouverneur Warren heard Longstreet's men "shouting in the most confident tones" as they attacked federal forces, while another remembered the whir of the bullets flying in "among the men" like swarms of deadly insects. Paul Jones Semmes was part of the attack these Union defenders so vividly described. At 4:00 p.m. on July 2, Longstreet ordered a charge toward the left flank of the Union line. In support of Kershaw's brigade, Semmes led his command through Rose's Woods and the wheat field and beyond it into the valley of Plum Run below Little Round Top.

There, Paul Jones Semmes's good luck came to an end. General Kershaw remembered that the federals "opened on these doomed regiments a raking fire of grape and canister, at short distance, which proved most disastrous." As Kershaw recalled, "General Semmes promptly responded to my call, and put his brigade in motion toward the right, preparatory to moving to the front. While his troops were moving he fell, mortally wounded." After the gruesome fighting finally subsided that evening, an ambulance conveyed the injured Confederate brigadier all the way to Martinsburg, West Virginia, ahead of the overall Confederate retreat that began when Pickett's Charge failed on the third, and final, day of battle. His leg no doubt throbbing, Semmes must have found the sixty-mile excursion unbearably excruciating. Nonetheless, from Martinsburg a week later he gamely wrote again to his beloved Emily, hopeful that the worst was behind him and he would soon be home to recover further. This is what he said—in handwriting so uneven and nearly indecipherable it is reasonable to assume he was already consumed by fever:

My Dearest Wife:
I telegraphed you today: "Severely wounded. Main danger over. Stay at home. Will write." I was wounded on the 2 inst. at Gettysburg Penn—I arrived there in an ambulance yesterday, a distance of 60 miles—Abner, Tom Cleveland & Cody are with me—Will write soon again[.] The wound has done remarkably well though I traveled 4 days in an ambulance—which was very uncomfortable not having it after being

placed in it at the Hospital until I got here. I now am flat on my Back in a Comfortable room in a [residence of?] family, who treat me with every Kindness.

I was wounded in the leg but stopped the flow of blood in the field by a Tournequet [*sic*] applied by myself & drawn by one of my men & lost but little blood—Col Harm—Ltt Chamber Hd—Killd—Jack Jones Kill—& a long list—My Brigade suffered severely & behaved well— Much love to all Yr affect Hd

Paul J Semmes

Ellis escaped—God mercifully spared my life. We all have Cause to be thankful to *Him*.

In the end, God did not spare Paul Jones Semmes after all. Infection evidently overtook him, and his life ebbed away. His final words came not in another letter to his wife but purportedly in a whispered statement of patriotic defiance to a war correspondent: "I consider it a privilege to die for my country." He breathed his last in a Martinsburg hospital on July 10. In a terse letter to Jefferson Davis on July 7, General Lee reported his successful retreat, unmolested, back into Virginia and added almost as a postscript: "In addition to the general officers killed or wounded, of whom I sent you a list in my former letter, I have to mention General Semmes" and others.

But the martyred brigadier need not have worried that Lee no longer appreciated him. Paul Jones Semmes may have died believing he had lost Lee's confidence and respect, but after his death the Confederate commander wrote that Semmes and the other important officers who fell at Gettysburg had "died as they had lived, discharging the highest duty of patriots with devotion that never faltered and courage that shrank from no danger. . . . I cannot speak of these brave men as their merits and exploits deserve."

Paul Jones Semmes was one of 3,903 Confederates killed at the Battle of Gettysburg. The Union lost nearly as many: 3,515. Some 43,000 more were either wounded, missing, or captured on both sides. With total casualties exceeding an almost unimaginable 50,000, Gettysburg proved

Gen. Paul J. Semmes (1815–1863), engraving, n.d.

the most costly battle yet in American history. "I am gradually losing my best men," Lee mournfully wrote to President Davis. He would never again venture an offensive into the North. A South Carolina colonel reflected the shift in strategy when he wrote home the day after Semmes's death to explain: "Genl. Lee can whip with this army double as many Yankees in Virginia as he can in Penn. Better prolong the war by defending then [*sic*] ruin ourselves by failures at invasion."

Northerners immediately heralded Meade's victory and Lee's retreat as "the turning point in the war." Making that bold prediction, the *New*

PLATE 28–2

York Times, which often accompanied news reports of Union victories with predictions that they heralded imminent Confederate surrender, headlined its exuberant report "Splendid Triumph of the Army of the Potomac" and ventured to suggest that "it might seem that the rebellion would come to a speedy end, and without further effort on the part of the North." In fact, the war was only halfway over.

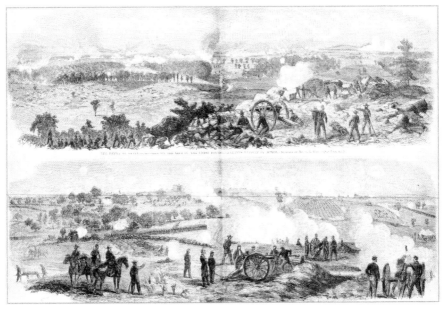

The Battle of Gettysburg—Union Position Near the Centre—
Gettysburg in the Distance—Cemetery on the Hill,
wood engravings, 1863

PLATE 28–3

29

Emancipated by War

Arrival at Chickasaw Bayou of
Jefferson Davis' Negroes from His Plantation on
the Mississippi Below Vicksburg, Mississippi,
Drawing by Frederick B. Schell, ca. 1863

I N RESPONSE TO SOME MODERN OBSERVERS WHO PERSISTENTLY MAKE the unsustainable argument that the Emancipation Proclamation freed no actual slaves, here is powerful evidence to the contrary in the form of an on-the-spot sketch by one Frederick B. Schell (d. ca. 1905). The Philadelphia-born illustrator covered the western theater of the war as a "special artist" for *Frank Leslie's Illustrated Newspaper*, sending personally observed sketches of incidents large and small back to New York to be adapted into woodcuts for the popular weekly. This particular neglected piece of visual testimony inspired no major headlines at the time but is historically important nonetheless, for it shows slaves actually achieving freedom seven months after Lincoln's proclamation took effect half a continent from Washington—in this case, notably, slaves owned by Lincoln's Confederate counterpart, Jefferson Davis.

The deceptively simple 9⅝-by-13½-inch graphite drawing on wove paper—inscribed by the artist in the upper left-hand corner "Arrival at Chickasaw Bayou of Jeff. Davis [*sic*] Negroes, from his plantation on the Mississippi below Vicksburg"—is one of a trove of 107 surviving

Leslie's-commissioned original sketches from the John T. Kavanaugh Collection acquired by the Historical Society in 1945. The archive boasts priceless eyewitness visual accounts of the Union naval attack on the Carolina coast, eastern land battles at Acquia Creek, Antietam, New Berne, and elsewhere, and western engagements along the Mississippi, as well as sketches of Lookout Mountain, Murfreesboro, Atlanta, and Vicksburg. This example may be the most compelling among them, particularly because it demonstrates the actual impact of the Emancipation Proclamation half a continent from Washington and Richmond—and in Jefferson Davis's own household.

Like the Declaration of Independence, Lincoln's proclamation required the force of arms to fulfill its liberating promise. It freed no slaves

PLATE 29–1

by words alone, but its words authorized action. Thus, whenever Union troops conquered Confederate territory after January 1, 1863, they were encouraged to alert enslaved people that they were legally free by the president's order—although many so knew already. Quite often, in fact, slaves took the initiative and used the mere approach of Union forces—the irresistible confluence of government authorization and the opportunity presented by Union military presence—to free themselves.

One such incident involved the human property still owned in the summer of 1863 by no less a symbol of the slaveholding aristocracy than Jefferson Davis, president of the Confederate States of America. Davis was not only a slave owner himself but an unrepentant advocate of slavery as a humane condition designed to protect so-called inferior races (and of course put them to good use for superior ones). "My own convictions, as to negro slavery, are strong," he proudly told a visitor during the secession crisis. "It has its evils and abuses," he acknowledged, but "we recognize the negro as God and God's Book and God's Laws, in nature, tell us to recognize him—our inferior, fitted expressly for servitude." Indeed, as the biographer William C. Davis (no relation) has pointed out, Jefferson Davis convinced himself that freedom would only hurt African Americans, for "the innate stamp of inferiority is beyond the reach of change. . . . You cannot transform the negro into anything one-tenth as useful or as good as what slavery enables him to be."

Davis remained prepared to defend slavery to the last. When he first learned that the Lincoln administration was considering African American recruitment, the Confederate president issued this chilling decree: "That all negro slaves captured in arms be at once delivered over to the executive authorities of the respective States to which they belong to be dealt with according to the laws of said States." In other words, such captives could be sent back into slavery. Moreover, white officers leading black men with weapons in their hands were to be treated as men fomenting a servile insurrection—a crime punishable by death. Long after the war, Davis opened his memoirs with a lengthy defense of "African servitude" and its protected standing in America. He never repented. But events intervened much sooner.

As early as 1862, Davis began receiving disquieting news concerning the slaves he had left behind to work his Mississippi plantation, Brier-field, after he assumed leadership of the Confederacy first in Montgomery, then in Richmond. With Grant's forces menacing nearby Vicksburg, some of his slaves had been emboldened to rob the main house and flee. The overseer told Davis he had been unable to stop them. While Vicksburg itself was enduring a forty-seven-day siege that would end with the city's capitulation on July 4, 1863, Union soldiers found an opportunity to visit the Davis plantation. (Around the same time, Confederate forces marching through Pennsylvania toward Gettysburg torched the abolitionist Thaddeus Stevens's ironworks in Caledonia, confiscating all his transportable property; such homes were considered trophies of war.) Although federal forces spared the Davis mansion, 137 family slaves escaped, with more soon to follow. The remaining enslaved people were then liberated by federal troops, who took out their fury by plundering the contents of the Davis property. Chained—at least figuratively—to his desk in Richmond, Davis resisted the temptation to rush home to inspect the losses for himself. But the mass escape of his human "property" never convinced the unyielding white supremacist that African Americans yearned for, much less deserved, freedom. Instead, he regarded their flight as an act of ingratitude.

Worse, as noted previously, Davis's response to the Union's decision to recruit "colored troops" was to declare their service a capital crime. If captured, he warned, rebellious slaves would not be treated as ordinary prisoners of war; instead, they would be returned to their owners for suitable punishment or handed over to local courts as criminals for trial and hanging. Their white officers would be regarded as insurrectionists who deserved death sentences, too. But Davis's threats did little to arrest the tide of liberation—even at his own doorstep. The wife of a North Carolina congressman accurately observed: "I don't think we will have many slaves after Jeff and Abe get done fighting to free them."

On August 8, 1863, *Leslie's* published its woodcut engraving of Schell's sketch of the Davis slaves entering the safe haven of Union headquarters, along with a brief, front-page account of what had occurred, under the headline "The Slaves of Jefferson Davis Coming on to the Camp at Vicksburg." The former Confederate secretary of state Robert Toombs, a

Georgian (and no friend of Davis's) who had quit the administration to join the Confederate army and suffered injury at Antietam, had recently boasted that slavery would not only endure in the South, war notwithstanding, but ultimately spread as far north as Massachusetts. Though the space the editors devoted to the incident was small, *Leslie's* clearly viewed the flight of the commander in chief's own slaves as a stunning rejoinder to this racist braggadocio.

> Few incidents have been more curious and instructive than that witnessed some time before the fall of Vicksburg, when the slaves of Jefferson Davis from his plantation on the Mississippi came into camp. It seemed in itself the doom of slavery, and formed such a contrast to the vaunt of Toombs, that he would call the roll of his slaves on Bunker Hill, that none can help being struck by it. The President of the Confederate States may call the roll of his slaves at Richmond, at Natchez, or at Niagara, but the answer will not come.

Leslie's woodcut adaptation, rushed into print while the event it portrayed was still newsworthy, inevitably coarsened Schell's hastily drawn but respectfully detailed composition, which showed the Davis slaves walking proudly into the Union camp. Schell strove for individualized portraiture and a realistic environment. But in the published woodcut, retitled *Arrival at Chickasaw Bayou of the Negro Slaves of Jefferson Davis, from His Plantation on the Mississippi,* smoke can be seen belching from the stacks of what in Schell's original was a more believably idle steamboat. Shorn trees remarkably take on new foliage. And the slaves themselves assume more stereotypical physical features, postures, and attire. But even the insensitive visual editing could not rob the scene of its breathtaking meaning: that here was proof of freedom cast ever wider, even to the very doorstep of the slave republic's own chief executive.

True to his retrograde racial beliefs to the end, Davis clung to his faith in slavery. And when the Confederate president ran perilously short of funds in the early weeks of his final year in office, 1865, he responded in character: Davis disposed of "property" to raise much-needed cash, selling three horses for $7,330—and two slaves for $1,612. Only when Union troops closed in on Richmond a few weeks later did the beleaguered president finally decide to set aside a lifetime of racist conviction and propose enlisting black troops to fight for Confederate survival in return for their subsequent freedom. But by then such gestures held no meaning. Davis's own slaves at Brierfield had signaled two years earlier that their liberty was already fairly won—and permanent.

The Emancipation Proclamation actually "freed" as many as 500,000 slaves before war's end. That is, enslaved African Americans like those forced to labor at Jefferson Davis's plantation rushed into army camps at the first sign of Union troops. The proclamation's effectiveness as a freedom document has been vastly underestimated. But then, so has the determination and courage of the slaves who based their risky escapes on its promise of legal freedom.

Arrival at Chickasaw Bayou of the Negro Slaves of Jefferson Davis, from his Plantation on the Mississippi, wood engraving, 1863

PLATE 29–2

30

---⟞⟨⟩⟞---

Wallpaper News for Cave Dwellers

The Daily Citizen, Newsprint on Wallpaper, 1863

E VEN THE PERENNIALLY OPTIMISTIC *CONFEDERATE STATES ALMANAC* admitted midway through the Civil War that a Southern newspaper might be "short enough for a pocket handkerchief one day, and big enough for a paper tablecloth another."

The problem was paper itself—that is, the chronic lack of it. The South could claim only a fraction of the nation's paper mills before the war began, and after federal troops occupied Nashville in 1862, one of the region's last prime sources of this essential raw material fell under Union control. The paper supply to the Confederacy's voracious publishers quickly dwindled to a trickle. At best, available stock became inferior, expensive, and scarce—made from rags or straw, incapable of holding ink; at worst, it disappeared altogether. As one Savannah editor admitted: "We are reduced to printing on paper, which, half the time, nobody can read." Most journals had no choice but to curtail their frequency and size, publishing hitherto routine "extra" bulletins on small slips only a column wide. Others closed down in the wake of unrelieved shortages. In 1862, an imperturbable Baton Rouge editor, forced to suspend publication for want of supplies, used the final edition of his newspaper to good-naturedly advertise himself for other employment. "The editor of this paper being now out of employment, owing to a temporary suspension of the same," read the notice, "is anxious and willing to do something for a livelihood . . . [and] has no objection to serving as a

THE DAILY CITIZEN.

J. M. SWORDS.......Proprietor

VICKSBURG, MISS.

THURSDAY, JULY 2, 1863.

Mrs. Cisco was instantly killed on Monday, on Jackson road. Mrs. Cisco's husband is now in Virginia, a member of Moody's artillery, and the death of such a loving, affectionate and dutiful wife will be a loss to him irreparable.

We are indebted to [illegible] Gillespie for a steak of Confederate beef *alias* meat. We have tried it, and can assure our friends that if it is rendered necessary, they need have no scruples at eating the meat. It is sweet, savory and tender, and so long as we have a mule left we are satisfied our soldiers will be content to subsist on it.

Jesse Askew, one of our most esteemed merchant-citizens, was wounded at the works in the rear of our city a few days since, and breathed his last on Monday. Mr. Askew was a young man of strict integrity, great industry and an honor to his family and friends. He was a member of Cowan's artillery, and by the strict discharge of his duties and his obliging disposition, won the confidence and esteem of his entire command. May the blow his family have sustained be mitigated by Him who doeth all things well.

Grant's forces did a little firing on Tuesday afternoon, but the balance of that day was comparatively quiet. Yesterday morning they were very still, and continued so until early in the afternoon, when they sprung a mine on the left of our centre, and opened fire along the line for some distance. We have not been able to ascertain anything definitely as to our loss, but as our officers were on the look out for this move of the enemy, the expectations of the Yankees were not realized by a great deal.

Among many good deeds we hear spoken of with pride by our citizens, we cannot refrain from mentioning the case of Mr. F. Kiser. This gentleman, having more corn than he thought was necessary to last him during the siege of this place, portioned off what would do him for the brief interval [illegible] before the arrival of succor [illegible], and since that time has relieved the wants of many families *free of charge!* May he live long and prosper, and his name be handed down to posterity when the siege of Vicksburg is written, as one in whose breast the "milk of human kindness" had not dried up.

Porter is enjoying a season of rest, and his men are doubtless obliged to him for his kind consideration for their welfare. On Tuesday he fired a few shells from his parrots, and kept his men tolerably busy sharpshooting across the river, with no other result than might be expected. The mortars have not been used for nearly forty-eight hours. Poor fool, he might as well give up the vain aspiration he entertains of capturing our city or exterminating our people, and return to his master to receive the reward such a gasconading dolt will meet at the hands of the unappreciating Government at Washington.

Death of Lieut.-Col. Griffin.—General Smith's Louisiana division seems singularly unfortunate. He has lost many gallant men whose valor and worth the siege has fully developed, and whose death is a great public calamity. Lieut.-Col. Griffin, commanding the 31st Louisiana regiment, was killed on Saturday. He was a popular and efficient officer. Gifted by nature with undaunted courage, indomitable resolution and energy, he was also possessed of quick determination, keen glance and coolness in danger, which are the most essential qualities of an officer, while by his mingled firmness and clemency of his conduct, he won the confidence and good will of his men. May the soft south winds moan their sweet requiems o'er his manes, and the twilight dews fall gently like an angel's tear-drop and moisten his turfy bed.

If aught would appeal to the heart of stone of the extortioner with success, the present necessities of our citizens would do so. It is needless to attempt to disguise from the enemy or our own people that our wants are great, but still we can conscientiously assert our belief that there is plenty within our lines, by an exercise of prudence, to last until long after succor reaches us. We are satisfied there are numerous persons within our city who have breadstuffs secreted, and are doling it out, at the most extortionate figures, to those who had not the foresight or means at their command to provide for the exigency now upon us. A rumor has reached us that parties in our city have been, and are now, selling flour at five dollars per pound! molasses at ten dollars per gallon! and corn at ten dollars per bushel! We have not as yet proved the fact upon the parties accused, but this allusion to the subject may induce some of our citizens to ascertain whether such prices have been paid, and to whom; and if so, let a brand not only be placed upon their brow, but let it be seared into their very brain, that humanity may [illegible] and shun them as they would the [illegible] of hell [illegible]

Good News.—In devoting a large portion of our space this morning to Federal intelligence, copied from the Memphis Bulletin of the 25th it should be remembered that the news, in the original truth, is whitewashed by the Federal Provost Marshal, who desires to hood wink the poor Northern white slaves. The former editors of the Bulletin being rather pro-southern men, were arrested for speaking the truth when truth was unwelcome to Yankeedom, and placed in the chain-gang working at Warrenton, where they now are. This paper at present is in duress, and edited by a pock-nosed, slab-sided, toad-eating Yankee, who is a lineal descendant of Judas Iscariot and a brother germain of the greatest Parliamental sycophantic, howling scoundrel unhung—Parson Brownlow. Yet with such a character, the paper cannot cloak the fact that Gen. Rob't. E. Lee has given Hooker, Milroy & Co. one of the best and soundest whippings on record, and that the "glorious Union" is now exceedingly weak in the knees.

Gen Rob't E. Lee Again.

Again we have reliable news from the gallant corps of Gen. Lee in Virginia. Elated with success, encouraged by a series of brilliant victories, marching toward crossing the Rappahannock, defeating Hooker's right wing and thence through the Shenandoah Valley, driving Milroy from Winchester and capturing 6000 of his men and a large amount of valuable stores of all descriptions, re-entering Maryland, holding Hagerstown, threatening Washington City, and within a few miles of Baltimore—onward and upward their war cry—our brave men under Lee are striking terror to the heart of all Yankeedom. Like the Scottish chieftain's braves, Lee's men are springing up from moor and brake, crag and dale, with flashing steel and sturdy arm, ready to do or die in the great cause of national independence, right and honor. To-day the mongrel administration of Lincoln, like Japhet, are in search of a father—for their old Abe has departed for parts unknown. Terror reigns in their halls. Lee is to the left of them, the right of them, in front of them, and all around them; and daily do we expect to hear of his being down on them. Never were the French in Algeria more put out by the mobile raids of Ab Del Kader than are the Federals of Maryland, Washington City, Pennsylvania and Ohio by the mercurial movements of Lee's cavalry. Like Paddy's flea are they to the Federals [illegible] they have got them and now they haven't. The omnipresence of our troops and that throwing dust in the eyes, or rather on the heels of the panic-stricken Federals in Maryland and Pennsylvania, clearly prove that Lee just now is the right man in the right place.

We lay before our readers in this issue an account of Lee's brilliant and successful onslaught upon the abolition hordes, which show plain from their own record, how our gallant boys of the cavalry have fleshed their swords to the hilt with their vaunting foes, and how each musket of our infantry has told its fatal leaden tale.

To-day Maryland is ours, to-morrow Pennsylvania will be, and the next day Ohio—now midway, like Mahommed's coffin—will fall.

Success and glory to our arms! God and right are with us.

We have heretofore refrained from alluding to a matter which has been a source of extreme annoyance and loss to our citizens. We refer to the lax discipline of some of our company officers in allowing their men to prowl around, day and night, and purloin fruit, vegetables, chickens, etc., from our denizens, and, in the majority of cases, from those whose chief subsistence is derived therefrom. This charge is not confined solely to those at the works, but is equally, if not mainly, attributable to the wagoners and others in charge of animals. Several cases have come to our knowledge wherein the offenders have, in open daylight, entered premises, seized cattle and other things, and defied the owners to their teeth. We are pained to learn that an esteemed citizen of our Vicksburg, Wm. Porterfield, was under the necessity, in protecting his property, to wound one or two soldiers and deprive another of his life. We fully appreciate the fatigue, hardships and privation to which our men are subjected; but upon inquiry it may be ascertained that our city is second to none in contributing to the welfare of those gallant spirits who risk their life and limb for the achievement of an end which will make us one of the most honored people of the earth, and such conduct of which we complain is but base ingratitude. A soldier has his honor at much a stake as when a civilian; then let him preserve his good name and reputation with the same jealous care as before he entered his country's ranks. But so long as this end is lost sight of, so long may we expect to chronicle scenes of bloodshed among those of our own people. We make this public exposure, mortifying as it is to us, with the hope that a salutary improvement in matters will be made by our military authorities.

On Dit.—That the great Ulysses—the Yankee Generalissimo, surnamed Grant—has expressed his intention of dining in Vicksburg on Saturday next, and celebrating the 4th of July by a grand dinner and so forth. When asked if he would invite Gen. Jo. Johnston to join he said, "No! for fear there will be a row at the table." Ulysses must get into the city before he dines in it. The way to cook a rabbit is "first catch the rabbit," &c.

Yankee News From All Points.

Philadelphia, June 21, 2 33 a. m.—The following is all the news of interest in the Washington Star:

Major Brazell, of the United States volunteers, received intelligence from Fayette county, Penn., this morning that the rebels in heavy force were advancing on Pittsburg via the National road leading from Cumberland across the Allegheny Mountains. Their pickets had reached Grantsville, Md., thirty-eight miles from Uniontown, Fayette county, Penn., on Wednesday evening last.

It is reported in Washington to-day that two members of Hooker's staff were gobbled up by guerrillas last night in the vicinity of Fairfax.

Harrisburg, June 20.—Operations were commenced on our side to-day by a portion of a New York cavalry regiment, capturing twenty rebel prisoners at McConnellsburg, in Fulton county.

Col. Lawrence, with a portion of the 127th Pennsylvania regiment, (mounted) captured a squad of rebels who were marauding on this side of the river.

We hold Chambersburg and the citizens are arming and fortifying the city. Gen. Couch had ordered that the place be held.

The Fortifications opposite this city are finished, and are considered impregnable.

The rebels are known to be 8000 strong at Hagerstown and Williamsport.

The rebels hold the north bank of the Potomac river, from Cumberland to Harper's Ferry. Gen. Kelly drove the rebels out of Cumberland, and when they left they threatened to return and furnish themselves with horses and forage. The rebels have done an immense amount of damage.

It is thought Gen. Rhodes is opposite Williamsport with 20,000 men. The rebel Gen. Imboden is reported as advancing, but this is considered doubtful.

Frederick, Md., June 20.—The enemy's cavalry left Boonsboro last evening, after capturing a number of horses, and returned to Hagerstown yesterday.

Six thousand infantry are reported to have crossed at Williamsport. It is not believed that they will visit Frederick.

The enemy has nearly 6000 infantry this side of the Potomac, under General Rhodes. Two regiments of infantry and a squad of cavalry are at Sharpsburg, and the remainder are encamped between Williamsport and Hagerstown. No artillery has been sent over, nor have any troops crossed since yesterday morning.

Gen Ewell has left Williamsport and gone to the main body of his command, stationed at Charlestown. Lee's army is not known to be within supporting distance of Ewell, and it is very probable that the force now in Maryland will not penetrate further north. The cavalry force numbers about twelve hundred, under Jenkins.

The party which first advanced upon Greencastle and Chambersburg numbered only six hundred and fifty.

Washington, June 22.—The Richmond Dispatch of the 21st contains the following: "Dispatches received yesterday from Savannah announce the capture by the enemy of the Confederate ironclad steamer Fingal, commanded by Captain Webb, of Atlanta. An other steamer outside the harbor was attacked and captured after an action of thirty minutes, by two Federal ironclads."

Richmond papers of the 20th say the city of Darien, Georgia was burned by the Federals on the 11th inst., and is now one plain of ashes and blackened chimneys. Seven Federal ironclads were at Brunswick, Georgia, and large forces had landed from transports. Vallandigham has run the blockade from Wilmington. He is going to Nassau and thence to Canada.

Washington, June 21.—A Harrisburg, Pa., dispatch to the Herald states that Jenkins passed through Greencastle last evening with 700 mounted infantry, in the direction of Waynesboro. The rebels are reported to have sixteen pieces of artillery with their large force. They occupy the south bank of the Potomac between Cumberland and Harper's Ferry. Rhodes has 24,000 men at Williamsport.

The opinion in official circles at Harrisburg is, that the rebels have serious designs on Baltimore. Their movements indicate this, and fears are entertained for the safety of that city. Three hundred rebel cavalry fired Mercersburg in several places.

A Chambersburg dispatch says the rebels are scouring the country for horses, and have got about 2000 head of cattle and 2000 horses. They are reported near Waynesboro and Gettysburg. Jenkins left Greencastle to night with eight days rations, on a foraging expedition.

Harrisburg, June 21.—A dispatch received here late this evening states that a rebel cavalry force is within eight miles of Gettysburg and had crossed South Mountain, evidently advancing to the Northern Central Railroad. An ample force is prepared to resist the attack.

New York, June 21.—A Harrisburg dispatch to night, contains the following: The rebels are reported 40 000 strong at Hagerstown, and fortifying. Milroy's headquarters are still at Bloody Run. Troops here are expecting marching orders immediately. It is feared Ewell is at Williamsport, but opinion here is that he is not at that point unless Lee is about to cross below. Heavy rains may have raised the Potomac and hurried him. Gov. Curtin to night received a dispatch from Chambersburg, stating that Jenkins had arrived at Waynesboro and had thrown out pickets five miles this side, but withdrew them this morning. There is no information at Waynesboro of rebel infantry at Hagerstown. Jenkins has been plundering horses in the mountains. General Couch received a dispatch to-night confirming the report of rebel cavalry at Gettysburg.

Baltimore, June 21, 8 p. m.—Latest advices from Point No 4 say that heavy firing has been heard there at intervals throughout the day.

Baltimore, June 21.—The rebels made their appearance at Frederick yesterday evening, and about 7 o'clock a body of cavalry reached Monocacy bridge, four miles this side of Frederick. The rebels paroled all the sick in the hospital and every Government employe. They searched the stables for horses, seizing all marked U. S. A very large force of rebel infantry, cavalry and artillery crossed at Antietam during yesterday. Refugees say they number from 10,000 to 50,000, but pickets report them at 25,000. Earthworks are being erected around the west and north sides of Baltimore, thus completing the chain of fortifications. Barricades are being erected within the city, extending from the high ground on the east to the southwestern ex[illegible] tremity of the city. These will be defended by Union League men, who are being armed by Gen. Schenck. The Union men are confident that the rebels will not be so rash as to attempt a raid in that direction. The disloyal among us are evidently uneasy, and begin to realize that any hostile movement of the rebel army against Baltimore might result disastrously among themselves.

A Herald's special from Monocacy Station, Md., the 21st, says: About 4 o'clock p. m., Major Cole, of the 1st Maryland cavalry, made a gallant dash into Frederick, with forty men driving out the enemy, killing two and capturing one. No loss on our side. Our cavalry passed through the city, and immediately after about 1500 rebel cavalry re-occupied the town.

Rebel cavalry entered Frederick yesterday, p. m., about 6 o'clock, and dashed furiously through the city, capturing nine of our men on duty at the signal station, and paroled the invalid soldiers, numbering about sixty, in the hospital. A number of horses were seized. Secession flags were displayed at the Central Hotel, and some citizens collected there to welcome the rebels. A majority of the population evinced no pleasure at the visit. The ladies were exceedingly expressive in their demonstrations of disgust, and showered words of sympathy upon our prisoners as they passed through the town. The party which entered the city did not number over twenty, and many of these seemed to be intoxicated, as they reeled in their saddles. Pickets were stationed on the outside of town. No one was allowed to leave until about midnight, when the cavalry all left, going toward Middletown. This morning they entered the city again, and established pickets in the outskirts. The telegraph poles were cut down and the wires destroyed. There was supposed to be about thirty rebels in the city this p. m., The enemy has no force between Frederick and Boonsboro except a small cavalry camp at Middletown. No attempt had been made to destroy the bridge over the Monocacy river, although the enemy came down last night within a few rods of the junction.

The rebels are reported to be fortifying South Mountain. They have in the vicinity of Williamsport about 6000 infantry, 1000 cavalry, and a few pieces of artillery. A squadron of cavalry could undoubtedly capture the entire force this side of South Mountain.

Mid the din and clash of arms, the screech of shells and whistle of bullets, which are a continual feature in the status of our beleaguered city, incidents of happiness often arise to vary in a cheery way the phases of so stern a scene. On the evening of the 20th ult, with gaiety, myrth and good feeling, at a prominent Hospital of this city, through the ministerial offices of a chaplain of a gallant regiment, Charles Royall, Prince Imperial of Ethiopia, of the Barberigo family, espoused the lovely and accomplished Rosa Glass, Arch Duchess of Senegambia, one of the most celebrated Princes of the Laundressina Regime. The affair was conducted with great magnificence, though as is usual in troublesome times the sabler element was predominant.

> The foe may hurl their deathly bolts,
> And think we are affrightened,
> Well may we scorn them, silly dolts,
> Our Blacks are now united.

Victimized.—We learned of an instance wherein a "knight of the quill" and a "disciple of the black art," with malice in their hearts and vengeance in their eyes, ruthlessly put a period to the existence of a venerable feline that has for time, not within the recollection of the "oldest inhabitant," faithfully discharged the duties to be expected of him to the terror of sundry vermin in his neighborhood. Poor, defunct Thomas was then prepared, not for the grave, but the pot, and several friends invited to partake of a nice rabbit. As a matter of course, no one would wound the feelings of another, especially in these times, by refusing a cordial invitation to dinner, and the guests assisted in consuming the poor animal with a relish that did honor to their epicurean taste. The "sold" assure us the meat was delicious, and that pussy must look out for her safety.

The Federal General McClernand until recently outside the rear of our city has been superceded. He and Grant could not run in the same harness. He was for splurging and Grant for gassing, both got the loggerheads. So poor Mc. had to leave, and Grant has all his own way.

The Yanks outside our city are considerably on the sick list. Fever, dysentery and disgust are their companions, and Grant is their master. The boys are deserting daily and are crossing the river in the region of Warrenton, cussing Grant and abolitionists generally. The boys are down upon the earth delving, the burrowing, the bad water, and the hot weather.

Gone Out.—The National Intelligencer of Washington has closed its long career in a suspension and a sale of its effects at auction.—It has been highly respectable and very mischievous in its day and generation. An old union prop falls with it. If we had the writing of its epitaph we should say, "Old Grimes is 'dead'

NOTE.

JULY 4th, 1863.

Two days bring about great changes. The banner of the Union floats over Vicksburg. Gen. Grant has "caught the rabbit;" he has dined in Vicksburg, and he did bring his dinner with him. The "Citizen" lives to see it. For the last time it appears on "Wall-paper." No more will it eulogize the luxury of mule-meat and fricassed kitten—urge Southern warriors to such diet never more. This is the last wall paper edition, and is excepting this note, from the types as we found them. It will be valuable hereafter as a curiosity.

deck-hand on a flat-boat, selling ice-cream, or acting as paymaster to the militia."

Although the supply crisis caused many established newspapers to shut down, a few new ones did open—at least for a time. Convinced in the teeth of the paper famine that the Confederacy required the equivalent of the North's *Harper's Weekly* and *Frank Leslie's* to sustain civilian morale through patriotic pictures, the intrepid Richmond publishers E. W. Ayres and W. H. Wade gamely launched a pictorial weekly, the *Southern Illustrated News,* in 1862. The first edition boasted the hopeful motto "Not a luxury, but a necessity." The periodical limped along for about two years, regularly advertising for ink and engravers, but soon began appearing irregularly as employable artists, the wood required for making engraved pictures, and paper for printing all became scarcer. Once, when the Confederate military took control of a nearby railroad station "and prevented the arrival of our useful supply of paper," the proprietors were forced to cancel an entire 1863 issue. The last known edition was published early the following year. The Southern publishing industry was by then so crippled it had barely found the resources to celebrate the inspiring bravery of Vicksburg, the citadel city on the Mississippi River that resisted Union conquest for nine months and two separate military campaigns.

Resourceful and desperate, newspapers there and in other cities took to issuing one-sided editions on any scrap they could find stored in idle warehouses—including brightly hued wallpaper. Even amid such humiliating deprivation, one crippled Southern journal that had once advocated strongly for secession would now offer "no apology for the . . . color and quality of the paper." Its variety, it proudly maintained, reflected "the hardships of war." None became more famous than the so-called wallpaper editions published in Vicksburg.

For two months beginning in May 1863, the Union fleet operating under a strategy devised by Ulysses S. Grant laid siege to the strategically located "Hill City." The shelling drove its starving citizens underground, where they literally took up residence in caves, a perilous situation glorified into myth by the intrepid Baltimore artist Adalbert Johann Volck in one of the Society's best-known Confederate war etchings. But as

PLATE 30–1 (opposite)

demonstrated in chapter 26, Volck's potentially morale-building tributes did not find their way into the Confederate marketplace while the war raged—especially to places like Vicksburg, once it came under attack by Union forces. In plate 30–2, Volck's horrific but uplifting vision shows a brave and somehow still beautifully dressed and coiffed Southern heroine kneeling in prayer in her ersatz parlor, a crucifix inspiringly nailed to one of the wooden posts precariously supporting her cave. Volck, a Catholic himself, perhaps meant to suggest that faith alone would save these courageous women. In the end, it did not.

One acute observer who managed to keep a more realistic record of the appalling conditions in the besieged city was the diarist Mary Ann Webster Loughborough. The young Arkansas-born mother had chosen, despite the danger, to follow her husband into active war zones when he left their hometown of Jackson with his regiment. In early May, however, she found herself trapped in imperiled Vicksburg. When authorities advised noncombatants to leave, she refused, instead retreating with her daughter to one of the bomb-resistant but rat-infested caves just outside town. Within a year she had revised and completed her journal under the title *My Cave Life in Vicksburg*—publishing it not in the South but, unsurprisingly, in New York. In one of the most compelling of her entries, Loughborough described the bombing that drove her underground with her child—and the constant fear, danger, and pathos of cave life:

> In the evening, we were terrified and much excited by the loud rush and scream of mortar shells; we ran to the small cave near the house and were in it during the night, by this time wearied and almost stupefied by the loss of sleep.
>
> The caves were plainly becoming a necessity, as some persons had been killed on the street by fragments of shells. The room that I had so lately slept in had been struck by a fragment of a shell during the first night, and a large hole made in the ceiling. I shall never forget my extreme fear during the night, and my utter hopelessness of ever seeing the morning light. Terror stricken, we remained crouched in the cave, while shell after shell followed each other in quick succession. I endeavored by constant prayer to prepare myself for the sudden death I was

almost certain awaited me. My heart stood still as we would hear the reports from the guns, and the rushing and fearful sound of the shell as it came toward us. As it neared, the noise became more deafening; the air was full of the rushing sound; pains darted through my temples; my ears were full of the confusing noise; and, as it exploded, the report flashed through my head like an electric shock, leaving me in a quiet state of terror the most painful that I can imagine—cowering in a corner, holding my child to my heart—the only feeling of my life being the choking throbs of my heart, that rendered me almost breathless. As singly they fell short, or beyond the cave, I was aroused by a feeling of thankfulness that was of short duration. Again and again the terrible fright came over us in that night.

I saw one fall in the road without the mouth of the cave, like a flame of fire, making the earth tremble, and, with a low, singing sound, the fragments sped on in their work of death.

Morning found us more dead than alive, with blanched faces and trembling lips. We were not reassured on hearing, from a man who took refuge in the cave, that a mortar shell in falling would not consider the thickness of earth above us a circumstance.

. . . Sitting in the cave one evening, I heard the most heartrending screams and moans. I was told that a mother had taken a child into a cave about a hundred yards from us; and having laid it on its little bed, as the poor woman believed, in safety, she took her seat near the entrance of the cave. A mortar shell came rushing through the air and fell with much force, entering the earth above the sleeping child—cutting through into the cave—oh! most horrible sight to the mother—crushing in the upper part of the little sleeping head, and taking away the young innocent life without a look or word of passing love to be treasured in the mother's heart.

I sat near the square of moonlight, silent and sorrowful, hearing the sobs and cries—hearing the moans of a mother for her dead child.

Cave dwellers were hardly the most reliable newspaper subscribers—they had other necessities foremost on their minds—but one local journal somehow continued for a while to cover the siege for the benefit of the

Cave Life in Vicksburg During the Siege,
etching by Adalbert Johann Volck, 1863

few news-starved readers brave enough to emerge from their shelters long enough to buy the daily. The publisher J. M. Swords ran out of his paper stock in June, but on the sixteenth, eighteenth, twentieth, twenty-seventh, and thirtieth he issued four-column-wide, single-sheet editions 16⅞ by 9⅛ inches in size on the back of wallpaper fragments. Some of the newspapers appeared on the reverse of rose-and-purple brocade designs, others on pink-and-red floral patterns set against cream-colored or pale-blue backgrounds. Swords used what he could get.

On July 2, the publisher prepared what turned out to be his last issue. It offered belated news of General Lee's "brilliant and successful" triumph against Joseph Hooker at the Battle of Chancellorsville the previous month. "Today Maryland is ours," the paper mistakenly reported, vowing, "To-morrow Pennsylvania will be, and the next day—Ohio—now midway like Mohammed's coffin—will fall." Little did Swords know that even as his July 2 edition hit the streets, Lee's forces were furiously engaged in their ill-fated contest at Gettysburg. Closer to home, the

PLATE 30–2

paper managed to acknowledge and admonish "the lax discipline of some of our company officers in allowing their men to prowl around, day and night, and purloin fruit, vegetables, chicken, etc. from our denizens, and, in the majority of cases, from those whose chief subsistence is derived therefrom. . . . A soldier has his honor as much at stake as when a civilian; then let him preserve his good name and reputation with the same jealous care as before he entered his country's ranks. . . . We make this public exposure, mortifying as it is to us, with the hope that a salutary improvement in matters will be made by our military authorities."

In fact, discipline among Vicksburg's Confederate defenders no longer mattered. His ranks of defenders reduced by disease and starvation, the commanding general John Pemberton surrendered his twenty-nine-thousand-man army to Grant on July 4.

In that final July 2 edition, J. M. Swords had mocked "the great Ulysses—the Yankee Generalissimo, surnamed Grant," for expressing "his intention of dining in Vicksburg . . . and celebrating the 4th of July with a grand dinner and so forth." Taunted the *Daily Citizen:* "Ulysses must get into the city before he dines in it. The way to cook a rabbit is 'first catch the rabbit.'"

Not long after the issue hit the streets, as it happened, Grant did just that. Swords fled town while his newspaper's metal type was still in its racks. Union conquerors stormed into the office and reset the story appearing in the paper's lower right-hand corner. A handful of surviving July 4 editions of the *Daily Citizen* concluded with the following acerbic update—the Union conquerors' last laugh after a brutal season of Confederate weeping:

NOTE

JULY 4th, 1863.

Two days bring about great changes. The banner of the Union floats over Vicksburg. Gen. Grant has "caught the rabbit"; he has dined in Vicksburg, and he did bring his dinner with him. The "Citizen" lives to see it. For the last time it appears on "Wall-paper." No more will it eulogize

> the luxury of mule-meat and fricasseed kitten—
> urge Southern warriors to such diet nevermore.
> This is the last wall-paper edition, and is, except-
> ing this note, from the types as we found them. It
> will be valuable hereafter as a curiosity.

Indeed, few Civil War papers are more valuable today than surviving copies of the last wallpaper editions of the *Daily Citizen*—with or without the Union-authored July 4 postscript. It remains not only among the rarest but the most frequently reproduced of all Civil War newspapers. At least thirty reprint editions are known, many passed off as genuine over the years, and their owners have often mistakenly believed they possessed the scarce originals. The New-York Historical Society owns four unquestionably genuine copies of the precious July 2 edition—three containing the last-minute inserted notice of Union occupation, and one without. In donating his "relic of the war" to the Society in 1875, the former Ohio cavalry officer Edward Crapsey offered unquestionable provenance: he had found the papers in Vicksburg himself—on the very day Union troops marched in. Together with Loughborough's recollections and Volck's etching, they constitute the most reliable record in existence of an instance of Southern endurance—and Union relentlessness—that changed the course of the war and evolved into myth.

31

———⟨∅∅⟩———

Wheel of Misfortune

Draft Wheel, ca. 1863

T HE ADMINISTRATION IS ACTING WISELY IN ORDERING THE immediate enforcement of the draft," the *New York Times* editorialized on July 10, 1863. "We have just achieved two great victories which it seems should paralyze the war power of the rebellion"—meaning Gettysburg and Vicksburg—but now, the paper recommended, "a new army of 300,000 men must be got ready to move upon the Confederacy. Let the rebel States see that not only are they beaten now, by the forces at present in the field, but that in the Fall they must meet the same veteran armies, recruited, and 300,000 stronger. And then, if they mean to stop short of annihilation, they will certainly see the propriety and necessity of yielding." Surely, the *Times* reasoned, even the "chiefs of faction" opposed to conscription would never "deter the Government from carrying it out to its complete execution."

In this prediction, the *Times* proved correct—but at what enormous cost in life, property, and civic image they could not have prophesied. In mid-July, provost marshals throughout New York City began drawing the first names of draft-eligible men from large, hand-cranked wooden wheels like this exceptional surviving original. Officials used this very relic that day on the Lower East Side.

Standing on a trestle frame held in place by bracketed wooden feet, the wheel features a lockable hatch and an iron-and-wood handle to rotate it, along with some one hundred of the small draft cards it

originally contained for that initial drawing—all bearing the names and occupations of men who, it turned out, were never drafted: an ethnic tapestry of names and occupations like tailor David Jones, mason Joseph Huber, upholsterer John Jacobs, shoemaker Joseph Illwitzer, carpenter Mike Johnson, and "colored waiter" George Jones.

The federal conscription act that Congress passed in March 1863 was by no means perfect. Though it applied to most male citizens between the ages of twenty-five and forty-five, it exempted any draftee who could provide a substitute to serve in his place or could pay a bounty of three hundred dollars to the government—an amount equal to the average *annual* salary of the Irish American laborers who so vociferously opposed the Lincoln administration, emancipation, and the military ser-

PLATE 31–1

vice the Union now required. To head off any show of opposition, Lincoln suspended the privilege of the writ of habeas corpus nationwide and established the offices of provost marshals, constituted almost as a secret police force with the power to seize spies, deserters, and war critics. These initiatives in some ways made a bad situation worse.

With the first conscription lottery scheduled for July 11, the blatantly racist anti-administration *Freeman's Journal* fanned the flames of discord by advising New Yorkers to resist the draft in order to prove that they were not an "enervated, emasculated, and slavish people." Other Democratic organs similarly denounced conscription as part of a plot by Republicans in Washington to override local and state rights, impose black equality, and force Irish-born Democrats into what some of them called a "nigger war"—requiring them to risk their lives to free black men who would soon compete for their low-paying jobs.

Nonetheless, the provost marshal drew the initial conscript names without incident on Saturday, July 11, and after a day off for Sabbath observance resumed the lottery on Monday the thirteenth. But early that steamy morning, enraged protesters stormed the uptown draft headquarters on Third Avenue between Forty-sixth and Forty-seventh streets, beating policemen who stood in their way. The mob tossed bricks through its plate-glass window and proceeded to smash the draft wheel, scatter the cards, trash the interior, and set the office ablaze. Then the rioters stormed downtown, their numbers increasing as they moved south toward the city's armories to seize guns and ammunition to continue their rampage, leaving the entire Forty-seventh Street block burning. Meanwhile, aroused residents in the city's poor Irish neighborhoods swarmed into black enclaves, torched businesses and homes, and menaced residents, beating hundreds, perhaps thousands of African Americans, maiming and sexually mutilating dozens, and lynching by some accounts eleven innocent victims. The New York City draft riots—more accurately race riots—were under way.

Other mobs targeted well-known Republicans and their personal and business properties. Protesters attacked the offices of Horace Greeley's *New York Tribune* on two separate occasions. At the newly opened nearby headquarters of the *New York Times,* the publisher Henry J.

Raymond took no chances, ordering guards manning Gatling guns to his roof to protect the lavish building. One mob pillaged the Brooks Brothers clothing store, and still another broke into a town house owned by two known Republican-inclined merchants, breaking up their expensive furniture and hurling a framed portrait of President Lincoln into the street, where cohorts merrily stomped it into smithereens. Mobs attacked abolitionists and so-called amalgamationists, including Mary Burke, a prostitute who reputedly took black men as clients, and Ann Martin and Ann Derrickson, two women married to black men. Imposing a reign of terror throughout Manhattan, rioters looted more stores and businesses, pummeled police officers, tore up railroad tracks, burned down the armory on Second Avenue and Twenty-first Street, and invaded the nearby Union Steam Works in an effort to gain control over the four thousand rifles stored inside. It took a huge police contingent to clear the factory in a horrific scene in which outnumbered occupiers leaped to their deaths from the steam works' windows or fell where they stood to gunfire or clubbing. When Archbishop John Hughes pleaded for calm, the predominantly Catholic mobs responded by setting fire to a number of Protestant churches and assaulting firemen who tried to extinguish the flames.

Not until July 17, when Union troops summoned to quell the riots reached New York from the vicinity of their recent triumph at Gettysburg, did order return to the shattered city after four days of plunder, arson, and death. Within days, against the urgent advice of the Democratic governor Horatio Seymour, federal officials resumed pulling names for the draft. But by then the city's Common Council had passed an emergency bill providing funds to underwrite the three-hundred-dollar bounties of every conscript who desired to avoid service by hiring a substitute. Many white men took advantage of the new loophole. Meanwhile, more than four thousand African Americans enlisted in all-black regiments voluntarily.

When officials tallied the human and financial costs of the worst urban violence in memory, the ugly riots had cost some 119 lives and left more than 110 soldiers and policemen wounded and untold hundreds of civilians, black and white, injured. It was, by all accounts, the bloodiest civil insurrection in the history of the country—save for the Civil War itself. But little evidence survived to attest to its ferocity: what was not burned to ashes was tossed into rivers or smashed and later discarded. Damaged buildings were torn down and new structures built on their sites. Whole communities disappeared. Unique relics like the Lower East Side draft wheel survived in far better condition than many battered New York neighborhoods and residents.

Provost Marshal Frederic C. Wagner, who donated the pristine memento of that rampage, later received ample political reward for his wartime loyalty and courage. A wealthy descendant of the seventeenth-century Lord of the Manor of Fordham, he went on to serve for more than twenty years as a deputy tax commissioner.

Sacking of Brownstone Houses in Lexington Avenue by the Rioters on Monday, July 13, wood engraving, 1863

PLATE 31–2

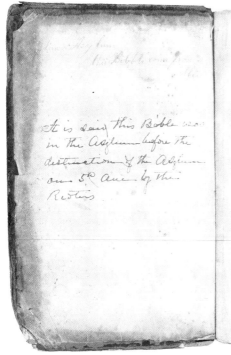

It is said this Bible was in the Asylum before the destruction of the Asylum on 5th Ave by the Rioters

25 When he raiseth up himself, the mighty are afraid: by reason of breakings they purify themselves.

26 The sword of him that layeth at him cannot hold: the spear, the dart, nor the habergeon.

27 He esteemeth iron as straw, *and* brass as rotten wood.

28 The arrow cannot make him flee; sling stones are turned with him into stubble.

29 Darts are counted as stubble: he laugheth at the shaking of a spear.

30 Sharp stones *are* under him: he spreadeth sharp pointed things upon the mire.

31 He maketh the deep to boil like a pot: he maketh the sea like a pot of ointment.

32 He maketh a path to shine after him; *one* would think the deep *to be* hoary.

33 Upon earth there is not his like, who is made without fear.

34 He beholdeth all high *things*: he *is* a king over all the children of pride.

CHAPTER XLII.

Job submitteth himself before God. 7 His friends are condemned for their wrong speaking. 10 Job's prosperity. 16 His age and death.

THEN Job answered the Lord, and said,

2 I know that thou canst do every *thing*, and *that* no thought can be withholden from thee.

3 Who *is* he that hideth counsel without knowledge? therefore have I uttered that I understood not; things too wonderful for me, which I knew not.

4 Hear, I beseech thee, and I will speak: I will demand of thee, and declare thou unto me.

5 I have heard of thee by the hearing of the ear: but now mine eye seeth thee:

6 Wherefore I abhor *myself*, and repent in dust and ashes.

7 ¶ And it was so, that after the Lord had spoken these words unto Job, the Lord said to Eliphaz the Temanite, My wrath is kindled against thee, and against thy two

friends: for ye have not spoken of me *the thing that* is right, as my servant Job hath.

8 Therefore take unto you now seven bullocks and seven rams, and go to my servant Job, and offer up for yourselves a burnt offering: and my servant Job shall pray for you: for him will I accept: lest I deal with you *after your* folly, in that ye have not spoken of me *the thing which* is right, like my servant Job.

9 So Eliphaz the Temanite and Bildad the Shuhite *and* Zophar the Naamathite went, and did according as the Lord commanded them: the Lord also accepted Job.

10 And the Lord turned the captivity of Job, when he prayed for his friends: also the Lord gave Job twice as much as he had before.

11 Then came there unto him all his brethren, and all his sisters, and all they that had been of his acquaintance before, and did eat bread with him in his house: and they bemoaned him, and comforted him over all the evil that the Lord had brought upon him: every man also gave him a piece of money, and every one an earring of gold.

12 So the Lord blessed the latter end of Job more than his beginning: for he had fourteen thousand sheep, and six thousand camels, and a thousand yoke of oxen, and a thousand she asses.

13 He had also seven sons and three daughters.

14 And he called the name of the first, Jemima; and the name of the second, Kezia; and the name of the third, Keren-happuch.

15 And in all the land were no women found so fair as the daughters of Job: and their father gave them inheritance among their brethren.

16 After this lived Job a hundred and forty years, and saw his sons, and his sons' sons, even four generations.

17 So Job died, *being* old and full of days.

PLATE 32–1

32

---∞∞∞---

Charred Survivor of an Urban Riot

Bible Used at Colored Orphan Asylum, ca. 1863

IN THE FIVE DAYS OF MOB VIOLENCE THAT RAGED THROUGHOUT Manhattan in mid-July 1863, rioters reserved their most unspeakable atrocities for African Americans. As noted in chapter 31, mobs outnumbered, overpowered, tortured, maimed, and murdered dozens of helpless black victims during the five days of hellish pandemonium. The historian Leslie Harris has recounted some of the specifics in painful detail; for example, one all-white gang of dockworkers beat and attempted to drown a man named Charles Jackson, while another brazenly roughed up a nine-year-old black boy on the corner of Broadway and Chambers Street—in full view of City Hall.

In another particularly horrific incident, a white man named George Glass seized the black coachman Abraham Franklin from his home and dragged him through the muddy streets, where a lynch mob soon strung him up from a lamppost. When a jeering crowd cut Franklin's body down, a sixteen-year-old white boy named Patrick Butler dragged the corpse along the streets by the genitalia, as onlookers shouted in amusement and approval. After another mob stabbed and stoned a black sailor named William Williams, a crowd of witnesses not only failed to intervene but cheered and vowed "vengeance on every nigger in New York."

But no act of racial violence against the innocent seemed more heartless than the brutal attack on the city's four-story Colored Orphan Asylum on Fifth Avenue between Forty-third and Forty-fourth streets on the initial afternoon of rioting, July 13, 1863. Founded in 1836 by charitable Quaker women from the New York Manumission Society, the institution had moved in 1843 into this spacious and well-ventilated new headquarters just a block from what is now the main branch of the New York Public Library—then the site of the municipal reservoir. The beautifully appointed orphanage featured basement playrooms, an ample first-floor kitchen, second-floor classrooms, a dining room, a laundry, a nursery, two infirmaries, and separate boys' and girls' dormitories in flanking wings. The imposing structure stood sheltered by a grove of trees that afforded the young residents—who ranged in age from infancy to the teenage years—a shady haven for outdoor recreation. No institution in the city offered stronger evidence of liberal-minded white philanthropists' commitment to indigent children of color. And that alone made it a target during the July 1863 unrest.

In its first twenty years of operation, the asylum had processed, aided, and educated more than twelve hundred orphans and abandoned children in need. Few knew that at the time of the riots a dozen of those in the asylum's care were the sons and daughters of black soldiers killed in action or of active recruits unable to care for children while they were off fighting in the ranks for the Union. In fact, just two days before the draft riots broke out in New York, one of the asylum's alumni, James Henry Gooding, had joined the heroic 54th Massachusetts Colored Infantry in its fabled attack against Battery Wagner near Charleston, South Carolina.

At 4:00 p.m. on July 13, 1863, according to well-preserved Orphan Asylum records, "the children numbering 233, were quietly seated in their school rooms, playing in the nursery, or reclining on a sick bed in the Hospital, when an infuriated mob, consisting of several thousand men, women, and children, armed with clubs, brick bats, etc. advanced upon the Institution." In a whirlwind of horror that lasted twenty minutes, the rioters broke their way into the locked building and pillaged it from basement to attic, hauling away all the chairs, beds, blankets, food, and clothing they could carry. Then they torched the first floor of the building, making sure enough straw from the remaining mattresses had been scattered around to conduct the flames swiftly. When a handful of firefighters already exhausted from battling the flames at the draft office a few blocks east tried twice to douse the blaze, rioters beat them back.

Only minutes earlier, hearing shouts of "Burn the niggers' nest!" teachers had gathered the orphans into a common room. There, one of them implored the frightened boys and girls: "Children, do you believe that Almighty God can deliver you from a mob?" They answered yes. "Then I wish you now to pray silently to God to protect you from this mob. I believe that he is able and that He will do it. Pray earnestly to Him, and when I give the signal, go in order, without noise, to the dining-room." From there the teachers led the crying children outside amid "the yells and horrible sounds" directed at them from the rioters.

Though the mob prevented the firemen from extinguishing the blaze, by some miracle of forbearance even the enraged, liquor-fueled looters and arsonists swarming outside could not summon the cruelty to harm the frightened children as the superintendent and matron of the asylum together "noiselessly" escorted them out of the Forty-fourth Street doors and toward sanctuary at a police station nine blocks south.

During this exodus, as the orphans made their way to safety, one reportedly "Irish" voice cried out: "If there is a man among you, with a heart within him come and help these poor children." The mob "laid hold of him, and appeared ready to tear him to pieces," but his plea was successful. The *Times* reported that one benevolent "young Irishman, named Paddy M'Caffrey, with four stage-drivers of the Forty-second Street line and the members of Engine Co. No. 18, rescued some twenty of the orphan children who were surrounded by the mob, and in defiance of the threats of the rioters, escorted them, to the Thirty-fifth Precinct Station-house. It hardly seems credible, yet it is nevertheless true, that there were dozens of men, or rather fiends, among the crowd who gathered around the poor children and cried out, 'Murder the d——d monkeys,' 'Wring the necks of the d——d Lincolnites,' etc. Had it not been for the courageous conduct of the parties mentioned, there is little doubt that many, and perhaps all of those helpless children, would have been murdered in cold blood."

Such individual acts of bravery helped ameliorate the impact of the

Colored Orphan Asylum, albumen print, 1861

tragedy. A six-year-old orphan girl who wandered away from the procession to the police precinct all the way to Seventh Avenue was rescued by a man named Osborn, who bravely "took her into his own house." When a seven-year-old boy got lost, too, and tried to find refuge at a nearby home, the lady of the house, afraid the mob would burn her out for sheltering him, "appealed to an Irishman passing by for redress." The unidentified pedestrian, who fortuitously turned out to be a contractor at the orphanage, wrapped the child "in a cloth and carried him like a bundle to his own home," from which his daughter returned the boy to "a faithful colored officer of the Asylum."

Three days later armed police and Zouave guards escorted the dis-

PLATE 32–2

possessed children by boat across the East River to safety at an alms-house on Blackwell's (now Roosevelt) Island. Among the few inanimate objects that miraculously survived the invasion, fire, and dislocation is an immeasurably emotional relic now in the New-York Historical Society: the asylum's Bible.

The story of its rescue lives in the Society's collection as well. The library owns a century's worth (1836–1936) of minutes and records of the Association for the Benefit of Colored Orphans, among which is a meticulously detailed, handwritten account of the riot, highlighted by a heart-wrenching description of the children's escape from the doomed building—and an explanation for the survival of the holy book: "One little girl, as she walked through the Dining Room, took up a large family Bible, to which she had been accustomed to listen twice each day, and looking up at the Superintendent with a sweet smile, her whole face beaming with the love of God; she said, Mr Davis, I've got the Bible. This dear child carried this treasured volume from the Asylum to the Station House and thence to Blackwell Island."

This Bible still survives—the sole, improbable artifact to endure the sacking and destruction of the orphanage. Once the property of the Reverend Moseley Hooker Williams, it came to the New-York Historical Society through a donation by his son Clarence Williams in 1938.

As for the Colored Orphan Asylum, though it, too, survived, it never returned to its prime location on Fifth Avenue. When its philanthropic board made plans to rebuild there, neighboring residents did not exactly offer their welcome. Instead, they pressured the patrons to find another location. "Better build at a distance from the mob," advised an anonymous correspondent signing himself "An Old Subscriber" in an audacious letter to the *New York Times* a few weeks after the attack.

Short of funds, as the beneficiary Anna Shotwell lamented, "by the malice of a mob," organizers had little choice but to open a modest new temporary orphanage on Fifty-first Street. By this time, the city's clearly endangered black population had understandably dwindled to its lowest numbers in more than forty years. Reluctant to reenter long-integrated neighborhoods where they had been exposed to such deadly menace, many families relocated to Brooklyn or New Jersey. Others founded easier-to-defend new all-black communities uptown. In one such area, a neighborhood that would later become Harlem, a permanent Colored Orphan Asylum finally reopened in 1867 on 143rd Street between Broadway and Amsterdam Avenue.

"People who burn orphan asylums and murder inoffensive negroes because of their color," editorialized *Harper's Weekly* on August 8, a few weeks after the riots, "must expect a sharp and extreme punishment." But as far as we know, none of the rioters who plundered and torched the Colored Orphan Asylum on July 13, 1863, was ever brought to justice.

The Riots in New York: Destruction of the Colored Orphan Asylum,
wood engraving, 1863

PLATE 32–3

33

——⟨०/०⟩——

Traveling Light

Footlocker with Belongings, 1860–1890

ONLY GENERALS LIVED IN WHAT AMOUNTED TO LUXURY IN THE FIELD during the Civil War—often commandeering private homes near their encampments to use as headquarters or dwelling in capacious canvas tents, where they ate, drank, and smoked the best products that their aides could procure, and where they were faithfully attended by military personnel and civilian servants alike.

Privates, on the other hand, endured in comparative squalor, sleeping outdoors or inside inadequate tepee-shaped Sibley tents, "packed like sardines in a box." They survived on tasteless rations like hardtack, toting overloaded "knapsack, haversack, [and] three pound canteen, all full," on their frequent marches. In between these two extremes of luxury and privation, high-ranking officers at least made do with more compact and easily transportable living supplies. None was more ingeniously designed than the military footlocker—the nineteenth-century equivalent of modern carry-on luggage. Footlockers could hold a bounty of personal items in a remarkably small space.

Here is a rare example of these remarkable military footlockers—this one fully stocked with living supplies, military gear, and souvenirs—that appears to have remained intact, in much the same condition in which it was used and then left for posterity by its owner, Lieutenant Colonel William H. Paine (1828–1890) of the 4th Wisconsin. Paine was a New Hampshire–born, self-educated topographical engineer, surveyor, and

mapmaker who served with the Army of the Potomac through the entire war. The detail-oriented Paine must have appreciated the intricate, suitcase-like contraption he toted from battlefield to battlefield: he was responsible, after all, for modernizing and improving the systems used by military surveyors during the war. At one point the creative officer perfected and secured a patent for a coiled, flat-steel tape measure, the forerunner of today's familiar, retractable Stanley PowerLock models. Paine practiced innovation and surely appreciated it in others.

His lockable wooden footlocker, just 10¾ by 21½ by 15¼ inches in size, and made to be carried by two side handles, was itself a utilitarian marvel. Perhaps because it was not only highly useful but irresistibly attractive, Paine made sure it was sufficiently personalized to inhibit covetous comrades from purloining it. Painted on the lid is the bold identification: "Col. W. H. Paine / A.D.C. / HdQs Army of the Potomac / DC 1." Apparently, it remained safe. The footlocker still features its original two tray-like compartments, each still stocked with the personal and professional supplies Paine used on campaign and later: pince-nez-style engineering

PLATE 33–1

spectacles and a shaving kit that included a metal-handled shaving brush and a razor (the case is stamped "W. H. PAINE, 107 WEST 122 STREET, NEW YORK"). Also in the locker trays are a black comb and a wooden hairbrush with yellow bristles, a leather belt holster, a richly decorated leather-brass-and-cotton sword belt and buckles, paper fragments, a silver-colored skeleton key on a string, a single round metal grapeshot, a leather strap, a single gilt souvenir epaulet dating to the War of 1812, insignia of the U.S. Army Engineers, a miniature silk American flag on a metal flagpole (its stripes bearing the names of various Civil War battle sites), a wooden accessory box filled with personal items like ribbons, two coin purses with metal snap fasteners, a paper election roster, a dark-brown leather billfold, and two metal tape measures of the type Paine patented. Inside, too, was discovered a medal Paine earned from the American Institute, featuring on one side a female allegorical figure grasping a liberty pole and on the other an American eagle with a banner in its beak. The banner reads: "Awarded to Wm. H. Paine, for a Surveyors Measure & Case 1865." Paine apparently entered his tape-measure gadget in a postwar contest for new inventions—and won.

If these items could talk, they would no doubt offer a monologue on the most famous engagement they "witnessed," for after beginning his army career by mapping out the locations of all the destroyed bridges between Washington and Richmond in 1861, Paine saw service under General Irvin McDowell and a number of other commanders of the Army of the Potomac. For all of them he efficiently produced maps (several of which exist among his papers at the Society) in a singularly personal fashion: by placing a sketch board on the pommel of his saddle and drawing topographical features while riding horseback. "Making use of the lithographing process and having his assistants trained according to his own methods," *The National Cyclopaedia of American Biography* reported years later, "he would complete in a day a map that other engineers required three weeks to produce. Many of his maps are filed in the archives of the war department."

No doubt most memorably of all, Paine toted his gear all the way to Gettysburg. "Engaged in gathering information correcting maps securing guides etc.," Paine wrote from the village on the first day of battle there, July 1, 1863, in a diary that found its way into the collection in 1978 along with the footlocker. "At 10 pm guided Gen Meade and escort to near Gettysburg. . . . Spent the night in examining our position which is along a ridge extending SW and SE."

Paine made note of "a hard fought battle raging nearly all day" on July 2, then recorded his impressions of the loud Confederate bombardment that preceded Pickett's Charge the following afternoon—an attack "repulsed by a most terrible fire from our artillery as well as infantry the 2d corps which held the immediate front where the fire was most firm and met the infantry in front of the rifle pits. On visiting this part of the field after the action the ground was literally strown [*sic*] with dead and wounded rebels thousands lay in one small field." Conceivably, it was from this corpse-filled site that Paine picked up the grapeshot he subsequently consigned to his locker. "Their repulse was final," he said of the Confederates in the last entry in his account. "There is no danger of another attack from them. All the corps did well no one faltered. . . . It was the most fearfully magnificent scene imaginable. Shots & shells struck on every hand. . . . Having just repulsed the rebels after a hard fought battle we can celebrate with feeling."

Paine and his footlocker survived both the fight and the celebration intact. After the war, the former colonel married, moved to New York, produced some illustrations for Horace Greeley's and William Swinton's histories of the war, became chief engineer of the Flushing & Northern Railroad, worked on locating a new Hudson River tunnel, secured fourteen additional patents, became a trustee of the Harlem Savings Bank, and, in what was surely the highlight of his peacetime career, generated advance surveys in preparation for construction of the so-called eighth wonder of the world: the new Brooklyn Bridge. He evidently continued to use his footlocker on his postwar engineering assignments: one of its contents is a silk advertisement for Roebling & Sons, the designers and builders of the miraculous suspension span across the East River between Brooklyn and Manhattan.

34

⚬⚬⚬

Learning to Read, Dixie Style

The First Dixie Reader, 1864

MID THE DEPRIVATION THAT HELD MOST OF THE SOUTH IN ITS
unrelenting grip by mid-war, it is a source of surprise that the Raleigh, North Carolina, publisher Branson, Farrar & Company managed to assemble the talent—not to mention the ink and paper—to produce Mrs. M. B. Moore's *First Dixie Reader* in the tumultuous year of 1863. The New-York Historical Society owns a copy from a second printing issued, even more surprisingly, the following year of even greater scarcity: 1864. Printed on brittle, inferior paper—nothing better was likely available—by one A. M. Gorman, the book sold for seventy-five cents with the "usual discounts to the trade" and with ten cents on the dollar required for mail orders. The copy owned by the New-York Historical Society entered the collection in 1949.

"This little volume is intended to follow the Dixie Primer," Marinda Branson Moore declared in her preface, "also to accompany a Speller, which will be brought out as early as circumstances will permit. At no distant period we hope to complete the series of Readers." Designed "as a stepping-stone . . . to the large Speller," the primer alternated rote spelling lessons and reading exercises designed for children still unable "to understand properly the sounds of letters, and the rules of pronunciation." The publishers emphasized the primer's regional appeal: it was not only "well adapted to young readers," they advertised, but "entirely a Southern book" as well.

THE

First Dixie Reader;

TO FOLLOW

THE

DIXIE PRIMER.

BY MRS. M. B. MOORE,

Author of the Dixie Series.

RALEIGH :

BRANSON, FARRAR & CO.

1864.

PLATE 34–1

Few such titles were by then appearing in the South. As the historian Mary Elizabeth Massey observed in her classic 1952 study, *Ersatz in the Confederacy: Shortages and Substitutes on the Southern Homefront,* "Books were more scarce than either newspapers or magazines. Prior to 1861, books were brought into the South in quantity from the North and from England, for the works of the English authors were greatly admired by the Southern reading public. The blockade practically halted this importation, although a few books did come through. Whenever a new book made its appearance, it was received with much applause and passed around among many. The publishing houses . . . were handicapped by lack of paper, manpower, good ink, and by old worn-out, irreplaceable machinery. They published a fair number of new novels, histories, military works, textbooks, song books, and music" often in "brown paper editions, bound in any available material," but "they could not possibly keep up with the demand." In such a depressed and depressing market, Moore's little book must have been looked upon in its day as a literary and commercial triumph.

At first blush, *The First Dixie Reader* follows a familiar track typical of early childhood education in the mid-nineteenth century: repetition followed by more repetition. The book employed relentless rhyming to teach proper spelling: the words "cat," "bat," "fat," "mat," "pat," and "rat" introduced the publication, followed by such matching sounds as "bet," "get," and "met"; "bit," "fit," and "pit"; "cot," "dot," and "got"; and "cut," "gut," and "nut."

Many of the sentence-by-sentence reading exercises sound not unlike the numbing "Dick and Jane" stories of the next century. But there was surely more than a bit of proselytism behind the paralyzing tautology. In addition to such paeans to home-front industriousness, Moore managed to slip in moral and religious instruction alongside lessons about owls, colts, sheep, pigs, crows, dogs, and the mystery of rain. Character-building read-along passages emphasized sobriety, good behavior, Sabbath observance, and the constant presence of a judgmental God who watched children "all the day long." The book even contained a truly frightening nine-sentence explanation for the death and funeral of an infant, an all too common occurrence in nineteenth-century

America, North as well as South—but offered here as a warning against bad behavior: "It was well two days ago, and could play as you do; but now see its pale white face. God saw it would be best to take it to heaven now. Perhaps he looked away in the future, and saw that the child would not be good if it grew to be a man." Yet another lesson promised redemption in return for reverence:

1. Who made you, child?
2. God made me of dust.
3. For what did he make you?
4. To be good, and to do good.
5. Who loves good boys and girls?
6. Pa, and ma, and all good men.
7. Who else loves them?
8. God loves them.
9. Can you be good of yourself?
10. No, I must ask God to help me.
11. Will God hear a child pray?
12. He says he will.

Branson, Farrar & Company's surprisingly robust list of 1864 publications suggests that the yearning for instruction and the obligation for childhood education never deserted Southerners despite the absence of breadwinning men and the difficulty that home-front women experienced obtaining basic necessities like food. Emma Edwards Holmes, a South Carolina aristocrat who turned to tutoring during the war (being a "schoolmistress," she confided, was "what I have always wished myself to be"), found that maintaining discipline was difficult—especially with so many fathers and older brothers away at the front. "My little school does not progress very smoothly," she recorded in her diary in June 1862, "for neither of the boys are studious and give me a great deal of trouble— besides being very much spoiled & telling me 'I will and I won't' very frequently."

The New Dixie Primer was but one of eight spellers, rhyme books, and grammar manuals the publishers promoted in the endpapers for the

Moore primer. But despite Mrs. Moore's optimistic expectations for additional supplements, *The First Dixie Reader* turned out to be the last in her series of primers—and not only because the Southern publishing industry collapsed altogether in 1864. That year, Mrs. Moore herself died. This was her last book.

On the final leaf of its sixty-three pages of rote spelling instruction, chilling appeals to conscience, honesty, fair play, and industriousness, and the most mundane examples of animal lore, Marinda Branson Moore probably came closest to summarizing the Southern ideal of God-fearing education with a concluding poem titled "I'm Not Too Young for God to See." One can almost imagine entire classrooms full of impressionable children reciting the lines in abject terror. However "Southern" she thought such instruction to be, the author might have been surprised to learn a lesson for herself—that in 1864, Northern primers featured many of the same techniques, lessons, and warnings:

> *I'm not too young for God to see,*
> *He knows my name and nature too;*
> *And all day long, he looks at me,*
> *And sees my actions through and thro'.*
>
> *He listens to the words I say,*
> *And knows the thoughts I have within,*
> *And whether I am at work or play*
> *He's sure to know it if I sin.*

Presentation Address

OF THE

LADIES OF THE CITY OF NEW YORK

TO THE OFFICERS AND MEN

OF THE

Twentieth United States Colored Troops.

Soldiers:

WE, the Mothers, Wives, and Sisters of the members of the NEW YORK UNION LEAGUE CLUB, of whose liberality and intelligent patriotism, and under whose direct auspices, you have been organized into a body of National Troops for the defence of the Union, earnestly sympathizing in the great cause of American free nationality, and desirous of testifying, by some public memorial, our profound sense of the sacred object and the holy cause, in behalf of which you have enlisted, have prepared for you this Banner, at once the emblem of freedom and of faith, and the symbol of woman's best wishes and prayers for our common country, and especially for your devotion thereto.

When you look at this Flag and rush to battle, or stand at guard beneath its sublime motto: "GOD AND LIBERTY!" remember that it is also an emblem of love and honor from the daughters of this great metropolis, to her brave champions in the field, and that they will anxiously watch your career, glorying in your heroism, ministering to you when wounded and ill, and honoring your martyrdom with benedictions and with tears.

Names of Subscribers to the Flag.

Mrs. J. J. Astor	Mrs. M. Clarkson	Mrs. H. G. Thomson
" G. W. Blunt	" J. O. Stone	" F. C. Pendexter
" J. W. Beekman	" J. G. King, Jr.	" H. G. Chapman
" S. Wetmore	" H. Van Rensclaer	" G. Bancroft
" S. B. Chittenden	" J. A. King, Jr.	" M. K. Jesup
" G. Bliss, Jr.	" J. C. Cassegoe	" J. C. B. Davis
" S. J. Bacon	" J. L. Kennedy	" W. H. Scheiffelin
" R. B. Minturn	" F. Prime	" C. C. Dodge
" Charles King	" Barnwall	" John Jay
" S. W. Bridgham	" Wheelwright	" E. M. Young
" W. E. Dodge	" E. Collins	" J. T. Schultz
" R. Stebbins	" Bradish	" J. E. Brenly
" S. B. Schieffelin	" Bruce	" H. Chauncy
Miss King	" Tuckerman	" R. M. Hunt
Mrs. J. B. Johnston	" Shaw	Miss Jones
" N. D. Smith	" Williams	" J. Scheiffelin
" T. M. Cheeseman	" P. Richards	" Fish
" H. A. Coit	" R. Winthrop	" Jay
" A. P. Mann	" Weeks	" Anna Jay
" J. J. Phelps	" Jaques	" Young
" G. B. Deforest	" A. Brooks	" Schultz
" LeG. B. Cannon	" W. Felt	" Russell
" W. A. Butler	" J. W. Goddard	" J. M. King
" N. A. Murdock	" F. G. Shaw	" Cochrane
" A. Dunlap	" R. G. Shaw	Mrs. Vincent Colyer
" T. E. Howe	" G. B. Curtiss	" Catharine C. Hunt
" W. H. Lee	" R. C. Lovell	" Catharine Williams
" W. E. Dodge, Jr.	" C. G. Kirkland	" Emily H. Chauncey
" David Hoadley	" B. De Forest	" E. W. Crager
" C. Ludington	" Boerum	" W. C. Bryant
" G. Lemist	" Hamilton Fish	" F. B. Godwin
" E. C. Cowdin	" Alfred Pell	" Emily Boerum
" J. A. Roosevelt	" Kennedy	Miss Norsworthy
" J. Sampson	" J. Johnston	
" R. B. Minturn, Jr.	" T. L. Beekman	
" Alfred Pell, Jr.	" J. F. Gray	Mr. H. G. Chapman
" W. Hutchins	" J. Tuckeman	" Ira Brenly
" Geo. Opdyke	" F. A. Whittaker	" Peter Marié
" G. C. Ward	" J. H. Macy	" C. Berryman
" C. G. Judson	" F. H. Macy	" C. De P. Field
" S. W. Roosevelt	" J. McKaye	" C. H. Tuckerman
" E. D. Smith	" W. L. Felt	" O. A. Heckscher
" S. Gandy	" T. Haskell	" E. Scheiffelin
" R. L. Stuart	" Isaac Ames	" B. N. Field
" E. W. Stoughton	" L. F. Warner	" L. Scheiffelin
" J. W. Bigelow	" A. G. Phelps	" D. J. Clark
" M. O. Roberts	" N. Chandler	" W. H. Scheiffelin
" H. K. Bogart	" H. Potter	" Wadsworth
" E. C. Hall	" P. S. Van Renselaer	" S. A. Scheiffelin
" J. LeRoy	" Walter	" R. H. Hunt
" J. Brown	" H. Baldwin	" B. W. Griswold

WHITEHOLZE, PRINTER, 119 FULTON & 42 ANN STS, N.Y.

PLATE 35-1

35

⟨⟨⟨∂∂∂⟩⟩⟩

An Ovation—and a Banner—
for Black Troops

*Presentation Address of the Ladies of the City of
New York to the Officers and Men of the
Twentieth United States Colored Troops,* 1864

O N MARCH 5, 1864, "A VAST CROWD" OF 100,000 NEW YORKERS "OF EVERY
shade of color, and every phase of social and political life" thronged
into the city's principal outdoor rallying point, Union Square, to wave
flags and handkerchiefs and cheer themselves hoarse for a newly organized army regiment. This was no ordinary outpouring of appreciative
civilians. But then, this was no ordinary regiment. Less than a year after
the New York draft riots, the city's philanthropic liberal Republicans attempted to atone by financing, recruiting, training, outfitting, and now
robustly celebrating the brand-new 20th Regiment of the U.S. Colored
Troops—the first all-black unit raised in the Empire State.

That day, the police superintendent led a hundred city patrolmen at
the head of the parade, followed by members of the regimental sponsor,
the Union League Club, and hundreds of "Colored Friends of the Recruits marching with hands joined." The Governors Island Band provided musical accompaniment, and the crowd offered "cheers upon
cheers," according to one rather sanctimonious account, "given in a
manner which showed how truly the brave spirit of the once-despised
colored man was appreciated by the intelligent citizens of New-York."

The ceremony got under way at 1:00 p.m. on a specially built, flag-festooned wooden platform outside the club building, when a noted educator offered what was intended to be an inspiring lecture. Then, most dramatically, the club unfurled and presented the regiment with an "elaborately embroidered" regimental flag (designed by the *Washington Crossing the Delaware* artist, Emanuel Gottlieb Leutze, no less). Emblazoned with the words "God and Liberty," the banner was adorned with a "conquering eagle and broken yoke"—emblems intended to "speak as plainly as symbols can of the might of Freedom and the overthrow of Slavery."

Accepting it in behalf of his men, the regimental commander acknowledged that the banner "symbolizes our country" and declared: "It is this that makes death glorious beneath its starry folds." Echoing these sentiments, the principal orator that day predicted that the colors would "form a spell of such power as to bind up every generous heart with one firm, fierce resolve that these flags . . . shall not be surrendered—but shall go marching on, and marching on, and still marching on to triumph, and final victory!" The flag itself has long disappeared, but the ornate words that its female donors spoke and published that day in presenting it to the 20th survive in the collection in the form of a period handbill published especially for the regiment's dazzling send-off.

Trained on Rikers Island, then transported by boat across the East River hours earlier for the outdoor ceremony, the thousand soldiers of the 20th paraded that day from the riverfront to Union Square. Along the way, they enjoyed a Manhattan welcome every bit as enthusiastic and colorful as the flag-suffused parade given in honor of the members of the all-white 7th Regiment when they headed off for the seat of war back in the spring of 1861. George Templeton Strong, a Union League founder who attended both ceremonies, proudly noted of the latter, "Our labors of a year ago have borne fruit," adding that he thought the "phenomenon—Ethiopia marching down Broadway, armed, drilled, truculent, and elated—was" as memorable as the departure of the first white regiments for the front three years earlier. "The regiment was 'black but comely,'" he added in a somewhat unfortunate afterthought, "and marched well . . . not below the average of new regiments. Both sidewalks and all the windows were full of applauding spectators. There was hearty cheering and clapping and waving of handkerchiefs, and I neither heard nor heard of any expression of sound, constitutional, conservative disapproval."

The 20th had been the brainchild of the "Mothers, Wives, and Sisters" of the Union League, if they did say so themselves—which they proudly did, right in the handbill prepared for the flag-presentation ceremony: *Presentation Address of the Ladies of the City of New York to the Officers and Men of the Twentieth United States Colored Troops*. There was no doubting the ladies' charitable intentions, yet there was something excruciatingly patronizing about the published reminder (floridly composed by the writer Henry T. Tuckerman) that it was their own "liberality and intelligent patriotism" that had made it possible to fashion these soldiers "into a body of National Troops for the defense of the Union, earnestly sympathizing in the great cause of American free nationality."

Organizing a "colored" regiment in New York had not been an easy task. Although Lincoln's Emancipation Proclamation had specifically urged African American recruitment, prompting other Northern governors to respond enthusiastically by raising regiments, New York's Democratic chief executive, Horatio Seymour, fearful of alienating his downstate, predominantly Irish American supporters, did little to encourage it here—not even when proponents pointed out that every African American recruited would mean one less white conscript drafted. Significantly, Lincoln's most recent call for more men had made no reference to race. Finally, local white philanthropists organized their own New York Association for Colored Volunteers in November. After its first meeting the committee made it clear to Seymour that "justice and patriotism alike require that all men who are subject to a *draft,* shall have equal privileges in *volunteering*," and warned the governor to place "no impediments" in the way of "colored men who are willing to comply."

Seymour backed down, or at least he deferred to the War Department, but the challenge of recruiting in New York remained formidable. At first, no Manhattan landlord would rent an office for "such a purpose as a depot for recruiting negroes." Finally, the committee found space to share in a building on Broadway and Fourth Street, in rooms already occupied as a relief center for black draft riot victims. Although offered less pay than white recruits, African Americans were still eligible for a handsome seventy-five-dollar federal bounty just for signing up. Unfortunately, some were reportedly swindled by bounty brokers; others were drugged and virtually shanghaied into service. Worse, when the regiment shipped out to Rikers Island for training, the men were crammed into tents "without floors or warming, causing great suffering from cold." The committee took it upon itself to buy the extra tents the army had failed to provide, and purchased stoves to heat them, but not before many of the recruits fell ill. There was "no proper hospital" on the island to treat them. Miraculously, the enlistees recovered, survived, and learned their military drills. After only two months to learn how to be soldiers, they headed to Manhattan to receive their regimental colors.

On March 5, "desirous of testifying, by some public memorial, our profound sense of the sacred object and the holy cause, in behalf of which you have enlisted," the Union League women reminded the recruits that they had "prepared for you this Banner, at once the emblem of freedom and of faith, and the symbol of woman's best wishes and prayers for our common country, and especially for your devotion thereto." The mothers and sisters left the troops with this final piece of what they hoped would be inspiring advice: "When you look at this Flag and rush to battle, or stand at guard beneath its sublime motto . . . remember that it is also an emblem of love and honor from the daughters of this great metropolis, to her brave champions in the field, and that they will anxiously watch your career, glorying in your heroism, ministering to you when wounded and ill, and honoring your martyrdom with benedictions and with tears."

The notion of white women referring to black men as their "champions in the field" was radical indeed for 1864, but the soldiers for whom the compliment was intended probably paid more attention to its rather chilling reminder about the very real possibility of death. The entire passage was read aloud that afternoon from a copy engrossed on parchment and signed by 153 subscribers to the flag project—the crème de la crème of New York society—including the wives of John Jacob Astor, William

Presentation of Colors to the 20th U.S. Colored Infantry,
March 26, 1864

Cullen Bryant, Hamilton Fish, and of prominent men named Phelps, Dodge, Jay, Roosevelt, and Van Rensselaer. The New-York Historical Society's four pristine copies of the rare handbill version are undoubtedly among the thousands handed out to the throng that gathered that afternoon at Union Square.

"This march will be the subject of cords of historical paintings before 1900 A.D.," George Templeton Strong immediately predicted. Indeed, the March 5 event proved significant enough to inspire a beautiful E. L. Henry commemorative painting for the Union League clubhouse itself, along with widespread coverage in the press. This included a woodcut illustration published in *Frank Leslie's Illustrated Newspaper* on March 26, which showed the large, and integrated, crowd (the people of color, to be sure, relegated to the rear outskirts of the audience), cheering and waving as the regiment goes through its precision drills. As the *Times* reported in its own detailed coverage: "They are a fine, strong and hearty set of men, and their splendid appearance, combined with the apparent

PLATE 35–2

readiness and determination with which they enter their new profession, created a very favorable impression in the minds of all who saw them. . . . They marched to the front of the stand and performed one or two military movements in good style, their order of arms being almost, if not quite, equal to that of the famous 7th Regiment. They were then formed in square, open ranks, officers to the front, color-guard to the front and centre, the Colonel in front of his regiment and opposite President King of Columbia College, who presented the stand of colors to the regiment, then addressed them."

Surely it was not lost on the audience, particularly the African American attendees, that all the regiment's officers were white—including the regimental commander, Lieutenant Colonel Nelson B. Bartram, a former public school assistant principal, though a veteran of the Peninsula Campaign, Fredericksburg, and Chancellorsville. Bartram came with useful experience in managing African American soldiers. He had recently returned to New York after serving as commander of the brave and "resolute" men of the 8th USCT in Florida. Rounding out the contingent of officers were Lieutenant Colonel Andrew E. Mather of Cooperstown and Major Amos P. Wells, who had served in Ellsworth's Fire Zouaves early in the war. As in virtually all black regiments, the surgeons, quartermasters, line captains, and first and second lieutenants were Caucasian as well. Thanks to federal policy, the USCT was not only slow to organize regiments in New York State and unable to offer equal pay for its recruits but also resistant to the idea of bestowing rank on people of color.

That was evident when the March 5 ceremonies came to a close. Bartram mounted his handsome gray horse; called the 20th into close order; received three cheers for himself, his officers, and his men; and in return proposed three cheers for the Union League, which his soldiers offered "as only strong lungs and willing men can." Then the officers headed into the clubhouse to partake "of a splendid collation, which had been prepared for them" by members. The black recruits remained outside and according to one report got only coffee, albeit brewed "under the personal supervision of the ladies, who seemed well to understand the soldiers' tastes." Only then did the regiment begin its final march down

Broadway and across Canal Street to the Hudson River, where its men boarded the steamer *Ericsson* bound for service in New Orleans. There they began their military service not as warriors but as occupiers. Indeed, most African American troops were initially assigned to garrison duty or providing security for railroads and prison camps, but they also proved their valor, whenever asked, at battlefields from Port Hudson, Louisiana, to Petersburg, Virginia.

The 20th served at Port Hudson, too, but departed for a brief assignment at Point Cavalho, Texas, the month before the battles got under way at the more important Mississippi River target. In May 1864, the 20th returned to the New Orleans area. Stationed at nearby Carrollton, they saw little action, though by one report they became "the best drilled and best disciplined regiment in the department of the Gulf."

While the 20th saw none of the kind of memorable, heroic action that the 54th Massachusetts experienced at Battery Wagner in 1863, other New York USCT units did go on to earn their share of glory before the war ended. The year after the 20th mustered into service in the city where the draft riots had raged, the 102nd USCT helped seize the city where the rebellion itself had begun: Charleston, South Carolina. Altogether, New York State sent 4,125 African American soldiers into the ranks of the U.S. Colored Troops—far smaller totals than Southern states like Kentucky (23,703) and Tennessee (20,133), but notably fewer as well than Northern states like Pennsylvania (8,612) and Ohio (5,092). It is worth noting that African American soldiers from free states were predominantly free blacks who were in some cases decades removed from slavery, whereas blacks recruited in slave states tended to be escaped or liberated former slaves.

Attention soon shifted to the volatile issue of appointing black officers. "Why equal privileges are withheld from one class and not from the other, I am at a loss to conjecture," Sergeant James T. S. Taylor wrote in a letter to the editor of the *Anglo-African* after his own USCT regiment marched into Key West, Florida. "Are we still to be deprived of all these rights and privileges which, by our sacrifices, we justly merit? This nation had to be taught some very severe lessons by Providence before they would even let the negro have a musket, and now, not until equal rights are given us as soldiers will the God of all Wisdom lead the nation to a victorious triumph and a lasting peace."

It is likely that few of the tens of thousands of civilian onlookers massed in Union Square on March 5, 1864, for the Presentation of Colors to the 20th USCT gave a second thought to the inequity of the command structure among African American regiments. Instead, the *New York Times* spoke for many who thought that the mere enlistment of USCT volunteers constituted a revolutionary advance in race relations. "The scene of yesterday was one which marks an era of progress in the political and social history of New-York," wrote the reporter covering the event.

"In the month of July last the homes of these people were burned and pillaged by an infuriated political mob," the *Times* pointed out. "They and their families were hunted down and murdered in the public streets of this city; and the force and majesty of the law were powerless to protect them. Seven brief months have passed, and a thousand of these despised and persecuted men march through the City in the honorable garb of United States soldiers, in vindication of their own manhood, and with the approval of a countless multitude—in effect saving from inevitable and distasteful conscription the same number of those who hunted their persons and destroyed their homes during those days of humiliation and disgrace. This is noble vengeance—a vengeance taught by Him who commanded, 'Love them that hate you; do good to them that persecute you.'"

In the end, the legacy of the 20th had more to do with symbolism than sacrifice. The regiment served until October 1865—mustering out six months after the war ended. During its year and a half under arms, the 20th did suffer heavy casualties, losing a total of 283 soldiers. Nearly all fell victim to disease, but also to suicide, drowning, and sunstroke. Only a single soldier died of "wounds received in action."

36

⎯⎯⎯◦◦◦⎯⎯⎯

A Modern Major General

Ulysses Simpson Grant (1822–1885),
Painting by James Reid Lambdin, 1868

N O ONE EVER ACCUSED ULYSSES S. GRANT OF BEING A POPINJAY. WHEN
the greatest Union hero of the Civil War arrived in Washington in
1864 to formally receive his promotion to lieutenant general—the first
since George Washington to achieve that exalted rank—he tried regis-
tering at the plush Willard Hotel. Failing to recognize him, the desk
clerk there took one look at the scruffy little officer grasping a teenage
boy by the hand and wearing a stained linen duster over his field uniform and decided that a tiny room on the top floor would do fine. Only
when the clerk examined the guest book and saw the signature—"U. S.
Grant and son, Galena, Illinois"—did the best parlor suite in the house
suddenly become available, with apologies.

Grant's utter simplicity might have made good civilian accommoda-
tions hard to procure in 1864, but there was no doubt that this virtue
served him well with his own men, as well as with the image makers
who went on to transform him into a powerful symbol of Northern te-
nacity and egalitarianism. The war correspondent Sylvanus Cadwallader
saw nothing wrong with the fact that Grant's "clothing was unexcep-
tionable in quality and condition . . . his manner of wearing it . . . scarcely
up to military requirements. . . . His overcoat was generally the army
blue of regulation pattern no wise differing from those of officers or

PLATE 36–1

privates, with nothing on it to distinguish him or denote rank." This aversion to pretense set Grant apart—that and the useful intervention of Illinois politicians who believed that his everyman probity destined him for wider fame, if only his virtues were adequately communicated. Among the results were enough Grant portraits to fill a museum—including the Society's superb oil painting by James Reid Lambdin.

Modest as he remained, there was no denying Grant's understanding of his own appeal. Almost from the start of his stunning rise to fame in 1862, the innately unaffected general came to appreciate that his very lack of ostentation constituted the foundations of an irresistible—and potentially useful—public image. And notwithstanding his legendary disdain for vanity, he thereafter did whatever he could, whenever he could, to provide tangible examples for public consumption. In other words, as soon as he became famous, he proved ready, willing, and able to pose for artists.

Grant first catapulted to national attention in February 1862 by capturing Forts Henry and Donelson in Tennessee. The following month, *Harper's Weekly* immediately—and prematurely, as it turned out—heralded the victory as "the beginning of the end." The *New-York Illustrated News* went *Harper's* one better by publishing an almost unrecognizable engraving of "Major-General U. S. Grant, the Hero of the Recent Victories in Kentucky and Tennessee. From a Photograph by B. F. Chamberlain, of Cincinnati" (plate 36–2). Unfortunately, the artist who prepared this portrait apparently based it on not one but two sources—one outdated, the other unreliable. The first was an already passé photograph for which Grant posed in his Galena, Illinois, hometown before heading off for active duty. It showed him wearing an uncharacteristically flamboyant cockaded dress hat, cradling his sword in his lap, and sporting a long, flowing beard he would soon thereafter radically shave back. The second model was a more recent photograph apparently made in Cairo, Illinois, but it showed not the general but a beef contractor called William Grant who bore only passing resemblance to his famous namesake. In the absence of fresh photographs, charlatans had apparently begun hawking William's picture as a genuine image of Ulysses. For good measure, the *New-York Illustrated News* provided its

Major-General U. S. Grant, the Hero of the Recent Victories in Kentucky and Tennessee, woodcut engraving of a Grant look-alike, *New-York Illustrated News,* March 22, 1862

composite with epaulets! Over the next year, many printmakers continued to copy these absurd models. Grant apparently determined at some point to do something about the situation. Notwithstanding his growing command responsibilities, he began accommodating artists.

In November 1863, for example, with his army camped at Chattanooga,

PLATE 36–2

Grant welcomed to his headquarters a twenty-six-year-old English-born, formerly pro-Confederate painter named John Antrobus, who had evidently been sent to Tennessee by a friend of the general's in Chicago to craft a more heroic and realistic portrait. "Mr. Antrobus left here will [well] pleased with his success," Grant advised his friend the U.S. marshal of Chicago, J. Russell Jones, on November 17. "I hope you will be equally pleased." Not surprisingly, Jones was thrilled with the depiction of an anxious-looking Grant before Missionary Ridge (the scene of one of his triumphs), field glasses in one hand, the other resting on a captured Confederate fieldpiece. Enthusiastically telling the general that "if anything in this country beats it, I have yet to see it," Jones reported that "Antrobus' Studio is constantly thronged by people desiring to see it, but only the favored few get in," promising: "On Monday it is to be placed on exhibition, the proceeds to go to the Soldiers Home—and as soon as I am well enough & can leave, we shall take it to Washington."

The press was no less rhapsodic. "It is the man himself," raved the *Chicago Tribune,* calling the picture "a great historical painting." And with evident hometown pride, a Galena journalist called the canvas "a perfect masterpiece, that must give its author a place in the front rank of American artists." But clearly, Jones and Grant's other admirers had something more in mind for the picture than good local reviews. Jones made no secret (at least to Grant) of why he wanted the picture exhibited in the nation's capital: he evidently believed the mere sight of the general, even on canvas, would win him prompt military elevation and perhaps even a shot at unseating, or at the very least succeeding, Lincoln as president. "I took the liberty of saying in a recent letter to Mr. Washburne," admitted Jones, that if the president "and his friends" saw it for themselves, "Lincoln will then go in easy, and Grant must be made Lieut. Genl. . . . As things now stand you could get the nomination of the Democracy [the Democratic Party], but could not be elected against Lincoln. I tell everybody that I know nothing whatever of your views, but that I am satisfied that all you care for at present is to whip the Rebels and put down the Rebellion . . . and then the balance will take care of itself." Somewhat mortified, Grant quickly made clear in a private letter to the chairman of the Democratic Central Committee in Ohio that he was "not a candidate for any office nor for favors from any party," adding, however, in an eerie echo of Jones's blueprint for future success: "Let us succeed in crushing the rebellion, in the shortest possible time, and I will be content with whatever credit may then be given me."

With or without Grant's acquiescence, the Antrobus portrait did prove influential. It inspired a widely distributed popular print and earned a special exhibition in a House of Representatives committee room once Jones recovered and took it east. Such was the growing power of the Grant image—or the disquieting rumors about his political ambitions—that President Lincoln himself felt it prudent to head up to the Capitol to examine the painting himself. He had not yet laid eyes on Grant, but he diplomatically pronounced himself "highly gratified" by what he saw.

When Grant himself finally made his way to Washington to meet the president and receive his third star, an observer noted that the general was still dressed in "an ordinary-looking military suit, and doesn't put on any airs whatever." Lincoln threw him a White House reception where "the torrent" of guests eager to catch a glimpse of the "rather slightly built" hero forced many spectators, and eventually Grant himself, to step onto the nearest couch in order to see and be seen. Tellingly, when the well-regarded painter Peter Rothermel immortalized this scene in a canvas titled *The Republican Court in the Days of Lincoln,* he took pains to suggest that Grant had now ascended to a far higher iconographical pedestal than a sofa. Rothermel's depiction planted the general firmly on the East Room floor, right next to Lincoln—shorter than the president, to be sure, but not by much (in reality Lincoln had six or seven inches on him)—and by dint of his placement clearly the second-most-important figure in both the ballroom and the nation. Relegated to a nearby chair, too old and bloated to join the receiving line, sat General Winfield Scott (though he had in fact retired to West Point and was not present), his inclusion no doubt meant to symbolize the acquiescence of the old guard in Grant's rise.

His admirers and political backers would never again be without an adequate supply of Grant images. The general somehow managed to find time to pose often for suitable photographic models during the busy final year of the war (some of them outdoors, on campaign). The print publisher who brought out an etched adaptation of a Vicksburg portrait accurately claimed that "the paint of it was hardly dry when Grant entered the town as victor on the Fourth of July." Grant was aided in this widespread proliferation of images by his special patron, the Illinois congressman Elihu Washburne, whom Lincoln instructed "to superintend the getting up" of a gold medal in Grant's honor in late 1863.

Nothing did more to enshrine Grant as one of the signal heroes of the war—and of the art it inspired—than the myriad surrender scenes that proliferated after Robert E. Lee met him at Appomattox Court House, Virginia, on April 9, 1865. The inescapable contrast between the splendid Lee, adorned in full dress, a gleaming sword at his side, and the unself-consciously ill-clad Grant, wearing a mud-spattered field uniform, seemed to symbolize a working people's conquest of the aristocracy. Such images elevated Lee to the status of living martyr of the Lost Cause but also immortalized the man who had so calmly and generously accepted his surrender without a show of military pomp.

After the war, it seemed that every Northern military hospital, Union League Club, and veterans' organization commissioned a Ulysses S. Grant portrait of its own to adorn its walls. One of the best of these is the Society's resolute but refreshingly informal picture by James Reid Lambdin (1807–1889), created from life in 1868 when Grant was a candidate for president of the United States (plate 36–1). The Historical Society's four-by-three-foot canvas was acquired through the Beekman Fund in 1954.

Like most of the pictures created that election year, the Lambdin painting shows Grant still wearing his Civil War uniform, hand casually thrust into his pocket. Grant's martial image was shamelessly exploited that season. Posing later that year for another artist, Grant confessed, "I have sat so often for portraits that I had determined not to sit again." Of course he did so anyway, and repeatedly.

Lambdin, a Pennsylvania-born portrait artist who had studied for a time under Thomas Sully, also painted Daniel Webster, John Marshall, Lincoln, and such Union military heroes as Generals Ambrose Burnside, William Rosecrans, Don Carlos Buell, and George G. Meade. But his Grant ranks among his best—and perhaps with the best of all the portraits of the ever-elusive, chronically self-effacing, but reliably available subject.

To the end of his life, Grant remained of two minds about such projects. As often as he offered himself to artists and photographers, he never lost his Galena boy's sense that the fuss was unnecessary and the entire genre of military art imperfect. Long after the fighting had ended, Grant insisted: "I never saw a war picture that was pleasant. I tried to enjoy some of those in Versailles, but they were disgusting." Still, he never encountered a portrait of himself that elicited such a negative reaction, and he may have been thinking of the many useful examples when he added, "There was nothing in our war to be ashamed of, and I believe in cherishing the memories of the war so far as they recall the sacrifices of our people for the Union." In the end, none of those "people," save for Lincoln himself (perhaps), ended up more frequently and lovingly depicted by the portrait painters.

Unlike Lincoln, it might be noted, Grant had developed another talent while attending West Point that he demonstrated to good advantage as a student but sadly abandoned when he began his military career. As his surviving U.S. Military Academy records show, he was a passably good artist himself.

37

———◦⁄◦⁄◦———

All's Fair

Entry Ticket for the New York Metropolitan Fair, 1864

I N THE ERA BEFORE GOVERNMENTS ROUTINELY EARMARKED TAXPAYER-funded care for the casualties of war, the Union's private relief organizations—above all, the U.S. Sanitary Commission—worked tire-lessly to raise and direct enormous sums of money for this desperately needed philanthropic cause. New York led the way.

By the summer of 1863, Frederick Law Olmsted, who took time from his work as landscape architect for the city's new Central Park project to serve as the commission's general secretary, had proudly noted that the organization had already raised four million dollars "to relieve suffering among the sick & wounded of the Union." The commission's specific goals included educating the troops about health, nourishment, and sanitation; providing food, clothing, medicine, and writing material to the wounded in soldiers' convalescent homes and military hospitals; and financing direct nursing care to those injured in battle. That the U.S. Sanitary Commission pursued these objectives in the face of open hos-tility from the army's hidebound medical hierarchy made its accom-plishments all the more remarkable. By early 1864, the *New York Times* had acknowledged: "One of the most remarkable features of the present war, is the humane aspect given it by the non-combatant population of the North [who supply] comforts to the weary, shivering, bleeding sol-dier, to alleviate his distresses, to furnish balm for his wounds and linen for his sores."

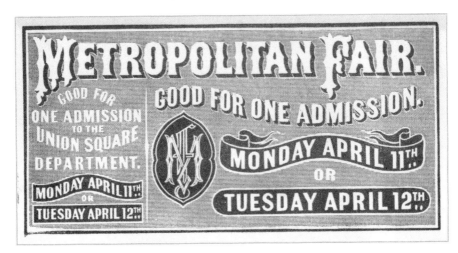

By then, Abraham Lincoln himself had become a contributor to the movement. In October 1863, the organizers of the Great Northwestern Sanitary Fair in Chicago asked the president to contribute his *"original manuscript"* of the Emancipation Proclamation to their event. Not surprisingly, the proclamation turned out to be the most valuable item donated to the Chicago charity benefit, for which Lincoln enjoyed the consolation of winning a gold watch that a Chicago jeweler had provided to reward its "largest contributor."

Other fairs attracted comparable crowds, similarly generous donations, and equally enthusiastic press coverage when they occurred in Brooklyn, Philadelphia, Cincinnati, Boston, St. Louis, Stamford, Albany, and later Baltimore. But no event of its kind produced the funds, the attendance, or the legacy generated by the Metropolitan Fair in New York City, which took place April 4–27, 1864, and raised a record total of $1.34 million for wartime relief. Altogether, the fair may have drawn more than 100,000 visitors (no one ever totaled the attendance) to its headquarters building at the extraordinarily transformed 22nd Regiment Armory and adjoining temporary structures along Sixth Avenue, a block from Union Square. It proved the biggest attraction in the city's history.

Planners decided at the outset that the New York fair must be *"national"* enough to be "worthy of the occasion, the place, and the necessity" but also *"universal"* in appeal, "enlisting all sympathies from the

PLATE 37–1

highest to the lowest." It would be "democratic, without being vulgar; elegant, without being exclusive; fashionable, without being frivolous; popular, without being mediocre . . . inspired from the higher classes" but designed to "include, and win the sympathies and interest of all classes." Goods would be made available for sale at no more than "current market value." Fine art would go on view for the enlightenment of the masses. An in-house journal would ballyhoo daily events. Punch would not be served.

The overwhelming result offered plenty to dazzle the soberest visitor. The Metropolitan Fair was a combination museum, curiosity shop, theater, state fair, sideshow, rummage sale, and mega–department store,

Ticket Office, Metropolitan Fair, New York,
stereograph by E. & H. T. Anthony & Co., 1864

PLATE 37–2

Entrance to the Grand Moving Diorama and
Miniature Battle Field, Metropolitan Fair, New York,
stereograph by E. & H. T. Anthony & Co., 1864

unquestionably the largest exposition of any kind yet organized in a single venue. Few in its throngs of visitors had seen anything quite like it. On entering the flag-festooned main pavilion through a temporary building erected in front of the armory, attendees could choose from a dizzying array of eye-catching options. One of the most popular attractions was a display in the hall of arms, trophies, and more than a thousand historic battle relics (including uniforms worn by Washington and Jackson and a drinking cup said to have been made by a heartless rebel from a Union soldier's skull after the Battle of Bull Run). Nearby stood an indoor "wigwam," complete with authentic Rocky Mountain Native Americans (few New Yorkers had ever before set eyes on an Indian) who periodically sang and performed war, scalp, and thanksgiving

PLATE 37–3

dances. A few steps away was a refreshment center that featured a restaurant serving such delicacies as turtle soup for fifty cents and porterhouse steak with mushrooms for seventy-five cents. Coffee, at an expensive fifteen cents per cup, could be accompanied by such treats as charlotte russe and meringue for a quarter dollar each. An adjacent ice-cream parlor offered vanilla or lemon at fifteen cents per scoop. Entertainment was never far away. Within yards, a spectacular fifty-horsepower steam engine imported from the Fishkill Works grandly belched out sound and fury, though signifying little except the churning of mammoth gears.

Exhibition Room, Metropolitan Fair, New York,
stereograph by the Bierstadt Brothers, 1864

PLATE 37–4

Department of Photographs & Engravings, Metropolitan Fair,
New York, stereograph by J. Gurney & Son, 1864

The vast armory drill room featured eight bins and counters offering children's clothing, hardware and furnishings, lingerie, perfumes,
sewing machines, rubber products, fine jewelry, soaps and candles,
leather products, architectural ornaments, harnesses and bridles, and
church goods abounding with a "bewildering profusion" of "afghans . . .
pincushions, tidies, and glove-boxes," all "triumphed over by wax-dolls
and fate-ladies." A cozy concert hall offered band concerts and school-
group recitals, along with a sold-out performance of *Cinderella*. Nearby,

PLATE 37–5

the visitor could enter a "curiosity shop" abounding with fossils and rare minerals or visit an autograph counter boasting signatures donated by literary and musical luminaries like Dickens, Macaulay, Thackeray, Rossini, Donizetti, and Verdi, not to mention Florence Nightingale, Garibaldi, and most of the crowned heads of Europe, Queen Victoria included.

This profusion of main-level displays all radiated from the fragrant central Floral Temple and Flower Department, which surrounded a lavish indoor fountain that somehow produced a lighting effect that resembled an ever-present ghost. Not many yards away, the braver curiosity seekers could submit themselves to a small electric shock from a new-fangled magnet. Close by stood the headquarters of the official newspaper, the *Spirit of the Fair,* and a knickknack stand featuring wax fruits, flowers, and a "wounded Zouave" doll fetchingly posed before a basket for donations.

Perhaps most dazzling of all was the cavernous art gallery "rich in pictures that had for years lurked in the seclusion of drawing rooms and private collections." In the age before public museums, the Metropolitan Fair gallery gave art lovers their greatest, and in many cases their very first, opportunity to see so large and important an exhibition of paintings—some 360 in all. The breathtaking installation boasted among its large-scale landscapes Frederic Edwin Church's *Heart of the Andes,* hung directly opposite Albert Bierstadt's equally formidable *Rocky Mountains*—with both treasures surrounded by works by the great painters of the day: Huntington, Inman, Durand, Cropsey, and Eastman Johnson. Dominating even these masterpieces was the floor-to-ceiling display of the ornately framed Emanuel Gottlieb Leutze painting *Washington Crossing the Delaware.* It took up an entire wall, but it failed to impress every viewer. A critic from the *New York Times* complained that Leutze's Washington had "the head and air of a dancing master" who looked as if he were planning to "dance a pirouette on the snow."

Occupying the armory's second floor was a library and bookstore, along with exhibits of stained glass, tapestry, and engravings and lithography. And one floor higher still was an exhibit of Mathew Brady photographs alongside a working photo studio manned by Gurney & Son, where visitors could sit for *carte-de-visite* portraits or purchase "nice

Art Gallery, Metropolitan Fair, New York,
stereograph by J. Gurney & Son, 1864

stereographic views of the Fair"—dozens of which later entered the
New-York Historical Society collections. And there was more. Featured
in adjacent wings were displays of musical instruments, international
exhibits, a science and medical display, and a "Knickerbocker Kitchen"
where Dutch-costumed volunteers demonstrated new recipes for spe-
cialties like mince pie while an "ancient darkey in the chimney corner
scraped away upon his still more ancient fiddle." For urban fairgoers cu-

PLATE 37–6

rious about rural life, a nearby structure on Seventh Avenue and Fifteenth Street offered a livestock exhibition that featured a representative population of cows, sheep, ponies, and horses, along with a 3,602-pound white ox.

The fair threw open its doors to the public on a dazzling spring day. Neighborhood residents marked the occasion by hanging flags from their windows. Music filled the streets, and military units marched to the armory for the opening ceremony. With ten thousand troops in the procession, it was the largest military display in civic history. At one point a "double line of bayonets" glistened "from Sixth to Second Avenue." The public response was strong and grew stronger. Steamboat companies whose vessels groaned with commuters and tourists heading to the event gratefully donated a share of their receipts to the fair; similarly, local rail lines sent between twenty-five hundred and five thousand dollars each in gratitude for the "enormous business" the fair generated.

Visits were costly. Patrons paid five dollars for "season tickets" to the Metropolitan Fair or fifty cents for daily entrance. By the end of its three-week run, some thirty thousand visitors had thronged the event each day, with the press fanning public interest by publishing breathless reports of its wonders almost daily. No one ever estimated how many thousands of products passed to buyers from its scores of booths and counters.

The New-York Historical Society's exceptional collection of relics and records from this unforgettable charity event includes a set of forty-eight stereographic cards of its displays; Mathew Brady's souvenir album, *Recollections of the Art Exhibition, Metropolitan Fair, New York, April 1864;* correspondence among its organizers; donor books; account ledgers; product lists; promotional broadsides; and one rare, surviving two-day ticket to the event for April 11 or 12, 1864 (plate 37–1).

Included in the trove as well are isolated copies of the long-forgotten official newspaper, *Spirit of the Fair,* in one of which its editor attempted to imagine how the city might appear one hundred years into the future—when, as it happened, another giant exposition took place in New York: the 1964 World's Fair. This is how the 1864 newspaper answered the question "How then will this city look in 1964?"

First, it will be the heart of the world, which electricity will thrill every instant with the pulses of all the earth. Midway between Asia and Europe, it will be to both their market, bank, mine, granary and library.

. . . There will be bridges across the East River, and tunnels beneath the North; and vast docks at Harlem and Brighton. A belt of marble and granite piers shall gird it. The Croton [reservoir] will be quadrupled.

The Central Park will weave secular elms, and find all its groves too small for the multitudes. Railways, or whatever succeeds them, shall thread all the depths of the island, and Broadway be but an alley. Two national holidays, the old Fourth, and that auspicious day which we shall see crowned with peace and reunion, will be exulted here by the millions.

Not all of these bold Metropolitan Fair dreams came true, but enough did become reality to remind the modern observer how much this thrilling municipal event inspired what seemed at the time to be incredibly bold aspirations for a limitless future.

38

—⦦ΘⁿΘ⦧—

The Faces of War

Photograph Album Presented to
Major M. S. Euen by Co. C, P.P.,
1860–1869

H ERE ARE THE GRIM, STIFFLY POSED VISAGES OF THE MEN WHO WENT
to war for the Union and New York—many of whom, no doubt,
never returned. Their portraits exist in this format because the armed
revolution against the Union unexpectedly coincided with a technological revolution in American photography. As a result, not only were many
of the unforgettable scenes of war recorded by some of the greatest photographic artists of the era—Mathew Brady, Timothy O'Sullivan, George
Barnard, and Alexander Gardner, among many others—but long-
forgotten enlisted men and officers who served on both sides of the conflict were able to carry pictures of their loved ones into battle and to
leave behind images of themselves in uniform so their wives, sweet-
hearts, and mothers would not forget them. Despite these dramatic
improvements, the Union inexplicably employed only one official photographer: Captain Andrew J. Russell of the 141st New York Volunteers,
who limited his work to landscapes and railroad bridges.

"The year 1861 is memorable for a revolution in pictures" is how the
editor of the *American Journal of Photography* put it at the time, noting
that "the card photograph has swept away everything before it, and is
the style to endure." By "card photograph" the observer meant the newly

PLATE 38-1

Major Eum

introduced *cartes-de-visite*, small prints the size of, and named for, visiting cards. They were taken simultaneously by a multiple-lens camera and mounted on two-and-a-half-by-four-inch cardboard. Patented in Paris by a flamboyant Frenchman named Adolphe-Eugène Disdéri—hence the Gallic appellation—the new process first took Europe by storm and then arrived in America sometime in 1860. Its appeal was instantaneous and obvious: sitters could now pose for four simultaneous images in a single exposure, quadrupling the number yielded by the suddenly outdated single-lens tintype camera. That meant a subject could retain one of the resulting prints for himself and give away three to loved ones—or, to fill albums like Euen's, to fellow members of an army regiment.

Photographers also lured celebrities into their galleries to pose free of charge for pictures they then reproduced by the thousands at significant profit—increasing the subjects' fame in return. By 1865, E. & H. T. Anthony, official distributors for Mathew Brady's vast portrait archive, advertised that their catalog had swelled to include *cartes* of 5,000 "eminent Americans," including 550 statesmen, 300 generals, 125 writers, 120 "divines," and 50 "prominent women," all priced at $1.90 per dozen, along with albums ranging in cost from fifty cents to fifty dollars. Countless families purchased and enthusiastically preserved portraits of favorite politicians, military heroes, and actors alongside images of their own families.

In 1863, Oliver Wendell Holmes would observe:

> Card portraits, as everybody knows, have become the social currency, the "green-backs" of civilization. . . . The sitters who throng to the photographer's establishment are a curious study. They are of all ages, from the babe in arms to the cold wrinkled patriarchs and dames whose smiles have as many furrows as an ancient elm has rings that count its summers. . . . Attitudes, dresses, features, hands, feet betray the social grade of the candidates for portraiture. The picture tells us no lie about them. There is no use in their putting on airs; the make-believe gentleman and lady cannot look like the genuine article. Ill-temper cannot hide itself under the simper of assumed amiability.

The *carte-de-visite* morphed from a novelty to a craze when another, unnamed innovator perfected leather albums to hold them: they featured thick multilayered leaves with open windows to display the images and a slot at the bottom of each page to insert pictures. Some included designated spaces for autographs. Their covers boasted attractive brass fastening clasps that made the larger albums look like Bibles. Indeed, in many homes, these treasured keepsakes bulging with memories became second in importance only to scripture.

Surviving undisturbed albums of the day are extremely rare—subsequent generations often removed and sold off the celebrity shots to collectors—but the Society owns this unusual presentation album, given as a gift to an otherwise unknown Civil War officer. In a tangible way, the collection reflects all the optimism and patriotism that characterized so many of the volunteers who first went off to war to save the Union.

Little is known about its original owner, Matthias Selah Euen (often misspelled "Ewan" in regimental records), except that he may have begun the war as a captain in Company C of New York's 71st, but later signed on as a captain in Company E of the 156th Infantry Regiment of volunteers drawn principally from the Hudson valley at the foot of the Catskill Mountains—hence its nickname, the Mountain Division. (Company E was organized in Plattekill, Newburgh, and surrounding towns.) According to an obituary published in the *New York Times* in 1898, Euen "served throughout the war, escaping without serious injury, and at its close was brevetted Colonel for bravery." His surviving album, which contains 119 mounted and loose images, features this gold-embossed inscription on its leather cover: "Presented to Major M. S. Euen by Co. C, P.P." It was evidently a gift from his fellow officers, and their pictures fill its pages.

Though Euen was said to have ended his association with that particular outfit early in the conflict, he evidently kept the album current during his subsequent years of military service. Most of the photographs are unsigned, and the vast majority unidentifiable. But like most owners of *carte-de-visite* albums, Euen supplemented the original collection of portraits of his extravagantly bearded, now-forgotten comrades-in-arms with easily obtainable *cartes* of public figures, which were sold by

Unidentified African American Soldier, carte-de-visite, from the Euen album, ca. 1861

newsdealers and other distributors. And these offer clues to his military loyalties and political orientations. For example, Euen included photographs of two generals under whom he probably served, George B. McClellan and Ambrose E. Burnside. Like the Lincolns, he added a *carte* of Major Robert Anderson, the commander of Fort Sumter when it fell to the Confederacy in April 1861. A picture showing a sculpted cross may have offered succor before battles.

Euen's strong sense of New York loyalty may explain his inclusion of a portrait of Secretary of State William H. Seward, a former governor of New York, while a possible hint of pro-abolitionist political sentiments might be discernible from a *carte* of the famous antislavery senator from Massachusetts, Charles Sumner. His longing for an end to the war is evident in his inclusion of the late New York–born writer John Howard

PLATE 38–2

Payne, best known for writing the song "Home, Sweet Home." Oddly, the book includes only one image of Euen himself (plate 38–1), relegated to the middle, and it also includes unexplained, thought-provoking portraits of unidentified African Americans. The album also features a *carte* of Nathaniel Banks, a onetime and future Massachusetts congressman who led a Union expedition up the Red River in Louisiana in 1864—a campaign in which Euen participated.

The 156th saw plenty of action during its three years of service beginning in November 1862. Euen and his men fought at Fort Bisland and Port Hudson, Louisiana, and, after performing garrison duty at the latter outpost, participated in the battles of Pleasant Hill, Alexandria, and Mansura during the Red River Campaign. Later reassigned to the East, the regiment confronted Jubal Early during Philip Sheridan's Shenandoah Valley Campaign, going into combat at such famous battlefields as Winchester, Fisher's Hill, and Cedar Creek. After William T. Sherman captured Savannah at Christmastime 1864, the unit joined Union occupying forces there, then marched with Sherman all the way to the Carolinas. When the final casualty tolls were calculated, the 156th New York had lost 231 men—not surprising, considering its exhausting schedule of deployments—64 in action and 167 to disease. Euen escaped unscathed—and with a tooled leather, gilt-embossed photo album in which to preserve his memories. His grandson Donald E. Morgan donated it to the Society in 1963.

Chicago Convention has nominated McClellan. That was expected. But the baseness of the "platform" on which he is to run was unexpected. Jeff-Davis might have drawn it. The word Rebel does not occur in it. It contemplates surrender & abasement. If McClellan can consent to be its representative, he condemns his name to ——— infamy. So shameful an avowal of dishonor has never been made by any political party North of the Potomac — nor even South of it. Gen —— thinks McC. will decline a nomination on such terms. We shall see. I have little faith in McClellan's principles. I could write at least a page of indignation about the insult these Chicago Resolutions have inflicted on the country. Were it not rather late, & were I not rather tired. If the People should endorse them next Nov', the country is not worth saving; the title "Citizen of the United States" is equivalent to that of Coward, fainéant, Serf & Craven, & I will emigrate, & become a citizen of some community of gregarious blue baboons in South Africa. It's a hopeful indication however that Gen: Dix (who does not love the Administration) denounces these Resolutions as shameful & scandalous. He tells me there will be no draft next Monday. So I expected. But I do not regret the $1100.00 I paid for a substitute. The big buckles-man thereon I much purchased looked as if he could do good service.

Sept: 3d   Sat: Glorious news this morning – viz: Atlanta taken at last!!! It comes in official form, seemingly most authentic, but there are doubters, who distrust it, and the appearance of no additional intelligence since morning give, a certain plausibility to their scepticism. So I suspend all jubilation for the present. If it be true it is (coming at this political crisis) the greatest event of the war. It would seem that Sherman moved to the South of Atlanta, leaving one corps to guard his communications, cutting off Hood's; that Hood thereupon also left his entrenchments, gave battle, — was beat — more or less — & that pending the battle this reserve corps walked into the beleaguered city by its back door. We shall probably know more tomorrow. God grant our first news prove true.

A very busy day. Letters, & a Complaint, Snyder v. Slocum, founded on a Contract for sale of a big lease on 5th Ave. Dined with Geo. A. at Maison dorée. Glad to learn that all but the most inveterate malignant Copperheads denounce & repudiate the Chicago Platform. Even the Herald condemns it. They say McC. will come out with a letter repudiating it, & consenting to run as an "independent candidate." This may be part of a politic scheme intended to secure the votes of both Peace & War Democrats. McClellan is in the hands of Belmont & Barlow, & I fear they can manipulate him as they please. — At U.L. Club to-night, watching for news. None came. Told OW S.B.R. that I would be glad if he could some how hint to his special friend Hon: Wash: Hunt, member of the Chicago Convention, that he was not particularly wanted as a visitor on these premises, Sunday ev'g or week days or at any time.

Sept: 5   Monday. Two days of cold Easterly storm. Thank God, the fall of Atlanta is fully confirmed. He hardly dared believe it till to day. Its importance both moral & military is immense. Hardee is said to be killed, and two less notorious Rebel generals. He is no great loss to Secession. Hood seems to have destroyed much rolling stock & stores, which he could not carry off. — We have news that the — rebel privateer Georgia has been bagged by the Niagara (her name makes the event a coincidence, for I suppose Sherman's success gives us mastery of nearly all that State) & there is some reason to fear a complication with England, as the Georgia was sailing under British colors. — Dined with Agnew after a busy day. He is over-worked, & —— or in danger of breaking down.

39

⭐

Strong Opinions

Entries from the Diary of
George Templeton Strong, 1864

ERE IS A DENSE SINGLE LEAF FROM A MASSIVE, TRULY EXCEPTIONAL archive. This one page specifically testifies to the excitement in New York that greeted a major turning point of the Civil War— Sherman's capture of Atlanta. But more important, the lengthy manuscript from which it comes is a monument to the disciplined scribe who dutifully recorded this event, just as he memorialized nearly every day of his life from his sophomore year at Columbia College in 1835 at age fifteen until three weeks before his death forty years later. His name was George Templeton Strong, and his diary is one of the most priceless Civil War treasures in the entire New-York Historical Society collection, and certainly the most rewardingly illuminating.

Not surprisingly, since so many men went off to war, nearly all of the great home-front diaries, Northern as well as Southern, were written by women. A rare exception—not to mention a universally acknowledged classic of the form—is the captivating daily journal kept by the New York attorney Strong and unpublished for nearly a century.

The printed edition lacks the startling appearance of Strong's original, meticulous jottings, which run to more than four million words filling 2,250 pages bound in four morocco volumes, each nine by fourteen inches, the unlined pages miraculously composed in a minuscule but beautifully even and legible hand in characters so tiny and densely packed that each page looks more like the Rosetta stone than a Victorian-era personal journal.

George Templeton Strong was already forty-one years old when the Civil War began and apparently too nearsighted to serve in the armed forces. He had graduated second in his class at Columbia at age eighteen, studied law with his father, a noted attorney, and then joined the elder Strong's Wall Street law firm, Strong & Bidwell—today Cadwalader, Wickersham & Taft, the oldest continually operating legal partnership in the country. Before the war, George became a trustee of Columbia College and a vestryman at Trinity Church. He was clearly a Renaissance man. Like his parents a devoted amateur musician, he mastered the piano, oboe, and viola, played from time to time in the Metropolitan Opera orchestra as a lark, and later served as president of the New York Philharmonic. His home on Gramercy Park North boasted a specially built three-manual organ so large he nicknamed it Goliath.

When war broke out, Strong performed what service he could from the wartime home front, serving first as paymaster of the New York Rifles ("only playing soldier," he admitted), then more usefully becoming treasurer of and doing "diligent service" for the U.S. Sanitary Commission and later helping to found the Union League Club. But his exemplary devotion to charitable causes, honest politics, the Union, and ultimately emancipation could hardly match his timeless contributions as a diarist, even though the public did not get a glimpse at his observations for decades. In fact, the friends who knew him best thought George a rather undemonstrative man who seldom commented about his surroundings or contemporaries. Little did they know! For all his talents, Strong might have disappeared into historical oblivion—just another well-meaning New York dilettante who avoided the military draft—had he not, every night before going to sleep, tenaciously recorded his acute and balanced observations of a rapidly changing New York as the city enthusiastically prepared for and then sometimes impatiently endured the rebellion.

Like most New Yorkers, regardless of party (the diarist was a Whig who later joined the Republicans), Strong was infuriated by the Confederate attack on Fort Sumter and enthusiastically succumbed to war fever as soon as local citizens began organizing into volunteer regiments. "Change in public feeling is marked, and a thing to thank God for," he wrote a few days after Anderson's surrender. "We begin to look like a United North." A later entry contained the fervent prayer "GOD SAVE THE UNION, AND CONFOUND ITS ENEMIES. AMEN." A sudden decline in wealth soured Strong for a time. "This is to be a terrible, ruinous war," he confided on April 23, 1861, "and a war in which the nation cannot succeed, it can never subjugate these savage millions of the South. It must make peace at last with the barbarous communities off its Southern frontier."

He regained his bearings once he committed himself to the Sanitary Commission. After digesting books about soldier health, he warned: "An epidemic of camp fever or dysentery or cholera among our volunteer regiments is inevitable within sixty days unless a sanitary system be created for them. . . . When this army is destroyed by disease, we shall have to raise another, and at a fearful cost. We cannot afford to waste life." By summer he was worried that New Yorkers were losing their enthusiasm for suppressing the rebellion: "We are not fighting in earnest, *not even yet*. Our sluggish, good-natured, pachydermatous Northern people requires a deal of kicking to beat its blood. Not a traitor is hanged after four months of rampant rebellion. We must change all this." We do not know whether he communicated these opinions as forcefully to his friends and allies as he did to his diary, if at all.

Strong approved of Lincoln's Emancipation Proclamation, but he may have underestimated its impact when he initially predicted: "It will do us good abroad, but will have no other effect." When the final proclamation took effect in January 1863, however, Strong celebrated: "The nation may be sick unto speedy death and past help from this and any other remedy, but if it is, its last great act is one of repentance and restitution." Strong denounced the draft rioters as a "purely Celtic . . . rabble," observing: "Their outbreak will either destroy the city or damage the Copperhead cause fatally. Could we but catch the scoundrels who have stirred them up, what a blessing it would be . . . agents of Jefferson Davis, permitted to work here in New York."

As part of his ongoing work for the Sanitary Commission, Strong occasionally traveled to Washington, where on one memorable morning in May 1864 he met with the forbidding, volatile, and voluble secretary of war, Edwin M. Stanton, who was no friend of civilian relief organizations (he had denounced the commission as a "swindling concern"). Strong bravely advised Stanton that if only the War Department began cooperating with the commission, it would "add fifty percent to the value and effect of every dollar we spend." By way of a response, Stanton unleashed a barrage of verbal abuse, but to Strong's delight he at least got to glimpse a surprise visitor toward the end of his interview: Abraham Lincoln.

On seeing the president for the first time back in October 1861, Strong had dismissed the "hard-featured" leader as "among the ugliest white men I have seen. Decidedly plebeian. Superficially vulgar and a snob. But not essentially. He seems to me clear-headed and sound-hearted, though his laugh is the laugh of a yahoo, with a wrinkling of the nose that suggests an affinity with the tapir and other pachyderms; and his grammar is weak." By January 1862, Strong had revised his opinion—but only somewhat—after listening to Lincoln spin frontier anecdotes with a peculiar, almost indecipherable backwoods accent. "He is a barbarian, Scythian, yahoo, or gorilla, in respect of outside polish," Strong confided to his diary, "but a most sensible, straightforward, honest old codger. The best President we have had since old Jackson's time, as I believe." Two years later, Lincoln seemed a ghost of his former robust self. This is what Strong recorded of that unforgettable May 6, 1864, encounter in Stanton's office:

> I was amazed by the discovery of our importance and that the Secretary of War keeps himself thoroughly posted as to our movements and doings. Whenever he referred to any publication, he rang in his messenger, and said, "Ben! get me so and so of the Sanitary Commission," which the faithful but seedy creature did with admirable accuracy and promptitude. He failed only once, when he brought in a copy of the *Medical Times* instead. Whereupon the Secretary damned him and sent him back, soliloquizing, as it were, *sotto voce*, "It contains another attack on me. I suppose the Commission got *that* up, *too*."

On the whole, this interview was a good thing, though without direct tangible results. We drew Stanton's fire and can estimate his weight of metal. It is not very heavy. He hates us cordially and would destroy us if he dared, but he fears our constituency. Public favor is the breath of his nostrils. He is not a first-rate man morally or intellectually. His eye is bad and cold and leaden and snakey, even when he is most excited. His only signs of ability at this conference were remarkable memory and capacity for details.

Pending our conference, the long, lean, lank figure of Uncle Abraham suddenly appeared at the door. [Cornelius] Agnew [head of the New York veterans' hospital and fellow sanitation commissioner] and I rose. Stanton didn't. Lincoln uttered no word, but beckoned to Stanton in a ghostly manner with one sepulchral forefinger, and they disappeared together for a few minutes, going into a side room and locking the door behind them. We saw Abe Lincoln in the telegraph office as we entered the office, waiting for dispatches, and no doubt, sickening with anxiety—poor old codger! But it's shameful to so designate a man who has so well filled so great a place during times so trying.

Summer 1864, however, found Strong questioning the president's chances for a second term. "The great election of next November looks more and more obscure, dubious, and muddled every day," he wrote on August 16. "Lincoln is drifting leeward. There is a rumor of a move by our wire-pullers and secret, unofficial governors to make him withdraw in favor of Salmon P. Chase, or somebody else, on whom the whole Republican party (if such a thing exist) can heartily unite." But the diarist's mood shifted dramatically during the first week of September. First, Strong found reason for hope in the Democratic Party's controversial antiwar platform, declaring of its notorious peace plank: "So shameful an avowal of dishonor has never been made by any political party north of the Potomac, nor even south of it."

The very next day came the Union military triumph that would so suddenly change the course of the war—and Lincoln's prospects for a second term. This is how Strong recorded the event—in the journal entries illustrated in plate 39–1.

Sept: 3d Sat: Glorious news this morning—viz: Atlanta taken at last*!!! It comes in official form, seemingly most authentic, but there are doubters who distrust it, and the appearance of no additional intelligence since morning gives a certain plausibility to their scepticism. So I suspend all jubilation for the present. If it be true, it is (coming at this political crisis) the greatest event of the war. . . .*

Sept: 5 Monday. . . . Thank God, the fall of Atlanta is fully confirmed. We hardly dared believe it till today. It's importance both moral & military is immense.

Two months later, Strong would greet news of Lincoln's November 8 victory by observing that "the most momentous popular election ever held since ballots were invented has decided against treason on disunion." A few months later, the diarist would join in the exuberant response to Lee's surrender at Appomattox, expressing his joy and thanks to heaven by writing in Latin, beginning with the words of the popular Christmas carol: "*Gloria in Excelsis Deo. Et in Terra, Pax hominibus bonae voluntatis*" ("Glory to God in the highest. Peace on earth and good will toward men").

At his death in 1875, the *New York Times,* entirely unaware of his copious journals, summarized George Templeton Strong's literary achievements by saying only: "Although not the author of any literary works, he contributed many articles of rare merit and essays of elaborate research to several of the leading periodicals." Even the *Times* occasionally got things wrong.

Published in four volumes in 1952 with notes and commentary by the great Civil War scholar Allan Nevins, Strong's diary enjoyed a resurrection in 1990 as a featured source in Ken Burns's hugely successful documentary on the Civil War. Voiced memorably by George Plimpton as Strong, it was for many Americans their first introduction to George Templeton Strong.

40

———— ❧❦❧ ————

Prison Art

Point Lookout Sketches, Watercolor Drawings, 1864

I
N SOME CASES, THE WAR BROUGHT OUT LATENT TALENTS AMONG
otherwise ordinary soldiers—particularly those who enjoyed months
of leisure between battles and used the time to start diaries, draw pictures of their comrades and surroundings, or transform found objects
like tree branches and human bones into carved sculptures. But perhaps
no population produced more amazing work than the men held for long
periods in Union and Confederate prison camps. Here, particularly after
the Lincoln administration suspended prisoner exchanges in mid-1862,
relegating thousands of soldiers to extended periods of captivity, those
in confinement turned to such callings as art and journalism (see chapter 45) to help pass the time.

That examples of their efforts survive comes as no surprise—
considering the sheer numbers of wartime prisoners. During the four-
year conflict, by most accounts, about 212,000 Confederates and 463,000
Union men fell into enemy hands, and since only some 265,000 were
paroled before 1862, that left more than 400,000 who were imprisoned
for the duration, resulting in starvation, exposure, sickness, or worse.
Those strong enough to endure the filthy, undersupplied, rodent-
infested, disease-ridden hellholes understandably searched for ways to
survive. Sheer creativity may have provided some of these durable men
reason to go on.

One of the most surprisingly talented and prolific of the artistic

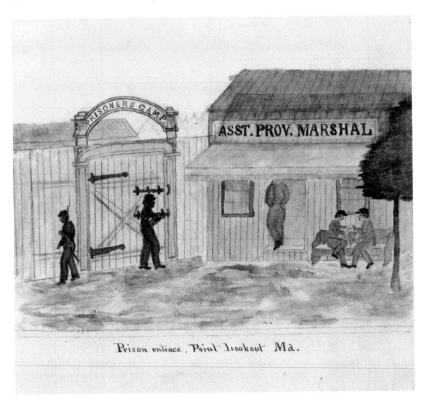

Prison entrace, Point Lookout Md.

primitives was John Jacob Omenhausser (1830–1877), a private in Company A of the 46th Virginia Infantry, who in 1864 was sent to the Union prison camp at Point Lookout, Maryland—a twenty-three-acre facility that, with as many as twenty thousand men incarcerated, was the largest in the North. At one point so many of his works began popping up in public and private collections around the country that many scholars concluded they must be the work of several different men: no single prisoner-artist, they reasoned, could possibly have produced such a huge body of work. They were wrong. The New-York Historical Society owns a portfolio containing forty-two vivid Omenhausser watercolors—later preserved and bound into a single volume by the son of James Barnes, commandant of the Point Lookout facility.

If we accept the authenticity and single authorship of all these pictures, Omenhausser was among the most prolific of all the self-taught painters

PLATE 40–1

who toiled away in Civil War prison camps: a total of 222 watercolors have been unearthed and attributed to date, not counting as many as a dozen isolated pieces that reportedly exist in other collections. The artist's surviving great-grandson, Richard Brooks, emerged around 1999 to add credence to the identification of his ancestor as the creator of all these works. Apparently, Omenhausser had been an accomplished folk artist before the war, and Brooks possessed an early landscape effort to prove it.

Omenhausser was either Austrian-born or second-generation Austrian American—sources disagree—and spent his early years with his parents in Philadelphia. The family resettled in Baltimore, but young John was left fatherless when still a child. By the 1840s, when he was still a teenager, he had begun painting—producing at least one urban street scene. Evidently, his early art did not sell. To earn a living, he became a professional candy maker. Why Omenhausser pledged his allegiance to the South no one knows for certain—it would not have been unusual in secession-minded Baltimore—but he appears to have joined the Richmond Light Infantry Blues early in the war. He was thirty or thirty-one years old. Omenhausser saw action around Big Sewell Mountain in western Virginia as part of a brigade commanded by the former Virginia governor General Henry A. Wise. In November 1861, Omenhausser, a recent widower, wrote to a female friend: "Enclosed you will find a true picture of camp life, and its mess that cooks together that I belong to and by their clothing you will see that we are not fit to stand much cold weather. It being such a true picture of camp life. I had to draw a great many of them for members of our company and others of the regiment. The Co's says it is a very good picture, some of them have been sent to different parts of the southern Confederacy, as far south as New Orleans."

Omenhausser subsequently fought in North Carolina, where he fell into the hands of Union troops, but he was almost immediately paroled to Richmond, a town he came to like. He proved less lucky when he returned to active service. On June 15, federal soldiers again captured an injured Omenhausser near Petersburg, Virginia. By this time, prisoner exchanges had ceased. The following month, he wrote to his lady friend to report: "I was left crippled on the Battle field of the 15th at a time that our men retreated from the breastworks, and was captured by the enemy. I expect you and my company all thought that I was Kill'd. I was captured by black soldiers, and did not expect any quarters, but god ordained it otherwise." Omenhausser remained confined at Point Lookout for more than a year.

Like most prisons, Point Lookout had too little food and too many malicious or corrupt overseers. Confederate prisoners were no doubt particularly galled to discover that most of their armed guards were African American. Prisons were often governed not only by abusive keepers but by self-appointed inmate gangs. On the other hand, many prisoners seemed to prefer life in captivity to life with the army. Hearing that they might be paroled in October 1863, a group of captives at Point Lookout actually petitioned authorities not to be returned to the rebel army. Some claimed they had been coerced to join the Confederate army in the first place, one such Point Lookout prisoner insisting that "it never was our intention that we should fight against the united States to support a rotten government for Jeff Davis." Another offered not only to take the oath of allegiance to the Union but even to join the federal army—if, as he scrawled, he could be "plaste whear thar will be no danger of falling in to the hands of the Confederate rebs."

Omenhausser himself did little such complaining. Instead, he spent his time writing poems and letters to his lady—with whom he reached an understanding about future marriage—and creating his thick portfolio of watercolors, no doubt to the wonder of the other inmates. Conceivably, he used some of the portraits as gifts to his fellow prisoners or perhaps traded them in lieu of payment for special consideration or extra rations. Judging from the Omenhausser works in the Historical Society portfolio, it appears that every convenience at Point Lookout cost something extra, be it jewelry, souvenirs, or perhaps art.

The Historical Society's unfailingly compelling pencil, ink, and watercolor works by Omenhausser cover a wide range of prison-life experience, from the facility's front gates to its inner workings. Omenhausser certainly knew how to tell a story and compose a picture, and he neatly balanced landscape with what passed for portraiture, almost always evocatively or amusingly presented. Thus his *Prisoners Post Office* shows not only inmates depositing mail in crude wooden boxes but also a broadly caricatured African American guard looming on patrol nearby. A crowded, almost Bosch-like scene at the prisoners' cookhouse focuses not on the revolting food but on a brawl erupting between prisoners over spilled—or thrown—soup. And a view of the prison schoolhouse is enlivened by a small image of a soldier in the foreground pumping water from a well while "students" lounge in the doorway, perhaps a subtle reminder that mere sustenance remained far more vital to prisoners than education. Omenhausser's depiction of the prison hospital, at first glance little more than a rendering of a series of cabins on stilts, is enhanced by the inclusion of the tiny figure of an amputee on crutches hobbling from its entranceway.

A fellow prisoner was probably referring to Omenhausser's work when he recorded in his diary in December 1864 that an inmate at Point Lookout was producing "some very amusing caricatures, or cartoons, depicting the humorous side of prison life." Indeed, Omenhausser often employed the device of voice balloons to provide comic dialogue for his little scenes. Thus, a view of nine prisoners heading off "to Swallow the Oath" offers a wry glimpse into the reluctant oath takers' attitudes as well, with one uneasy and resentful prisoner telling another, "If you push by me again I'll break your head," while another crouches in a corner scratching his insect-pocked leg, muttering: "I wonder what makes this place so lousy."

In Omenhausser's world, clever prisoners made the best of deprivation: inventive prisoners trade silver rings for soup crackers, somehow bake and sell pies and biscuits, brew and imbibe corn beer, stir ugly stews of rat liver hash, and hawk every kind of nourishment available from the land or water, from "appels" and "potators" to Maryland crabs and watermelon. They craft and sell paper fans to sunbaked Union officers and offer homemade molasses to starving comrades—at a price, of course.

Although Point Lookout was located on the southern tip of Maryland's St. Mary's County on a small tongue of land at the confluence of the Potomac River and the Chesapeake Bay, it was evidently never completely isolated from civilization. One Omenhausser scene shows an unscheduled inspection—we can surmise this because one of the prisoners has his shirt off in front of a lady—with hostile prisoners mocking the female visitor who had come "to see the sights." In yet another of the artist's clever and affecting scenes, a prison barber offers shaves in return for two crackers, and a half-naked prisoner unself-consciously launders his trousers in a cauldron of boiling water.

Omenhausser's subjects are feisty, rowdy, and irreverent (characters are constantly shouting epithets like "Go to the devil"). Their "sports" activities consist of gambling with handmade dice or cards. They bathe on the beach in sight of a Union gunboat and resentfully endure the evident humiliation of being supervised by black guards. Omenhausser's African American soldiers are invariably presented as racist stereotypes who speak in minstrelish dialect and are easily cheated or confused by their "superior" prisoners. "Git away from dat dar fence white man," commands one armed soldier in a typical print, rifle raised, "or I'll make Old Abe's Gun smoke at you. I can hardly hold de ball back now. De bottom rails on top now." In another such scene, Omenhausser expressed his obvious doubts about his guards' competence with firearms—a frequent, if inaccurate, canard about black soldiers—by suggesting that one African American had accidentally shot and killed one of his comrades. "Git up, Abram," the guard pleads to his prostrate, bleeding friend, "and don't act Possum . . . don't make a fool of your self, don't you see de white folk's laughing at you—for de Lord I believes the nigger dead for Sartain."

As for himself, an evidently stubborn Omenhausser never took the oath of allegiance to the Union—even after Lee's surrender. Instead, he remained a prisoner at Point Lookout until June 1865, then moved to Richmond, returned to his prewar occupation as a confectioner, married his faithful wartime fiancée, and died young of cancer in 1877. He left no known evidence of further artistic efforts.

When Point Lookout's remaining prisoners were removed from the camp at war's end in 1865, some, thirty-five hundred men were still behind its walls.

41

━◆◎◎◆━

Tribute from a Bad Man?

Colored Troops Before Richmond,
Engraved Silver, 1864–1865

ONTROVERSY STILL SWIRLS AROUND MAJOR GENERAL BENJAMIN Franklin Butler. It followed him through the war, dogged him during Reconstruction, and continues to haunt his reputation. He was, without question, an indifferent, if not entirely inept, field commander, and in the South he was excoriated for alleged corruption, especially as the officer in charge of occupied New Orleans. More recently, however, scholars have come to acknowledge his pioneering efforts to promote black freedom and later equality.

A Democrat before the war, Butler had not only opposed Lincoln for the presidency in 1860 but cast his vote at the Democratic convention for one Jefferson Davis of Mississippi. When Stephen A. Douglas prevailed instead, Butler backed the Southern Democrat John C. Breckinridge of Kentucky for the White House. Butler even ran unsuccessfully on the Breckinridge ticket for governor of Massachusetts.

Lincoln nevertheless appointed Butler a major general in the Union army, mainly because he needed the support of anti-secession War Democrats. Because Butler was one of the first generals named in the war, he was senior to many of the professional soldiers with whom he served. For the rest of the war, Lincoln had to find him assignments where his seniority did not give him the command of major Union armies. It did

not help that he was manifestly ugly, practically grotesque. Admire him or loathe him, he was one of the unique characters of the era. Whatever his shortcomings on the battlefield, the Civil War truly radicalized Benjamin Butler where race was concerned.

Born in New Hampshire in 1818, Butler lost his father to yellow fever when he was only five months old, and he grew up shuttled back and forth between relatives. Not until the age of ten was he reunited with his struggling, widowed mother, who had opened a boardinghouse in Lowell, Massachusetts. Short, stocky, homely, pugnacious, and cursed with an incurable eye defect that made him appear constantly to be squinting, Butler managed to graduate from Colby College, then studied law and launched a successful criminal practice that rapidly expanded from

PLATE 41–1

Lowell to Boston. An early and ardent supporter of banking reforms and shorter working hours for laborers, Butler next turned to politics, winning election to the Massachusetts state assembly as a Democrat in 1853 and to the state senate in 1859. Meanwhile, he invested his money wisely in a profitable new Lowell woolen mill.

Though he had supported conservative Southern Democrats for national office, when war broke out, Butler, a brigadier in the state militia mainly for its social cachet, immediately demonstrated his loyalty to the Union (and his own self-interest). He not only organized a regiment of Massachusetts militia, he saw to it that its men were outfitted in brand-new woolen overcoats purchased from Butler's own factory. Federal officials overlooked such conflicts of interest because the Lincoln administration desperately needed loyal and well-known Democrats—"political generals," they came to be called—in the volunteer army. It could not be a Republican fight alone.

Butler stirred up controversy almost immediately. On one hand, he became the first Union commander to reach Washington with his troops and unlock the capital from its isolation after the Baltimore riots of April 1861. On the other hand, it was Butler who announced that he would imprison any Maryland legislator who attempted to take the state out of the Union—arousing the enmity of many residents, including the Baltimore artist Adalbert Johann Volck (see chapter 26). Butler's flamboyant and, some said, illegal gestures included taking possession of the state seal so that a secession ordinance, if it passed, could not be officially stamped.

Although the commanding general Winfield Scott was outraged to learn that Butler had decided to occupy Baltimore without proper orders, Lincoln demonstrated his gratitude the next month by making Butler the first volunteer commander to earn the rank of major general. Butler betrayed his ineptitude almost immediately when his forces were humiliated at the Battle of Big Bethel, Virginia, in June. Assigned to a quieter command at Fort Monroe, Virginia, Butler quickly raised eyebrows—and made history—by welcoming, and giving an appealing new name to, the African American "contrabands of war" who began seeking refuge at his headquarters. Butler not only set a precedent by deciding to shelter these black refugees and to assign them to work at the fort despite protest by their owners, he made news in other fields by introducing such novelties as reconnaissance balloons and Gatling guns to his command.

In May 1862, Butler finally earned a new field assignment, taking an army all the way to New Orleans. He entered the city as its conqueror, even though the Union victory there had in fact been accomplished by naval forces under David G. Farragut. What followed, to put it mildly, was a stormy occupation. As military governor, Butler imposed martial law and infamously threatened to treat any angry New Orleans female who hurled verbal abuse at Union soldiers as "a woman of the town plying her avocation." The ungentlemanly order appalled residents, inspired his onetime political favorite Jefferson Davis to suggest he should be executed, and earned the general the nickname Beast Butler. Meanwhile, Butler's hard hand effectively reduced confrontations on New Orleans's streets. Sanitary conditions also improved, and yellow fever epidemics abated.

However effective in some areas, Butler imposed what some occupants protested was a reign of terror in New Orleans. When a pro-Confederate local gambler tore down an American flag and dragged it through the streets, for example, the general ordered him hanged. Butler bullied, menaced, and allegedly purloined funds from foreign consulates, triggering more than one diplomatic crisis. Locals whispered that he also plundered silverware from nearby homes. The jury is still out on whether or not Butler actually stole treasure or took bribes. He certainly left New Orleans wealthier than when he arrived, and at the very least he allowed his brother to enrich himself during his regime by selling banned goods on the river and conducting an illicit business in trade permits. Reports of these abuses brought increased pressure on Lincoln, and the president yielded in late 1862, replacing Butler with General Nathaniel Banks.

Butler's last field command was as the general in charge of the army-navy assault on Wilmington, North Carolina, in December 1864. After the explosion of a bomb vessel and a heavy naval bombardment, Butler declared that the rebel fort had not been sufficiently weakened to ensure a successful assault, and he reembarked his troops. Grant was furious and replaced him with another general, Alfred H. Terry, who captured the fort in January 1865. Butler resigned from the army and ran for Congress, this time as a Republican, and spent the postwar years arguing for tough Reconstruction policies and black voting rights in the South.

Though he became a champion in the struggle to extend rights to African Americans in peacetime, Butler's true epiphany may have come during wartime with the Army of the James, when in late September 1864 he admiringly observed troops from an all-black regiment fighting at New Market Heights near the Confederate capital. USCT regiments made up only a fifth of Butler's force during that two-day struggle but lost more than half of their men. In unexpected recognition of their valor, Butler commissioned the assistant engraver of the U.S. Mint, Anthony C. Paquet (1814–1882), to design a medal in their honor. He did so—as usual—without permission from higher authorities.

The obverse of the resulting medal shows two soldiers in high relief charging a Confederate position under a scroll reading "*FERRO IIS LIBERTAS PERVENIET*" ("Freedom Will Be Theirs by the Sword"). Below the action scene are the words "U.S. COLORED TROOPS" and "BUTLER DEL. PAQUET, F" (the credit line that indicates Butler wanted personal credit for the design). The reverse side features a wreath of oak leaves amid the legends "DISTINGUISHED FOR COURAGE" and "CAMPAIGN BEFORE RICHMOND 1864." A Boston company created the ribbons and fasteners.

The so-called Butler Medal, sometimes called the Army of the James Medal, is the only award of its kind created during the Civil War to mark a specific battle or celebrate a specific regiment. It is a memento not only of the bravery of the U.S. Colored Troops before Richmond but of the ever-audacious Benjamin Butler's remarkable wartime conversion from supporter of the white supremacist Jefferson Davis to white supremacy's worst nightmare. Butler used personal funds to strike the 197 silver and 11 bronze copies of the Army of the James Medal and took the opportunity to present many of them to veterans of the action personally. He also sent one to the Oxford University historian Goldwin Smith, who had observed the Army of the James in action in 1864. Butler accompanied the gift with a proud note: "I venture to send to you . . . the first medal ever struck in honor of the negro soldiers by the white man." The Society acquired its own silver copy of the extremely rare Butler Medal by purchase in 2011 from the widow of the furniture maker Duncan Phyfe's great-grandson. Surviving records offer no clue to how the family of a prominent white cabinetmaker came into possession of the war's most famous token of esteem for black soldiers.

Not that it should have surprised any of his contemporaries that Butler might act independently, but in his 1892 autobiography the general finally offered an explanation for what inspired him to create and finance this consummate expression of generosity and gratitude. As Butler put it:

> I had the fullest reports made to me of the acts of individual bravery of colored men on that occasion, and I had done for the negro soldiers, by my own order, what the government has never done for its white soldiers—I had a medal struck of like size, weight, quality, fabrication, and intrinsic value with those which Queen Victoria gave to her distinguished private soldiers of the Crimea. . . . These I gave by my own hand, save where the recipient was in a distant hospital wounded, and by the commander of the colored corps after it was removed from my command, and I record with pride that in that single action there were so many deserving that it called for a presentation of nearly two hundred. Since the war I have been fully rewarded by seeing the beaming eye of many a colored comrade as he drew his medal from the innermost recesses of his concealment.

As usual, not all of his fellow commanders shared Benjamin Butler's enthusiasm or embraced his methods. The two hundred soldiers who received these unsanctioned medals were never allowed to wear them on their uniforms. Butler's superior officers had the last laugh, delegitimizing a gesture of genuine beauty because it came from the hands of a "Beast."

42

—◦◦◦—

Political Dirty Tricks

The Miscegenation Ball, Lithograph, 1864

Few americans of the civil war generation doubted that the 1864 presidential campaign—often called the most important election in history—would ultimately boil down to the incendiary issue of race, at least in the tinderbox of New York City. In the metropolis where a draft riot had escalated into a race riot just one year earlier, the pro-Democratic, anti-emancipation newspaper the *New York World* produced several pieces of provocative evidence to testify to this ugly race-based strategy for defeating Lincoln and the Republicans and hopefully overturning his 1863 proclamation.

Most newspapers of the day openly aligned with one political party or the other and made no secret of their orientation. There was never any question of the *World*'s antipathy toward Abraham Lincoln. The paper had opposed him editorially ever since the beginning of the Civil War, excoriating him as a dictator, challenging the constitutionality of the military draft, and reserving particularly virulent attacks for the president's Emancipation Proclamation. Not long before his quest for reelection, Lincoln had further ensured the *World*'s enmity by personally ordering the paper shut down and its editor Manton Marble arrested. This occurred after the *World* published—innocently, it always unconvincingly maintained—an obviously forged presidential order calling for an additional 500,000 volunteers for the Union army. The administration believed that the hoax was calculated to ignite a run on

PLATE 42–1

stocks, after which insider traders, advised of the scheme in advance, would buy low and then profit enormously once prices recovered after the order for more troops was revealed as a fabrication. In other words, Lincoln believed the *World* had done more than act maliciously; it had acted fraudulently as well.

But the *World* had more than a persecution complex where Lincoln was concerned. In the view of its white supremacist editors, his reelection would do nothing less than undermine the rights of the country's white majority. It would encourage Republicans to create a repugnantly integrated society and supposedly result in a humiliating loss of jobs and status for its loyal readers, many of them Irish American Catholics who had already made their fears violently manifest during the previous summer's rioting. As the presidential campaign got under way, the *World* made its hatred for Lincoln clear enough in its editorial columns, charging the president with plotting to use a second term to establish a mixed-race society in which black men would be free to marry white women, and black masters would employ white servants. Even for this period of unprecedented partisanship, however, the *World* forged unusual alliances by campaigning against Lincoln through other genres, including book and picture publishing, that had long remained separate from the politically charged world of newspapers.

In one example, the *World* collaborated with a New York printmaker to issue a series of venomous cartoons that played to the racial fears of white voters. It is important to remember that most engravings and lithographs of the period, including politically inspired caricatures, were issued by nonpartisan entrepreneurs like Currier & Ives, who sought to profit from customers of all political persuasions. The racially charged series that appeared under the sponsorship of the *World* was unique. No one is absolutely certain how the resulting poster cartoons were displayed during the Civil War era. Too crude to adorn private homes like the concurrently mass-produced heroic portraits and battle scenes, these caricatures were probably toted in parades, affixed to outdoor walls, tacked up in political clubhouses, or laughed over in taverns. A broadside advertising them in 1864 emphasized their appeal to "the Democratic Social Circle"—whatever that was. The anti-Lincoln *World* series focused almost exclusively on race and was meant in particular to arouse fears that black men would soon be engaging in sexual relations with white women—just the kinds of charges that invariably triggered the most violent fear and hatred.

One particularly distasteful, but enormously revealing, example of the *World's* unrepentantly racist anti-Lincoln campaign is a colorful lithograph in the Society's collection, *The Miscegenation Ball*, published specifically for the presidential contest by the local firm of Bromley & Company. The result was more than a mere cartoon. This print purported to provide an accurate depiction of an event allegedly held at New York's Lincoln Central Campaign Club on Broadway and Twenty-third Street on September 22, 1864—perhaps not accidentally the second anniversary of the Preliminary Emancipation Proclamation. The *World* had reported that after a brief official meeting at the club, organizers had cleared the room so Lincoln supporters, including "prominent men," could cavort with black women at a scandalous "negro ball." Quoting the paper's toxic coverage of the alleged event, the print's caption assured viewers: "This fact WE CERTIFY, *that on the floor during the progress of the ball were many of the accredited leaders of the Black Republican party*, thus testifying their faith by their work in the hall and headquarters of their political gathering. There were Republican OFFICE-HOLDERS and prominent men of various degrees, and at least one PRESIDENTIAL ELECTOR ON THE REPUBLICAN TICKET." The lithograph portrayed mixed-race couples dancing or embracing indecently on the sidelines, while astonished white eyewitnesses peer onto the shocking scene from a skylight above. Gracing the hall in the distance is a portrait of Lincoln himself—his image here meant to imply he had somehow blessed the outrageous affair.

The Miscegenation Ball was but one of a series of Bromley & Company campaign lithographs issued that autumn in an effort to incite voter Negrophobia. In one similar attack, Lincoln was shown bowing to a mixed-race couple on the street and, in yet another, being thrown from a train wreck labeled "The Abolition Catastrophe" after crashing into the "obstructions of Emancipation, Confiscation, [and] Public Debt," according to an advertisement of the day also in the New-York

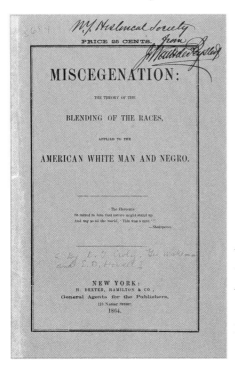

Miscegenation: The Theory of the Blending of the Races, Applied to the American White Man and Negro, pamphlet, 1864

Historical Society collection. Alone among these prints, *The Miscegenation Ball* was designed by a truly gifted printmaking outfit: the Canal Street firm of Kimmel & Forster, specialists in sporting and genre scenes, whose participation probably reflected no political bias—only a strong profit motive. A typical printmaker for hire, Kimmel & Forster issued pro-Lincoln lithographs as well. *The Miscegenation Ball* was an exception in its otherwise bland, though proficient, catalog. It was a picture meant to inflame racial tensions at the expense of truth—the equivalent of a twenty-first-century unfounded blog or tweet, except that a major daily newspaper masterminded it.

Around the same time the *Miscegenation Ball* calumny took hold, it should be noted, a brave black woman from New York made her own dramatic gesture toward equality. Mrs. Ellen Anderson, a Sabbath school teacher, got word in June 1864 that her husband, William, had been killed in action while serving as a sergeant in the 26th Colored Regiment. A few days later, Mrs. Anderson attempted to ride in the whites-

PLATE 42–2

only car of the Eighth Avenue railroad. A policeman was summoned to remove her, but Mrs. Anderson asked to be left where she was: she had just lost her husband, she explained, and she was "sick and wished" only "to ride up home." When the police officer insisted she leave at once, Mrs. Anderson tried pointing out that she had paid her fare and "had a right to ride anywhere." Unconvinced, the officer tried hauling her out of her seat, but Mrs. Anderson grabbed a strap and hung on. Not until a second officer was summoned was she dragged from the train as a crowd of apathetic spectators looked on. Mrs. Anderson ultimately retained counsel and pursued the matter legally; her courage helped desegregate New York's transit system. And it forcibly demonstrated that blacks would resist discrimination even if papers like the *New York World* tried to deflect their movement with diversions like the so-called scandal of the purported "miscegenation ball."

But the threatening idea of integration proved hard to eradicate. Surely the most hideous testimony to its intractable hold on the public imagination is evident in the form of another *World*-inspired product from the 1864 campaign: a seventy-two-page booklet titled *Miscegenation: The Theory of the Blending of the Races, Applied to the American White Man and Negro,* published that same year by the Manhattan firm of H. Dexter, Hamilton. Crafted as a wholly serious political document in an age in which pamphlets were regarded as important devices for the advancement of political philosophy, *Miscegenation* openly advocated the "blending of the white and black races on this continent" to achieve a fairer society. An innocent reader perusing its pages would be greeted with a laborious, if earnest, defense of what was for its time a radical fringe idea—racial equality—without ever realizing that it was designed as a deadpan, tongue-in-cheek farce. Scientific facts were presented along with supportive data from history and quotations from Shakespeare. The publication not only advocated racial amalgamation—in other words, interracial sex—which most whites of the day found appalling; it first proposed the entirely new word to describe it: "miscegenation," from the Latin *miscere* (to mix) and *genus* (race).

Most readers never realized that the uncredited pamphlet was actually the work of the New York *World* correspondents David G. Croly and

George Wakeman, whom London's *Morning Herald* once described, in something of an understatement, as "obstinate Democrats in politics." Not content with merely perpetrating the hoax, the authors dispatched complimentary copies anonymously to a number of the country's leading black and white antislavery men, accompanied by letters encouraging their endorsements—or what modern publishers call blurbs.

Signing their letters only "Author of 'Miscegenation,'" Croly and Wakeman actually sent one copy to Abraham Lincoln at the White House, reporting to him that the book had already sold thousands of copies and that its "leading ideas" had been "warmly endorsed by the progressive men of the country." Now the correspondents brazenly asked the president for permission to "dedicate it to your excellency."

"I am aware that the subject creates prejudice among depraved and ignoble minds," the audacious cover letter continued, "but I am sure that you in common with the foremost men of our age and time can see no other solution of the negro problem than the gradual and certain blending of the two races." The letter ended by flattering Lincoln for "giving liberty to four millions of human beings" during his first term and expressing the hope "that the next four years may find these freedmen possessed of all the rights of citizenship and recognized as one of the elements that will enter into the emancipation of the future American race." The perpetrators of the *Miscegenation* caper clearly hoped that Lincoln would fall for the scheme and reply with an acknowledgment they could reprint and circulate widely to prove to voters that the president indeed harbored integrationist sympathies. Such a charge could doom his reelection chances.

But Lincoln apparently saw through the hoax and remained silent. "This 'dodge' will hardly succeed," London's *Morning Herald* reported when it learned about the affair, proceeding to boast—in an insensitive acknowledgment of the racial prejudices reigning even among the president's supporters—"Mr. Lincoln is shrewd enough to say nothing on the unsavory subject."

Abraham Lincoln never commented on the episode publicly. Instead, he pasted the endorsement request onto the inside cover of his copy of *Miscegenation* and simply filed it away. His copy was discovered years later among the Lincoln papers donated by the president's son to the Library of Congress and not opened to historians until 1947.

Whether the New-York Historical Society's copy was one of the "thousands" actually sold to unsuspecting 1864 voters or an archival copy deposited as a curiosity is not known. But it remains one of the earliest examples of the political "dirty trick" in the collection—or on record—the ancestor of today's anonymous negative political advertising on television. It serves also as a reminder that while Civil War battles continued to rage, politics and race were never out of the national conversation.

Abraham Lincoln won reelection in November 1864. But he was overwhelmingly defeated in New York City.

FOR PRESIDENT,

ABRAHAM LINCOLN.

FOR VICE PRESIDENT,

ANDREW JOHNSON.

THE UNION AND THE CONSTIT

PLATE 43–1

43

~~~oⱰⱰ~~~

Lincoln's Worst Mistake?

Campaign Flag, 1864

ABRAHAM LINCOLN HAD LITTLE INFLUENCE OVER THE CHOICE OF A running mate when he was first, and unexpectedly, nominated for the presidency in 1860. In the mid-nineteenth century, delegates made such decisions on their own. Conceiving of Lincoln as a quintessential westerner, delegates to the Republican National Convention meeting in Chicago that year concluded that they must have an easterner for the vice presidency. They turned to Hannibal Hamlin, an antislavery senator from as far east as the map would allow: Maine. Neither man attended the convention, and neither could recall that they had ever shaken hands.

Two weeks later, the nominee headed to Chicago to meet the man with whom he would share the national ticket. At the city's Tremont House hotel, Lincoln and Hamlin exchanged greetings for the first time. Lincoln remarked that he had once heard his new running mate give an antislavery speech in the Senate. Hamlin remembered Lincoln delivering an oration in the House "so full of good humor and sharp points," he recalled, that it left him "convulsed with laughter." But when Lincoln asked if they had ever been formally introduced to each other, Hamlin thought for a moment and then replied: "No, sir; I think not." They were not expected to work together.

Such was the reigning tradition of the day, and to his credit Lincoln tried for a while to reform it. He spent the rest of his Chicago trip conferring with Hamlin on the pressing issue of Cabinet selection. Then, three months later, when he planned his inaugural journey, he arranged to meet Hamlin in New York so they could proceed to Washington together as a team. In Manhattan, the vice president–elect even stood in once for Lincoln, delivering a speech at their New York hotel following an especially exhausting late night at the opera. Otherwise, Hamlin stayed in the background.

Once Lincoln began his term on March 4, Hamlin had little further to do with the administration. Vice presidents of the day remained firmly tied to the legislative, not the executive, branch of government. Unlike today's vice presidents, they had no White House office of their own, attended no Cabinet meetings, and certainly enjoyed no routine luncheons or regularly scheduled briefings with the chief executive. In popular prints of the day showing crowded receptions at the mansion, Hamlin is nowhere to be seen—conspicuously absent, like nearly all of his predecessors. He had served his purpose as a candidate.

When news of the proclamation's announcement finally reached him, poor Hamlin was home in Maine and could do no more than write an ardent fan letter, congratulating Lincoln for what he predicted would "stand as the great act of the age," and adding confidently: "It will be enthusiastically approved and sustained, and future generations will, as I do, say God bless you for this great and noble act." In what he labeled a "Strictly private" reply, a deeply worried Lincoln confided, "My expectations are not as sanguine," admitting in an anguished, justly famous letter: "It is six days old, and while commendation in newspapers and by distinguished individuals is all that a vain man could wish, the stocks have declined, and troops come forward more slowly than ever. This, looked soberly in the face, is not very satisfactory." That exchange ended all known communications between Abraham Lincoln and Hannibal Hamlin on matters of substance.

By the time Lincoln stood for renomination less than two years later, few party professionals gave Hamlin a second thought as a serious candidate for another run as vice president, whatever his real or imagined experiences during the run-up to Lincoln's most historic act. Party politics still mattered most, and the exquisite art of ticket balancing remained the highest priority. Hamlin, Republicans concluded, simply no longer fit the bill. Like the proverbial bee, he had stung once in 1860 and now was dead. By then, Lincoln was known more as a Northern man than as a western man, and when it redesignated itself the National Union Party, the Republican organization looked for an anti-secession Southerner to balance the 1864 ticket. The choices were limited. Only one Southern senator had refused to leave his post during the formation of the Confederacy. Only one had remained fully loyal to the Union, albeit no friend of the African American. Though otherwise untested, Andrew Johnson of Tennessee had the potential to fill a political need.

The extent of Lincoln's involvement in the switch to Johnson from Hamlin, if any, has been much debated but never proven. One of his private secretaries, William Osborn Stoddard, later claimed in memoirs written only for the eyes of his children that Lincoln in fact dispatched him to the Baltimore convention to make sure that Johnson indeed won the coveted spot on the ticket for vice president. "I had somehow strengthened my idea that Lincoln did not want Hamlin, and that he had been leaning toward Johnson," Stoddard recalled. If such was indeed the case, it may rank as the worst political mistake Abraham Lincoln ever made. But presidents seldom consider their own mortality, even now, and Lincoln had no good reason to imagine he might soon be killed and succeeded by his vice president—even though he had received plenty of letters that threatened otherwise.

On paper, Johnson seemed a good political fit. Born in North Carolina and raised in eastern Tennessee, he had opened a tailor shop before he even knew how to read, a skill he did not learn until his fiancée gave him instruction. Nonetheless, he became mayor of Greeneville at a young age, went on to the state senate, then Congress, became governor of Tennessee in 1853, and a U.S. senator in 1857. Lincoln rewarded Johnson's loyalty by naming him military governor of Tennessee once Union forces took control of the state in 1862. Like most settlers from the eastern part of his state, Johnson disliked slavery, but he was deeply racist and, some hinted, too fond of drink as well. Stoddard thought he had a "not very good temper."

In another bow to tradition, neither candidate did any direct campaigning for the ticket in 1864. Johnson came to think of himself as so isolated from the administration he was about to join that he wrote to the president in January asking to be excused from attending the inauguration, since Tennessee was scheduled soon to vote on abolishing slavery. Besides, the state would be choosing a new governor the day of the inaugural ceremonies, March 4. Lincoln rejected Johnson's proposal, and the newly elected vice president reluctantly made his way to Washington. When the ceremony was over, Lincoln may have wished he had permitted Johnson to remain in Nashville. Johnson's drunken behavior at his inaugural—whether or not it was the result of too much alcohol-laced medicine to combat a cold—mortified the entire audience, the president included. Six weeks later, Lincoln was dead and Johnson was president. Stoddard, the clerk who claimed he had advocated for Johnson at the 1864 convention on Lincoln's instructions, later admitted both pride and regret in the result. "But for me," he insisted, Johnson "would never have been President and would never have been so dreadfully impeached."

Although the 1864 Lincoln-Johnson campaign inspired its share of broadsides, pictures, and tokens, they were no match in quantity for the avalanche of graphics that abounded during the four-way presidential race four years earlier. By 1864, Lincoln no longer needed the artist's help in introducing himself to a national public that had hardly heard of him; Johnson, too, had achieved a degree of fame. Prints and other homespun work faced increased competition from the growing proliferation of *carte-de-visite* photographs. Publishers spent more time on cartoons and caricatures, along with pictorial commentary on the Emancipation Proclamation.

Nonetheless, the Society owns a number of beautifully preserved pieces of 1864 campaign ephemera, including a large Lincoln-Johnson poster and a rare lantern containing a portrait of the president. But perhaps the most unusual of all these surviving relics suggests that not every Lincoln enthusiast appreciated the switch in running mates or thought the substitution important enough to trigger the purchase of a new campaign banner. In the Historical Society collection is the American flag in plate 43–1, originally affixed to which are the names of Lincoln and Hamlin, the Republican standard-bearers of 1860, though Hamlin's name is now invisible. The banner was no doubt tailored for the hurrah campaign before the war, when New Yorkers marched in parades jubilantly waving flags and banners. For the more subdued 1864 contest, the flag's owners decided to repair rather than replace. As this surviving flag shows, they simply covered Hamlin's name with Johnson's. The letters that spelled out the alliterative name of Lincoln's first vice president still linger like a ghostly shadow under close scrutiny and bright light—neither of which, in subsequent years, Andrew Johnson proved able to withstand.

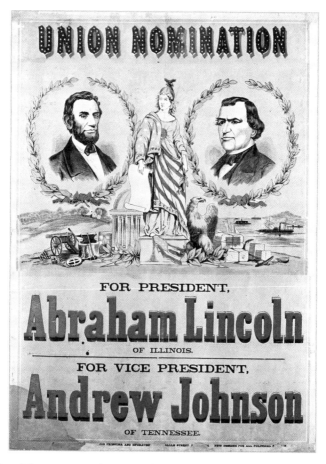

Union Nomination for President, Abraham Lincoln of Illinois.
For Vice President, Andrew Johnson of Tennessee,
election poster, 1864

PLATE 43–2

War Department
Washington City

Genl. McClellan		Abraham Lincoln 186	
New - York	33	New. England	39
Pennsylvania	26	Michigan	8
New Jersey	7	Wisconsin	8
Delaware	3	Minesota	4
Maryland	7	Iowa	8
Missouri	11	Oregon	3
Kentucky	11	California	5
Illinois	16	Kansas	3
	114	Indiana	13
		Ohio	21
		W. Virginia	5
			117

written in Mr. Stanton's
Room

    This is in the President's hand writing and purport
to be the probable result of the vote of the several states
in the November election, and was written about
the first week in October 1864 and prior to the
October election in the states of Penna. Ohio
and Indiana — A.E.H.S.

44

———⟨⟨⟩⟩———

Counting Votes, Lincoln's Way

Projection of November 1864 Election,
Abraham Lincoln, 1864

ABRAHAM LINCOLN'S PRIVATE SECRETARIES AND LATER BIOGRA-
phers John G. Nicolay and John M. Hay admired many things
about their boss, but one of the skills they esteemed most, yet discussed
least, was the president's remarkable acumen as a vote counter. Long before computerized record keeping and political track polling, Lincoln
seemed uncannily able to comprehend, retain, and analyze even the
most fragmented early voting trends.

"He was completely at home among election figures," marveled Nicolay and Hay. "All his political life he had scanned tables of returns with
as much care and accuracy as he analyzed and scrutinized maxims of
government and platforms of parties. Now, as formerly, he was familiar
with all the turning-points in contested counties and 'close' districts,
and knew by heart the value of each and every local loss or gain, and its
relation to the grand result." Indeed, as the two acknowledged, Lincoln
had been a serious student of voting trends ever since his days as a poll
watcher in rural New Salem.

The loyal staff aides made these comments on Election Day 1860
when they watched in awe as the then presidential candidate Lincoln
sifted through the initial returns that arrived on that historic night and

"understood at a glance whether" they represented "a loss or gain to his party" from the Frémont-Buchanan canvass four years earlier. Whatever Lincoln could not trust to his understanding of cold statistics, as he reminded friends four years later on election night 1864, he usually trusted to a higher power, occasionally interpreting minor incidents as major omens. For example, on the "dark, rainy, and gloomy night" in 1858 when his customarily astute reading of early returns indicated that Republicans would lose the 1858 Illinois legislative elections, thus guaranteeing his defeat for the U.S. Senate, he decided to head home early, hope gone. Although he was usually "surefooted," as he remembered, the "path had been worn hog-back and was slippery." As Lincoln recalled: "My foot slipped from under me, knocking the other one out of the way, but I recovered myself and lit square, and I said to myself, 'It's a slip and not a fall.'"

Lincoln rarely slipped politically again. And as a prized relic of his campaign for a second presidential term seems to indicate, by 1864 he had abandoned fate altogether and resumed his interest in raw numbers—sacrificing none of his sharp focus and frank self-analysis when it came to predicting his own prospects for reelection. That year, Lincoln believed he might well "fall" after all—jeopardizing not only his own legacy but also the future of the Union and emancipation. In this long-unknown document—tangible proof of his preelection jitters—Lincoln tallied the numbers and allowed himself to believe, just five weeks before Election Day and at the end of one of the most brutal presidential campaigns in American history, that he might just squeak by on November 8 after all. But only just. The autograph document from the Society's archive is published here for the first time.

Lincoln had done no campaigning in his own behalf during the 1860 presidential race and maintained his determination to remain similarly above the fray in 1864. But in a remarkable greeting to the 166th Ohio that August, he summed up what he believed the race was all about in a pep talk that could have served well as a campaign manifesto. "It is not merely for to-day, but for all time to come," he reminded the soldiers, "that we should perpetuate for our children's children this great and free government, which we have enjoyed all our lives. I beg you to remember this, not merely for my sake, but for yours. I happen temporarily to occupy this big White House. I am a living witness that any one of your children may look to come here as my father's child has. It is in order that each of you may have through this free government, which we have enjoyed, an open field and a fair chance for your industry, enterprise and intelligence; that you may all have equal privileges in the race of life, with all its desirable human aspirations. . . . The nation is worth fighting for, to secure such an estimable jewel."

However lofty those beautifully expressed sentiments, by early autumn Lincoln saw the political handwriting on the wall—and what it spelled out was far less eloquent. He came to believe he would in fact *not* be dwelling in that "big White House" much longer. Internecine Republican challenges had weakened him, and unrelieved Union battlefield setbacks had undermined his argument that the sections could ever be reunited with slavery destroyed. Supporters continued looking for alternatives. His own campaign chairman told him he could not possibly win reelection.

So convinced did Lincoln become of his own impending political doom that on August 23 he scribbled an extraordinary memorandum all but conceding defeat, then sealed it with paste and asked his Cabinet members to sign it sight unseen. To a man, they did so. What the pledge declared, they learned only later, was: "This morning, as for some days past, it seems exceedingly probable that this Administration will not be re-elected. Then it will be my duty to co-operate with the President elect, as to save the Union between the election and the inauguration; as he will have secured his election on such ground that he can not possibly save it afterwards." He was paving the way for a graceful exit, hoping that even during a four-month interregnum, his lame-duck administration might, with the help of a Democratic president-elect, crush the rebellion.

As it turned out, Sherman's victory in Atlanta, Farragut's heroics at Mobile Bay, and news of the destruction of the commerce raider *Alabama* by the USS *Kearsarge* in distant France conspired to brighten not only Lincoln's spirits but also his prospects for a second term. And no one understood the shifting momentum more incisively than the president. Encouraged, he reunited his fractured party, made a change in his Cabinet to placate congressional liberals, and worked behind the scenes to make sure that soldiers and sailors unable to obtain passes to return home in time to vote on November 8 would enjoy the opportunity to cast ballots in camp. Still, he remained understandably nervous and uncertain as the final weeks of the campaign arrived.

The proof of his anxiety is visible in the beautifully preserved handwritten ledger in plate 44–1. As it shows, just a month before Election Day, Lincoln apparently felt emboldened to summon his old vote-guessing prowess and make a stab at estimating how the electoral vote count would end up in the approaching presidential contest. During a visit to Secretary of War Edwin M. Stanton's office during the first week of October, he took up this sheet of departmental stationery and scrawled in one column the names of the states he expected to win together with the electoral vote value of each. In the other column he listed those he anticipated losing to the Democrats. When he added each column, he found he had awarded himself 117 votes to 114 for George B. McClellan—just one scant vote more than he needed to win.

Lincoln's preelection tally surprisingly ceded not only New York and Pennsylvania but even Lincoln's home state of Illinois—a whopping total of 75 electoral votes—to McClellan. The president must have dispirited himself with his accounting, for he left the paper behind when he left Stanton's rooms. A clerk named A. E. H. Johnson fortuitously picked it up and later added an affidavit of his own attesting to its authenticity. Still visible are these penciled sentences on the bottom: "Written in Mr. Stanton's Room. This is in the President's hand writing and purports to be the probable result of the vote of the several states in the November election, and was written about the first week in October 1864 and prior to the October election in the states of Penna, Ohio and Indiana. A.E.H.J." Precisely how and when it entered the New-York Historical Society collection remains a mystery.

Evidence exists that Lincoln took one more stab at vote prediction, on Military Telegraph Office stationery, not long after the heartening results arrived from these early statewide contests. A previously published copy of a remarkably similar tabulation sheet exists in the Huntington

Library. Lincoln's subsequent, hitherto unknown second crack at predicting the outcome varied not a whit from the copy owned by the Historical Society—except that in the revised tally the president awarded himself three additional electoral votes from the newly admitted state of Nevada. For now, he still believed he would secure no more than 120 electoral votes in all—enough for a clear majority, but still not by much.

As it turned out, Abraham Lincoln far underestimated his strength on both of these attempts at predicting his political future. On November 8, he swept to victory, winning every state but Delaware, Kentucky, and New Jersey and amassing a total of 212 electoral votes to McClellan's meager 21. For once, the old vote counter had miscalculated. That night, Lincoln grew sentimental as he awaited returns in the telegraph office. "It is a little singular," he confided to Hay, "that I, who am not a vindictive man, should have always been before the people in canvasses marked for the bitterness—always, but once; when I came to Congress it was a quiet time. But always besides that, the contests in which I have been prominent have been marked with great rancor." Of course, the latest results cheered him immeasurably.

Back in 1860, he had left the Springfield telegraph office armed with assurances of his first election to the presidency to inform his wife they were headed to Washington, explaining to his friends in the office that it was about time he "went home and told the news to a tired woman who was waiting up for him." He reached his house a few minutes later only to find Mary fast asleep. Lincoln "gently touched her shoulder" to wake her and announced: "Mary, Mary! *we are elected!*" Now, four years later, he thoughtfully sent the first congratulatory fruit basket of the night over to the White House with a message assuring Mary they were *reelected.* As he explained to his friends in the War Department telegraph office, "She is more anxious than I." One can hardly believe so, judging from the razor-thin margin he initially predicted he would win that evening.

Three days later, Lincoln assembled his Cabinet and at last unsealed and read aloud the blind memorandum he had asked his ministers to sign a few months earlier. Thinking back to his desperation in August, he admitted that while he would have been prepared to cooperate with

George B. McClellan had the Democratic candidate prevailed, he doubted whether McClellan, if elected, would have helped him in "finishing the war." Secretary of State William H. Seward agreed that he "would have done nothing at all."

"At least," said Lincoln, "I should have done my duty, and have stood clear before my own conscience."

Abraham Lincoln (1809–1865),
albumen silver print from glass negative, 1864

PLATE 44–2

45

—◦◦◦—

Publish or Perish?

Prison Times, Newspaper, 1865

HERE IS A CONVINCING REMINDER THAT EVEN WHEN THEIR LUNGS filled with gunpowder, their mouths choked back vile food, and their heads overflowed with fear, soldiers never lost their nose for news—even if it came in the form of makeshift examples like the meticulously hand-lettered ersatz journal shown in plate 45–1. It qualifies as the limited edition of all limited editions of Civil War publishing. The inhabitants of one crowded prisoner-of-war camp for whom it was published may well have been compelled to share scant copies, but they were undoubtedly thrilled to have the chance to read any newspaper at all, even briefly.

Overall, the Civil War inspired a huge demand for speedily issued, widely distributed news, and it spawned a generation of information addicts no less insistent on rapidly delivered information than today's aficionados of the World Wide Web. While many Northern publishers responded to this opportunity by making their publications larger, their circulation broader, and their profits greater than ever, Southern publishers enjoyed no such bonanza during this golden age for the journalism business. The Southern demand for newspapers expanded just as the Southern supply of reporters, paper, ink—and even the coins readers needed to buy their favorite dailies—dwindled. By October 1861, the Atlanta-based *Southern Confederacy* had reduced itself to half the size it had been before the war and was appearing on brown paper. The

299

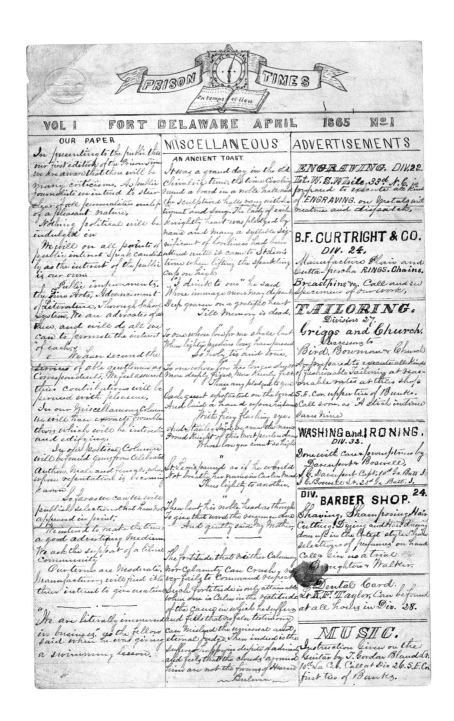

PRISON TIMES

VOL I   FORT DELAWARE   APRIL   1865   No I

OUR PAPER

In presenting to the public this our first edition of the Prison Times we are aware that there will be many criticisms. As public journalists we intend to steer clear of all personalities unless of a pleasant nature.

Nothing political will be indulged in

We will on all points of public interest speak candidly as the interest of the public is our own.

Public improvements, the Fine Arts, Advancement of Literature, Thorough School System. We are advocates of all these, and will do all we can to promote the interest of each.

We have secured the services of able gentlemen as Correspondents. We feel assured their contributions will be perused with pleasure.

In our Miscellaneous column we will give extracts & writings, those which will be interesting and edifying.

In our political column will be found Gems from Celebrated Authors, Male and Female, whose reputation is becoming known.

So far as we can we will publish selections that have not appeared in print.

We intend to make the times a good advertising Medium. We ask the support of a liberal community.

Our terms are Moderate, Manufacturers will find it to their interest to give us a trial.

"We are literally immersed in business" so the fellow said when he was giving a swimming lesson.

MISCELLANEOUS

AN ANCIENT TOAST.

It was a grand day in the old Chivalric time, the time Circling round a board in a noble hall with triment and song. The lady of each knightly heart was pledged by name and many a syllable significant of loveliness had been uttered until it came to St Leon's time when lifting the sparkling cup on high

"I drink to one" he said
Whose image never may depart
Deep graven on a grateful heart
    Till Memory is dead.

To one whose love for me shall last
When lighter passions long have passed
    So holy too and true,

To one whose love has longer dwelt
More deeply fixed, More Keenly felt
    Than any pledge to you
Each guest upstarted on the word
And laid a hand on his flashing sword
    With fiery flashing eye.
And "Stanley" "Say'st we crave the name
Proud Knight of this most peerless dame
    Whose love you count so high"

St Leon paused as if he would
Not breathe her name in Carless Mood
    Thus lightly to another.

Then bent his noble head as though
To give that word the reverence due
    And gently said "My Mother"

The fortitude that neither Calamity Nor Calamity can Crush, or even fails to command respect. Such fortitude is only attainable when one is calm in the rectitude of the cause in which he suffers and feels that no false testimony can mislead the universal and eternal Judge. Then indeed is the sufferer happy in despite of admiration and feels that the clouds around him are not the frowns of Heaven.

— Bulwer —

ADVERTISEMENTS

ENGRAVING. DIV. 22.

Mr. W. S. White 33d N. C. is prepared to execute all kinds of ENGRAVING on metals with neatness and dispatch.

B.F. CURTRIGHT & CO. DIV. 24.

Manufacture Plain and Gutta-percha RINGS, Chains, Breastpins &c. Call and see Specimens of our work.

TAILORING.

Division 27.
Griggs and Church.

Successors to Bird, Bowman & Church.

Are prepared to execute all kinds of fashionable Tailoring at reasonable rates at their shop S.E. Cor. upper tier of Bunks. Call soon as "A stitch in time Saves nine

WASHING and IRONING. DIV. 33.

Done with care & promptness by Davenport & Boswell.
M. C. Davenport Capt. 10th La Batt. 1
E. C. Boswell Lt. 20th La. Batt. 1

DIV. BARBER SHOP. 24.

Shaving, Shampooing, Hair Cutting, Dyeing and Hair dressing done up in the latest style. Choice selections of perfumes on hand Call give us a trial
Broughton & Walker.

Dental Card.

Dr. R. F. Taylor, Can be found at all hours in Div. 28.

MUSIC.

Instruction given on the Guitar by J. Gordon Blandds. 10th La Cav. Call at Div 26. S.E.Cor. first tier of Bunks.

PLATE 45-1

following June, all four principal Richmond papers, the *Enquirer, Dispatch, Whig,* and *Examiner,* began publishing on single sheets—no real surprise in a city where even bread soon grew scarce. And in besieged Vicksburg, as noted earlier, a newspaper appeared on the back of floral-patterned wallpaper (see chapter 30).

Meanwhile, Northern editors like Horace Greeley of the *New York Tribune* and his competitors James Gordon Bennett of the *Herald* and Henry J. Raymond of the *Times* all flourished between 1861 and 1865. Investing wisely in the hiring of war correspondents, these publishers gained in wealth, stature, and power as readers came increasingly to rely on them for prompt reports of the latest battles—sometimes as breath-takingly early, by nineteenth-century standards, as a day or two after the smoke had cleared; longer, of course, if reports had to be sent from the distant western theater. Like many of their peers, Greeley and Raymond dabbled in politics as well, not only inflecting news reports with their strong partisan views but occasionally questing for public office them-selves, seeking to place their acolytes in patronage jobs, demanding lu-crative government advertising, raising funds for political parties, and seeking to influence, not just report, administration policy. While the Lincoln administration and the Union military occasionally censored, or closed, dissident papers they judged had crossed the line from politi-cal opposition to treason, the remarkable thing about the state of news-paper publishing during the Civil War was that freedom of the press generally thrived.

Additional evidence exists that soldiers, too—even those in woeful prison camps—had an insatiable hunger for news from home. News-dealers maintained a lively business at Union encampments, even when regiments took up occupying positions in the distant South. Among the favorites were illustrated weeklies like *Harper's* and *Leslie's,* which even illiterate soldiers could appreciate for their woodcuts. Enlisted men par-ticularly coveted a publication called *Waverly Magazine,* which con-tained rather scandalous personal advertisements from women looking for "a soldier correspondent." But given the choice, enlisted men always preferred to read publications by and for civilians, preferably the variety that carried news from their hometowns. They trusted them more. In desperate circumstances, deprived of all other sources of information, soldiers, as this relic shows, not only made news but made newspapers.

Sometime after the war, the New-York Historical Society acquired this awe-inspiring example of journalistic perspicacity: a four-page newspaper, handwritten in ink, produced by Confederate detainees at the remote Fort Delaware prison camp on Pea Patch Island on the Delaware River. It must have required intense labor and devotion to put it together, considering the circumstances in which its creators lived.

The U.S. Army Corps of Engineers had built the formidable, polygonal masonry fort during the decade before the war as a harbor defense installation; interestingly, among the engineers who worked on the construction was the future Civil War general George B. McClellan. According to an architecture research report published in 1999, the interior alone required two million bricks. No doubt it was freezing in winter and steamy in summer. Beginning in 1862, the fort doubled as a prison—not only for captured Confederates but also for Northern political prisoners and Union soldiers convicted of crimes like sleeping on duty or desertion. Most of the Confederate captives seized at the Battle of Gettysburg in 1863 ended up at Fort Delaware. That year, the prison population swelled, according to one report, to eleven thousand. Among the units assigned to guard duty at the overcrowded facility—no doubt to the white Southerners' further displeasure—were members of the all-black Corps d'Afrique.

Conditions were, of course, appalling, though significantly better than at truly horrific death camps like Andersonville. One survivor remembered receiving four meals a day at Fort Delaware—but complained that together they still amounted to an "exceedingly light diet" consisting only of bread and unsweetened coffee for breakfast, "a cup of greasy water misnamed soup" for lunch, a two-inch-square cube of beef and more bread for dinner, and another serving of bread and coffee for supper. At the very least, one prisoner conceded, the men got "sufficient" quantities of "well baked" bread there. Others complained of abundant but fetid water, no doubt responsible for the cholera and typhoid epidemics that periodically swept through the facility. A single outbreak of smallpox allegedly claimed twenty-five hundred lives. And yet this swarming, unhealthy, isolated prison somehow produced a sense of community—and a newspaper.

"One of the most remarkable productions of Fort Delaware was the *Prison Times*," the onetime inmate Edward R. Rich remembered in his 1898 memoirs, "a newspaper published in April, 1865, by Capt Geo. S. Thomas, 64th Georgia Regiment, and Lieut. A. Harris, 32d Virginia Cavalry who proved himself a most expert penman." Rich failed to credit several others responsible for its production, including the officer listed first on the masthead of "Editors & Proprietors": J. W. Hibbs, captain in the 13th Virginia Infantry, and co-editor William H. Bennett, also of the 64th Georgia. Obviously, the paper enjoyed both a severely limited run (each copy had to be written by hand) and an extremely brief "newsstand" life, for this maiden issue bore the date of April 1865, the month the war ended. Harris probably took so long to pen each copy that there was no time to produce a sequel before the war ended. This is one of only four known surviving copies of the one and only issue of *Prison Times*.

Readers of that first and last issue may have included the remaining members of the so-called Immortal Six Hundred, a group of captured Confederate officers who had been used briefly as human shields at Morris Island, South Carolina, in retaliation for a similarly inhumane scheme employing fifty Union captives as human shields in Charleston. The surviving "Six Hundred" became living Southern martyrs—though they never faced enemy fire as shields—but remained in Union captivity. They were first transported to Fort Pulaski, where their ranks thinned owing to dysentery and scurvy. In March 1865, the survivors ended up at Fort Delaware, where fellow detainees reportedly treated them like royalty. Yet *Prison Times* surprisingly made no reference to their arrival. Perhaps because it took so long to handwrite duplicate copies of "Volume 1, Number 1," the editors concluded they could not change the layout even for such a newsworthy special bulletin. Still, what appeared within the paper's densely packed four pages shines a revealing light onto Civil War prison life—reflecting a displaced society remarkably determined to re-create the commercial and social amenities of home.

Although its tone suggests that in some ways the entire enterprise may have been something of a lark for its bored creators, *Prison Times* (whose tongue-in-cheek motto was *"En temps et lieu"*—"In time and place") did offer highly useful miscellany. Paid advertising included "commercial" notices for such undoubtedly essential services as laundering and haircuts (ten cents), shampoos (fifteen cents), and shaves (five cents); along with guitar lessons; dental work; "fashionable Tailoring at reasonable rates" ("A stitch in time saves nine," reminded the advertiser); shoe repair; chess clubs; a musical association; and even a debating society ("The Debating Club of Division '22' meets every Thursday night"). A prisoner named B. F. Curtright offered handcrafted "gutta-percha RINGS, Chains, Breastpins, &c.," while "Davenport & Boswell" offered to do "Washing and Ironing" at a price.

One column featured original inmate poetry ("The Low, Soft Music of the Pines" by A.H. of Florida and "Midnight Musings" by T.G.B. of Louisiana). And yet another provided a "Christian Association Directory," which noted that regular meetings of the group were held every Friday night. Perhaps the most useful feature of all was a back-page column called "Barracks Directory"—listing the locations of the self-appointed chiefs, adjutants, and postmasters serving each of the prison's ten inmate "divisions." The newspaper was probably designed for officers only, but there were more than enough of them packed into the island fortress to constitute a large "captive" audience. As the lead editorial noted:

> There are more than Sixteen Hundred officers in our Barrack in an enclosure containing scarce five acres of ground.
>
> One would suppose that the fact of so many men being thus crowded together would tend to create the greatest possible amount of sociability and afford unrivaled facilities for forming and cementing extreme personal friendships.
>
> But there seems to be as much isolation of individuals and as many little cliques and communities as in the largest cities of the world outside.
>
> This is a phenomenon of prison social life to which we can only call

attention at present and leave for a longer experience or more profound and skillful annotation to explain.

As our knowledge of the "Great World" outside is fast becoming traditionary or at best confined to "Fresh fish" stories, our news items will be necessary of a purely local character.

In our humble efforts to portray the Prison Times at this place we shall labor to keep our readers posted upon all the events of our little world worthy of record and afford them every facility of knowing who is here and what is being done.

Otherwise, the entire issue carried the tone of rather acid parody—understandable among creative souls trapped in maddening confinement—but the modern reader is left wondering whether the paper may have been designed primarily to consecrate as many individual names as could fit into a four-page periodical. For the savvier reader, it provided some needed relief through dark humor. A column titled "The Markets," for example, obviously designed to mimic the financial reports in hometown journals, reflected the cynicism of prisoners forced to spend money for black-market "extras." "Every thing but Tobaco [*sic*] is still held at extravagantly high rates," it reported, including poultry and butter—inexcusable, the paper sardonically contended, since the waters outside the prison were "no longer blockaded by ice."

That initial editorial also clearly indicated that its editors preferred that the paper enjoy no more than a limited run—for one obvious reason aside from the hard work it took to issue the first number: they desperately wanted to go free. "Trusting that the difficulties of conducting an enterprise of this kind under the circumstances are duly appreciated by an intelligent public, we send forth this our first number hoping that ere we can have time to issue many numbers our prison times will be discontinued forever and our patrons and ourselves be far away in our loved Sunny South."

That is precisely what happened. As Rich would remember: "*Prison Times, Vol. 1, No. 1* died almost as soon as it was born, for the ink was scarcely dry on its pages ere the news of Lee's surrender reached Fort

Delaware. No doubt hoping for a speedy parole, the editors suspended further publication of the newspaper." It had indeed enjoyed a very brief life, but in Rich's estimation "it was full of interest to its readers, and should anyone whose eye glances over these pages have a copy of it, they will surely prize it as a treasured memento of their Prison life in Fort Delaware."

Today Fort Delaware is no less isolated but has been reinvented as a state park—accessible, however, only by jitney. For those unable to undertake the challenging journey thousands of Civil War prisoners once made, the Syfy channel has televised two "investigations" on the site, not of prison life there in the 1860s, but of reported paranormal activity haunting the place since.

46

—◦◦◦—

The Draft That
Really Ended the War

Terms of Surrender, April 9, 1865, Ulysses S. Grant

O N APRIL 9, 1865, A FLUSHED AND UNMISTAKABLY AGED ROBERT E. LEE, his hair and beard, one startled observer noted, now looking "as white and as fair as a woman's," slowly rode his famous horse Traveller to Wilmer McLean's brick home at Appomattox Court House, Virginia. Soon thereafter, Ulysses S. Grant arrived on the scene to accept the surrender of the Army of Virginia—in effect, to end the four-year Civil War.

Among the Union staff aides who gathered for the historic event were Grant's military secretary, a Seneca Indian named Ely S. Parker ("Do-Ne-Ho-Geh-Weh," or "the Wolf," to his tribe), and Captain Robert T. Lincoln (whose own sobriquet was the "Prince of Rails"), recently attached to Grant's military family as a personal favor to his father, the president. The enthusiastic young Lincoln later brought a Lee photograph home to show off to his family at the White House. But the veteran Parker acquired a souvenir of considerably greater value: this original copy of the generous surrender terms Grant wrote out that day inside the McLean parlor in Lee's presence. Military conscription had already swelled Union ranks to a level that made them unbeatable, but here is the "draft" that really ended the Civil War.

"Those who watched his face to catch a glimpse of what was passing in his mind could gather thence no trace of his inner sentiments,"

The document below is one of the original impressions from
the manifold on which I wrote the terms of surrender of Gen. Lee

(2)   Appomattox C.H. Va
                        Apl. 9th 1865

Gen. R. C. Lee
Comdg C.S.A.
              Gen

                      In accordance
with the substance of my letter
to you of the 8th inst. I propose to
receive the surrender of the Army of
N. Va. on the following terms, toadt
    Rolls of all the officers and
men to be made in duplicate
one copy to be given to an officer
designated by me, the other to be
retained by such officer or officers
as you may designate. The officers
to give their individual paroles
not to take up arms against the

The above is an original in Genl Grant's own handwriting, of the terms of surrender given by him
to Genl Lee at Appomattox Court-House. It is one of 3 or 4 impressions as written in the "Manifold
Order book"; said book being now on file either at Hdqrs of the Army, or in the War Office. The interlineations

PLATE 46-1

until properly exchanged

Government of the United States, that
each Company or Regimental Commander
sign a like
Parole for the men of their
own Commands.

The Arms, Artillery and public
property, to be parked and stacked
and turned over to the officer
appointed by me to receive them.
This will not embrace the side
Arms of the officers, nor their
private horses or baggage. This done
each officer and man will be
allowed to return to their homes
not to be disturbed by United
States Authority so long as they
observe their Parole and the
laws in force where they may
reside.

Very respectfully
U.S. Grant Lt Gen

another eyewitness remembered of Lee on April 9, 1865. His countenance "wore its habitual calm, grave expression." Not even Grant could detect any hint of emotion from the dignified warrior who had extended the costly fighting so long yet remained such a flawless hero to his men. "As Lee was a man of much dignity, with an impassible face," Grant wrote in his memoirs, "it was impossible to say whether he felt inwardly glad that the end had finally come, or felt sad over the results, and was too manly to show it." Little did the Union victors know, but the previous day, as he pondered what to do next with his battered and starving army, Lee was observed in "a savage mood," pacing "backwards and forwards . . . like a caged lion." The Confederate general John B. Gordon heard Lee state that he "would rather die a thousand deaths" than surrender. "What man," one of Lee's other field commanders subsequently marveled, "could have laid down his sword at the feet of a victorious general with greater dignity than he did at Appomattox?"

Overshadowed by this legendary show of nobility—which was amplified by Lee's magnificent appearance that day in what Grant described as an "entirely new" full-dress uniform with "a sword of considerable value" at his side—was not only the sharply contrasting simplicity of his Union counterpart but also the extraordinary generosity of the surrender terms he proposed. Grant had found no time to change clothes before the meeting and was forced to wear his usual "rough traveling suit, the uniform of a private with the straps of a lieutenant-general." As he admitted: "I must have contrasted very strangely with a man so handsomely dressed, six feet high and faultless of form." But to Grant, words meant far more than show.

When Lee had sent word the day before that he would meet Grant "with reference to the surrender of this army," the Union commander had made clear in his reply that he would not address the overall questions of peace and reunion. As he explained with typical bluntness: "I have no authority." Grant had received scant instruction on how he should treat the Confederates should they be brought to heel, only that he attempt to negotiate nothing more than "the capitulation of Gen. Lee's army." At his final war conference with President Lincoln a few

The Draft That Really Ended the War · 311

weeks earlier, the commander in chief had been conciliatory but vague. He hoped to avoid further bloodshed. He should be glad if Jefferson Davis escaped out of the country so Northerners and Southerners alike could be spared the divisive spectacle of a postwar treason trial. As for the rest of the Confederate fighting force, William T. Sherman left the meeting with the impression that Lincoln preferred to "restore all the men of both sections to their homes" or, in the vernacular of the day, to "let 'em up easy." As Lincoln later put it more directly, if jocularly, he did not want to *hang* Confederates; he wanted to hang *on to* them.

But all that Grant would allow himself to advise Lee before their climactic meeting was: "By the South laying down their Arms they will hasten that most desirable event, save thousands of human lives and hundreds of Millions of property not yet destroyed." Grant ended his terse preliminary message by expressing the sincere hope "that all our difficulties may be settled without the loss of another live [*sic*]." Lee had little choice but to accede. His aides selected the McLean home as the venue for a formal surrender.

Cautiously, the two commanders began their meeting there that day by chatting about "old army times." Grant remembered Lee well from the Mexican War, he offered—gushing, "I think I should have recognized you anywhere"—but Lee stiffly replied that he could not recollect "a single feature" of his opponent, much as he had tried to conjure up his appearance in recent years. Grant took no offense; he thought it natural enough because of "the difference in our rank and years." In fact, their "conversation grew so pleasant," Grant recalled, "that I almost forgot the object of our meeting." General Lee had to call Grant's "attention to the object of our meeting, and said that he had asked for this interview for the purpose of getting from me the terms I proposed to give his army." Grant responded that "his army should lay down their arms, not to take them up again during the continuance of the war unless duly and properly exchanged." Lee acknowledged that he understood and agreed, and he suggested that the terms be consecrated on paper.

It was then that Grant asked Ely Parker for writing materials "and commenced writing out the following terms" at one of McLean's parlor tables as Lee sat opposite, silently watching. To compose what was argu-ably the most important document of his entire life, Grant employed a newfangled "manifold writer" that he had probably picked up from a Pennsylvania Avenue stationer during his visit to the capital the year before. By inserting thin yellow paper between its waxy sheets—precursors of carbon paper—a writer could make multiple copies of an original composition simultaneously. Grant reportedly inserted three sheets of paper and began writing. No one kept track of how much time he took.

"When I put my pen to the paper I did not know the first word that I should make use of in writing the terms," Grant later admitted. "I only knew what was in my mind, and I wished to express it clearly, so that there could be no mistaking it. As I wrote on, the thought occurred to me that the officers had their own private horses and effects, which were important to them, but of no value to us; also that it would be an unnec-essary humiliation to call upon them to deliver their side arms." The terms were simple, straightforward, and devoid of pretense—much like the man who wrote them:

Appomattox C.H. Va

Apl. 9th 1865

Gen. R. E. Lee
Comd.g. C.S.A.
          Gen:

          In accordance with the substance of my letter to you of the 8th inst. I propose to receive the surrender of the Army of N. Va. on the following terms, towit:

          Rolls of all the officers and men to be made in duplicate. One copy to be given to an officer designated by me, the other to be retained by such officer or officers as you may designate. The officers to give their indi-vidual paroles not to take up arms against the Government of the United States until properly exchanged and each company or regimen-tal commander sign a like parole for the men of their commands.

          The Arms, Artillery and public property to be parked and stacked and turned over to the officer appointed by me to receive them. This will not embrace the side Arms of the officers nor their private horses or baggage.—This done each officer and man will be allowed to return to their homes not to be disturbed by United States Authority so long as they observe their parole and the laws in force where they may reside.

Very respectfully
U.S. Grant Lt. Gn

When Grant finished composing this two-page document, Lee put on his spectacles, crossed his legs, and carefully read the terms over twice, remarking that Grant's magnanimous gesture regarding horses and sidearms would "have the best possible effect upon the men" and would "do much toward conciliating our people." Lee asked for but a few minor changes, which were made, then called for writing supplies of his own and inked a formal letter of reply: "General: I received your letter of this date containing the terms of the surrender of the Army of Northern Virginia as proposed by you. As they are substantially the same as those expressed in your letter of the 8th inst., they are accepted. I will proceed to designate the proper officers to carry the stipulation into effect."

At this point, Grant asked that his own terms, which now bore penciled emendations, be copied professionally and requested that his adjutant, Colonel Theodore S. Bowers, make a clean copy in ink. Bowers, however, was apparently so nervous that he faltered and after several aborted attempts handed the task over to Parker. When it was accomplished and signed on letterhead marked "Head Quarters Armies of the United States," Parker folded the official holograph letter into an envelope, sealed it, and handed it to Lee's aide Charles Marshall, who in turn presented it to Lee.

Before General Lee departed the scene, he told Grant that his army was painfully short of food and asked one more concession: Might he supply them with rations? Grant asked how much was required, and Lee requested food for twenty-five thousand. Grant immediately agreed to provide it. The Union commander later said he never entertained a thought about asking Lee to surrender his gleaming sword that day. He had no desire to humiliate him. Nor did he want his own men to celebrate in a way that might embarrass or arouse their vanquished enemies. When one of his officers jubilantly ordered the commencement of a hundred-gun salute to celebrate the victory, Grant halted it midway. The time for firing cannon was over.

After Robert E. Lee stepped back outside onto the McLean house's "comfortable wooden porch," mounted Traveller, and headed back to tell his soldiers that their fighting days were over, Grant remained for a time in the parlor. There, he took the copies of the draft terms he had composed on his "Philp & Solomons' Manifold Writer" and gave one—the second, by most accounts—to Ely Parker as a keepsake. No one knows whether Lee had fully appreciated the irony of the fact that the man who had written out the terms for surrendering an army that had fought to preserve slavery and white supremacy was himself a person of color, albeit what people of the day called a "red man."

Not that the North had been much more hospitable to him. Though an accomplished attorney and successful engineer before the war, Parker had not found it easy to enter, much less rise in, the Union army—this despite his friendship with its leading general. He had met Grant back in the general's Galena, Illinois, hometown in the 1850s, and Grant, then down on his luck, had taken an instant liking to him. Not until 1863, however, was the general able to overcome racist resistance to Parker's commission and name him as a captain on his staff. Parker had since earned promotion to the rank of lieutenant colonel. For his loyalty and good service he now received one of the most coveted mementos of the final act of the long and bloody drama that had claimed some 750,000 lives.

Parker kept the priceless relic for the rest of his life. After the old colonel's death in 1895, ownership passed to his widow. She in turn sold it to the New York Commandery of the Military Order of the Loyal Legion of the United States. In April 1926, not long after the sixty-first anniversary of its composition at Appomattox, MOLLUS donated it to the New-York Historical Society. Today it is housed in a hinged, book-like wooden frame.

When the surrender conference ended that April 1865 day, Grant introduced Lee to his entire staff, and the Confederate general shook hands with a few and bowed "in a formal manner" to the rest. When he reached Parker, it is said that Lee paused for several seconds, scrutinized what an onlooker called Parker's "swarthy" features, and, in the only caustic lapse he allowed himself during his surrender ordeal, commented: "I am glad to see one real American here."

To which Ely Parker replied, no doubt hoping for a more egalitarian postwar future: "We are all Americans."

Washington April 25th

My dear Mary:

I received your
kind note last week, &
I should have answered
it before, but that I have
really felt, as though
could not settle myself
quietly, even to the
performance of such
a slight duty as that
Henry has been suffering
a great deal with his
arm, but it is now

though I try my best to think
of them as little as possible.
I cannot sleep, & really feel
wretchedly - only to think
that fiend is still at large—
There was a report here
yesterday that every house
in the District of Columbia
was to be searched to-day—
I hoped it was true, as
the impression seems to
be gaining ground that
Booth is hidden in
Washington— Is not that
a terrible thought!
Mr. Johnson is at
present living in Mrs—

47

Bloody Good Friday

Letter from Clara Harris to Mary, April 25, 1865

HER FATHER WAS AN IMPORTANT REPUBLICAN U.S. SENATOR FROM New York State, but young Clara Harris was not President and Mrs. Lincoln's first choice to accompany them on their excursion to the theater on the night of April 14, 1865.

Others had been asked—and had declined. Maybe it was the wrong play for a city swelling with patriotic pride: a boisterous English drawing room comedy that made Americans look oafish and stupid. Perhaps it was the inconvenient date: April 14 was Good Friday, the holiest day on the Christian calendar, and the more observant would understandably resist even a presidential summons to a heathen playhouse on so sacred an evening. A few weeks earlier, in fact, the bishop of New Hampshire, Carlton Chase, had strongly urged Lincoln to mark the occasion a different way, by appointing *"Good Friday,* the fourteenth day of April next—to be observed as a day of Fasting and Prayer throughout the United States. I have reason to believe," the bishop added, "that day would be agreeable to Christian people of all denominations." But the plan was not agreeable to Abraham Lincoln. Worn out and desperate for relief, he determined instead to go to Ford's Theatre on April 14 to laugh along with *Our American Cousin.*

For a time, no one wanted to attend as his guests. General Grant had been the first choice to share the double-sized presidential box at Ford's with the Lincolns. But Julia Dent Grant understandably had no desire to see Mrs. Lincoln again—anywhere. During the Lincolns' last visit to Grant's headquarters at City Point, Virginia, Mary had repeatedly pulled rank and demanded acknowledgment as Mrs. Grant's superior, at one point castigating her host, "I suppose you think you will get to the White House yourself?" Julia had not forgotten. Even though the theater's manager, John T. Ford, put out a handbill advertising the Grants' presence for that night's gala performance, Julia would have no part of it. The general made a feeble excuse—they had to rush off to New Jersey to see their children—so the Lincolns began looking elsewhere for replacements. Thomas Eckert, the assistant secretary of war, turned them down, too. Even their son Robert declined, claiming he was exhausted by his Appomattox ordeal and wanted only to enjoy a good night's sleep in a real bed. Desperate to fill the box, Mrs. Lincoln finally turned to Miss Harris—and to her twenty-seven-year-old fiancé, Major Henry Rathbone.

That afternoon, the president invited Mary for an afternoon carriage ride and this time specified that he wanted no other guests along. "I prefer to ride by ourselves today," he insisted. Mary's recent public outbursts had revealed her to be close to a complete nervous breakdown. But her husband evidently still harbored a deep affection for his spouse of nearly twenty-three years. "He was almost boyish, in his mirth," Mary later told the artist Francis B. Carpenter of that final afternoon together, "& reminded me, of his original nature, what I had always remembered of him, in our own home—free from care. I never saw him so supremely cheerful—his manner was even playful. . . . During the drive he was so gay, that I said to him, laughingly, 'Dear Husband, you almost startle me by your great cheerfulness,' he replied, 'and well may I feel so, Mary, I consider *this day,* the war has come to a close'—and then added, 'We must *both* be more cheerful in the future—between the war & the loss of our darling Willie—we have both, been very miserable.'" As Mary remembered it, they made plans that afternoon to visit California and the Holy Land some day.

Mary, in her own way, had been as worried about her husband as he was about her. Not long before this day, he had almost sadistically confided to his fragile wife the details of a strange dream. As he remembered the chilling experience:

About ten days ago, I retired very late. I had been waiting up for important dispatches. I could not have been very long in bed when I fell into a slumber, for I was weary. I soon began to dream. There seemed to be a death-like stillness around me. Then I heard subdued sobs, as if a number of people were weeping. I thought I left my bed and wandered downstairs.

I was puzzled and alarmed. What could be the meaning of all this? Determined to find the cause of a state of things so mysterious and so shocking, I kept on until I arrived in the East Room, which I entered. There I met with a sickening surprise. Before me was a catafalque, on which rested a corpse in funeral vestments. Around it were stationed soldiers who were acting as guards; and there was a throng of people, some gazing mournfully upon the corpse, whose face was covered, others weeping pitifully.

"Who is dead in the White House?" I demanded of one of the soldiers.

"The president," was his answer. "He was killed by an assassin."

Then came a loud burst of grief from the crowd, which awoke me from my dream. I slept no more that night.

"That is horrid," Mary burst out in response. "I wish you had not told it. I am glad I don't believe in dreams, or I should be in terror from this time forth." Lincoln sheepishly tried to console her: "It was only a dream, Mother. Let us say no more about it, and try to forget it."

By the day of their carriage ride, both of them may indeed have forgotten it—or at least nervously confined it to the backs of their minds. For days, the city had been ablaze in illumination in celebration of Lee's surrender, with church bells loudly ringing and bands marching in the streets playing music. This was a time to celebrate, not worry.

After returning to the White House, Lincoln took care of remaining business, saw a few callers, and only then began dressing for the theater. His last-minute chores would make the couple late. The play was already under way when the Lincolns boarded the presidential carriage. A few minutes later, they pulled up at Senator Ira Harris's house at Fourteenth and H streets to pick up Henry and Clara. Then they set off for the theater, a redbrick building a few blocks away on Tenth Street. When they finally entered Ford's, they walked up to the mezzanine level, then circled their way around the back aisle toward their box at stage left. The audience quickly caught sight of them and began to applaud, and the actors stopped mid-performance to join in the ovation. By the time the Lincoln party reached the box, the orchestra was in the midst of a full-blast rendition of "Hail to the Chief." Lincoln acknowledged the welcome and then took his seat in an upholstered rocking chair drawn close to the rail. Mary sat down next to him in an upright chair. Miss Harris and Major Rathbone settled on a settee along the back wall.

When a shot rang out, most members of the audience at first thought it was part of a special effect in the play. No one remembered who screamed first, but many thought it must have been Mrs. Lincoln calling almost incoherently for help. "I struck boldly," John Wilkes Booth icily boasted in his diary of what happened next, shortly after 10:00 p.m. "I walked with a firm step through a thousand of his friends, was stopped but pushed on. A col. [*sic*] was at his side. I shouted Sic Semper ['Thus Ever to Tyrants,' the motto of Virginia] before I fired. . . . I shall never repent it."

As the audience erupted in pandemonium, Booth leaped to the stage, injuring his leg, limped unmolested toward the wings, and fled without interference. He remained a fugitive for days. The scene inside the box was no less frantic. Booth had jammed a thick wooden beam against the door before attacking the president, and people now straining to come to the president's aid could not force their way in from the outside. Finally, spectators in the closest rows lifted a surgeon toward the box, which the physician found to be spattered with blood.

The New-York Historical Society has a handwritten letter from the remarkably composed eyewitness Clara Harris written to a friend we know only as Mary, describing the shocking events of April 14, 1865, in all their bloody detail. Harris had a victim of her own to worry about, for right after Booth shot Lincoln, Rathbone made a belated effort to seize the assassin, who sliced deeply into his arm with a large knife. The major fell back, spurting blood. Even when Dr. Charles Leale and others came to the president's aid, Rathbone lay in the box all but ignored, bleeding profusely. That he survived the loss of so much blood was something of a miracle. This is the harrowing update Clara provided just eleven days after the assassination:

> Henry has been suffering a great deal with his arm, but it is now doing very well,—the knife went from the elbow nearly to the shoulder, inside,—cutting an artery, nerves, & Veins. He bled so profusely as to make him very weak. My whole clothing, as I sat in my box was saturated literally with blood, & my hands & face. You may imagine such a scene. Poor Mrs. Lincoln all through that dreadful night would look at me with horror & scream, oh! my husband's blood,—my dear husband's blood—which it was not, though I did not know it at the time. The President's wound did not bleed externally at all. The brain was instantly suffused.

Just as Clara hoped, Henry Rathbone ultimately recovered. Two years after the Lincoln assassination, in 1867, the couple married and relocated to Germany when the major was appointed American consul to Hannover. But Rathbone could never forget the events of April 14, 1865. Racked by guilt, he tormented himself that he had been unable to do anything to save the president. He began taking drugs to relieve his depression, but addiction only increased his paranoia. On December 23, 1883, he took out a gun and brandished it at Clara as he accused his wife of secretly plotting to leave him. "There is devilment afoot!" Clara screamed to the household help. "Lock the children's door." The last sounds her maid heard were a gunshot and Clara Harris Rathbone's cry "Henry, let me live! Oh don't!" Police rushed to the scene, but it was too late. Clara was dead of a bullet and stab wounds. Her dazed husband was curled up in the kitchen, once again bleeding—but this time from a few halfhearted self-inflicted knife slashes, muttering as if still in the throes of a nightmare: "Who could have done this to my darling wife?"

A court judged Rathbone to be criminally insane and committed him to a mental asylum in Hildesheim, Germany. He was still confined there when he died at age seventy-four in 1911—the last survivor of the bloody presidential box at Ford's Theatre the night Abraham Lincoln was murdered.

Laurel lay on ...... sw at Lincoln's bust,
while lying in state for three days in
City Hall in New York April 28th
1865

PLATE 48–1

48

—◈◈◈—

A Sprig from Lincoln's Bier

Framed Leaves from Abraham Lincoln's Bier, 1865

THAT ABRAHAM LINCOLN'S DEATH ELEVATED HIM TO THE STATUS OF secular saint practically overnight should surprise no one. His almost sacrilegious decision to go out in public on Good Friday ironically worked to sanctify his reputation. By Sunday, when the churchgoing American public gathered at their places of worship to observe what many later described as a "Black Easter," ministers throughout the North openly compared Lincoln to Jesus. Like the Messiah, he had died for his nation's sins. For the nation's Jews, Sunday marked the final weekend of the equally important festival of Passover, and rabbis took to the pulpit to liken the martyred leader to the hero of that holiday, Moses. Like the Hebrew prophet and lawgiver, they pointed out, Lincoln had led an enslaved people to freedom but had not lived to see the promised land. It was said that Jews actually chanted the mourners' Kaddish prayer in his memory, the first time a non-Jew was ever so honored in an American synagogue. No American tragedy had ever stirred such deep emotions. In a single day a controversial politician had morphed into a second George Washington, equally revered. Foes who dared to whisper that they were glad of his death were beaten on the streets.

"Lincoln's death," Walt Whitman ruminated when news of the murder first reached New York, "—thousands of flags at half mast & on numbers of them long black pennants—from the shipping densely crowding the docks, the same—numerous ferry boats constantly plying

323

across the river, the same solemn signal—black—business public & private all suspended, & the shops closed—strange mixture of horror, fury, tenderness, & a stirring wonder brewing. . . .

"Black, black, black," continued Whitman, "—as you look toward the sky—long broad black like great serpents slowly undulating in every direction. . . . All Broadway is black." The ubiquitous diarist George Templeton Strong similarly noticed that "not a building on Wall Street, Broadway, Chambers Street, Bowery, Fourth Avenue, is without its symbol of the profound public sorrow. What a place this man, whom his friends have been patronizing for four years as a well-meaning, sagacious, kind-hearted, ignorant, old codger, had won for himself in the hearts of the people! What a place he will fill in history!"

No single funeral could possibly accommodate such widespread and overwhelming grief. In an eerie re-creation of his portentous recent dream, Lincoln's body first lay in state in the East Room at the White House, where an initial memorial service took place on April 19. Six hundred people thronged the ceremony, crowded onto specially built indoor risers, though an inconsolable Mary Lincoln was unable to summon the strength to come downstairs and attend. Somehow Robert Lincoln, no less consumed with guilt than poor Henry Rathbone, took over as family representative and chief planner for his father's long and emotional journey home. Robert and the late president's closest advisers devised an ingenious itinerary, dictated by the vagaries of still-limited railroad connections but surely informed as well by a sense of history and nostalgia. Lincoln's body would be taken home along the almost identical route the living man had traveled from Springfield to Washington to assume the presidency only four years before.

The first stop was Baltimore. Only this time, unlike 1861, neither fears over security nor mania for secrecy shrouded the event from the population. Thousands turned out in the once-hostile city to pay their respects. After additional, equally effusive demonstrations of public grief at Harrisburg and Philadelphia, Lincoln's remains arrived in New York City on April 24, ten days after the assassination. The passionate mourning had not abated. Now the biggest funeral of all got under way, as a huge but largely silent procession accompanied the horse-drawn hearse

NEW YORK CENTRAL RAILROAD.

Time Table of Special Train & Pilot

WITH THE

REMAINS OF ABRAHAM LINCOLN, LATE PRESIDENT OF THE UNITED STATES,

Wednesday, April 26th, 1865.

	Pilot Engine.	Funeral Train.
Leave Albany	3.50 P. M.	4.00 P. M.
" Schenectady	4.35 "	4.45 "
" Hoffman's	4.58 "	5.08 "
" Cranesville	5.08 "	5.18 "
" Amsterdam	5.15 "	5.25 "
" Tribes Hill	5.30 "	5.40 "
" Fonda	5.45 "	5.55 "
" Yosts	5.58 "	6.08 "
" Palatine Bridge	6.15 "	6.25 "
" Fort Plain	6.22 "	6.32 "
Arrive St. Johnsville	6.37 "	6.47 "
Leave St. Johnsville	6.50 "	7.00 "
" East Creek	6.57 "	7.07 "
" Little Falls	7.25 "	7.35 "
" Herkimer	7.40 "	7.50 "
" Ilion	7.46 "	7.56 "
" Frankfort	7.52 "	8.02 "
Arrive Utica	8.15 "	8.25 "
Leave Utica	8.35 "	8.45 "
" Whitesboro	8.45 "	8.55 "
" Oriskany	8.53 "	9.03 "
" Rome	9.05 "	9.15 "
" Greens Corners	9.17 "	9.27 "
" Verona	9.28 "	9.38 "
" Oneida	9.40 "	9.50 "
" Wampsville	9.48 "	9.58 "
" Canastota	9.55 "	10.05 "
" Canaseraga	10.04 "	10.14 "
" Chittenango	10.15 "	10.25 "
" Kirkville	10.26 "	10.36 "
" Manlius	10.33 "	10.43 "
Arrive Syracuse	11.05 P. M.	11.15 P. M.

This Train and Pilot will have the right to the track over all other trains, and no train will run within thirty minutes of their time.

E. FOSTER, Jr., } Ass't Supt's.
Z. C. PRIEST, }

H. W. CHITTENDEN, General Superintendent.

New York Central Railroad. Time Table of Special Train & Pilot with the Remains of Abraham Lincoln, Late President of the United States, Wednesday, April 26th, 1865

down Broadway to the sound of rolling wheels, cadenced boot steps, muffled drumbeats, and the chimes of Trinity Church's tower bells tolling "Praise God, from Whom All Blessings Flow."

Thousands of marchers followed the hearse that day, among them civic leaders, military companies, labor groups, uniformed police and firemen, veterans, and religious, political, and fraternal organizations. Looking on, rich and poor competed for a glimpse of the procession from thickly crowded sidewalks, "the velvets and rustling silks of the rich" mingling in one tearful throng with "the humbler garments of the honest poor." Reporters spied solemn groups of mechanics and benevolent associations on parade, rows of politicians twenty abreast, German "turners" (gymnasts) in "plain linen coats" in step with Irish children "in green blouses, and hand in hand." In an inexcusably cruel

PLATE 48-2

Lincoln's Funeral Procession in New York City, stereograph, 1865

gesture, city officials had earlier decided to ban African Americans from the funeral march entirely, but the mourners persisted. The *Evening Post* complained, "We have accepted the service of colored citizens in the war and it is disgraceful ingratitude to shut them out of our civil demonstration," and by order of the secretary of war himself, the heartless municipal order was overturned. Two hundred marchers of color ended up walking at the very back of the endless line, proudly car-

PLATE 48–3

rying banners that read "Two Million of Bondsmen He Liberty Gave" and "ABRAHAM LINCOLN Our Emancipator."

When the hearse finally reached Chambers Street that day, pallbearers deposited the president's ornate, fifteen-hundred-dollar walnut-and-silver coffin on a dais atop the grand double staircase on the second floor of City Hall, the building's facade now draped in black and adorned by a huge banner that read "The Nation Mourns." For their final stop in the biggest city in the country, Lincoln's remains, hastily and imperfectly retouched by an embalmer, went on public view in the open coffin just outside the rooms where President-elect Lincoln had uneasily attended a reception with the city's secession-minded mayor in February 1861. This time, no expressions of disloyalty greeted him. But there would be one more demonstration of New York–style audacity. The photographer Jeremiah Gurney, who had manned the cameras at the Metropolitan Fair a year before, ventured early to City Hall and climbed to the walkway ringing the interior of the rotunda dome, from which he made one final portrait of the lamented leader: a distant photograph of Lincoln in death. (Outraged, Secretary of War Edwin M. Stanton later confiscated the prints.) Despite this distraction, Lincoln's private secretary John G. Nicolay declared, "The reception in New York was worthy alike of the great city and of the memory of the man they honored."

All through the night and into the next morning, mourners patiently stood on line, often for hours, for a brief glimpse of the face so familiar from the countless photographs and prints in circulation—many of them published over the war years on Fulton or Nassau Street, not far from this very spot. By the time the lid was closed on Lincoln's coffin in Manhattan, some 150,000 people had viewed the remains. It was, the *New York Times* summarized, "a day long to be remembered as one marked by the most tremendous crowds ever seen in this city." The throng included "young boys, who will live to tell of this great day to their children when this century has passed," as well as "old men, who have seen the wars of 1812 and of 1861–5, and now come out into the genial sunshine to see our second WASHINGTON carried to his tomb. Their aged and tear-dimmed eyes," the analysis breathlessly concluded, "have beheld the country twice convulsed by war, and are now preparing to go to that

The Body of the Martyr President, Abraham Lincoln, Lying in State at the City Hall, N.Y., April 24th & 25th, 1865, lithograph, 1865

bright abode to which our heroic LINCOLN has gone before." The *Times* judged the outpouring to be not only an expensive tribute to a hero but also "a prompt, spontaneous and deliberate sacrifice by the industrious, the frugal, the pecuniarily responsible body of the people." It was not just "the grandest oblation ever made on the altar of departed worth." It had disproved "the theory that republics are ungrateful."

PLATE 48–4

From Manhattan, Lincoln's body headed toward New Jersey, then north for another public funeral in Albany, and ultimately west for ceremonies in Buffalo, Indianapolis, Chicago, and finally Springfield. Lincoln was laid to rest inside a temporary receiving vault at Oak Ridge Cemetery outside the town he left, never to see again, just over four years before—what must have seemed to his old neighbors a lifetime ago. For the hundreds of thousands who personally witnessed any or all of these spectacular events, and for the millions more who did not but wished they had, souvenirs again provided a tangible link to the mass mourning long after Lincoln had been interred. Once again, just as at all the peak periods of public hunger for Lincoln images and artifacts, New York entrepreneurs supplied the majority of keepsakes—and profited royally from the demand.

The New-York Historical Society's large holdings in artifacts from Lincoln's various funerals include an unexpected number of accomplished, on-the-spot, firsthand sketches showing the president's catafalque on view in sites in various cities, including the White House, the main Chicago courthouse, and the Springfield state capitol. They are all part of the vast trove of original model drawings that unidentified artists supplied to *Frank Leslie's Illustrated Newspaper* from 1861 to 1865. Among the collection's mass-produced mementos are a timetable of the special funeral train for April 26, 1865, and original lithographic prints and photographic stereo cards depicting the funeral procession as well as mourners filing past the coffin at City Hall in New York.

But perhaps no relic more evocatively symbolizes the city's grieving than the simple spray of laurel taken from Lincoln's bier at City Hall by a man named Jeremiah Wood and preserved ever after in a gilded oval frame together with a small photograph of the late president and a black-and-white crossed ribbon. It was given to the Society in 1947.

Similar keepsakes must have inspired the New York poet Walt Whitman, though he expressed his grief in words, not relics. We do not know whether he saw Lincoln's remains during those extraordinary days, but we do know that when he returned to the theme of mourning, this time in his acclaimed poem "When Lilacs Last in the Door-Yard

Bloom'd," the subject was not only a dead president but living flora like the sprig preserved by Jeremiah Wood:

Coffin that passes through lanes and streets,
Through day and night, with the great cloud darkening the land,
With the pomp of the inloop'd flags, with the cities draped in black,
With the show of the States themselves, as of crape-veil'd women, standing,
With processions long and winding, and the flambeaus of the night,
With the countless torches lit—with the silent sea of faces, and the unbared heads,
With the waiting depot, the arriving coffin, and the sombre faces,
With dirges through the night, with the thousand voices rising strong and solemn;
With all the mournful voices of the dirges, pour'd around the coffin,
The dim-lit churches and the shuddering organs—Where amid these you journey,
With the tolling, tolling bells' perpetual clang;
Here! coffin that slowly passes,
I give you my sprig of lilac.

(Nor for you, for one, alone;
Blossoms and branches green to coffins all I bring:
For fresh as the morning—thus would I chant a song for you, O sane and sacred death.

All over bouquets of roses,
O death! I cover you over with roses and early lilies;
But mostly and now the lilac that blooms the first,
Copious, I break, I break the sprigs from the bushes;
With loaded arms I come, pouring for you,
For you, and the coffins all of you, O death.)

49

—◦/◦/◦—

A Helping Hand
for the Wounded Veteran

Autograph Letter from
Joe W. Mersereau to William Oland Bourne, 1865

HERE IS POWERFUL EVIDENCE THAT NEW YORK LITERALLY OFFERED A helping hand to its disabled Civil War veterans—at a price, of course. Immediately following the war, a healthy postwar commercial market grew up in response to the heartbreaking demand for artificial limbs. At least, as this singular testimonial suggests, some of the devices functioned astoundingly well. Wartime amputation was a subject that the afflicted soldiers could never forget, yet most home-front civilians—at least those who failed to profit from it—understandably preferred to ignore.

"My fingers are getting better," a Confederate soldier named Richard Slade wrote home optimistically to his sister in 1864 after undergoing a finger amputation moderate enough to make him feel grateful for the outcome. "I did not have but one of them taken off the second one was broken & the Doctors insisted on taking it off but I would not let them & I saved my finger by this means," he reported manfully. "It looks rather hard to see them take off legs & arms & fingers & cut the men into pieces but thank God they have not got only a small part of me." Slade was fortunate indeed. The reigning amputation authority of the period, Samuel Cooper, whose book *The First Lines of the Practice of Surgery* served as a manual for battlefield medical treatment, usefully recommended "pinching the vessels"

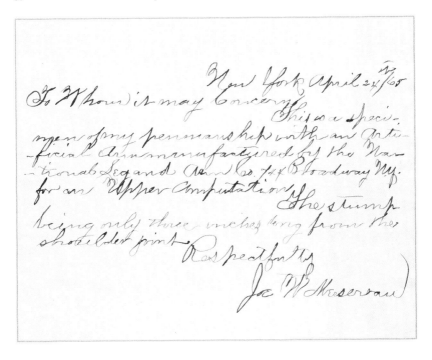

to stanch the bleeding that inevitably followed after fingers were shorn off, but otherwise admitted: "I can say nothing from my own experience."

Other soldiers who took shot and shell in their arms and legs were not as lucky as Slade. Projectiles like Minié balls, made of soft lead, routinely shattered bones and quickly contaminated the resulting wounds when remnants of soiled uniforms and unwashed human skin smashed into the body. Amputations were among the most frequently applied "treatments" for war wounds, easy and relatively quick to perform in lieu of more conservative and time-consuming methods in shockingly overcrowded facilities filled with mangled, screaming battle victims. Doctors working under the green flag with unsanitary instruments in emergency conditions made quick work of human extremities that modern medicine would never be compelled to sacrifice.

Nonetheless, wounded soldiers who refused the procedures often regretted their decisions. After taking a serious hit to a limb during the Battle of Peachtree Creek, Georgia, in July 1864, an Irish-born colonel named Thomas J. Reynolds begged the doctors to spare his valuable leg

PLATE 49–1

because it was "imported." Reynolds lived to write about the incident in his memoirs—more than forty years later. He was an exception. As the historian James I. Robertson Jr. has noted: "More arms and legs were removed in the Civil War than at any other time in the nation's history."

Soldiers recuperating in field hospitals from other complaints never forgot the horrible shrieks and groans that emanated from so-called operating rooms. Ether and chloroform were in short supply on campaign, and liquor was used more often to fuel elation than sedation. Patients with access to none of the above were given a stick to bite down on when the sawing commenced. A New Jersey enlisted man who watched doctors perform amputations on two of his comrades remembered: "Neither of them seemed to be under the influence of cloreform [*sic*], but were held down by some four men, while nothing but a groan escaped them, as the operation proceeded."

Régis de Trobriand, an officer who spent four years with the Army of the Potomac and recorded his impressions of the war in an 1889 memoir, left a particularly gruesome account of the day he came face-to-face with a battlefield amputation mill during McClellan's 1862 costly failures on the Virginia Peninsula:

> A little stream of coagulated blood reddened the steps coming from the half-opened door. On pushing it to enter I felt a resistance, the cause of which I soon recognized. It was a pile of amputated legs and arms thrown into a corner of the room, waiting the coming of a Negro to take them out and bury them in the garden. . . . Near the hole there lay by itself a leg white and slender, terminating in a foot almost as small as that of a child. The knee had been shattered by a ball. "You see we have had some work to do," said a surgeon to me. "Come in, colonel." Around the room . . . the amputated were on the floor in rows with the head to the wall. All these mutilated creatures turned their eyes, hollow with suffering, towards me, the greater part of them listless but a few with an air having a shade of defiance. I looked for the one to whom the leg with the child's foot had belonged. I had no trouble in recognizing him. He was, really, almost a child, with blue eyes, long blond hair, and with emaciated features.

334 • *The Civil War in 50 Objects*

Most soldiers who endured or even witnessed battlefield amputations remained traumatized for life. A Massachusetts enlisted man recovering in a field hospital never got the sights and smells out of his mind. "A large hole was dug in the yard," he recalled, "about the size of a small cellar, and into this the legs and arms were thrown as they were lopped off by the surgeons, with a coolness that would be a terror to persons unaccustomed to the sights of military surgery after a battle." The day he made these observations "was hot and sultry," he recalled, "and the odor of the ether used in the operations and the effluvia from the receptacle of mangled limbs, was sickening in the extreme. Flies came down upon us in clouds, torturing us with their bite."

On the other hand, when the luckier amputees returned home, diminished but alive, a surprising number took themselves to their local photography studios to make a record of their disfigurement. Lieutenant Legh Wilber Reid of Company E, 25th Virginia Cavalry, posed on crutches when he reached home in 1865 or 1866, wearing a longer-than-normal left trouser leg to discreetly cloak the fact that he had lost his leg. He lived until 1908. Some amputees even posed nude or with the barest of coverings for medical photographers determined to make a record of all manner of deformities caused by the weapons of war or botched surgeries; one hopes that the poor survivors were at least paid for exposing their battered bodies. Even the renowned Mathew Brady (or one of the camera operators in his employ) could not resist taking what amounted to atrocity pictures—portraits of skeletal, limbless, gangrene-afflicted Union soldiers who had survived the Andersonville prison in Georgia. The pictures proved so gruesome they remained unpublished until 1879, and even then appeared only in sanitized woodcut adaptations.

The soldiers who came home without arms or legs had to learn to make do with meager pensions and limited opportunities, though shortly before his second inauguration Lincoln acknowledged "the paramount claims" of "disabled and discharged soldiers." Most returned to family life or married and raised families. Some miraculously acquired the skills to regain nearly as much dexterity as they had boasted before the war—thanks to modern technology. It was a boom time for the manufacturers of artificial limbs; one historian later claimed that the most expensive item in the postwar budgets of Louisiana and other Southern states was the underwriting of prostheses.

Such struggles were not confined to the South. In New York, a soldier named Joe W. Mersereau even learned to write again using his newfangled artificial arm and, to prove his ability, wrote a testimonial to that effect on April 24, 1865—the very day a hearse bearing the body of his assassinated commander in chief rolled down Broadway toward City Hall. There is no evidence that Mersereau braved the inevitable jostling to attend that momentous event. Instead, he took up a pen that day and showed with his easily decipherable handwriting, shown in plate 49–1, albeit in a stumbling style of expression, that at least one determined life threatened by the Civil War would somehow go on:

New York April 24 1865

To Whom it may Concern

This is a specimen of my penmanship with an artificial arm manufactured by the National Leg and Arm Co. of 44 Broadway N.Y. for an upper amputation.

The stump being only three inches long from the shoulder joint.

Respectfully

Joe W Mersereau

No one kept precise statistics of the numbers of amputations performed during the Civil War (surely in the many thousands on both sides) or of the number of wounded veterans who survived and spent the rest of their days hobbling on prosthetic legs or struggling to perform the simple chores of life with only one arm. But Joe Mersereau at least had the benefit of the best New York–made technology. Compare his postwar fate with that of a North Carolina corporal named Spencer O'Brien, whose leg was amputated after four separate battle wounds. When he returned to his rural home after the war, he made his own wooden leg—out of a wagon axle.

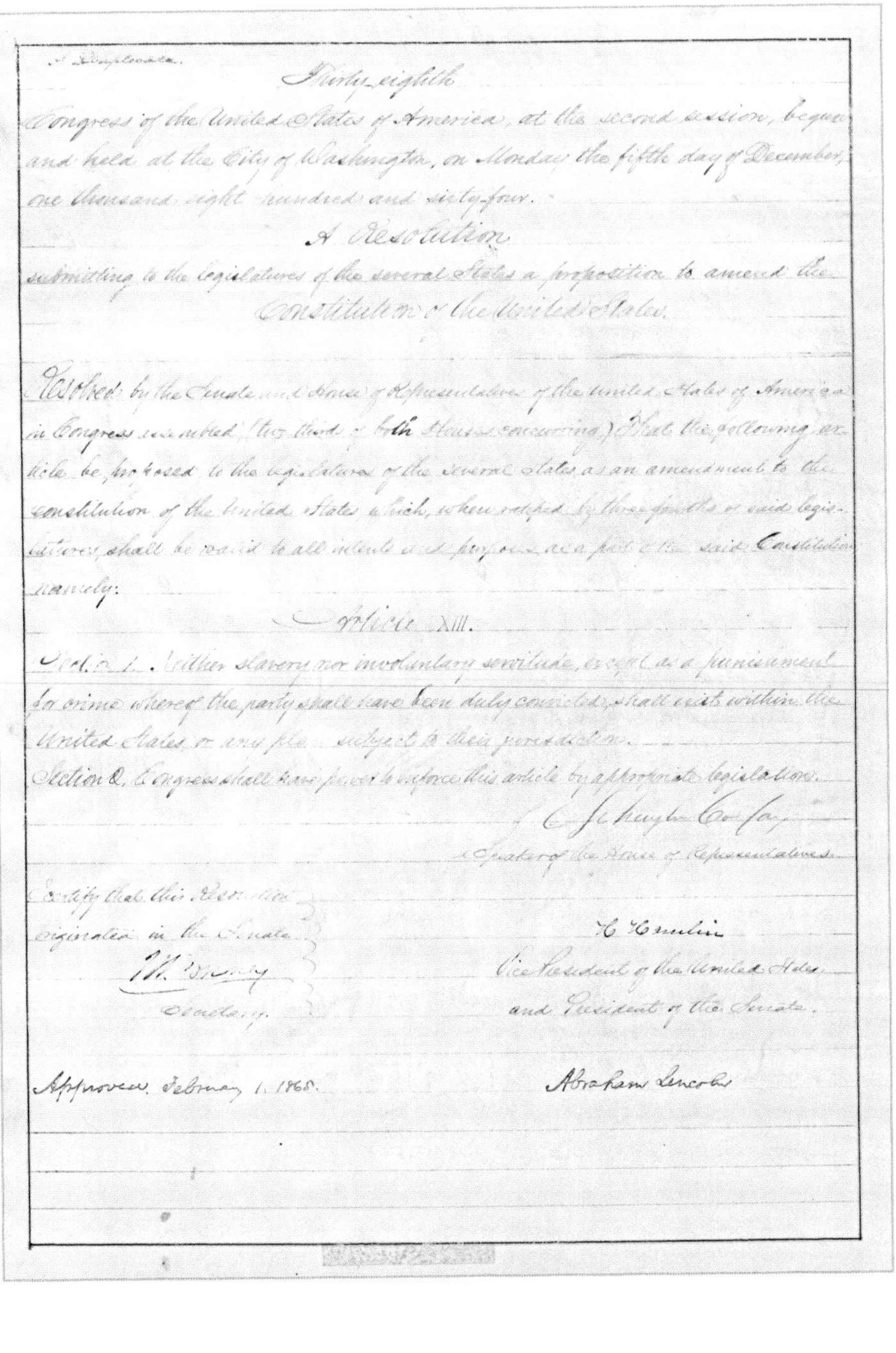

Thirty-eighth

Congress of the United States of America, at the second session, begun
and held at the City of Washington, on Monday the fifth day of December,
one thousand eight hundred and sixty-four.

A Resolution

submitting to the Legislatures of the several States a proposition to amend the
Constitution of the United States.

Resolved by the Senate and House of Representatives of the United States of America
in Congress assembled, (two thirds of both Houses concurring,) That the following article be proposed to the Legislatures of the several States as an amendment to the
constitution of the United States which, when ratified by three fourths of said Legislatures, shall be valid to all intents and purposes as a part of the said Constitution,
namely:

Article XIII.

Section 1. Neither slavery nor involuntary servitude, except as a punishment
for crime whereof the party shall have been duly convicted, shall exist within the
United States, or any place subject to their jurisdiction.
Section 2. Congress shall have power to enforce this article by appropriate legislation.

Schuyler Colfax
Speaker of the House of Representatives.

I certify that this Resolution
originated in the Senate.
W. Hickey
Secretary.

H. Hamlin
Vice President of the United States
and President of the Senate.

Approved, February 1, 1865.

Abraham Lincoln

PLATE 50-1

50

⊷⊷⊷⊷⊷

It Winds the Whole Thing Up

The Thirteenth Amendment
to the U.S. Constitution, Manuscript, 1865

HERE IS THE MOST SUPERFLUOUS, YET AT THE SAME TIME THE MOST significant, signature Abraham Lincoln ever affixed to a document: his approval of the congressional resolution for the Thirteenth Amendment to the U.S. Constitution abolishing slavery everywhere in the United States.

For days, President Lincoln had waited anxiously for the House of Representatives to pass this resolution—waited, counted votes, hosted secret strategy meetings with undecided representatives, made a few unsavory promises, offered raw political deals, and, wherever necessary, twisted arms with a ferocity he rarely exerted on members of the legislature. It was January 1865. No addition to the Constitution had been approved in more than six decades.

Lincoln even rode up one day to the Capitol himself—not to lobby Congress for passage of the amendment, but to join the audience for a specially arranged charity concert. There, he was so touched by a rendition of a maudlin tune called "Your Mission" that he asked the singer Philip Phillips to perform an encore. But not even the sentimental music he loved eased his anxiety about the future of the freedom amendment or diminished his determination to fulfill his mission to end slavery before the lame-duck Congress adjourned.

Months earlier, the House of Representatives had failed by a handful of votes to approve the amendment with the required two-thirds majority. Even its leading advocates thought their best option would be to wait for the next Congress to be seated in late 1865, when the Republican majority would increase significantly. Perhaps Lincoln could advance that timetable slightly by calling a special session as he had done at the commencement of the war on Independence Day 1861. But Lincoln made it clear that he desired—insisted—that the lame-duck House reconsider the measure sooner rather than later. His reasons were complicated but, as usual, eminently sensible from a political and diplomatic point of view. At the time, the president still harbored the hope that he could persuade Confederate leaders to lay down their arms without further casualties on both sides. But he also remained firm that he would not negotiate away the terms of the Emancipation Proclamation—as many in the North now advocated.

To prevent that subject from even coming up at any future conference, Lincoln urgently needed the issue of freedom to be taken away from the executive branch, beyond the fragile legality of a presidential proclamation, and enshrined into law by the legislature and the states. Even as the House resumed debate on the amendment late in January, a delegation of Confederate "peace commissioners" quietly set off for Washington to seek an armistice. Lincoln ordered them detained at Hampton Roads, Virginia. In an effort to keep the initiative secret so it would not anger Republicans and jeopardize the upcoming vote, Lincoln was forced to deny that such a summit was even contemplated. "Honest Abe" skirted the truth that day—but came close enough to get away with it—by assuring Congress that as far as he knew, no rebel peace emissaries were expected *in Washington*. Left unsaid was the fact that the delegation awaited his arrival in Virginia.

The ploy worked beautifully. This time, a sufficient number of congressmen—some already defeated for reelection and thus emboldened to vote their consciences regardless of political consequences, the braver ones destined for punishing defeats in return for their enlightened votes—changed their minds. On January 31, 1865, with votes to spare, the House of Representatives moved to send the Thirteenth Amendment to the legislatures of all the states of the Union. Now, if three-fourths of them approved it, the amendment would become an official part of the Constitution—a document that had recognized the existence of African slavery for nearly four score years and had accepted no new amendments of any kind since 1804.

The next day, February 1, 1865, a clerk brought a copy of this document to Lincoln's desk. The president had waited months for this moment. Here at last was the simple but broad language he had wanted: "Neither slavery nor involuntary servitude, except as a punishment for crime . . . shall exist within the United States." As he could see, the official notice boasted the signatures of both Speaker of the House Schuyler Colfax and outgoing Vice President Hannibal Hamlin (the latter acting in his capacity as president of the Senate). Almost by instinct, Lincoln took up a pen and added his own endorsement: "Approved, February 1. 1865. Abraham Lincoln." This is the very copy on lined vellum paper with ruled borders that the president signed and returned to Colfax, on loan to the Historical Society by the collector David Rubenstein. This is the only known signed copy of the joint resolution designated for any of the individual leaders who shepherded the amendment through Congress.

And then Lincoln paid a modest but embarrassing political price. Perhaps he had failed to realize that presidents were not required to sign resolutions on constitutional amendments (although his predecessor had affixed his name to an earlier, un-ratified Thirteenth Amendment that would have enshrined slavery permanently). Conceivably, Lincoln meant only to add his autograph to those of the others. One thing was certain: he was not about to be left out of this great moment—or this priceless document. He had fought too hard for its passage and believed that his name belonged on it, too. Whether or not he was required—or entitled—to approve, he signed his name. On February 7, the U.S. Senate actually passed yet another resolution, complaining that Lincoln's approval had been "unnecessary." As one irritated senator explained, presidents simply had "nothing to do" with amendments to the Constitution.

Their signatures were not required, and Lincoln's was apparently not appreciated. Worst of all, the criticism had come from the lips of a senator from Lincoln's own home state, Illinois.

If this latest vote upset Lincoln, he did not allow it to show. By then, Illinois had done something far more important. It had become the first state in the Union to ratify the Thirteenth Amendment, and just hours after Congress approved it.

Within weeks, as other states rushed to ratify as well, the Thirteenth Amendment became much more than a resolution adopted by Congress. It became a precious object, mass-produced copies of which ordinary Americans were soon able to purchase to display at home. One artist responded to public demand with a composite picture of all the congressmen and senators who had voted for it. Lincoln's portrait appeared at the very top. In reproductions of the document itself, legal or not, his signature usually appeared on the bottom—just where he had written it out in ink on February 1. From then on, and for all time to come, the name Abraham Lincoln would be associated with the amendment that, once and for all, did away with America's original sin: slavery.

On the evening of February 1, the same date he boldly signed the resolution, a band of musicians gathered outside on the White House lawn and began to serenade the president. A crowd braved the winter cold to join the throng and shouted for Lincoln to appear. Before long, the large windows on the second floor of the mansion opened, and Lincoln appeared to acknowledge the ovation. He looked exhausted but elated. He had no written text that night; instead, he spoke from the heart. Lincoln thanked the audience for its compliments but insisted that the occasion called for congratulations not to him alone but "to the country and the whole world."

The Thirteenth Amendment, he declared, had been desperately needed. Passage meant that another terrible "disturbance"—another bloody civil war—would never again tear the country apart over the issue of slavery. Yes, he was also proud of his Emancipation Proclamation, now two years old. The proclamation had begun the important work of ending slavery, but it had not gone far enough. It applied only to areas fighting a war against the Union—and not to loyal Southern slave states like Kentucky, where Lincoln had been born. There, slavery still existed, protected by the Constitution. As Lincoln put it that night, the proclamation alone simply could not "cure . . . all the evils" of slavery. But the amendment would. It was, in Lincoln's words, "a King's cure for all the evils." To another hearty round of loud applause, he declared: "It winds the whole thing up."

By then, no vote in Congress, no petty complaint, could ever separate Abraham Lincoln's name from this grand achievement.

Abraham Lincoln, who had led the war to preserve the Union he loved and then to eradicate the flaw he hated, did not live to see the Thirteenth Amendment to the Constitution ratified by the requisite number of states. By the time Georgia became the twenty-seventh state to approve the amendment in December 1865, finally outlawing slavery everywhere in the re-United States, Lincoln had been dead for eight months.

But old resentments died harder. Kentucky, the state Lincoln proudly called "the place of my nativity," rejected the amendment a few weeks before the president died. It did not reconsider and approve it until 1976.

Mississippi, the adopted home state of Lincoln's wartime Confederate counterpart, Jefferson Davis, took longest to ratify. Its approval of the official end of slavery did not come until 1995.

❋ ACKNOWLEDGMENTS ❋

THIS BOOK COULD NOT HAVE BEEN WRITTEN WITHOUT THE FAITH AND encouragement of Louise Mirrer, the president and CEO of the New-York Historical Society, to whom I am truly grateful for inviting me to serve as its author. Fortunately, she threw the full resources of the institution behind the project, which made the task not only less difficult but infinitely more rewarding and enjoyable. I am particularly thankful to have again relied on the able and patient editing of Valerie Paley, with whom I've now enjoyed a second rewarding opportunity to work closely on a Civil War project. Her energy, talent, and good cheer are really beyond compare. In turn, both of us benefited from the crucial work of our inexhaustible research assistant, Jeanne Gardner, and from the support of our publisher and editor at Viking, Wendy Wolf. My special thanks go to Roger Hertog, chairman of the New-York Historical Society, who honored me during the year 2012 by asking me to serve as a Hertog Fellow at the institution and who consistently provides so much encouragement to all who study and enjoy history.

I want as well to express my gratitude to my sometime co-author and full-time friend Craig L. Symonds, professor emeritus of history at the U.S. Naval Academy and eminent authority on both the land and the sea wars, for so quickly and expertly reviewing the manuscript of this book. His comments helped to prevent a number of factual errors and sharpened the analysis throughout. I also thank Professor Eric Foner of Columbia University for agreeing to write the introduction and helping me early on to crystallize an overall approach to this undertaking. My wife, Edith Holzer, proofread every line of manuscript and provided countless suggestions for stylistic improvements. Perhaps a more knowledgeable technocrat than either of us can explain why that seductive catch basin, spell-check, somehow never corrects "oif" to "of."

This is a book about incurably mute archives and relics, so to bring life to the original materials, I endeavored as often as possible to summon the voices of the people who created, commissioned, or collected them, along with those of contemporaries who lived through the Civil War era and recorded illuminating experiences of their own. I could never have met these goals in so brief a time without relying on important original and interpretive material in the Historical Society archives. I also turned for context and quotations to period newspapers, diaries, memoirs, and recollections, as well as to previously published works by several generations of superb historians. During the course of my own research and writing, I found myself increasingly and rewardingly returning with pleasure to old favorites I had not consulted for years. I want very much to take this opportunity to acknowledge my debt to all these invaluable sources and their authors and editors.

First there is the seminal work produced over the years for the Historical Society by such scholars as Kenneth T. Jackson, George C. Groce, David H. Wallace, Roberta J. M. Olson, Kimberly Orcutt, Barbara Gallati, Ira Berlin, Leslie M. Harris, and Linda S. Ferber. Their essential guides to both the permanent collection and the Society's recent special exhibitions inform the essays that accompany this book's fifty chapters.

I have also relied heavily on the work of many other scholars and wish to acknowledge all of them: Carrie Rebora Barratt, Michael Barton, Roy P. Basler, Kenneth Bernard, Iver Bernstein, John D. Billings, Paul and Meta Bleier, David W. Blight, Gabor S. Boritt, Catherine Clinton, Ronald S. Coddington, Henry Steele Commager, Don Congdon, Richard Nelson Current, Rodney O. Davis, William C. Davis, David Herbert Donald, Clifford Dowdey, Don and Virginia Fehrenbacher, Michael Fellman, Paul Finkelman, Eric Foner, Philip Foner, John Hope Franklin, Doris Kearns Goodwin, Rod Gragg, William C. Harris, James O. Horton and Lois Horton, Michael Kammen, Alvin Robert Kantor and Marjorie Sered Kantor, Dorothy Meserve Kunhardt, Philip B. Kunhardt Jr., Larry

M. Logue, A. L. Long, Stefan Lorant, Francis A. Lord, Carlton McCarthy, Maurie D. McInnis, James M. McPherson, Thomas Mallon, Chandra Manning, and John Marszalek.

Also Mary Elizabeth Massey, Milton Meltzer, Roy Meredith, Earl Schenck Miers, Reid Mitchell, Jim Murphy, Mark E. Neely Jr., Allan Nevins, Ralph G. Newman, Lloyd Ostendorf, Carla L. Peterson, Merrill D. Peterson, Emerson Reck, John Rhodehamel, Leonard L. Richards, James I. Robertson Jr., Kirk Savage, Barnet Schecter, Loren Schweninger, Stephen W. Sears, John Y. Simon, Jean Edward Smith, Edward Steers Jr., Craig L. Symonds, Louise Taper, Annette Tapert, Yuval Taylor, William F. Thompson, Hans L. Trefousse, Noah Andre Trudeau, Justin G. Turner and Linda Levitt Turner, Richard Wheeler, Ronald White Jr., Hermann Warner Williams, Douglas L. Wilson, H. Donald Winkler, and those irreplaceable memoirists Benjamin Franklin Butler, Francis Bicknell Carpenter, Jefferson Davis, Varina Davis, Frederick Douglass, Ulysses S. Grant, Oliver Wendell Holmes, George McClellan, Horace Porter, and William T. Sherman.

Whatever insights I arrived at for this book, I owe in large measure to the strong foundation established by all of the prodigious and pioneering work cited above. Whatever mistakes have somehow crept into the text despite all this expert guidance, I attribute with apologies to no one but myself.

⁂ BIBLIOGRAPHY ⁂

Primary Sources and Memoirs

Arnold, J. G. *The History of Abraham Lincoln and the Overthrow of Slavery.* Chicago: Clarke, 1866.

Basler, Roy P., ed. *The Collected Works of Abraham Lincoln.* 8 vols. New Brunswick, N.J.: Rutgers University Press, 1953–1955.

Bates, Edward. *The Diary of Edwards Bates, 1859–1866.* Edited by Howard K. Beale. Washington, D.C.: U.S. Government Printing Office, 1933.

Bellows, Henry W. "The Sanitary Commission." *North American Review* 98 (1864): 153–94.

Billings, John D. *Hardtack and Coffee; or, The Unwritten Story of Army Life.* Boston: George M. Smith, 1887.

Brooks, Noah. *Washington in Lincoln's Time.* Edited by Herbert Mitgang. New York: Rinehart, 1958.

Burlingame, Michael, and John R. Turner Ettlinger, eds. *Inside Lincoln's White House: The Complete Civil War Diary of John Hay.* Carbondale: Southern Illinois University Press, 1997.

Butler, Benjamin F. *Butler's Book: Autobiography and Personal Reminiscences of Major-General Benj. F. Butler: A Review of His Legal, Political, and Military Career.* Boston: A. M. Thayer, 1892.

Cadwallader, Sylvanus. *Three Years with Grant.* 1955. Lincoln: University of Nebraska Press, 1983.

Carpenter, Francis B. *Six Months at the White House with Abraham Lincoln: The Story of a Picture.* New York: Hurd & Houghton, 1867.

Chase, Salmon P. *Inside Lincoln's Cabinet: The Civil War Diaries of Salmon P. Chase.* Edited by David Donald. New York: Longmans, Green, 1954.

Chesnut, Mary. *Mary Chesnut's Civil War.* Edited by C. Vann Woodward. New Haven, Conn.: Yale University Press, 1981.

Coffin, Charles Carleton. *The Boys of '61; or, Four Years of Fighting: Professional Observation with the Army and Navy, from the First Battle of Bull Run to the Fall of Richmond.* Boston: Estes and Lauriat, 1882.

Croly, David G., and George Wakeman. *Miscegenation: The Theory of the Blending of the Races, as Applied to the American White Man and Negro.* New York: Dexter & Hamilton, 1864.

Davis, Jefferson. *The Rise and Fall of the Confederate Government.* 2 vols. 1881. Richmond: Garrett & Massie, 1938.

Davis, Varina Howell. *Jefferson Davis, Ex-president of the Confederate States of America: A Memoir by His Wife.* 2 vols. 1890. Baltimore: Nautical & Aviation Publishing Company, 1990.

Douglass, Frederick. *Life and Times of Frederick Douglass.* Hartford: Park, 1882.

———. *Men of Color, to Arms! A Call by Frederick Douglass.* Rochester, N.Y., 1862.

Dowdey, Clifford, ed. *Wartime Papers of R. E. Lee.* Richmond: Virginia Civil War Centennial Commission, 1961.

Foner, Philip S., and Yuval Taylor, eds. *Frederick Douglass: Selected Speeches and Writings.* Chicago: Lawrence Hill Books, 1999.

Grant, Ulysses S. *Personal Memoirs of U. S. Grant.* 2 vols. New York: Charles L. Webster, 1892.

Holzer, Harold, ed. *Lincoln's White House Secretary: The Adventurous Life of William O. Stoddard*. Carbondale: Southern Illinois University Press, 2007.

Johnson, Robert Underwood, and Clarence Clough Buell, eds. *Battles and Leaders of the Civil War*. 4 vols. New York: Century, 1888.

Lincoln, Abraham. Papers. Robert Todd Lincoln Collection. Library of Congress.

Livermore, Mary Ashton Rice. *My Story of the War: A Woman's Narrative of Four Years Personal Experience as Nurse in the Union Army . . .* Hartford: Worthington, 1888.

Long, A. L. *Memoirs of Robert E. Lee*. London: Low, Marston, Searle & Rivington, 1886.

Loughborough, Mary Ann. *My Cave Life in Vicksburg, with Letters of Trial and Travel*. New York: D. Appleton, 1864.

McCarthy, Carlton. *Detailed Minutiae of Soldier Life in the Army of Northern Virginia, 1861–1865*. 1882. Lincoln: University of Nebraska Press, 1993.

McClellan, George B. *McClellan's Own Story: The War for the Union . . .* New York: Charles L. Webster, 1887.

Moore, Mrs. M. B. *The First Dixie Reader*. Raleigh, N.C.: Branson, Farrar, 1863.

Nicolay, John G., and John Hay. *Abraham Lincoln: A History*. 10 vols. New York: Century, 1890.

Olmsted, Frederick Law. *Papers of Frederick Law Olmsted. Vol. 4, Defending the Union— The Civil War and the U.S. Sanitary Commission, 1861–1863*. Edited by Jane Turner Censer. Baltimore: Johns Hopkins University Press, 1977.

Pember, Phoebe Yates. *A Southern Woman's Story*. New York: G. W. Carleton, 1879.

Perkins, Frederic B. *The Picture and the Men: Being Biographical Sketches of President Lincoln and His Cabinet . . .* New York: A. J. Johnson, 1867.

Pollard, Edward A. *Southern History of the War*. 1866. New York: Fairfax Press, 1990.

Porter, Horace. *Campaigning with Grant*. New York: Century, 1897.

A Record of the Metropolitan Fair in Aid of the United States Sanitary Commission, Held at New York in April, 1864. New York: Hurd & Houghton, 1867.

Russell, William Howard. *My Diary North and South*. Edited by Fletcher Pratt. 2 vols. London: Bradbury & Evans, 1863.

———. *William Howard Russell's Civil War: Private Diary and Letters, 1861–1862*. Edited by Martin Crawford. Athens: University of Georgia Press, 1992.

Sherman, William T. *Memoirs of General W. T. Sherman*. 2 vols. 1886. New York: Library of America, 1990.

Simon, John Y., and John M. Marszalek, eds. *The Papers of Ulysses S. Grant*. 33 vols. Carbondale: Southern Illinois University Press, 1967–2012.

Strong, George Templeton. *The Diary of George Templeton Strong*. Edited by Allan Nevins and Milton Halsey Thomas. 4 vols. New York: Macmillan, 1952.

Taylor, Walter H. *Four Years with General Lee*. 1877. Bloomington: Indiana University Press, 1962.

The Tribune Almanac for the Years 1838 to 1868, Inclusive . . . New York: New York Tribune, 1868.

Tuckerman, Henry T. *Book of the Artists: American Artist Life . . .* 1867. New York: James F. Carr, 1967.

Turner, Justin G., and Linda Levitt Turner. *Mary Todd Lincoln: Her Life and Letters*. New York: Alfred A. Knopf, 1972.

Volk, Leonard W. "A Lincoln Life-Mask and How It Was Made." *Century Magazine*, December 1881. Reprinted in *Intimate Memories of Lincoln*, edited by Rufus Rockwell Wilson. Elmira, N.Y.: Primavera Press, 1945.

The War of the Rebellion: A Compilation of the Official Records of the Union and Confederate Armies. 128 vols. Washington, D.C.: Government Printing Office, 1880–1901.

Welles, Gideon. *Diary of Gideon Welles, Secretary of the Navy Under Lincoln and Johnson*. Edited by Howard K. Beale. 3 vols. Boston: Houghton Mifflin, 1911.

———. *Selected Essays by Gideon Welles: Lincoln's Administration*. Edited by Albert Mordell. New York: Twayne, 1960.

Whitman, Walt. *Memoranda During the War.* Edited by Peter Coviello. 1875–1876. New York: Oxford University Press, 2004.

Newspapers

Chicago Press and Tribune
Douglass' Monthly
Frank Leslie's Illustrated Newspaper
Freeman's Journal
Harper's Weekly
Journal of Commerce
New York Evening Post
New York Herald
New-York Illustrated News
New York *Independent*
New York Journal of Commerce
New York Times
New York Tribune
New York Weekly Caucasian
New York World
Prison Times
Southern Illustrated News
Vicksburg Daily Citizen

Secondary Sources

Abels, Jules. *Man on Fire: John Brown and the Cause of Liberty.* New York: Macmillan, 1971.
Anbinder, Tyler. *Five Points: The 19th-Century Neighborhood That Invented Tap Dance, Stole Elections, and Became the World's Most Notorious Slum.* New York: Free Press, 2001.
Anderson, George McCullough. *The Work of Adalbert Johann Volck, 1828–1912.* Baltimore: George McCullough Anderson, 1970.
Axelrod, Alan. *The Real History of the Civil War: A New Look at the Past.* New York: Sterling Books, 2012.
Bak, Richard. *The Day Lincoln Was Shot.* Dallas: Taylor, 1998.
Baker, Jean H. *Mary Todd Lincoln.* New York: W. W. Norton, 1987.
Barratt, Carrie Rebora, Lance Mayer, Gay Myers, Eli Wilner, and Suzanne Smeaton. *"Washington Crossing the Delaware": Restoring an American Masterpiece.* New York: Metropolitan Museum of Art, 2011.
Barton, Michael, and Larry M. Logue, eds. *The Civil War Soldier: A Historical Reader.* New York: New York University Press, 2002.
Beringer, Richard E., Herman Hattaway, Archer Jones, and William N. Still Jr. *Why the South Lost the Civil War.* Athens: University of Georgia Press, 1986.
Berlin, Ira, and Leslie M. Harris. *Slavery in New York.* New York: New Press and New-York Historical Society, 2005.
Bernard, Kenneth A. *Lincoln and the Music of the Civil War.* Caldwell, Idaho: Caxton Printers, 1966.
Bernstein, Iver. *The New York City Draft Riots: Their Significance for American Society and Politics in the Age of the Civil War.* New York: Oxford University Press, 1990.
Bleier, Paul, and Meta Bleier. *John Rogers' Groups of Statuary: A Pictorial and Annotated Guide for the Collector.* New York: Paul and Meta Bleier, 1971.
Blight, David W. *Beyond the Battlefield: Race, Memory, and the American Civil War.* Amherst: University of Massachusetts Press, 2002.

Boime, Albert. *The Art of Exclusion: Representing Blacks in the Nineteenth Century.* Washington, D.C.: Smithsonian Institution Press, 1990.

Boyer, Richard O. *The Legend of John Brown: A Biography and a History.* New York: Alfred A. Knopf, 1973.

Bremer, Robert H. *The Public Good: Philanthropy and Welfare in the Civil War Era.* New York: Alfred A. Knopf, 1970.

Brummer, Sidney D. *Political History of New York During the Civil War.* New York: Columbia University Press, 1911.

Burrows, Edwin G., and Mike Wallace. *Gotham: A History of New York City to 1898.* New York: Oxford University Press, 1999.

Carroll, John F. *A Brief History of New York's Famous Seventh Regiment.* New York: Veterans of the Seventh Regiment, Civil War Centennial Committee, 1960.

Cashin, Joan, ed. *The War Was You and Me: Civilians in the American Civil War.* Princeton, N.J.: Princeton University Press, 2002.

Cheney, Glenn Alan. *How a Nation Grieves: Press Accounts of the Death of Lincoln, the Hunt for Booth, and America in Mourning.* Hanover, Conn.: New London Librarium, 2012.

Clinton, Catherine. *Mrs. Lincoln: A Life.* New York: HarperCollins, 2009.

Clinton, Catherine, and Nina Silber, eds. *Divided Houses: Gender and the Civil War.* New York: Oxford University Press, 1992.

Coddington, Ronald S. *Faces of the Civil War: An Album of Union Soldiers and Their Stories.* Baltimore: Johns Hopkins University Press, 2004.

———. *Faces of the Confederacy: An Album of Southern Soldiers and Their Stories.* Baltimore: Johns Hopkins University Press, 2008.

Commager, Henry Steele, ed. *Living History: The Civil War—the History of the War Between the States in Documents, Essays, Letters, Songs, and Poems.* 1950. New York: Black Dog & Leventhal, 2000.

Congdon, Don, ed. *Combat: The Civil War.* 1967. New York: Konecky & Konecky, 1992.

Cornish, Dudley Taylor. *The Sable Arm: Negro Troops in the Union Army, 1861–1865.* New York: Longmans, Green, 1956.

Current, Richard N., ed. *Encyclopedia of the Confederacy.* 4 vols. New York: Simon & Schuster, 1993.

Curtis, Newton Martin. *From Bull Run to Chancellorsville: The Story of the Sixteenth New York Infantry Together with Some Personal Reminiscences.* New York: G. P. Putnam's Sons, 1906.

Darrah, William C. *Cartes de Visite in Nineteenth-Century Photography.* Gettysburg, Pa.: William C. Darrah, 1981.

Davis, William C. *Jefferson Davis: The Man and His Hour—a Biography.* New York: HarperCollins, 1991.

Dobak, William A. *Freedom by the Sword: The U.S. Colored Troops, 1862–1867.* Washington, D.C.: Center of Military History, United States Army, 2011.

Farrow, Anne, Joel Lang, and Jenifer Frank. *Complicity: How the North Promoted, Prolonged, and Profited from Slavery.* New York: Ballantine Books, 2005.

Faust, Drew Gilpin. *This Republic of Suffering: Death and the American Civil War.* New York: Alfred A. Knopf, 2008.

Faust, Patricia L., ed. *Historical Times Illustrated Encyclopedia of the Civil War.* New York: Harper & Row, 1986.

Fehrenbacher, Don E., and Virginia Fehrenbacher. *Recollected Words of Lincoln.* Stanford, Calif.: Stanford University Press, 1996.

Foner, Eric. *The Fiery Trial: Abraham Lincoln and American Slavery.* New York: W. W. Norton, 2010.

Freehling, William W. *The Road to Disunion. Vol. 2, Secessionists Triumphant.* New York: Oxford University Press, 2007.

Gallati, Barbara Dyer, ed. *Making American Taste: Narrative Art for a New Democracy.* New York: New-York Historical Society, 2011.

Gates, Henry Louis, Jr., ed. *Lincoln on Race and Slavery.* Princeton, N.J.: Princeton University Press, 2009.

Gladstone, William A. *Men of Color.* Gettysburg, Pa.: Thomas, 1993.

———. *U.S. Colored Troops, 1863–1867.* Gettysburg, Pa.: Thomas, 1990.

Glatthaar, Joseph T. *Forged in Battle: The Civil War Alliance of Black Soldiers and White Officers.* New York: Free Press, 1990.

Gragg, Rod, ed. *The Illustrated Confederate Reader: A Collection of Personal Experiences, Eyewitness Accounts, Diverting Vignettes, and Interesting Facts by and About Southern Soldiers and Civilians.* New York: Harper & Row, 1989.

Groce, George C., and David H. Wallace. *The New-York Historical Society's Dictionary of Artists in America, 1564–1860.* New Haven, Conn.: Yale University Press, 1957.

Guelzo, Allen C. *Fateful Lightning: A New History of the Civil War.* New York: Oxford University Press, 2012.

Hattaway, Herman, and Archer Jones. *How the North Won: A Military History of the Civil War.* Urbana: University of Illinois Press, 1983.

Heidler, David S., and Jeanne T. Heidler. *Encyclopedia of the American Civil War: A Political, Social, and Military History.* New York: W. W. Norton, 2000.

Hess, Earl J. *The Union Soldier in Battle: Enduring the Ordeal of Combat.* Lawrence: University Press of Kansas, 1997.

Hogg, Ian V. *Weapons of the Civil War.* New York: Military Press, 1987.

Holzer, Harold. *Emancipating Lincoln: The Emancipation Proclamation in Text, Context, and Memory.* Cambridge, Mass.: Harvard University Press, 2012.

———. *Lincoln at Cooper Union: The Speech That Made Abraham Lincoln President.* New York: Simon & Schuster, 2005.

———. *Lincoln President-Elect: Abraham Lincoln and the Great Secession Winter, 1860–1861.* New York: Simon & Schuster, 2008.

———, ed. *Lincoln and New York.* New York: New-York Historical Society, 2009.

———, ed. *Lincoln as I Knew Him: Gossip, Tributes, and Revelations from His Best Friends and Worst Enemies.* Chapel Hill, N.C.: Algonquin Books, 1999.

———, ed. *The Lincoln Mailbag: America Writes to the President, 1861–1865.* Carbondale: Southern Illinois University Press, 1998.

———, ed. *State of the Union: New York and the Civil War.* New York: Fordham University Press, 2002.

Holzer, Harold, Gabor S. Boritt, and Mark E. Neely Jr. "Francis Bicknell Carpenter (1830–1900): Painter of Abraham Lincoln and His Circle." *American Art Journal* 16 (Spring 1984): 66–89.

———. *The Lincoln Image: Abraham Lincoln and the Popular Print.* New York: Charles Scribner's Sons, 1984.

Holzer, Harold, and Mark E. Neely Jr. *Mine Eyes Have Seen the Glory: The Civil War in Art.* New York: Orion Books, 1993.

Holzer, Harold, and Craig L. Symonds, eds. *"The New York Times" Complete Civil War.* New York: Black Dog & Leventhal, 2010.

Homberger, Eric. *The Historical Atlas of New York City: A Visual Collection of 400 Years of New York City's History.* New York: Henry Holt, 1994.

Horwitz, Tony. *Moonlight Rising: John Brown and the Raid That Started the Civil War.* New York: Henry Holt, 2011.

Hubbell, John T., and James W. Geary, eds. *Biographical Dictionary of the Union: Northern Leaders of the Civil War.* Westport, Conn.: Greenwood Press, 1995.

Jackson, Kenneth T., ed. *The Encyclopedia of New York City.* New Haven, Conn.: Yale University Press, 1995.

Johnston, James H. *From Slave Ship to Harvard: Yarrow Marmont and the History of an African American Family.* New York: Fordham University Press, 2012.

Jones, Katharine M. *Heroines of Dixie: Confederate Women Tell Their Story of the War.* Indianapolis: Bobbs-Merrill, 1955.

Kantor, Alvin Robert, and Marjorie Sered Kantor. *Sanitary Fairs: A Philatelic and Historical Survey of Civil War Benevolences.* Glencoe, Ill.: SF, 1992.

Katz, Harry L., and Vincent Virga. *Civil War Sketch Book: Drawings from the Battlefront.* New York: W. W. Norton, 2012.

Kessner, Thomas. *Capital City: New York City and the Men Behind America's Rise to Economic Dominance, 1860–1900.* New York: Simon & Schuster, 2003.

Kunhardt, Dorothy Meserve, and Philip B. Kunhardt Jr. *Twenty Days: A Narrative in Text and Pictures of the Assassination of Abraham Lincoln and the Twenty Days and Nights That Followed—the Nation in Mourning, the Long Trip Home to Springfield.* New York: Harper & Row, 1965.

LaFantasie, Glenn W. *Gettysburg Heroes: Perfect Soldiers, Hallowed Ground.* Bloomington: Indiana University Press, 2008.

Leonard, Elizabeth. *Yankee Women: Gender Battles in the Civil War.* New York: W. W. Norton, 1994.

Linderman, Gerald. *Embattled Courage: The Experience of Combat in the American Civil War.* New York: Free Press, 1987.

Livingston, E. A. *Brooklyn and the Civil War.* Charleston, S.C.: History Press, 2012.

Long, David E. *The Jewel of Liberty: Abraham Lincoln's Re-election and the End of Slavery.* Mechanicsburg, Pa.: Stackpole Books, 1994.

Long, E. B. *The Civil War Day by Day: An Almanac, 1861–1865.* Garden City, N.Y.: Doubleday, 1971.

Lorant, Stefan. *Lincoln: A Picture Story of His Life.* Rev. ed. New York: W. W. Norton, 1969.

Lowenfels, Walter, and Nan Braymer, eds. *Walt Whitman's Civil War: Compiled and Edited from Published and Unpublished Sources.* New York: Alfred A. Knopf, 1960.

McInnis, Maurie D. *Slave Waiting for Sale: Abolitionist Art and the American Slave Trade.* Chicago: University of Chicago Press, 2011.

McKay, Ernest. *The Civil War and New York City.* Syracuse, N.Y.: Syracuse University Press, 2008.

McPherson, James M. *Battle Cry of Freedom: The Civil War Era.* New York: Oxford University Press, 1988.

———. *The Negro's Civil War: How American Negroes Felt and Acted During the War for the Union.* New York: Pantheon Books, 1965.

———. *War on the Waters: The Union and Confederate Navies, 1861–1865.* Chapel Hill: University of North Carolina Press, 2012.

Mallon, Thomas. *Henry and Clara: A Novel.* New York: Ticknor & Fields, 1994.

Manning, Chandra. *What This Cruel War Was Over: Soldiers, Slavery, and the Civil War.* New York: Alfred A. Knopf, 2007.

Marten, James. *The Children's Civil War.* Chapel Hill: University of North Carolina Press, 1998.

Marvel, William. *Andersonville: The Last Depot.* Chapel Hill: University of North Carolina Press, 1994.

Massey, Mary Elizabeth. *Ersatz in the Confederacy: Shortages and Substitutes on the Southern Homefront.* Columbia: University of South Carolina Press, 1952.

———. *Women in the Civil War.* Lincoln: University of Nebraska Press, 1966.

Masur, Louis P., ed. *The Real War Will Never Get in the Books: Selections from Writers During the Civil War.* New York: Oxford University Press, 1993.

Meltzer, Milton. *Voices of the Civil War: A Documentary History of the Great American Conflict.* New York: Thomas Y. Crowell, 1984.

Miers, Earl Schenck, ed. *Lincoln Day by Day: A Chronology.* 3 vols. Washington, D.C.: Lincoln Sesquicentennial Commission, 1960.

Mitchell, Reid. *Civil War Soldiers: Their Expectations and Their Experiences.* New York: Viking Press, 1988.

———. *The Vacant Chair: The Northern Soldier Leaves Home.* New York: Oxford University Press, 1993.

Murphy, Jim. *The Boys' War: Confederate and Union Soldiers Talk About the Civil War.* New York: Clarion Books, 1990.

Mushkat, Jerome. *Fernando Wood: A Political Biography.* Kent, Ohio: Kent State University Press, 1990.

Neely, Mark E., Jr., and Harold Holzer. *The Lincoln Family Album: Photographs from the Personal Collection of a Historic American Family.* New York: Doubleday, 1990.

———. *The Union Image: Popular Prints of the Civil War North.* Chapel Hill: University of North Carolina Press, 2000.

Neely, Mark E., Jr., Harold Holzer, and Gabor S. Boritt. *The Confederate Image: Prints of the Lost Cause.* Chapel Hill: University of North Carolina Press, 1987.

Nevins, Allan. *The War for the Union.* 4 vols. New York: Charles Scribner's Sons, 1959–1971.

Oakes, James. *The Radical and the Republican: Frederick Douglass, Abraham Lincoln, and the Triumph of Anti-slavery Politics.* New York: W. W. Norton, 2007.

Olson, Roberta J. M. *Drawn by New York: Six Centuries of Watercolors and Drawings at the New-York Historical Society.* New York: New-York Historical Society, 2008.

Orcutt, Kimberly, ed. *John Rogers: American Stories.* New York: New-York Historical Society, 2010.

Pakula, Marvin, ed. *Uniforms of the United States Army.* New York: Thomas Yoseloff, 1960.

Peterson, Carla L. *Black Gotham: A Family History of African Americans in Nineteenth-Century New York City.* New Haven, Conn.: Yale University Press, 2011.

Peterson, Merrill D. *John Brown: The Legend Revisited.* Charlottesville: University of Virginia Press, 2002.

Pleasants, Stanley. *Fernando Wood of New York.* New York: Columbia University Press, 1948.

Reilly, Bernard F., Jr. *American Political Prints, 1766–1876: A Catalog of the Collections in the Library of Congress.* Boston: G. K. Hall, 1991.

Reynolds, David S. *John Brown, Abolitionist: The Man Who Killed Slavery, Sparked the Civil War, and Seeded Civil Rights.* New York: Alfred A. Knopf, 2005.

Robertson, James I., Jr. *Soldiers Blue and Gray.* Columbia: University of South Carolina Press, 1988.

Ross, Ishbel. *Rebel Rose: Life of Rose O'Neal Greenhow, Confederate Spy.* New York: Harper & Brothers, 1954.

Schecter, Barnet. *The Devil's Own Work: The Civil War Draft Riots and the Fight to Reconstruct America.* New York: Walker, 2005.

Sears, Stephen. *George B. McClellan: The Young Napoleon.* New York: Ticknor & Fields, 1988.

———. *Gettysburg.* Boston: Houghton Mifflin, 2003.

Silber, Nina. *Daughters of the Union: Northern Women Fight the Civil War.* Cambridge, Mass.: Harvard University Press, 2005.

Smith, Jean Edward. *Grant.* New York: Simon & Schuster, 2001.

Smith, Robin. *American Civil War Zouaves.* London: Osprey, 1996.

Spann, Edward K. *Gotham at War: New York City, 1860–1865.* Wilmington, Del.: SR Books, 2002.

Spassky, Natalie. *American Paintings in the Metropolitan Museum of Art.* Vol. 2, *A Catalogue of Works by Artists Born Between 1816 and 1845.* New York: Metropolitan Museum of Art, 1985.

Stauffer, John. *Giants: The Parallel Lives of Frederick Douglass and Abraham Lincoln.* New York: Twelve, 2008.

Steers, Edward, Jr. *Blood on the Moon: The Assassination of Abraham Lincoln.* Lexington: University Press of Kentucky, 2001.

Stevenson, Lauralee Trent. *Confederate Soldier Artists: Painting the South's War.* Shippensburg, Pa.: White Mane, 1998.

Symonds, Craig L. *The Civil War at Sea.* 2009. New York: Oxford University Press, 2012.

————. *Lincoln and His Admirals.* New York: Oxford University Press, 2008.

Tapert, Annette. *The Brothers' War: Civil War Letters to Their Loved Ones from the Blue and Gray.* New York: Times Books, 1988.

Thompson, William F. *The Image of War: The Pictorial Reporting of the American Civil War.* 1960. Baton Rouge: Louisiana State University Press, 1994.

Trudeau, Noah Andre. *Like Men of War: Black Troops in the Civil War, 1862–1865.* Boston: Little, Brown, 1998.

Vorenberg, Michael. *Final Freedom: The Civil War, the Abolition of Slavery, and the Thirteenth Amendment.* New York: Cambridge University Press, 2001.

————. "The Thirteenth Amendment Enacted." In *Lincoln and Freedom: Slavery, Emancipation, and the Thirteen Amendment,* edited by Harold Holzer and Sara Vaughn Gabbard. Carbondale: Southern Illinois University Press, 2007.

Wallace, David H. *John Rogers: The People's Sculptor.* Middletown, Conn.: Wesleyan University Press, 1967.

Warner, Ezra J. *Generals in Blue: Lives of the Union Commanders.* Baton Rouge: Louisiana State University Press, 1964.

————. *Generals in Gray: Lives of the Confederate Commanders.* Baton Rouge: Louisiana State University Press, 1959.

Waugh, Charles G., and Marlon H. Greenberg, eds. *The Women's War in the South: Recollections and Reflections of the American Civil War.* Nashville: Cumberland House, 1999.

Waugh, Joan. *Ulysses S. Grant: American Hero, American Myth.* Charlotte: University of North Carolina Press, 2009.

Wheeler, Richard. *Lee's Terrible Swift Sword: From Antietam to Chancellorsville: An Eyewitness History.* New York: Harper & Row, 1992.

————. *Sword over Richmond: An Eyewitness History of McClellan's Peninsula Campaign.* New York: Harper & Row, 1986.

————. *Voices of the Civil War.* New York: Thomas Y. Crowell, 1976.

————. *Witness to Appomattox.* New York: Harper & Row, 1989.

————. *Witness to Gettysburg.* New York: New American Library, 1987.

Wiley, Bell Irvin. *Embattled Confederates: An Illustrated History of Southerners at War.* New York: Harper & Row, 1964.

————. *The Life of Billy Yank: The Common Soldier of the Union.* Indianapolis: Bobbs-Merrill, 1952.

————. *The Life of Johnny Reb: The Common Soldier of the Confederacy.* Indianapolis: Bobbs-Merrill, 1943.

Williams, Hermann Warner, Jr. *The Civil War: The Artists' Record.* Boston: Beacon Press, 1961.

Wilson, Mark R. *The Business of Civil War: Military Mobilization and the State, 1861–1865.* Baltimore: Johns Hopkins University Press, 2006.

Winkler, H. Donald. *Stealing Secrets: How a Few Daring Women Deceived Generals, Impacted Battles, and Affected the Course of the Civil War.* Naperville, Ill.: Cumberland House, 2010.

Wise, Arthur, and Francis A. Lord. *Bands and Drummer Boys of the Civil War.* New York: Thomas Yoseloff, 1966.

Zeller, Bob. *The Blue and Gray in Black and White: A History of Civil War Photography.* Westport, Conn.: Praeger, 2005.

⚜ LIST OF OBJECTS ⚜

PLATE 1–1

Unidentified maker
Slave shackles intended for a child, ca. 1800
Wrought iron
1⅞ × 4⁹⁄₁₆ in.
Gilder Lehrman Collection (GLC 06151)

PLATE 1–2

Unidentified maker
Slave shackles, ca. 1866
Steel
4¼ × 23 × ¼ in.
Gift of Mrs. Carroll Beckwith, 1921.20

PLATE 2–1

Unidentified artist
Caesar: A Slave, ca. 1850
Cased daguerreotype
3¾ × 3¼ × ½ in.
PR 012.002.323

PLATE 3–1

Eastman Johnson (1824–1906)
Negro Life at the South, 1859
Oil on linen
37 × 46 in.
The Robert L. Stuart Collection, on permanent loan from the New York Public Library
  (S-225)

PLATE 4–1

John Rogers (1829–1904)
The Slave Auction, 1859
Painted plaster
13⅜ × 8 × 8¾ in.
Gift of Mr. Samuel V. Hoffman, 1928.28

PLATE 5–1

Charles Blair (1865–1893), blacksmith
"John Brown" pike, ca. 1857–1859

Steel, wood
81 × 4½ in.
INV.5736

PLATE 6–1

Thomas Satterwhite Noble (1835–1907)
John Brown's Blessing, 1867
Oil on canvas
84¼ × 60¼ in.
Gift of the children of Thomas S. Noble and Mary C. Noble, in their memory, 1939.250

PLATE 7–1

Cast by Augustus Saint-Gaudens (1848–1907) from original by Leonard Wells Volk
    (1828–1895)
Right Hand of Abraham Lincoln (1809–1865), 1886
Bronze
3⅝ × 6¼ × 5 in.
Gift of Mrs. John V. Irwin, 1939.584

PLATE 7–2

Cast by Augustus Saint-Gaudens (1848–1907) from original by Leonard Wells Volk
    (1828–1895)
Life Mask of Abraham Lincoln (1809–1865), 1886
Bronze
9 × 7½ × 6 in.
Gift of Mrs. John V. Irwin, 1939.583

PLATE 8–1

Fernando Wood (1812–1881)
To the People of Louisiana, their Executive and Representatives Greeting,
January 29, 1861
Broadside
16 × 12⅞ in.
Misc.MSS.Wood, Fernando

PLATE 8–2

Fernando Wood (1812–1881)
Communication from His Honor the Mayor, Fernando Wood, January 7th, 1861
New York: Edmund Jones & Co., printers to the Corporation, No. 26 John Street, 1861
20 pages, 7⅛ × 4⅝ in.
Pamph.JS1234.A14.1861

PLATE 9–1

Alma A. Pelot (active 1860–ca. 1900)
South-Western Angle of Fort Sumter, Charleston Harbor, S.C., April 15, 1861
Photographic print
9½ × 11 in.
PR.164.2.18

PLATE 10-1

Mrs. John E. Forbes
Flag, 1861
Wool, cotton, bast cord
38¾ × 52¾ in.
Gift of Mrs. Irving McKesson, 1955.53

PLATE 10-2

Thomas Nast (1840–1902)
Study for "Departure of the Seventh Regiment for the War, April 19, 1861," ca. 1865–1869
Oil over graphite on brown paper, varnished, laid on heavy board, nailed and mounted
on wood panel
22½ × 32¾ in.
Gift of George A. Zabriskie, 1946.174

PLATE 11-1

Unidentified maker
Confederate Palmetto Flag, 1861
Cotton
9¼ × 9½ in.
Gift of Mr. Charles C. Leigh, through E. C. Estes, 1865.9

PLATE 11-2

Unidentified maker
Confederate Navy Jack, or "Southern Cross," 1861–1865
Cotton
24½ × 32½ in.
Charles M. Lefferts Collection

PLATE 12-1

Unidentified artist
A Great Rush to Join the 36th Regiment, New York Volunteers, ca. 1862
Woodcut and letterpress
New York: Baker & Godwin
37¾ × 24¹³⁄₁₆ in.
PR 055

PLATE 13-1

Unidentified maker
Zouave uniform worn by Private David P. Davis of the 5th New York Volunteer Infantry,
ca. 1861–1863
Wool, linen
Jacket 2½ × 20½ × 28½ in.; shirt 1½ × 24 × 31¾ in.; pantaloons 1½ × 48 × 33½ in.; sash ¼ ×
8¼ × 104½ in.; leggings each 1 × 15¾ × 13¼ in.
Gift of Mr. Walter F. Davis, 1948.427a–g

PLATE 13–2

Unidentified artist
Ephraim Elmer Ellsworth (1837–1861), ca. 1861
Photographic print
6¼ × 4½ in.
PR 52

PLATE 14–1

Howard Cushing Wright to his mother, New Orleans, Monday, July 29, 1861
Autograph letter signed, two sides of three folded sheets
7½ × 12 in.
MSS.AHMC.Wright, Howard

PLATE 15–1

Louis Lang (1814–1893)
Return of the 69th (Irish) Regiment, N.Y.S.M. from the Seat of War, 1862–1863
Oil on canvas
87 × 140 in.
Gift of Louis Lang, 1886.3

PLATE 16–1

Francis Bicknell Carpenter (1830–1900)
The Lincoln Family in 1861, ca. 1865
Oil on canvas
27 × 36¾ in.
Gift of Warren C. Crane, 1909.6

PLATE 17–1

Unidentified maker
Snare drum, ca. 1860–1865
Wood, hide, rope, paint
13½ × 17 in.
Gift of Miss Louise I. Corell, 1944.120a

PLATE 17–2

Unidentified artist
Charles F. Mosby, Age 13. Confederate Drummer Boy, Served Throughout the War, ca. 1865
Photographic print
4¾ × 3¼ in.
PR 068

PLATE 18–1

Edwin White (1817–1877)
Thoughts of the Future (Thoughts of Liberia, Emancipation), 1861
Oil on canvas

18 × 21 in.
The Robert L. Stuart Collection, on permanent loan from the New York Public Library
(S-200)

PLATE 19–1

Thomas Fitch Rowland (1831–1907)
Half model of the USS Monitor, 1862
Wood, metal
14½ × 98 × 12 in.
Gift of Thomas Fitch Rowland, 1862.9

PLATE 19–2

Charles Parsons (1821–1910)
The First Naval Conflict Between Iron Clad Vessels, 1862
Lithograph of Endicott & Co.
13¹¹⁄₁₆ × 21 in.
PR 100

PLATE 20–1

Cipher key, ca. 1861
1¾ × 8⅞ × 1¼ in.
MSS.Alexander Robert Chisolm Papers

PLATE 21–1

Victor Nehlig (1830–1909)
An Episode of the War—the Cavalry Charge of Lt. Henry B. Hidden, 1862
Oil on canvas
45¾ × 75 in.
Gift of William H. Webb, 1875.2

PLATE 22–1

William Rothert (ca. 1842–1862)
Diary, 1861–1862
5⅛ × 3¼ × ⅝ in.
MSS.BV.Rothert

PLATE 23–1

Unidentified makers
Military buttons mounted on card, 1860–1864
Brass, paper
Card 11 × 8½ in.; largest button 1 in.
Gift of the Military Order of the Loyal Legion of the United States, New York
Commandery, 1926.95a–j

PLATE 23–2

Unidentified makers
Confederate buttons mounted on card, 1860–1865

Brass, paper, silk
Card 11 × 7 in.; largest button ⅞ in.
Gift of the 7th Regiment, National Guard, New York, 1951.501a–m

PLATE 24–1

Petition to Abraham Lincoln for Recruitment of Black Troops, 1862
Multiple sheets of paper, pasted together
9 in. × 25 ft.
MSS.BV.Petitions

PLATE 25–1

Abraham Lincoln (1809–1865)
By the President of the United States of America. A Proclamation, 1863
Folio broadside printed by Charles G. Leland and George H. Boker for the Philadelphia
    Great Central Sanitary Fair, June 7–29, 1864
21⅝ × 17⅜ in.
Y1863

PLATE 25–2

Abraham Lincoln (1809–1865)
General Orders, No. 1, January 2, 1863
War Department, Adjutant General's Office
3 pages, 6⅞ × 4¾ in.
Y1863.L

PLATE 26–1

Adalbert Johann Volck (1828–1912)
Print #3, Writing the Emancipation Proclamation, 1863
Etching
8 × 10¼ in.
PR.010.1.05

PLATE 26–2

Adalbert Johann Volck (1828–1912)
Print #19, Offering of Bells to Be Cast into Cannon, 1863
Etching
8 × 10½ in.
PR.101.1.21

PLATE 27–1

Frederick Douglass (1818–1895)
Men of Color, to Arms!
Broadside
Rochester, N.Y., 1863
8⅔ × 6⅓ in.
SY1863.50

PLATE 27–2

Unidentified artist
Fred[erick] Douglass (1818–1895), n.d.
Albumen print, *carte-de-visite*
3½ × 2⅛ in.
Gift of Mr. Rodman Gilder, PR 011

PLATE 28–1

Emily J. Semmes to Paul Jones Semmes, June 1, 1863
Autograph letter signed, four pages
7⅞ × 5⅛ in.
Gilder Lehrman Collection (GLC0075.10)

PLATE 28–2

Unidentified artist
Gen. Paul J. Semmes (1815–1863), n.d.
Engraving
8¾ × 11¾ in.
PR 052

PLATE 28–3

A. R. Waud (1828–1891)
*The Battle of Gettysburg—Union Position Near the Centre—Gettysburg in the
    Distance—Cemetery on the Hill*
Wood engravings
Published in *Harper's Weekly*, July 25, 1863
8 × 22⅓ in.
E171.H29

PLATE 29–1

Frederick B. Schell (d. ca. 1905)
*Arrival at Chickasaw Bayou of Jefferson Davis' Negroes from His Plantation on the
    Mississippi Below Vicksburg, Mississippi*, ca. 1863
Graphite on beige paper
9⅝ × 13½ in.
Museum purchase, James B. Wilbur Fund, 1945.580.107

PLATE 29–2

Frederick B. Schell (d. ca. 1905)
*Arrival at Chickasaw Bayou of the Negro Slaves of Jefferson Davis, from his Plantation
    on the Mississippi*
Wood engraving
Published in *Frank Leslie's Illustrated News*, August 8, 1863
11½ × 16 in.
E171.L63

PLATE 30–1

J. M. Swords, publisher
The Daily Citizen, Vicksburg, Miss., July 2 and 4, 1863
Newsprint on wallpaper
16⅞ × 9⅛ in.
New-York Historical Society Newspaper Collection

PLATE 30–2

Adalbert Johann Volck (1828–1912)
Print #28, Cave Life in Vicksburg During the Siege, 1863
Etching
7¹³⁄₁₆ × 10⁷⁄₁₆ in.
PR.010.1.30

PLATE 31–1

Unidentified maker
Draft wheel, ca. 1863
Wood, metal
11 × 16½ in.
Gift of Frederic C. Wagner, 1865.6

PLATE 31–2

Unidentified artist
Sacking of Brownstone Houses in Lexington Avenue by the Rioters on Monday, July 13
Wood engraving
Published in *The New-York Illustrated News,* July 25, 1863
11 × 16½ 3 in.
E171.D38

PLATE 32–1

Bible used at Colored Orphan Asylum, Fifth Avenue and Forty-third Street
Open to inscription regarding the burning of the asylum during the draft riots,
    July 1863
6¼ × 9¼ × 3 in.
Records of the Association for the Benefit of Colored Orphans

PLATE 32–2

Unidentified artist
Colored Orphan Asylum, 1861
Albumen print mounted on card (stereograph)
3 × 6⅛ in.
PR.065.0334.0004

PLATE 32–3

Unidentified artist
The Riots in New York: Destruction of the Colored Orphan Asylum
Wood engraving

Published in the *Illustrated London News*, August 15, 1863
7⅜ × 9¹¹⁄₁₆ in.
PR 100

PLATE 33–1

Unidentified maker
Footlocker with belongings, 1860–1890
Wood, leather, paper, silk
Locker 10¾ × 21½ × 15¼ in.
Gift of the Estate of Isidore L. Rosenzweig, in Memory of Bessie and Isidore L.
　Rosenzweig, 1978 (INV.8671a–ww)

PLATE 34–1

Marinda Branson Moore (1829–1864)
The First Dixie Reader; to Follow the Dixie Primer
Raleigh, N.C.: Branson, Farrar & Co., 1864
5½ × 4 × ¼ in.
Gift of L. J. Bailey, YC1864.Moore

PLATE 35–1

*Presentation Address of the Ladies of the City of New York to the Officers and Men of the
　Twentieth United States Colored Troops*
New York: Whitehorne, 1864
14⁹⁄₁₆ × 5½ in.
SY1862.43

PLATE 35–2

Unidentified artist
Presentation of Colors to the 20th U.S. Colored Infantry
Wood engraving
Published in *Frank Leslie's Illustrated Newspaper*, March 26, 1864
10⅞ × 15½ in.
E171.L63.4

PLATE 36–1

James Reid Lambdin (1807–1889)
Ulysses Simpson Grant (1822–1885), 1868
Oil on canvas
50⅛ × 36 in.
Museum purchase, Beekman Fund, 1954.36

PLATE 36–2

Unidentified artist after B. F. Chamberlain
Major-General U. S. Grant, the Hero of the Recent Victories in Kentucky and Tennessee
Woodcut engraving of a Grant look-alike
Published in the *New-York Illustrated News*, March 22, 1862
7⅛ × 5½ in.
E171.D38

PLATE 37–1

Entry ticket for the New York Metropolitan Fair, 1864
3 × 5 in.
Metropolitan Fair Papers

PLATE 37–2

E. & H. T. Anthony & Co.
Ticket Office, Metropolitan Fair, New York, 1864
Stereograph
3 × 6 in.
PR 065-0500-0010

PLATE 37–3

E. & H. T. Anthony & Co.
Entrance to the Grand Moving Diorama and Miniature Battle Field, Metropolitan Fair, New York, 1864
Stereograph
2¾ × 6⅛₆ in.
Gift of Charles W. Kirby, 1936, PR 065-0500-0036

PLATE 37–4

Bierstadt Brothers
Exhibition Room, Metropolitan Fair, New York, 1864
Stereograph
5¹³⁄₁₆ × 3 in.
PR 065-0500-0037

PLATE 37–5

J. Gurney & Son
Department of Photographs & Engravings, Metropolitan Fair, New York, 1864
Stereograph
5⅝ × 3 in.
PR 065-0500-0041

PLATE 37–6

J. Gurney & Son
Art Gallery, Metropolitan Fair, New York, 1864
Stereograph
5⁵⁄₁₆ × 3 in.
Gift of Charles W. Kirby, 1936, PR 065-0500-0052

PLATE 38–1

Photograph album presented to Major M. S. Euen by Co. C, P.P., 1860–1869
Album
8¾ × 6 × 3 in.
PR 002, Album 99

PLATE 38–2

Unidentified artist
Unidentified African American Soldier, ca. 1861
Carte-de-visite
4 × 2¼ in.
PR 002.99

PLATE 39–1

George Templeton Strong (1820–1875)
Diary entries from September 3 and 5, 1864
Manuscript journal with attached photographs and newspaper clippings
9 × 13¾ × 2⅛ in.
BV Strong, George Templeton

PLATE 40–1

Attributed to John Jacob Omenhausser (1830–1877)
Point Lookout sketches, 1864
Forty-two watercolor drawings, bound with associated material in 1880
Each sheet 10 × 12 in.
Gift of the Naval History Society, NHSC Point Lookout

PLATE 41–1

Benjamin Franklin Butler, designer (1818–1893), and Anthony C. Paquet, engraver
    (1814–1882)
Colored Troops Before Richmond, 1864–1865
Engraved silver
1⁹⁄₁₆ × 1⁹⁄₁₆ in.
Gift of J. Ellis Phyfe, 2011.23

PLATE 42–1

Unidentified artist
The Miscegenation Ball, 1864
Hand-colored lithograph, Kimmel & Forster, lithographers
18½ × 22½ in.
PR 010.1864.3

PLATE 42–2

David G. Croly, George Wakeman, and E. C. Howell
*Miscegenation: The Theory of the Blending of the Races, Applied to the American White
    Man and Negro*
Pamphlet
New York: H. Dexter, Hamilton, 1864
72 pages, 7½ × 5 in.
Gift of J. Watts de Peyster, E185.62.C76.186

PLATE 43–1

Unidentified maker
Campaign flag, 1864
Cotton
16½ × 25½ in.
Samuel T. Shaw Memorial Collection, 1946.243

PLATE 43–2

Unidentified maker
*Union Nomination for President, Abraham Lincoln of Illinois. For Vice President,
 Andrew Johnson of Tennessee,* 1864
Election poster
99⅞ × 43¾ in.
PR 055

PLATE 44–1

Abraham Lincoln (1809–1865)
Projection of November 1864 Election, 1864
9¾ × 7¾ in.
MSS.Lincoln

PLATE 44–2

Mathew B. Brady (ca. 1823–1896)
Abraham Lincoln (1809–1865), January 8, 1864
Albumen silver print from glass negative
Published in Meserve Historical Portraits
3¼ × 2⅛ in.
PR 231

PLATE 45–1

J. W. Hibbs, Geo. S. Thomas, Wm. H. Bennett, A. Harris
Prison Times, 1865
Four-page manuscript newspaper
12¼ × 7¾ in.
Misc.MSS.Fort Delaware

PLATE 46–1

Ulysses S. Grant (1822–1885)
Terms of Surrender, April 9, 1865
Two-page impression from manifold with interlinear revisions written by Ely S. Parker
 at Grant's dictation
14¾ × 20¼ in.
MSS.BV.Grant

PLATE 47–1

Clara Harris to Mary, April 25, 1865
Autograph letter signed, two sides of one folded sheet and one single sheet

5¼ × 8¼ in.
MSS.AHMC.Harris, Clara

PLATE 48–1

Unidentified maker
Framed leaves from Abraham Lincoln's bier, 1865
Laurel leaves, ink, silk ribbon, wood, gilding
8¾ × 7¼ × 1 in.
Gift of Mrs. Georgine Wood Charlton, 1947, Z.2603

PLATE 48–2

New York Central Railroad. Time Table of Special Train & Pilot with the Remains of Abraham Lincoln, Late President of the United States, Wednesday, April 26th, 1865
11 × 6¹¹⁄₁₆ in.
SY1865.584

PLATE 48–3

Unidentified photographer
Lincoln's Funeral Procession in New York City, 1865
Stereograph
3¼ × 6½ in.
PR 065.0509.0007

PLATE 48–4

Currier & Ives
The Body of the Martyr President, Abraham Lincoln, Lying in State at the City Hall, N.Y., April 24th & 25th, 1865, 1865
Lithograph
18⅛ × 13 in.
PR 052.54

PLATE 49–1

Joe W. Mersereau to William Oland Bourne, April 24, 1865
Autograph letter signed
8 × 9⅞ in.
MSS.69.William Oland Bourne Papers

PLATE 50–1

Abraham Lincoln (1809–1865)
The Thirteenth Amendment to the U.S. Constitution, February 1, 1865
Manuscript document on lined vellum with ruled borders, signed by President Abraham Lincoln, co-signed by Hannibal Hamlin as vice president of the United States and president of the Senate, Schuyler Colfax as Speaker of the House, and John W. Forney as secretary of the Senate
1 page, 20 × 15¹⁄₁₆ in.
Exhibited at the New-York Historical Society through the generosity of David Rubenstein

⁂ INDEX ⁂

Page numbers in *italics* refer to illustrations.